# Attention

# Series in Human–Technology Interaction

## Series editor: Alex Kirlik

# Attention

## From Theory to Practice

*Edited by*

**Arthur F. Kramer**
**Douglas A. Wiegmann**
**Alex Kirlik**

OXFORD

UNIVERSITY PRESS

2007

# OXFORD
## UNIVERSITY PRESS

Oxford University Press, Inc., publishes works that further
Oxford University's objective of excellence
in research, scholarship, and education.

Oxford   New York
Auckland   Cape Town   Dar es Salaam   Hong Kong   Karachi
Kuala Lumpur   Madrid   Melbourne   Mexico City   Nairobi
New Delhi   Shanghai   Taipei   Toronto

With offices in
Argentina   Austria   Brazil   Chile   Czech Republic   France   Greece
Guatemala   Hungary   Italy   Japan   Poland   Portugal   Singapore
South Korea   Switzerland   Thailand   Turkey   Ukraine   Vietnam

Copyright © 2007 by Arthur F. Kramer, Douglas Wiegmann, and Alex Kirlik

Published by Oxford University Press, Inc.
198 Madison Avenue, New York, New York 10016

www.oup.com

Oxford is a registered trademark of Oxford University Press.

Library of Congress Cataloging-in-Publication Data
Attention: from theory to practice / edited by Arthur Kramer, Douglas Wiegmann, and Alex Kirlik.
p. cm. – (Series in human-technology interaction; v. 4)
Includes bibliographical references and index.
ISBN-10: 0-19-530572-8
ISBN-13: 978-0-19-530572-2

1. Attention.   2. Human-machine systems.   I. Kramer, Arthur F.   II. Wiegmann, Douglas A.
III. Kirlik, Alex.   IV. Series.
BF321.A833 2006
153.7′33–dc22        2006010098

1 3 5 7 9 8 6 4 2

Printed in the United States of America
on acid-free paper

# Preface

This book was written for two reasons. First, the chapters presented here serve as a tribute to the long and distinguished career of Christopher D. Wickens. Chris has made many important contributions to our understanding of attention. His research has ranged from the empirical study of attention in the laboratory to studies of attentional deployment in tasks such as driving and piloting, and in populations from young to older adults. His multiple-resource model of attention has become the standard in the field of human factors and applied psychology, and is used both to study attention in complex and multiple tasks, and to make decisions about the design of interfaces for complex systems. More recently, Chris has extended and elaborated his attentional model into what has now become the SEEV model (see Part VII in the current volume). Second, the chapters in this book bring together contributions by many of the current leaders in the field of applied attention and present the best of the integration of theory and practice.

The first part of the book, entitled "Toward a Practical View of Attention: Theoretical and Methodological Issues," includes four chapters that provide critical reviews of historical and contemporary literature on divided attention, selective attention, and attentional capture; describe elaborations of old models or offer new models of attention; and describe how converging operations might be used to address both basic questions and applications of attention to real-world and simulated real-world tasks. For example, Hancock, Oron-Gilad, and Szalma describe how Wickens' multiple-resource model might be further elaborated to address unresolved questions in attentional theory and practice. Sheridan offers an engineering approach to attentional control, discussing how concepts such as fuzzy logic, Kalman estimators, Yufix virtual associative networks, and Bayesian logic might be used to provide quantitative predictions concerning the manner in which attention is allocated in complex tasks. Moray provides a brief historical description of early models of visual and auditory attention. He also discusses two real-world examples of modeling and understanding the role of attention beyond the laboratory, both in terms of the design and use of radar displays, and the design of navigation displays and signals for train engineers. Finally, Boot, Kramer, and Becic provide a critical review of the literature on attentional capture and guidance, and discuss how laboratory research does (or does not) scale up to address real-world problems. They conclude by discussing two recent experiments that ask how best to alert operators to important changes on cluttered dynamic radar displays.

Part II presents research on a variety of emerging topics in applied attention theory. Parasuraman and Greenwood note that many performance laws in applied psychology do not adequately capture individual differences, and these authors introduce a neuroergonomics approach to individual performance prediction based on molecular genetics and neuroscience. Their work breaks new ground in the effort to provide a neural and genetic basis for characterizing individual differences in various cognitive functions, including attention and memory. Lee similarly takes the study of attention into new realms by considering the role of affect in information processing. Lee observes that a rapidly growing body of empirical evidence now demonstrates that factors such as the emotional content of stimuli and responses to technology should no longer be ignored in the application of psychology to design. Vicente seeks to broaden our understanding of attention in yet another direction through field investigation. In his study of monitoring a nuclear power plant (NPP), Vicente demonstrates the rich diversity of information sources used to support attention allocation in an operational context, and the clever strategies and devices used by operators to compensate for their limited cognitive resources, concluding that "it is simply not possible to monitor an NPP using attentional resources alone." On a related note, Gray, Neth, and Schoelles argue that understanding attention and performance in interactive systems requires a detailed functional analysis of the external resources available to support performance in addition to internal cognitive resources. Gray and his colleagues conclude that it may be most fruitful to consider behavior to be adapted to a task environment comprised of a mix of these internal and external resources.

The understanding of driver distraction, which is closely related to failure of selective attention, has become an increasingly important topic given the rapid proliferation of cellular phones, global positioning satellite navigation systems, in-vehicle entertainment and information management systems, and other automotive telematic devices. Indeed, a substantial percentage of automobile accidents are now attributed to driver distraction of inattentiveness. Part III addresses the important issue of driver distraction. The Strayer and Drews chapter is unique in that it brings a number of converging methodologies to bear, including observational field studies, well-controlled simulator studies, and a psychophysiological study, in the examination of the human information processing costs associated with hands-free cell phone use during driving. The conclusions of the study, in terms of the nature and magnitude of performance and safety costs, are both theoretically and practically important, and suggest that recent legistration on cell phones and driving should be reexamined in light of the data. Fisher and Pollatsek examine the important issue of teenage drivers. Why do teen drivers have such a high accident rate and what can be done about it? Both of these questions are addressed by the studies described in the chapter.

Changes in attentional processes across the life span have become an increasingly important topic, with both theoretical and practical implications, given the "aging" of most industrialized societies. Tsang provides a critical review of models of attention and, more specifically, of attentional control during the performance of multiple concurrent tasks in the context of aging. She then goes on to discuss the results of a number of studies conducted in her laboratory during which converging operations are used to localize age-related costs in multitask processing within the context of Wickens' multiple-resource model. Finally, Tsang describes the important influence of experience or expertise, in the presented case in the context of piloting, as a moderator of age-related decline of attentional control. Like Tsang, Fisk and Rogers begin by providing a review of the literature on skill acquisition and maintenance, focusing on their important research on the development of automatic processing for young and older adults. They then discuss how such data can be used to design products to enhance the independence of older adults. In particular, they describe some very interesting research on aging and independence in the context of the Aware Home at the Georgia Institute of Technology.

Part V covers the implications of multiple-resource theory for interface design. In Chapter 13, Sarter presents examples of the successful implementation of multimodal interfaces in support of concurrent task performance and information processing. The chapter also describes the additional benefit of distributing information across sensory channels, including redundancy, complementarity, and substitution. In Chapter 14, Theeuwes and colleagues summarize the results of their research on cross-modal interactions between sensory modalities and the implications for the design of multisensory displays. Their findings support the multiple-resource theory's assumption of independent resources for auditory and visual processing. However, their research also indicates that cross-modal interference can occur when central processing is necessary for information consolidation. Hence, the extent to which multisensory displays will have large advantages over unimodal displays may depend heavily on whether one or more of the modalities compete for limited-capacity central processes.

Part VI focuses on attention and training, particularly as they apply to multitasking. Chapter 15 by Gopher focuses on "emphasis change," which is a training protocol that requires individuals to change systematically their emphasis, efforts, and attention allocation policy on a major subcomponent of the performed task. Gopher also introduces a new concept of "task shell," which is a mental model of the integrated structural and dynamic properties of a task. A task shell developed through emphasis change training can lead to greater sensitivity to changes in task difficulty and load, and to better adaptation to changes through attention reallocation. In Chapter 16, Dismukes and Nowinski also focus on a relatively new but rapidly growing topic in cognitive psychology called prospective memory. Prospective memory is the process of recalling and performing an action that could not be executed at the time the original intention was formed. Intentions or goals are often deferred as a result of other concurrent tasks in the environment competing for attentional resources. Failures of prospective memory often occur because concurrent tasks win this competition for resources that guide the retrieval of memory items associated with each task. Dismukes and Nowinski provide real-world examples in aviation that illustrate the impact that prospective memory failures can have on flight safety and they provide some recommendations for training individuals to overcome prospective memory failures.

The final chapter in this volume, written by Christopher Wickens, provides both a critical review and discussion of the topic of attention over the past 100 years and a prescription for the future. Several cautions and suggestions are offered for the future. First, that researchers become less focused on attentional paradigms and more focused on explaining important attentional phenomena. In the past, paradigms have been studied as an end in and of themselves rather than as a means to understanding important real-world attentional phenomena. Second, that the focus on mean effects has, to date, often precluded the study of extreme responses. Given that errors often arise from unusual or extreme events, it is important that they be more frequently examined during the study of human performance in complex systems. Finally, that computational models become more of a focus in the study of applied attention. Although our models will rarely provide the final answer, they serve to formalize our understanding and enable the testing of our hypotheses.

# Contents

# Contributors

ENSAR BECIC, Beckman Institute for Advanced Science and Technology; and Department of psychology, University of Illinois at Urbana-Champaign

WALTER R. BOOT, Beckman Institute for Advanced Science and Technology; and Department of Psychology, University of Illinois at Urbana-Champaign

ADELBERT BRONKHORST, TNO Human Factors, The Netherlands

KEY DISMUKES, NASA Ames Research Center

FRANK A. DREWS, Department of Psychology, University of Utah

DONALD L. FISHER, Department of Mechanical and Industrial Engineering, University of Massachusetts at Amherst

ARTHUR D. FISK, School of Psychology, Georgia Institute of Technology

DANIEL GOPHER, Technion-Israel Institute of Technology

WAYNE D. GRAY, Department of Cognitive Science, Rensselaer Polytechnic Institute

PAMELA GREENWOOD, Department of Psychology, George Mason University

PETER A. HANCOCK, MIT[2] Laboratories, University of Central Florida

ALEX KIRLIK, Beckman Institute for Advanced Science and Technology and Human Factors Division, University of Illinois at Urbana-Champaign

ARTHUR F. KRAMER, Beckman Institute for Advanced Science and Technology; and Department of Psychology, University of Illinois at Urbana-Champaign

JOHN D. LEE, Department of Mechanical and Industrial Engineering, The University of Iowa

NEVILLE MORAY, Magagnosc, France

HANSJÖRG NETH, Department of Cognitive Science, Rensselaer Polytechnic Institute

JESSICA NOWINSKI, National Aeronautics and Space Administration, Ames Research Center

CHRISTIAN N. L. OLIVERS, Cognitive Psychology, Vrije Universiteit, The Netherlands

TAL ORON-GILAD, MIT$^2$ Laboratories, University of Central Florida

RAJA PARASURAMAN, Department of Psychology, George Mason University

ALEXANDER POLLATSEK, Department of Psychology, University of Massachusetts at Amherst

WENDY A. ROGERS, School of Psychology, Georgia Institute of Technology

NADINE SARTER, Department of Industrial and Systems Engineering, University of Michigan

MICHAEL J. SCHOELLES, Department of Cognitive Science, Rensselaer Polytechnic Institute

THOMAS B. SHERIDAN, Massachusetts Institute of Technology and Volpe National Transportation Systems Center

DAVID L. STRAYER, Department of Psychology, University of Utah

JAMES L. SZALMA, MIT$^2$ Laboratories, University of Central Florida

JAN THEEUWES, Cognitive Psychology, Vrije Universiteit, The Netherlands

PAMELA S. TSANG, Department of Psychology, Wright State University

ERIK VAN DER BURG, Cognitive Psychology, Vrije Universiteit, The Netherlands

KIM J. VICENTE, Department of Mechanical and Industrial Engineering, University of Toronto

CHRISTOPHER D. WICKENS, Human Factors Division; and Department of Psychology, University of Illinois at Urbana-Champaign

DOUGLAS WIEGMANN, Human Factors Division, University of Illinois at Urbana-Champaign

# Part I

# Toward a Practical View of Attention: Theoretical and Methodological Issues

# Chapter 1

# Attention: From History to Application

## *Neville Moray*

Modern work on attention began with the development of Broadbent's filter theory (Broadbent, 1953, 1958). Broadbent once pointed out that interest in attention had continued in Europe from the time of Titchener (1903), but hardly a single paper appeared in journals of the American Psychology Association after the malignant influence of Watson and the Ur-behaviorists took control of the discipline in the 1920s. Consider, for example, Stevens's (1953) *Handbook of Experimental Psychology.* There are three pages on how animals may attend to only one part of the stimulus during learning, and several pages on the intensity of illumination and attention span—apart from that, nothing. Attention did not figure even in Fitts's chapter on engineering psychology.[1] The renaissance of attention theory in the 1950s was truly radical.

Broadbent worked almost entirely on auditory attention. Much of his work was applied and, together with the famous "split-span" memory experiment (Broadbent, 1953), led him to formulate his filter theory: the single-channel model of selective attention. However, it did not lead to detailed quantitative predictions. Broadbent's philosophy of experimental design was to eliminate a large class of alternative explanations by a single experiment, not to predict in detail what would happen in real time in real-world tasks. Almost no work captured the richness and, above all, the temporal dynamics of the real world, although Broadbent always emphasized the importance of applied research.

It may be something of a surprise to Chris Wickens to be reminded that in my early days I tried to convince Broadbent that some parallel processing was possible. For example, in split-span experiments we have two ears but only one mouth, so that output must be serial and sequential. When we gave listeners a stenographer's keyboard, on which several keys can be pressed simultaneously, we found almost parallel performance. In addition, Broadbent's original split-span subjects only had about 10 trials. We found that after 100 trials their performance on the classic split-span task greatly improved—a result that was confirmed by Geoff Underwood using a listener, one "Moray," with years of practice at two-channel listening. He found almost perfect ability to listen to two messages at once (Underwood, 1974). We also found that small changes in pitch and loudness could be perceived in parallel (Moray, Fitter, Ostry, Favreau, & Nagy, 1976).

Early modern research on attention was concerned with underlying mechanisms, rather than predictions about situations unconstrained by laboratory experimental design. Typically, laboratory experiments are not dynamic. They consist of a series of statistically independent trials of fixed duration, with the task specified by the experimenter. Participants play no part in determining what will happen next. Real tasks are dynamic, and people decide when attention will be paid to what, how long a "trial" (the word is hardly applicable) will last, and, by their interaction with the environment, alter the future that they will experience. In real tasks, the "experiment" is controlled by the participant as much as by the experimenter (Rasmussen, Pejtersen, & Goodstein, 1995, pp. 219–224).

#### VISUAL ATTENTION: "THE EYES HAVE IT"

Because of the structure of the retina, with its small area of foveal vision, "real" visual attention is necessarily single channel at the level of gaze direction. Of course, one can pay attention to different parts of the retinal array, as Erikson and his group here at Illinois have shown. There are also earlier works, including a rather charming little paper by Babington-Smith (1961) that also shows this, and recently coaches have begun to teach players to pay attention to the periphery of vision in soccer and other sports. However, evolution has provided us with a system of visual attention that is primarily mediated by switching fixation.

I have heard it said that attention mediated by eye movements is "uninteresting," presumably because moving the eyes does not seem to involve "deep" processes inside the head and hence does not seem "truly cognitive." This seems to me, a very strange attitude. Although movements of the head and eyes may be simple, great cognitive subtleties remain in the choice of what to look at, where to look for it, and when. The most important aspects of visual attention in the working environment are the strategy and tactics of gaze.

I offer two examples of successful quantitative modeling on the assumption of single-channel visual attention.[2] In neither study are we concerned with the selection of one message and the rejection of others, but with the dynamic tactical distribution of attention over many sources in real time, all of which require attention. This kind of attention is akin to the "traveling salesman's problem": how to visit the maximum number of places with minimal travel (Dessouky, Moray, & Kijowski, 1995). The empirical study of eye movements has a surprisingly long history (Woodworth, 1938), but only recently has the technology improved to a level where it is (fairly) easy to collect and analyze data outside the laboratory. On the other hand, there is a plethora of mathematical models for how attention may direct eye movements (Moray, 1986). Here I want to show how one can develop an analytic model of attention and then verify it with empirical measures of eye movements.

#### Example 1: Visual Attention to Radar Displays: From Analytic Models to Behavior

Probably the earliest quantitative model is that of Senders (1964, 1983), inspired by the empirical data of Fitts and his coworkers, who 50 years ago recorded pilots' eye movements and estimated the probabilities of looking at different instruments and the transition probabilities among instruments (Jones, Milton, & Fitts, 1949, 1950). Senders proposed that the purpose of attention was to reduce uncertainty and thus support adaptive behavior in a dynamic environment. He used information theory's Nyquist sampling theorem to model eye movement dynamics, predicting that observers would fixate quasi-random functions of time at twice the bandwidth of the sources, with the fixation duration dependent on the perceptual accuracy required. He found the predicted linear relations, although high frequencies were undersampled and low frequencies oversampled. He also discussed an early form of urgency model, in which the time until the next fixation depended not just on the bandwidth, but on how close to a constraint boundary the variable was when it was observed (Senders, Elkind, Grignetti, & Smallwood, 1965).

Other models have considered signals of different value, the effects of responses made by the operator, expected payoff rather than simply signal magnitude, and several other characteristics of the task, but by and large they were not validated using real tasks. For a summary, see Moray (1986).

In the late 1970s, I was asked to investigate the behavior of radar operators (Moray, Neil, & Brophy, 1983; Moray, Richards, & Low, 1980). How many aircraft could a fighter controller handle? The problem is the inverse of that of the air traffic controller. The fighter controller must bring aircraft into close proximity with one another, rather than prevent close approaches. One could, of course, simply measure performance as a function of the number of aircraft involved, but it is potentially more valuable to develop a general model that can be used to evaluate existing or new radar systems, to develop training strategies for operators, and so forth. We therefore need a model of the strategic and tactical control of dynamic visual attention that incorporates the task variable constraints of radar as well as cognitive mechanisms.

A fighter controller (hereafter called simply *the controller*) must detect the presence of aircraft, decide whether their track requires present or future intervention, dispatch aircraft into the airspace appropriately, and monitor the movements of all the aircraft. Controllers may use advanced electronic processing or may have to monitor fading echoes and measure manually angles and distances on the screen. They may have to consult information off the radar screen, such as displays with meteorological information, flight strips, or a "tote board" indicating the aircraft available. Aircraft have different importance, and although some keep to predetermined flight paths, others may fly anywhere. Displayed information may be updated quite quickly or only at intervals of several seconds. The radar we investigated was a very long-range military radar, with an antenna that rotated about once in 12 seconds; so information about a particular echo could not change more frequently than that.

There were four sources of information other than echoes: the control panel of the radar, the tote board, the rim of the display (which was used for measuring course angles manually), and "other" (such as momentary glances at people in the room, hard-copy messages, and so on). In addition, there were the echoes representing aircraft, which could be divided into "friendly"

aircraft, "target" aircraft, and "strangers" (i.e., aircraft that suddenly appeared in the airspace and were not, until then, part of the operator's scenario). A task analysis suggested that Senders's model would not apply. Information was generated intermittently (one update per each rotation of the antenna) and at the ranges used, the movement of the echo at each rotation was extremely small (less than the width of the echo itself), so that the bandwidth of the displayed information was extremely low, except for the pulse of information as the echo was updated (Crossman, 1974). The situation was at the low-bandwidth end of Senders's experiment, where operators tend to oversample, and previous work suggested that when to take a sample is partly a function of how rapidly forgetting occurs. The observer has a threshold of uncertainty for the memory of the last observation, and when that is exceeded, a new sample is taken (Moray, Synnock, & Sims, 1973).

To study forgetting, participants were shown drawings of radar-like displays and were asked to recall the positions of echoes after various delays. Their accuracy was measured as the standard deviation (s.d.) of the distribution of their estimates of position. Forgetting as a function of time was well fitted by Equation 1.1, where t is the time in seconds since the echo was observed and k is a constant that depends on how many echoes were monitored.

$$\text{s.d.} = k + 0.02(t)^{3/2} \qquad (1.1)$$

Equation 1.1 can be used to describe a circle within which the observer believes the echo to lie with a given probability, as a function of time since it was last observed. Although new information about the location of an echo appeared only once per rotation of the antenna, even with only two aircraft displayed, the controllers' gaze returned to each several times during the period of rotation. More time was spent attending to the location of the echoes than was needed on the basis of exogenous uncertainty, suggesting forgetting as a factor.

The controllers must ensure that the friendly aircraft (F) approaches the suspicious aircraft (T) closely but does not hit it. Furthermore, the closer F comes to T, the less time there is to correct its flight path, because rates of turn are limited by physics and the reaction times of pilots. Hence, the closer two aircraft are, the shorter the interval that can be allowed to elapse before they are next observed, and it is reasonable to assume that the urgency of the need for a new observation increases exponentially as the distance between the aircraft diminishes. (This is also known to be the case in bat echolocation.) Although the course and speed of the aircraft are known, as time passes and forgetting grows according to Equation 1.1, the area of uncertainty around the memory of each echo will grow, and these will eventually overlap. The region of overlap represents the probability that the aircraft are in collision, and because these areas are represented by a standard deviation, we can associate a probability with the area of overlap. We assume that there is a threshold of intolerability such that if the probability of both aircraft being in the same location exceeds this threshold, the observer will look at the echo about which the uncertainty is greatest. This can be generalized to three or more aircraft located, and further by weighting the uncertainty thresholds by the relative importance of the aircraft. We further assume that as the distance between aircraft decreases, the threshold of tolerability decreases. Constraints on the maximum rate of changing fixation were added from the known distribution of eye movement times (Boff & Lincoln, 1988), modified by empirical data from a pilot study of eye movements in our operators. Equations representing these dynamics were embodied as a computer program. The model was written in FORTRAN and run on an IBM mainframe. The output of the model is the sequence of fixations and the times at which these occurred.

The model makes the following predictions:

1. There will not be more than about two fixations (acts of attention) per second.
2. The intervals between successive looks at an aircraft (the mean first passage time, or MFPT) will be long when aircraft are far apart and will shorten as they approach one another.
3. If there are more than two aircraft on the display, and some of them are in the final stages of a close approach and others are far apart, attention will be absorbed more and more by the former, and in the limit no attention will be paid to distant aircraft as some aircraft become close enough for a potential collision.
4. Observations on features other than the aircraft will decrease (in the sense that the interval between them will increase) as aircraft close on one another.
5. Controllers will suffer from mental overload, and will lose control of the situation, when the number of aircraft being controlled results in MFPTs that are long enough to allow significant forgetting

as predicted by Equation 1.1. We believe this value to occur where the curves begin to accelerate upward—that is, at about 6 seconds. (This value agrees quite well with the mean time for self-paced sampling found by Moray and colleagues [1973], and with the point in Senders's [1964] experiment when oversampling begins.)

We were able to compare the predictions of the model with two sets of data: one for which we recorded eye movements from radar operators in a realistic mission simulator and the other while they were controlling real jet fighters, which played the roles of targets and friendlies. The data obtained both from the computer runs of the model and the records of eye movements from operators consist of long sequences of fixations of the general form

$$\ldots F_1 \text{-} T_1 \text{-} T_2 \text{-} S \text{-} F_1 \text{-} t \text{-} F_1 \text{-} F_2 \ldots$$

where fixations $F_1$-$F_2$, are friendly aircraft nos. 1 and 2, $T_1$-$T_2$, are targets 1 and 2, S is a stranger, t is the tote board, and so on, together with the times at which each fixation would occur. Earlier work showed that it was sufficient to sample the eye movement records twice a second. (See Figure 1.1.)

The most appropriate way to analyze this kind of data is to use Markov analysis. The sequence of observations is cast into a table containing the frequencies of transitions between the different classes of observations (states), and from these tables a table of state transition probabilities is derived. By appropriate mathematical transformations, several interesting statistics can be derived (Kemeny & Snell, 1960). If the transition probability matrix is raised to successively higher powers, we obtain a table in which all the rows are identical. This is the limiting matrix, and the entry in a column is an estimate of the proportion of time spent in that state. The second is the table of MFPTs. If we look at any cell $x_{rc}$ at the intersection of row $r$ and column $c$, its value is the mean number of samples that will occur from the last time the observer was in state $r$ before state $c$ is entered. For example, if we look at the intersection of $F_1$ and $T_2$, the value in that cell estimates the mean number of states passed through (other things looked at) from the last time $F_1$ was fixated until the next time $T_2$ is fixated. If samples are taken every $t$ seconds, then multiplying the MFPT by $t$ coverts the MFPT to a measure of time. A table can also be obtained of variance of the MFPTs, from which the standard deviation of the MFPT can be derived. If data include self-transitions where for cells $x_{rc}$ r = c, we can also estimate the mean duration of fixation time for each variable.

These are very powerful ways of looking at temporal sequences. They capture the dynamics of real-time operations in a way that traditional means (which usually reduce to the values of the limiting matrix) do not. Some examples are given from the work on radar operators in Figures 1.2 to 1.5.

All the predictions were validated at least to a first approximation. The computer model predicted that the maximum number of aircraft that could be handled would be four, because with that number the MFPTs were approaching the point of significant forgetting, and if we added the range of values implied by the variance of the MFPT, many MFPTs would lead to serious forgetting. Our empirical studies supported

this prediction. With four aircraft performance not only began to deteriorate, but one operator flew one of his aircraft off the radar plot and never found it again. (Fortunately this was in a simulated mission!) It is also interesting with respect to prediction 3, that at the end of one sortie with real aircraft, the operator suddenly glanced at another part of the radar and said, "Oh my God!" He had so ignored everything but the two aircraft that were close together that he had failed to attend to another of his aircraft for many seconds and had allowed it to stray into a designated flight path for civil aircraft leaving the United Kingdom for the continent.

We can conclude that a quantitative single-channel model of visual dynamic attention can predict significant details of the real-time behavior of humans performing real tasks to "a good engineering approximation."

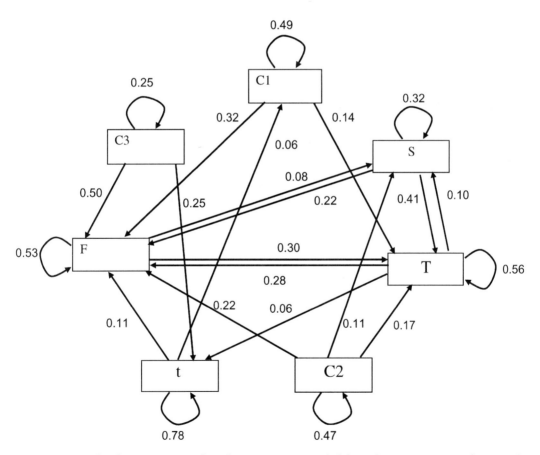

FIGURE 1.1. Graphical representation of eye fixation transition probabilities during a sortie using live aircraft. Given that the entity on the tail of an arrow is currently fixated, the probability is that the next fixation will be on the entity at the head of the arrow. F, friendly; S, stranger; T, target; t, tote board. C1, C2, and C3 are features on the console other than the screen.

A

|   | F | T | S | C | O |
|---|---|---|---|---|---|
| F | 0.00 | 0.73 | 0.23 | 0.02 | 0.02 |
| T | 0.54 | 0.00 | 0.38 | 0.03 | 0.05 |
| S | 0.48 | 0.42 | 0.00 | 0.00 | 0.10 |
| C | 0.00 | .040 | 0.60 | 0.00 | 0.00 |
| O | 0.10 | 0.50 | 0.30 | 0.00 | 0.10 |

B

|   | F | T | S | C | O |
|---|---|---|---|---|---|
| F | 1.56 | 0.76 | 1.64 | 33.19 | 10.04 |
| T | 1.03 | 1.36 | 1.49 | 33.05 | 9.72 |
| S | 1.08 | 0.91 | 2.07 | 33.75 | 9.42 |
| C | 1.56 | 1.07 | 1.10 | 33.94 | 10.06 |
| O | 1.49 | 0.95 | 1.52 | 33.84 | 9.26 |

C

| F | T | S | C | O |
|---|---|---|---|---|
| 0.32 | 0.37 | 0.24 | 0.01 | 0.05 |

FIGURE 1.2. Analysis of empirical eye movement data from controllers handling one friendly and one target. (A) Example of empirical transitional probability matrix for an experienced controller with two aircraft, one friendly (F) and one target (T). (B) The mean first passage time for data in A. Time is in seconds from last looking at an entity in the left-hand column to next looking at any entity in the top row. (C) Limiting matrix for the data in A. The numbers represent the proportion of time spent in each state. F, friendly; T, target; S, stranger; C, any fixation of console or instruments; O, any other fixation.

A

|   | F | T | C1 | C2 | C3 | t |
|---|---|---|---|---|---|---|
| F | 2.30 | 1.54 | 79.6 | 38.3 | 26.2 | 81.0 |
| T | 1.45 | 2.30 | 81.1 | 39.7 | 25.7 | 79.5 |
| C1 | 2.45 | 1.00 | 82.1 | 40.8 | 26.7 | 80.5 |
| C2 | 2.73 | 2.77 | 82.3 | 20.5 | 28.0 | 82.3 |
| C3 | 2.47 | 2.02 | 82.1 | 39.3 | 27.3 | 82.1 |
| t | 1.00 | 2.30 | 81.1 | 39.7 | 25.7 | 79.5 |

B

| F | T | C1 | C2 | C3 | t |
|---|---|---|---|---|---|
| 0.44 | 0.44 | 0.01 | 0.05 | 0.05 | 0.01 |

FIGURE 1.3. Example of computer simulation of eye movements with one friendly and one target. (A) The mean first passage time matrix generated by the model for one friendly (F) and one target (T). (B) Limiting matrix for data from which A was calculated. Proportion of time spent looking at each type of information. F, friendly; T, target; t, tote board; C1, C2, C3, three parts of the console excluding the screen. No S or O was included in this simulation.

### Example 2. The Analysis of SPADs: Why Do Train Drivers Pass Red Lights?

On British railways, a SPAD is a "signal passed at danger" and this occurs when a driver takes his train past a red signal ("signal showing a red aspect"). Although some SPADs are trivial, such as when a train stops at a platform but overruns a signal at red by 2 or 3 m, SPADs are taken extremely seriously, because they can often put a train in the path of another. Recently there were SPADs at Southall and at Ladbroke Grove that resulted in horrific crashes with many deaths. During the public inquiries into these accidents, I appeared as an expert witness for ASLEF, the train drivers' union. We were asked if we could explain why train drivers would pass signals having a red aspect. One good result of the inquiries was that the railways were made to set up

A

| | Friend | Target | Stranger | Console 1 | t | Console 2 | Console 3 | Console 4 |
|---|---|---|---|---|---|---|---|---|
| Friend | 1.78 | 1.11 | 3.58 | 151.1 | 170.8 | 20.9 | 25.0 | 7.08 |
| Target | 1.58 | 1.36 | 3.54 | 150.6 | 170.8 | 20.7 | 25.0 | 6.92 |
| Stranger | 1.94 | 1.44 | 2.97 | 151.6 | 169.9 | 20.8 | 25.1 | 6.74 |
| Console 1 | 1.59 | 1.54 | 4.30 | 101.0 | 171.7 | 20.5 | 25.7 | 6.61 |
| t | 3.52 | 2.70 | 5.73 | 152.8 | 39.5 | 22.9 | 27.1 | 7.78 |
| Console 2 | 2.19 | 1.48 | 3.72 | 151.7 | 171.5 | 13.6 | 20.7 | 6.73 |
| Console 3 | 1.90 | 1.53 | 4.36 | 151.6 | 171.7 | 20.9 | 14.8 | 7.20 |
| Console 4 | 1.90 | 1.44 | 3.51 | 150.5 | 171.3 | 20.5 | 25.0 | 5.54 |

B

| Friend | Target | Stranger | Console 1 | t | Console 2 | Console 3 | Console 4 |
|---|---|---|---|---|---|---|---|
| 0.28 | 0.37 | 0.17 | <0.01 | 0.01 | 0.04 | 0.03 | 0.09 |

FIGURE 1.4. Averaged data for 16 experienced controllers early in the sortie when aircraft are distant from one another. (A) Mean first passage time (in seconds) averaged for 16 experienced controllers. (B) Limiting matrix averaged for 16 experienced controllers. Proportion of time spent looking at each entity.

a research program into human factors, under which Prof. John Groeger, a colleague of mine at the University of Surrey, collected what we believe are the first driver eye movement data from real trains on a standard railway route. Furthermore, the chairman of the inquiry accepted our claim that to say that something was the result of "driver human error" was not an explanation of what happened, but should, in the future, be the start—not the end—of any inquiry.

I shall concentrate on Ladbroke Grove because it shows how an attention model can throw quantitative light on very complex field data. The situation at Ladbroke Grove is shown in Figure 1.6. Signals on this section of track are "four aspect." They can show green (G; "Proceed at speed."), double yellow (YY; "Prepare to slow down, the next signal may be YY, Y, or R.); single yellow (Y; "Slow down, the next signal

will be R or Y."), or red (R, "Stop. Do not proceed."). When approaching a G, the driver may drive the train up to the speed limit for that section of track, limits being indicated by trackside signs or on overhead gantries. At YY, speed need not be reduced, and may even be increased, but the driver should be prepared to slow down if the following signal is Y. A Y implies that the next signal will probably be a Y or an R, so speed should be reduced and the driver should prepare to stop. In addition to the light signals there is an auditory advanced warning system (AWS) signal located about 200 m before each signal. When the train passes the AWS, a bell sounds in the cab if the signal being approached is showing G, and a horn sounds if it is showing Y, YY, or R. (That is, the horn is equivalent to a "not G" message.) The driver must respond to show he has heard the AWS.

A

|  | Friend | Target | Stranger | Console 1 | t | Console 2 | Console 3 | Console 4 |
|---|---|---|---|---|---|---|---|---|
| Friend | 1.22 | 1.09 | 8.60 | ∞ | 109.2 | 26.5 | 59.3 | 16.8 |
| Target | 1.13 | 1.17 | 8.60 | ∞ | 109.2 | 26.0 | 59.3 | 16.8 |
| Stranger | 1.26 | 1.26 | 7.37 | ∞ | 109.9 | 25.9 | 59.2 | 16.5 |
| Console 1 | 1.52 | 1.05 | 9.12 | ∞ | 109.2 | 26.1 | 59.8 | 17.8 |
| t | 2.65 | 2.62 | 9.99 | ∞ | 28.2 | 26.1 | 61.3 | 18.8 |
| Console 2 | 1.55 | 1.39 | 8.81 | ∞ | 108.3 | 19.6 | 60.0 | 16.7 |
| Console 3 | 1.55 | 1.08 | 9.32 | ∞ | 109.9 | 26.7 | 44.2 | 16.3 |
| Console 4 | 1.35 | 1.33 | 8.71 | ∞ | 109.9 | 25.8 | 58.2 | 13.0 |

B

| Friend | Target | Stranger | Console 1 | t | Console 2 | Console 3 | Console 4 |
|---|---|---|---|---|---|---|---|
| 0.41 | 0.43 | 0.07 | 0 | 0.02 | 0.03 | 0.01 | 0.04 |

FIGURE 1.5. Averaged data for 16 experienced controllers late in the sortie when aircraft are close to one another. Compare with Figure 1.4 for empirical validation of the prediction concerning early and late periods in sorties. If first passage time = ∞, then the controller looked at the entity at the moment data collection began and never returned to it. Note the decrease in mean first passage time (MFPT) for the active aircraft, the increase for stranger, and the inverse changes in proportion of time spent attending to these variables, as predicted by the model. (A) MFPT averaged for 16 experienced controllers. Time is in seconds. (B) Limiting matrix averaged for 16 experienced controllers late in sortie when aircraft are close to one another. Proportion of time in each state.

Many SPADs seem to involve a loss of "situation awareness" (Endsley, 1995). Why did the driver not notice that the upcoming signal was red? Did he not look at it? If he did see the R, why did he not act accordingly? Why did the AWS not ensure that he looked at the signal in time to notice which aspect of the light was showing? The underlying problem is one of the dynamic allocation of attention.

Details of the public inquiry can be found in Cullen (2000). The skill with which accident investigation is carried out and the detailed analysis produced in public inquiries of this kind are extremely impressive. The site of the crash is measured meticulously, meteorological data are reconstructed, real-time "black box" records of the trains' movements, drivers' actions, settings of switch points, signal state, and so forth, are analyzed in detail, and observations of passengers and people who happened to observe the trains as they passed are considered. The following is a summary of the relevant facts.

In the early morning, with a bright, low sun behind him, Driver Hodder drove his commuter train

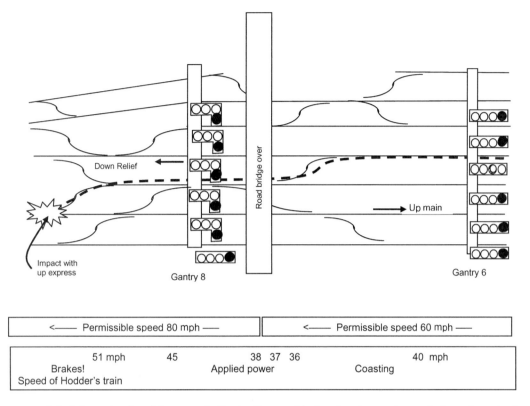

FIGURE 1.6. Schematic of track layout at Ladbroke Grove, with signal settings and record of speeds attained by Driver Hodder (not to scale). Note that signals are to the left of the line to which they apply. Distance between the gantries is 600 m. The tracks weave left and right over this distance, so the alignment of the signals with the tracks frequently changes. Lamps shown here in black were at red.

westward from Paddington Station through the section of track toward Ladbroke Grove. This is a very complex set of track, with six or more parallel tracks, including slow and fast lines in both directions, many places where trains must switch from one track to another and in so doing cross the paths of other trains, and where there are many signals, gantries, bridges, superstructures carrying electric catenaries, and so on. Often, signals are hidden for several seconds by other equipment, or a signal is not clearly seen until quite late in the driver's approach. Sometimes drivers have to count across a gantry to make sure which signal is which. The critical problem was that Hodder's train had to cross from one down track to another, and in doing so had to cross the path of trains coming in the opposite direction on the high-speed up line. The critical signal that guarded the crossing was SN109, preceded at a distance of several hundred meters by SN87. Figure 1.6 shows what happened.

The evidence suggests that as Hodder approached the crucial signal, SN109, he did the following:

1. He correctly read SN87 as having a yellow aspect (Y) and passed it coasting (i.e., at relatively low speed with the throttle closed).
2. He shortly afterward began to accelerate. Although he had just seen a Y, he was traveling more slowly than was necessary and one assumes he was trying to keep to his schedule, expecting the next signal to be a Y.
3. After he passed SN87 and approached SN109, the latter was showing an R.
4. At 239 m before SN109, he increased his acceleration substantially, despite the fact that he would be expecting SN109 to be either Y or R.
5. At 104 m before SN109 he again increased his acceleration.
6. At about 150 m before SN109 he would have heard the AWS horn in the cab, indicating a

"not G" state of upcoming SN109. We know that he heard this, because he pressed the button to cancel the AWS.

7. He passed SN109 (at R) with power still engaged at about 45 mph.
8. There were no "distractors" in his environment, in the sense of people working trackside, vandals, unusual trains or events, and so forth.

After he had passed SN109, he was on the track occupied by an up express coming in the opposite direction at about 100 mph, and a few seconds later the crash occurred. Both drivers and many passengers were killed.

One would like to answer the following questions:

1. Did Hodder look at least once at SN109?
2. If so, what did he see?
3. Is it likely that Hodder misread SN109 as not R and if so, why?
4. Why did Hodder not interpret the AWS alert as indicating a danger aspect that required him to slow or stop?
5. Is it likely that Hodder failed to look again at SN109 when he was close to it (after the AWS sounded) and if so, why?
6. More generally, if he failed to pay attention appropriately to SN109, is this something that was the result of some abnormal culpable behavior by Hodder or is it in some sense a "reasonable" thing that any driver might do?

Clearly the last question is vital. SPADs are rare, although not negligibly so, and if they occur because of "normal" behavior, rather than because of behavior that might be considered especially culpable in the driver, it could call for major redesign of the system.

Because trains run on tracks, driving a train may seem a simple task, but apart from the skill needed to control the enormous kinetic energy involved, the visual environment is highly dynamic and very rich in detail. In their study of train driver eye movements, Groeger and associates (2004) needed the following classification to describe what drivers looked at:

- Own signal
- Other signals (signals to the left and right of the driver's own signal)
- Own gantry (anywhere on the gantry holding the driver's own signal except a signal)
- Other gantry (and signals not facing the driver, or other gantries not facing the driver)

- Signage (speed restrictions, AWS hardware, direction indicators, TV monitors in stations, and so on)
- Moving objects (traveling trains, trackside work crews, and so on)
- Off track (fields, trees, and so on)
- Sky
- Track ahead (own or other)
- In cab (control panel, speedometer, windows, controls, and so on)

Note that some categories contain multiple sub-categories. It is this set of targets that visual attention samples. So when it was stated that there were no "distractions" in Hodder's environment just before the crash, that is misleading. With the exception of the sky and some off-track features, all the other features in Groeger's list *require* attention if the driver is carrying out his job conscientiously—*and all of them are distractors for each other.* His task is *not* just to look at signals.

Several characteristics of the approach to SN109 made it particularly hard for the driver to identify this signal. Road bridges, other gantries, posts, and a super-structure supporting catenary cables carrying electric current obscured the signals from time to time. The tracks weave from left to right and back, so that the alignment of signals with their tracks constantly changes, and signals disappear and reappear, making it even harder to identify the signal relevant to a particular train. The set of signals on gantry 8 was complex and numerous. From information theory we know this slows decisions and increases the probability of perceptual error. Moreover, there was one very important oddity about the signals on this gantry. Almost all four-aspect signals in Britain are arranged as shown in Figure 1.7A, but those on the critical gantry were as shown in Figure 1.7B. This had three effects:

1. The red aspect light of SN109 was obscured partially or wholly by an insulator until the driver was quite close to the signal, at about 150 m, whereas the YGY lights could be seen.
2. The driver's dominant mental model would expect the R to be below the YGY group. If the red aspect, although illuminated, could not be seen because it was obscured, then the driver, if fixating on the vertical YGY lamps, might assume that it was vertically below the visible lights and was not illuminated. Because there was no bright G illuminated, Hodder may have interpreted what he saw of SN109 from 270 m to 220 m as

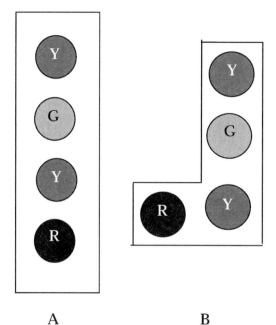

**A**                    **B**

FIGURE 1.7.  (A) Normal layout of four-aspect signal. (B) Layout of SN109, a four-aspect signal.

indicating that SN109 was in a state of "not G," as well as "not R," which would be compatible with SN87 having been Y.

3. The very low, bright sun shining from behind Hodder could have made the Y lamps of SN109 appear to be illuminated by reflection, which would be compatible with not G and not R.

We can now propose a sequence of cognitive events constraining Hodder's situation awareness:

1. SN87 at Y leads to an expectation that SN109 will be Y or YY.
2. The masking of SN109 and other signals on the approach to gantry 8 leads to uncertainty regarding which signal is which.
3. Nonetheless, SN109 is fixated, but the mental model of expected signal geometry, including the fact all the signals passed since leaving Paddington had the normal geometry, leads the driver to expect that if there is an R it will be vertically below the YGY of SN109.
4. No red is visible below the YGY of SN109.
5. The driver concludes that the state of SN109 is not R.
6. Because no bright G is visible and the signals are reflecting sunlight, he concludes that the not R state of SN109 is also not G and hence is Y or YY.

7. He therefore applies power and accelerates.
8. There is acute time pressure on the scheduling of visual attention. The environment contains many items that demand attention, as we saw from Groeger's classification. The task of driving a train, and in particular the task of driving defensively, requires Hodder to scan many parts of the visual environment.

Hodder had an extremely demanding visual environment that would have challenged his attention at the best of times. Given the work of Groeger and colleagues (2004), we can go considerably further toward a quantitative analysis of Driver Hodder's attention. Let us see what we can learn from Drivers' eye movements.[3]

During an earlier public inquiry into the crash at Southall, the train operating companies stated that when approaching a signal, drivers always look at signals and always see the signal before the AWS sounds. I pointed out that this was a specious belief, because no research had been done on drivers' visual attention, and I gave reasons from cognitive psychology that made it unlikely that this belief was correct. Groeger and colleagues recorded eye movements during approaches to 470 signals using 10 drivers. On nearly 30% of approaches, the drivers did not look at the signal until after the AWS sounded. During the last 15 seconds before reaching a signal, drivers fixate on the signal for only about 20% of the time. For another 44% of the time they are fixating on other parts of the environment (side of the track, rails, speed signs, oncoming trains, details inside the cab, and so forth). The remaining 36% of the time they are not fixating on anything: Their eyes are moving, and therefore no information is processed. The mean number of fixations in the last 15 seconds is 17.05 and, on the average, the first time the driver looked at the signal as he approached it was about 25% closer to the signal than when it first appeared and could have been fixated, leaving about 8.75 seconds before the signal was reached. What is the probability that after the first fixation the drivers fixate on it again to check it before passing it?

We could use Groeger's data to measure the transition probabilities among the drivers' fixations, but this has not yet been done. We can, however, make a first approximation by taking the proportions just mentioned and using them to drive a random number generator to generate strings of simulated fixations that satisfy the observed proportions. We can then use these simulated data to develop a Markov model as we did for the radar data.

Such modeling suggests the MFPT would be between 1.6 and 3 glances with a standard deviation of approximately 4.0. Taking the middle value of this estimate, we have an estimate of MFPT of about 2.2 fixations. Taking account of the time when the drivers are looking at nothing, this gives an estimate of the time between successive looks at the signal being approached on the order 2.5 seconds. Groeger found empirically that the mean fixations per second on signals is about 0.4, with a standard deviation of about 0.3, meaning that a fixation on a signal occurs about once every 2.5 seconds. This agrees well with the model. Furthermore, given the value of the standard deviation, there will be a substantial proportion of occasions on which fixations on signals occur less often than every 2.5 seconds. Indeed, about 15% of occasions should have an FPT of more than 7 seconds. Furthermore, Groeger measured how long it took, on average, for the drivers to fixate their signal for the first time after it became visible, and found that they traversed about a quarter of the distance to the signal before taking the first look. Because the standard deviation of this mean was about 0.25, there will be a substantial proportion—say, 0.05 or 0.1—of occasions on which the signal is not fixated until the driver has almost reached it (or even passed it?). Remember that we are not interested in whether this happens frequently. If an SPAD happens on even 0.1% of occasions, that is extremely hazardous. For safety it must *never* happen. In Hodder's case, SN109 only became fully visible (red light plus the vertical lights) for about the last 10 seconds of his approach. If Groeger's data are representative, there is a substantial probability—by which I mean greater than 1% and perhaps as high as 5%—of his only looking once more at the signal after it first appears.

Groeger also found that when approaching a signal the mean proportion of time spent fixating signals (rather than some other part of the environment) is 0.16. The standard deviation is ± 0.14. Hence, on about 15% of occasions we would expect the proportion of time spent looking at the signal to be as little as 0.02. The point at which SN109 was first fixated was at about 220 m, and this is about 15 seconds before passing the gantry, and 0.02 × 15 = 0.3 seconds. The R aspect is occluded until the last 10 seconds, and 0.02 of 10 seconds is 0.2 seconds.

It seems we can conclude, based on this statistical model, that only a small minority of approaches would result in more than one additional fixation on the signal after the first time it is fixated. It is therefore not unexpected that expert drivers working conscientiously will have time only for one look. We can conclude that if Hodder was behaving as drivers did on some 25 to 30% of Groeger's approaches, he could quite easily not have looked to check on what he had seen and what appeared to be the expected Y or YY aspect.

Would not the sound of the AWS horn draw his attention to the signal? Why did the AWS not lead him to check? If he saw the Y aspect on signal SN87, then he would expect to see a Y or YY on SN109. Because the red light was obscured until quite late in the approach, and because unlike all the other signals it was to one side of the Ys and not below them, the first thing he would have seen may well have been an apparent yellow caused by sun backscatter. There was no R visible, and no brightly illuminated G, but two weak Ys made somewhat bright by reflected light. Given that he expected a Y, then the sound of the AWS would have confirmed this, because the horn means either Y or YY or R (not just R) and he was expecting Y or YY.

A strong case can be made that driver Hodder passed SN109 at red without noticing it, and was under the impression that it was showing either a Y or YY aspect. This claim is supported by an analysis of the cognitive systems involved in attention, perception, and memory decision making while driving the train through the environment that contains SN87 and SN109. Apart from exonerating Driver Hodder (who was killed in the crash) from irresponsible behavior, the analysis also points to a fundamental defect in systems design. The AWS, by failing to distinguish between Y and YY on the one hand, and R on the other, leads drivers into danger. The AWS should have a specific sound to signal R.

## SUMMARY AND CONCLUSIONS

I hope that these two studies show convincingly that attention theory can be used to predict and analyze behavior quantitatively in real "field" situations. Of course I have, in both cases, used a single-channel model of attention, because of the nature of visual attention. It seems that my career has been somewhat "contrarian," as they say in investment circles. In earlier years I tried to convince Donald Broadbent that there were cases when parallel processing seemed to occur, and in recent years I have similarly insisted to Chris Wickens that attention should be modeled as single channel rather than multiple resources. It has been a privilege to know and to work with both of these colleagues and I want to end this chapter by acknowledging not just the quality of their work, but the value of their friendship and encouragement in my own career. It has been more than a century since Titchener (1903) published his book, and more than half a century since Broadbent (1953) performed the split-span experiment. I look forward to the book by Chris Wickens that will lead the next 100 years of work on attention.

## ACKNOWLEDGMENT

The author thanks Prof. John Groeger for information about his eye movement data.

## Notes

1. Woodworth (1938) and Woodworth and Schlosberg (1953) did considerably better. I recommend a look at Woodworth (1938); it is a remarkable collection of experimental work, some of which has never been better presented, and a rich source of ideas for research.

2. As I have noted elsewhere, to assume single-channel attention in real tasks is conservative. If people can use multiple resources they will do better than predicted. If we assume the contrary and are incorrect, they will do worse. In applied situations it is better to be pleasantly surprised.

3. Groeger's data were gathered on a different section of track, but the body of data is sufficient to use his results as a basis for general statements.

## References

Babington-Smith, B. (1961). Effect of attention in peripheral vision. *Nature, 189,* 776.

Boff, K., & Lincoln, J. (1988). *Engineering data compendium.* Dayton, Ohio: Wright–Patterson Air Force Base.

Broadbent, D. E. (1953). The role of auditory localization in attention and memory span. *Journal of Experimental Psychology, 47,* 191–196.

———. (1958). *Perception and communication.* Oxford: Pergamon.

Crossman, E. R. F. W. (1974). Automation and skill. In E. Edwards & F. Lees (Eds.), *The human operator in process control* (pp. 1–24). London: Taylor and Francis.

Cullen, Rt. Hon. Lord. (2000). *The Ladbroke Grove rail inquiry.* London: HSE Books, Her Majesty's Stationary Office.

Dessouky, M. I., Moray, N., & Kijowski, B. (1995). Taxonomy of scheduling systems as a basis for the study of strategic behavior. *Human Factors, 37*(3), 443–472.

Endsley, M. R. (1995). Towards a theory of situation awareness in dynamic systems. *Human Factors, 37*(1), 32–64.

Groeger, J. A., Bradshaw, M. F., Everatt, J., Merat, N., & Field, D. (2004). *Pilot study of train-drivers'*

*eye-movements.* Report to Rail Safety Research Programme. London: Rail Safety and Standards Board.

Jones, R. E., Milton, J. L., & Fitts, P. M. (1949). *Eye fixations of aircraft pilots, I. A review of prior eye-movement studies and a description of a technique for recording the frequency, duration and sequences of eye-fixations during instrument flight.* USAF technical report no. 5837. Dayton, Ohio: Wright–Patterson Air Force Base.

———, Milton, J. L., & Fitts, P. M. (1950). *Eye fixations of aircraft pilots, IV. Frequency, duration, and sequence of fixations during routine instrument flight.* USAF technical report no. 5975. Dayton, Ohio: Wright–Patterson Air Force Base.

Kemeny, J. G., & Snell, J. L. (1960). *Finite Markov processes.* New York: Van Nostrand.

Moray, N. (1986). Monitoring behavior and supervisory control. In K. R. Boff, L. Kaufman, & J. P. Thomas (Eds.), *Handbook of perception and human performance* (vol. 2, pp. 40.1–40.5). New York: John Wiley & Sons.

———. (1993). Designing for attention. In A. Baddeley & L. Weiskrantz (Eds.), *Attention: Selection, Awareness, and Control* (pp. 111–134). Oxford: Oxford University Press.

———, Fitter, M., Ostry, D., Favreau, D., & Nagy, V. (1976). Attention to pure tones. *Quarterly Journal of Experimental Psychology, 28,* 271–283.

———, Neil, G., & Brophy, C. (1983). *Selection and behaviour of fighter controllers.* Contract report. London: Ministry of Defence.

———, Richards, M., & Low, J. (1980). *The behaviour of fighter controllers.* Contract report. London: Ministry of Defence.

———, Synnock, G., & Sims, A. (1973). Tracking a static display. *IEEE Transactions on Systems, Man and Cybernetics, SMC-2,* 518–521.

Rasmussen, J., Pejtersen, A.-M., & Goodstein, L. (1995). *Cognitive engineering: Concepts and applications.* New York: John Wiley & Sons.

Senders, J. W. (1964). The human operator as a monitor and controller of multi-degree of freedom systems. *IEEE Transactions on Human Factors in Electronics, HFE-5,* 2–5. [Reprinted in Moray, N. (Ed.) 2005. *Ergonomics: Major writings* (vol. 1, pp. 47–55). London: Taylor and Francis.]

———. (1983). *Visual sampling processes.* Tilburg, The Netherlands: Katholieke Hogeschool.

———. Elkind, J. I., Grignetti, M. C., & Smallwood, R. (1965). *An investigation of the visual sampling behavior of human observers.* Technical report no. NASA-3860. Cambridge, Mass.: Bolt, Beranek and Newman.

Stevens, S. S. (1953). *Handbook of experimental psychology.* New York: John Wiley & Sons.

Titchener, E. B. (1903). *The psychology of feeling and attention.* London: Macmillan.

Underwood, G. (1974). Moray vs. the rest. *Quarterly Journal of Experimental Psychology, 26,* 368–372.

Woodworth, R. S. (1938). *Experimental psychology.* Boston, Mass.: John Holt.

———, & Schlosberg, H. (1953). *Experimental psychology.* New York: Holt, Rhinehart.

# Chapter 2

# Attention and Its Allocation: Fragments of a Model

## Thomas B. Sheridan

I will start by suggesting that attention is the focusing of sensory, motor, and/or mental resources on aspects of the environment to acquire knowledge. Attention allocation is deciding what to focus those resources on, whether the decision making is conscious or subconscious, based on current task needs and the benefits and costs relative to what is known.

Maybe one should say attention is *focusing the nervous system,* but that still begs the question of just what "focus" really means in this context. Hopefully, functional magnetic resonance imaging is beginning to show us!

Attention can be either voluntary or involuntary, and it can be either *exteroceptive* (done in conjunction with external visual, hearing, touch, taste, smell, or force sensing) or it can be *nonexteroceptive* (independent of external sensing, done only in the mind and possibly involving interoceptors as well). Thus we have a 2 × 2 matrix of attention conditions (an example is given in Table 2.1). (One might even make a further distinction between conscious and subconscious

attention, but I won't go there.) This chapter will deal mostly with exteroceptive attention, because what produces attention by the brain in the absence of overt, observable triggering events seems much more difficult to grapple with. Nonexteroceptive attention typically occurs over longer time periods (e.g., reflecting on last night's party).

Attention has never seemed to me to be able to be well defined in an operational sense. Many different words seem to relate to attention but are not quite the same in meaning: *situation awareness, mental workload, vigilance, fatigue, drowsiness, alertness, activation,* and *distraction* (and one could cite others). Most would seem to correlate either positively or negatively with what we commonly call attention, although probably not very well with each other. Workload is a special case, because at the high and low extremes it is undesirable. Within a particular individual there may be differences in how skilled one is in different ways of attending. Some of the terms mentioned earlier attenuate attention generally (e.g., drowsiness), whereas

TABLE 2.1.  2 × 2 Matrix of Attention Conditions.

|  | Exteroceptive | Non-exteroceptive |
|---|---|---|
| Voluntary | Driving a car | Planning tomorrow |
| Involuntary | Surprise by loud noise | Feeling sick |

others refocus attention (e.g., distraction) (Sheridan, 2004). I believe we have not sufficiently sorted out these differential meanings, at least in any objective way. We need to try.

Attention allocation may be said to be hierarchical. Attending to income taxes or cutting the lawn or writing this chapter subsumes attention to many subtasks of those larger tasks. Given that any task analysis can be broken into smaller tasks, and given that each gross task and subtask has an attention requirement, one can distinguish between *macro attention* at the gross task level and *micro attention* at the subtask level. Attention allocation is a form of decision behavior that depends heavily on stored information (what we already know) about objects and events with respect to their interrelationships in time, space, magnitude, and relevance (utility or worth). In this sense, attention can be contrasted to what Gibson (1979) has called *affordances*. Gibson's affordances are opportunities for action made available by observations of (attraction of attention to) the external environment, whereas stored information (as a basis for decision to allocate attention) is internal. Obviously, the two must somehow coordinate (which we wish we understood better!).

To me as an engineer (and hopefully to others interested in understanding and predicting attention and attention allocation in design applications), it is helpful to represent what we observe in models (abstract representations of interrelations). The purpose of a model is to be able to *generalize* the interrelations from multiple sets of observed data and ultimately to *predict* some (dependent, or endogenous) variables as a function of other (independent, or exogenous) variables. There are many different ways to model (words, mathematics, graphic diagrams, and so on) and no one way is best. Certainly no tractable model can represent interrelations of more than a small set of variables, and the usefulness of a model is usually inversely proportional to the number of variables represented. Models can operate at the gross behavior level (e.g., attention) or at the level of the biochemistry of synaptic junctions. Obviously this chapter is aimed at the former and not

the latter. Models can also be *descriptive* (of what *did* happened in the past) or *predictive* (of what *will* happen in the future) or *normative* (given certain assumptions this is how the variables *should* behave) or some combination of these.

I subtitle this chapter "fragments of a model" (of attention and its allocation) because the models I discuss only encompass some elements of what must be going on, and I make no claim to being even close to modeling the complete story. In the spirit of this book honoring Chris Wickens, I review several different behavior modeling ideas proffered by myself and my students during the past 40 years. I'm fully aware that my perspective on what attention and attention allocation are, and how to model them, may differ from the norms that Wickens (2002) has so nicely established.

## MECHANISTIC MODELS FOR ATTENDING AND ACQUIRING MENTAL MODELS OF THE WORLD

Attending would be a meaningless activity were it not built upon a foundational structure of preacquired knowledge, and the coding of that knowledge in the brain, which includes attributes of both function and relative worth. As Chomsky (1965) has shown, much of linguistic ability (not linguistic knowledge) is prewired in the neonate. Even then, as developmental neurobiologists tell us, the synapses are furiously searching out and rejecting connections to make sense of the "blooming, buzzing confusion" being encountered by the wide-eyed infant in the new world outside the mother's womb. Amazingly, during those early months things manage to get sorted out and we come to attend to what is important as best we know what is important in time and sensory space. However, we also have our mental resource limits that Wickens (1980, 2002) has so eloquently characterized. Some might assert that, in addition, we are inherently lazy or otherwise constrained by attention inertia.

So how might we model attention as a focusing of sensory, motor, and/or mental resources on aspects of the environment to acquire knowledge? The following subsections present two mechanistic modeling ideas that seem relevant: the Kalman estimator and the Yufik virtual associative network (VAN). Both models assume sensory, motor, and/or mental resources already focused on some part of the environment (they are not models for *allocating* attention).

### Attention and Knowledge Acquisition by the Kalman Estimator

Let us start with the procedure (Kalman, 1960) that has proved invaluable in control engineering—an algorithm that, when embodied in a computer, really works in control tasks. It is suggested here as a normative representation of how knowledge is gained in situations when the variables are continuous in time. It is a way of compromising between making decisions based on an internal representation of reality, such as "dead reckoning," and responding simply to external stimuli, such as classic "error nulling" feedback control.

Neither dead reckoning nor error nulling works well in the face of noise. If the internal representation of space or initial conditions is in error, the dead-reckoning actions taken will be in error. If measurement of the

external stimulus is in error, the error-nulling control actions will be in error.

Figure 2.1 diagrams the process of estimation, as commonly considered by control engineers and estimation theorists. The boxes represent operations that in various applications are well defined and usually mathematical, typically linear differential equation transfer functions. To the left of the dashed line is the intelligent estimator, the animal or computer, and to the right is its environment. The blob on the right represents the true reality "out there." We assert that this true reality can never be known but can only be estimated, because of "filters" that lie between the information processing internal to the animal or machine and the outside world. There is a sensory filter on the afferent side and an action filter on the efferent side, and these filters cause distortions such as noise, nonlinearities, nonstationarities, and time delay—and, in effect, cut us off from measuring or affecting all but a minute portion of the potential spectrum of variables that are "out there." For example, one does not normally attend to the ceiling or the floor. The arrows represent causality or signal flow, and their lowercase letter labels are the key variables. In general, all the variables are vectors, quite large ones. For qualitative characterization purposes we need not be concerned with their size.

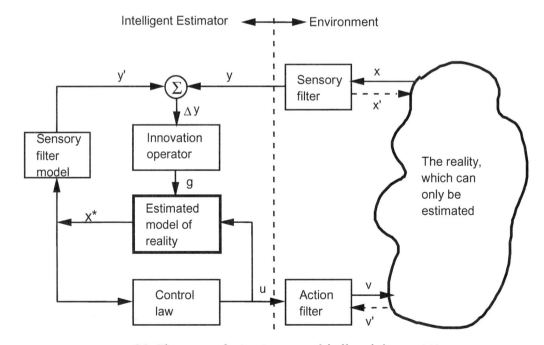

FIGURE 2.1. The process of estimation as a model of knowledge acquisition.

At the upper right, x is the state of reality, the unknown that we seek to know (and therefore must estimate). It is sensed by a constraining sensory filter that is represented (to the extent that it is known from experience) in the biological or electronic brain on the left of the dashed line. x′ is the covariable that always exists when two systems interact. In physical interactions, for example, if x were voltage measurement, x′ would be the current drawn from the environment by the voltmeter. If x were mechanical position, x′ would be the force imposed by the strain gauge or other device. Mostly, x′ is a small effect, but one can never measure something without affecting it (the Heisenberg principle). In social interactions, x′ is the effect the observer has on the observed.

On the left side, x* is the sought-after estimate of x (we will see in a moment how it is derived). On the basis of a best estimate of the state of reality x*, the animal or machine decides what to do about it (a control law), generating a command to the action filter (muscles or motors), the output of which is v, a mechanical force or position. (Animal or robot actions are only mechanical actions.) v′ is the covariable for v, the mechanical position or force complement to v′, where the product of v and v′ is energy. In this case, the action on the environment generates an action back on the muscles or motors, and the intelligent entity is changed in the process of making a change, this time (at least in a physical sense) to a more significant extent than with sensing, because the energy level with muscles is greater.

The heavy-lined box on the left is a model of reality (including a model of the action filter), which is driven by u in the same manner as the action filter and true reality, and in turn generates x*, which can be seen to be an input to the sensory filter model as well as the control law. This model is initially posited as a best guess, but gradually it is improved, based on a discrepancy between the output y′ of the sensory filter model and the output y from the real sensory filter. This discrepancy Δy is input to an *innovation operator* that determines how the model is driven into conformity with sensed reality (by g, the innovations change variable).

Thus the sensory, estimator, and action elements together *attend* to some part of the environment to acquire and refine knowledge on the basis of continuous feedback, not the simple form of feedback of the servomechanism, but rather a scheme that bootstraps a model into progressively closer matching with the measured environment. In modern (or "optimal") control there is a related theory (which need not concern us here) for shaping the control law, given x*, to optimize with respect to a given objective function. Through such attention, knowledge is acquired (refining the model) and a basis for further attention is established.

### Knowledge Acquisition by the Yufik Virtual Associative Network

The model of knowledge acquisition just described is a "black-box" characterization at the most abstract level. Perhaps a little closer to biological reality is a characterization originally developed by Yufik (Yufik & Sheridan, 1996), which hypothesizes the brain as a network of interconnections between storage (knowledge representation) elements that can be gradually shaped by interaction with stimuli (not unlike other network models of synaptic connection). Assume in Figure 2.2 (left) a pool of storage elements X (small dots) each of which is initially randomly connected to a large fraction of other elements. With use (environmental stimulation of certain elements but not others), these connection bonds are strengthened; with disuse, they are weakened. Over time, clusters form, but with much overlap (Fig. 2.2, center). The criterion for cluster formation is that the

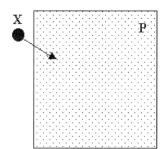 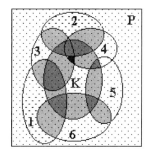 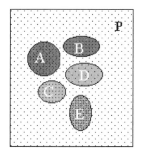

FIGURE 2.2. The virtual associative network as a model of knowledge acquisition.

sum of transitions between states within a cluster exceeds the sum of transitions from internal states to states outside the cluster by some confidence parameter. In time, the clusters are discrete and independent (Fig. 2.2, right). Computer simulation was used to show that this algorithm produced efficient learning.

Yufik and Sheridan (1996) further hypothesize that (1) clusters respond as synchronous units and (2) partitioning the resource pool into clusters enhances discrimination between the stimuli that caused the partitioning, and that "clusterization" suppresses spurious responses.

Clusters are assumed to have different stability, depending on the ratio of internal to external associative forces. The higher the ratio, the more stable the cluster. Changing cluster stability establishes an energy landscape over the resource pool. The more stable the cluster, the higher the energy barrier at its boundary. Because there are no areas in the landscape inaccessible to unit traffic, all boundary adjustments are globally coordinated. The landscape facilitates transfer of units between the clusters in which the weaker clusters dissolve and/or merge with the stronger ones (Fig. 2.3). In this way, the landscape suppresses spurious resource combinations using energy barriers.

VAN clusterization can represent stored knowledge (from past attention) or current allocation of sensory, motor, or cognitive resources (i.e., current attention). The VAN model was applied to a simulated air traffic controller situation, during which the controller's eye movements were measured, and attention to separation violations of aircraft was successfully modeled (Landry, Sheridan, & Yufik, 2001).

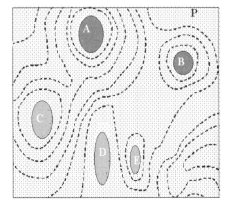

FIGURE 2.3. Virtual associative network clusters with energy barriers (as in a topographical map).

## NORMATIVE MODELS FOR DECIDING WHERE TO ATTEND

The models described here assumed attention already focused on some part of the environment, resulting in acquisition of knowledge. Given a knowledge base, mechanisms of *attention allocation* (a *decision process*) then become tractable. Several modeling ideas are presented in the following pages that characterize how "best" to estimate the state of the world to decide what is best to attend to: Bayesian updating, information value, dynamic programming, optimal temporal sampling, and fuzzy rules.

### Probability and Bayesian Updating

We know that humans are rational in attending more often to events that are more likely to change with time (Senders, Elkind, Gringnetti, & Smallwood, 1966). Insofar as relative probabilities of objects and events are relevant to deciding where to direct attention, Bayesian updating (Sheridan & Ferrell, 1974) should apply:

$$\frac{p(H_1|D_1, D_2, \ldots D_n)}{p(H_2|D_1, D_2, \ldots D_n)} = \frac{p_0(H_1)}{p_0(H_2)} \cdot \frac{p_0(D_1|H_1)}{p(D_1|H_2)}$$
$$\cdot \frac{p_0(D_2|H_1)}{p(D_2|H_2)} \ldots \frac{p_0(D_n|H_1)}{p(D_n|H_2)}$$

$$(2.1)$$

where $H_1$ and $H_2$ represent any pairing of hypotheses or tentative representations of the state of the world, and all $D_i$ represent the data or stimuli that are observed. The first term after the equals sign is the prior odds ratio (or even indifference: a ratio of 1). As more data are acquired, more terms are added to the bottom line to deduce better estimates of ratios of probabilities of current states, and this information is finally used to direct attention to the most likely H, other things being equal. Although the equation remains correct for either numerators or denominators, the likelihood ratios filling out the bottom line (ratios of some observation D, given $H_1$ or given $H_2$) are more amenable to the way people think; humans are not good at judging absolute probabilities p(D|H).

By comparing probabilities of different hypotheses (about, say, opportunities or threats in the environment), one can decide what to attend to next. When contingent probabilities are readily recordable (e.g., in eye tracking) there are emerging models that show promise, such as hidden Markov models (Rabiner, 1989).

## Using Information Value When Stimuli Are Only Known as Probabilities

When a set of events can be identified, along with the best action to take with respect to each (in this context I mean attention by the brain, not necessarily physical action), then the value over all such events is easily computed. Let $V(u_j|x_i)$ be the gain or reward or *objective function* for taking action $u_j$ when a process $x$ is in state $i$. If $x_i$ is known exactly, then a rational decision maker adjusts $u_j$ (selects $j$) to maximize $V$ for each occurrence of $x_i$, in each instance yielding $\max_j[V(u_j|x_i)]$. In this case, the average reward over a set of $x_i$ is

$$V_{avg} = \Sigma_i p(x_i)\{\max_j[V(u_j|x_i)]\} \qquad (2.2)$$

If $x_i$ is known only as a probability density, $p(x_i)$, then the best a rational decision maker can do is to adjust $u_j$ once to be the best in consideration of the whole density function $p(x_i)$. In this case, the average reward over a set of $x_i$ is

$$V'_{avg} = \max_j[\Sigma_i p(x_i)\, V(u_j|x_i)] \qquad (2.3)$$

Information value, then, is the difference between the gain in taking the best action, given each specific $x_i$ as it occurs, and the gain in taking the best action in ignorance of each specific $x_i$—in other words, knowing only $p(x_i)$:

$$V^*_{avg} = V_{avg} - V'_{avg} \qquad (2.4)$$

This difference is called *information value* (Howard, 1966) and is to be distinguished from Shannon information (Sheridan, 1995). In situations when current objects and events are known only probabilistically, but there is stored knowledge about $V(u_j|x_i)$, one can use the information value calculation to decide how to allocate attention relative to any set of $x_i$.

### Dynamic Programming to Optimize Attention to Previewed Stimuli

In many tasks (walking, driving a car) a human can "preview" an environment visually to anticipate and coordinate control actions to be taken in the near future. Tulga and Sheridan (1980) represented this situation in a laboratory setting by the display shown in Figure 2.4.

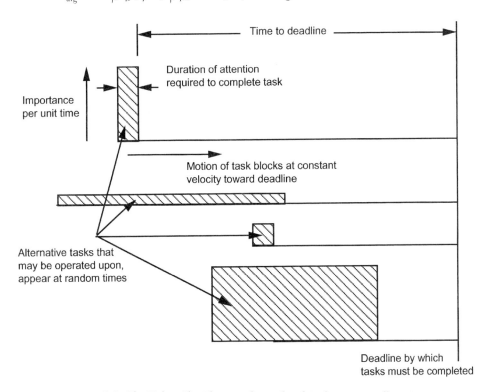

FIGURE 2.4. The Tulga–Sheridan paradigm of multitask attention allocation.

Each rectangle represented an independent object that needs attention to gain value from it, its height being the relative value gained per unit time of attention and the width being the relative duration of attention. These rectangles appeared at random (they need not have) and moved toward a deadline (that could be thought of as "now" for previewed objects). "Attending" in the experiment required the subject to move a computer cursor to within any rectangle, at which time the width of that rectangle would decrease at a constant rate (earning points). The goal was to maximize one's score.

The authors developed a T-path dynamic programming algorithm as a normative model to fit the data. The algorithm used a discount rate for expected future rewards, and branch and bound elimination rules to minimize the enumeration space. The mathematics will not be elaborated here. Suffice it to say that dynamic programming well suits the optimization of attention in multitask situations that are not too complex. Sheridan (1966) showed how dynamic programming could be applied to avoiding previewed obstacles in driving, and to a physician allocating "personal presence" to patients as well, some of whom posed the added cost of transportation to see them (Sheridan, 1970a).

A very simple example of dynamic programming is given in Figure 2.5. One works from the initial state and keeps track of (1) the least cumulative cost, C, to get to each state at each stage; and (2) the least cost path P (last state) to get to the current state. Then, at the least cost state at the final stage (1 in the example), one can trace back the least cost path (heavy line) to get there (in this case, state 2 at stage 2, state 3 at stage 1).

Moray and colleagues (1981) proposed a scheduling theory approach to the previous Tulga task. Dessouky and associates (1995) offered a taxonomy of scheduling systems as a basis for the study of strategic behavior and argued that several models from operations research might be useful in the allocation of function.

### Optimal Temporal Sampling

In many situations the value of information is a function of how recently a particular display or source of information has been observed. At any instant an operator observes a display that is the most current information, but as time passes after one observation (action) and before a new one, the information becomes "stale," eventually converging to some statistical expectation. How often should a person sample to gain information and readjust controls, given that there is some finite cost for sampling as well as the gradually increasing cost of inattention?

A way of considering information content together with costs is depicted in Figure 2.6 (Sheridan, 1970b), when the supervisory operator observes a system "state" vector $x$ and tries to take action $u$ to maximize some given objective function $V(x, u)$. Specifically, the question is how often to sample $x$ and/or update $u$. We assume that the state $x$ in this case includes any directly observable inputs and/or outputs relative to the system that will help the operator decide what further sample or action to take (a more inclusive definition than is usually assumed in control problems). The operator also is assumed to have statistical expectations about such signals.

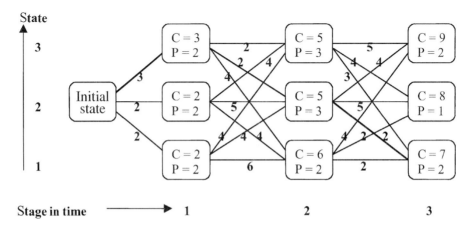

FIGURE 2.5. A simple example of dynamic programming.

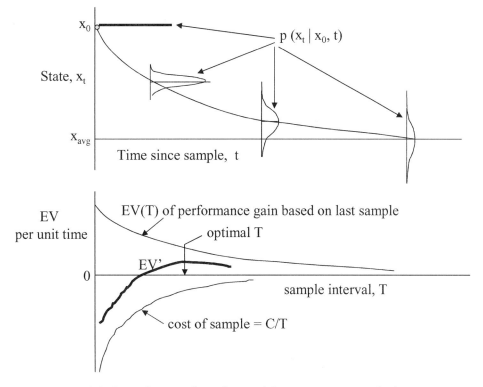

FIGURE 2.6.  Optimal temporal sampling model to maximize expected value (EV).

The analysis is easier when x and u are scalars. Given assumptions about the probability of x and how rapidly it is likely to change, given a value (objective) function for consequences resulting from a particular x and a particular u in combination, and given a discrete cost of sampling, one can derive an optimal sampling strategy as follows to maximize expected gain.

Assume that x has a known prior probability density $p(x)$, that $x_0$ is its particular value at the time of sampling, and that $p(x_t|x_0, t)$ is a best available model of expectation of x at time t following a sample having value $x_0$. (Necessarily, when $t = 0$, $p(x_t|x_0, t) = 1$ for $x_t = x_0$ and 0 elsewhere. Thereafter the density $p(x_t|x_0, t)$ spreads out, approaching $p(x)$ as t becomes large.) Assume also that $V(x, u)$ is the reward for taking action u when the state is x. The goal is to maximize EV, the expected value of V.

Clearly, without any sampling the best one can do is adjust u once and for all to maximize EV:

EV for no sampling
= max over u of [$\Sigma$ over x of  $(V|x, u) \cdot p(x)$]    (2.5)

If one could afford to sample continuously, the best strategy would be to adjust u continuously to maximize over u for each $(V|x, u)$ for the particular x encountered, so that

EV for continuous sampling
=$\Sigma$ over $x_0$ of [max  over u of $(V|x_0, u)] \cdot p(x_0)$
(2.6)

where $p(x_0) = p(x)$.

For the intermediate case of intermittent sampling,

$E(V|x_0, t)$ at t after sample $x_0$
= max over u of [$\Sigma$ over $x_t$ of $(V|x_t, u)$
$\cdot p(x_t|x_0, t)]$    (2.7)

Then $E(V|t) = \Sigma$ over $x_\phi$ of $E(V|x_0, t) \cdot p(x_0)$, remembering again that $p(x_0) = p(x)$.

In this case, for any sampling interval T and sampling cost C, the net EV is

$EV^* = (1/T)$ [$\Sigma$ over t from
0 to T of $E(V|t)] - C$]    (2.8)

So the best one can do is to maximize EV* with respect to T. The components of these tradeoffs are represented in Figure 2.6 as a function of time. The maximum of the heavy line EV' is thus the optimum.

Sheridan and Rouse (1971) found in an experiment that, even after the V(x,u) functions were made quite evident to subjects, their choices of T were suboptimal relative to this model. Moray (1986) points out that subjects with even moderate training are quite likely to demonstrate suboptimal behavior, and only after they "live the experience of the costs" for a long time are they likely to converge on optimality. Moray (1981) suggests approaches similar to that presented earlier in discussing the role of attention in error detection and diagnosis. More recently Moray and Inagaki (unpublished) have suggested a similar approach to that presented previously that draws on earlier work by Carbonell (1966).

### Fuzzy Rules to Decide Where to Attend

As noted earlier, language is intrinsic to all peoples, the ability hard wired and the particular language learned. There is also a strong suggestion in everyday language use and experience with semantics that words and thought are *fuzzy*. Fuzzy "if-then" rules applied to current stimuli (the "if" part) individually or in combination imply the strength of the alternative actions (the "then" part). In the current context, the "then" is where to allocate attention.

*Fuzzy rules* are different from *crisp rules* because *fuzzy sets* are fundamentally different from *crisp sets*. *Fuzzy* mathematics was introduced by Zadeh (1965) and has been extensively developed in Japan and other nations—perhaps more than in the United States, where it is controversial. For some people the term *fuzzy* seems a contradiction to rationality (which it is not!). Kosko (1992) is a good reference for those not familiar with fuzzy logic.

The membership M of objects or events of a fuzzy set can be 0 or 1 or anything in between. The meanings of words (the symbols of natural language) are fuzzy, in the sense that a word can apply very well (clearly, obviously) to some objects or events, can clearly exclude other objects or events, and can apply somewhat (more or less, partially) to still other objects and events. The membership is the degree of fit.

Figure 2.7 gives a simple example of plausible meanings, in terms of membership function M (fit, relative truth, applicability, and so on) for each of two physical variables relating to landing a private aircraft at a nearby field rather than going on to the planned destination. The first variable is gradations of *engine roughness*, for example, as measured by an accelerometer,

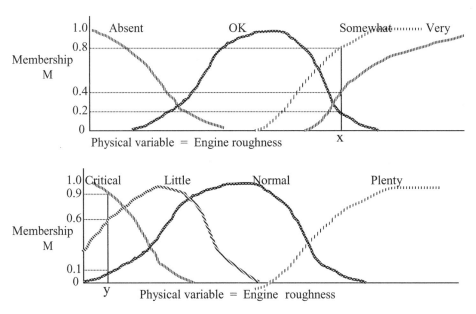

FIGURE 2.7. Fuzzy membership functions and the procedure to evaluate landing rules. From Sheridan (1992).

and the second physical variable is gradations of *remaining fuel*, for example, as measured in gallons. Each of the four curves for engine roughness and the four for remaining fuel specifies membership in a fuzzy set (labeled by a corresponding verbal term) relative to the associated quantitative and objectively measurable variable. Then, any given quantitative value maps to a fuzzy vector M of different memberships corresponding to each of several different fuzzy terms. In this example the engine roughness indicated by the mark "x" on the abscissa (physical continuum) of Figure 2.7 has membership M = 0.8 for "*somewhat* rough," 0.4 for "*very* rough," and 0.2 for "*okay*." The fuzzy vector for the *remaining fuel* mark "y" maps to 0.9 for "critical," 0.6 for "little fuel," and 0.1 for "normal."

Thus, any physical state vector maps to a corresponding membership M for every fuzzy term or symbol. We show next how it follows that any logical if-then statement made up of fuzzy symbols (such as, "If the engine is somewhat rough or very rough and there is little fuel, or, if fuel is critical, then land.") yields a net membership or relative applicability for the given physical situation. It is common to assume that the conjunction OR (logical union) means the *maximum* of the memberships of the two or more associated terms and the conjunction AND (logical intersection) means the *minimum* of their memberships. (Intuitively one can think of the memberships as tighter and looser degrees of constraint: OR means either is acceptable, so there is no point in using the tighter constraints; AND means they all must hold, so there is no choice but to impose the tightest constraint.) Then we can evaluate the net M for the given rule by parsing each rule. For example:

{[(*somewhat* rough) OR (*very* rough)] AND
[(*little* fuel)]} OR {(fuel *critical*)} → Land   (2.9)

This statement, for specified values of roughness and fuel, therefore has relative membership

$$M = max\ \{min[max\ (0.8), (0.4)],$$
$$[(0.6)]\}, \{(0.9)\} = 0.9 \qquad (2.10)$$

Figure 2.7 shows how the numbers are derived from the curves.

There may be other rules that recommend different actions. For example, "If A is the case, then take action 1; if B is the case, then take action 2." One procedure for determining final action in a given situation is to let the rule or combination of rules that has relatively greatest applicability dominate. In other words, the action with the greatest membership M should be taken, as is done in the text under the fuzzy variable plots in Figure 2.7. (Another procedure, applicable when the candidate actions are different degrees of the same physical variable, is to weight each action according to its membership so that the final action is a compromise.) Thus, the decision on where to attend can be modeled by fuzzy rules.

## CONCLUSION

Attention (the exteroceptive kind) is the process of focusing sensory, motor, and/or mental resources on particular elements of the environment to acquire knowledge. Attention allocation is decision making about how best to allocate sensory, motor, and mental resources, given a prior knowledge base of objects and events coded with respect to probability, functional meaning, and relative importance. Several models relating to attention are reviewed, both for the attention/knowledge acquisition process and for attention allocation. The models presented are "fragment" ideas that might be useful in building a comprehensive model of attention, but no such comprehensive model is offered here.

### References

Carbonell, J. R. (1966). A queuing model for many-instrument visual sampling. *IEEE Transactions on Human Factors in Electronics*, HFE-7, 157–164.

Chomsky, N. (1965). *Aspects of the structure of syntax.* Cambridge, Mass.: MIT Press.

Dessouky, M. I., Moray, N., & Kijowski, B. (1995). Taxonomy of scheduling systems as a basis for the study of strategic behavior. *Human Factors*, 37(3), 443–472.

Gibson, J. J. (1979). *The ecological approach to visual perception.* Boston, Mass.: Houghton Mifflin.

Howard, R. (1966). Information value theory. *IEEE Transactions on Systems Science and Cybernetics*, SSC-2, 22–26.

Kalman, R. E. (1960). A new approach to linear filtering and prediction problems. *Journal of Basic Engineering, Transactions of the ASME*, 82D, 33–45.

Kosko, B. (1992). *Neural networks and fuzzy systems.* Englewood Cliffs, N.J.: Prentice Hall.

Landry, S. J., Sheridan, T. B., & Yufik, Y. (2001). Cognitive grouping in air traffic control. *IEEE Transactions on Intelligent Transportation Systems*, 2, 92–101.

Moray, N. (1981). The role of attention in the detection of errors and in the diagnosis of failure in man–machine systems. In J. Rasmussen & W. Rouse (Eds.), *Human detection and diagnosis of system failures* (pp. 185–198). New York: Plenum Press.

———. (1986). Monitoring behavior and supervisory control. In K. Boff, L. Kaufman, & J. Thomas (Eds.), *Handbook of perception and human performance* (vol. 2). New York: Wiley.

———, Dessouky, M. I., Kijowski, B. A., & Adapathya, R. (1991). Strategic behavior, workload, and performance in task scheduling. *Human Factors, 33*(6).

Rabiner, L. (1989). A tutorial on hidden Markov models and selected applications in speech recognition. *Proceedings of the IEEE, 77*(2), 257–286.

Senders, J. W., Elkind, J. I., Grignetti, M. C., & Smallwood, R. P. (1966). An investigation of the visual sampling behavior of human observers. NASA-CR-434. Cambridge, Mass.: Bolt, Beranek and Newman.

Sheridan, T. B. (1966). Three models of preview control. *IEEE Transactions on Human Factors in Electronics, HFE-6*, 91–102.

———. (1970a). Optimum allocation of personal presence. *IEEE Transactions on Human Factors in Electronics, HFE-10*, 242–249.

———. (1970b). On how often the supervisor should sample. *IEEE Transactions Systems, Science and Cybernetics, SSC-6*(2), 140–145.

———. (1992). *Telerobotics, automation and human supervisory control.* Cambridge, Mass.: MIT Press.

———. (1995). Reflections on information and information value. *IEEE Transactions on Systems, Man and Cybernetics, 25*(1), 194–196.

———. (2004). Driver distraction from a control theory perspective. *Human Factors, 46*(4), 587–599.

Sheridan, T., & Ferrell, W. (1974). *Man–machine systems: Information, control and decision models of human performance.* Cambridge, Mass: MIT Press.

Sheridan, T. B., & Rouse, W. B. (1971). Supervisory sampling and control; sources of suboptimization in a prediction task. *In Proceedings of the 7th annual conference on manual control.* University of Southern California.

Tulga, M. K., & Sheridan, T. B. (1980). Dynamic decisions and workload in multi-task supervisory control. *IEEE Transactions on Systems, Man and Cybernetics, SMC-10*(5), 217–231.

Wickens, C. D. (1980). The structure of attentional resources. In R. Nickerson (Ed.), *Attention and performance VIII* (pp. 239–257). Hillsdale, N.J.: Erlbaum.

Wickens, C. D. (2002). Multiple resources and performance prediction. *Theoretical Issues in Ergonomic Science, 3*, 159–177.

Yufik, Y., & Sheridan, T. B. (1996). Virtual networks: New framework for operator modeling and interface optimization in complex supervisory control systems. *Annual reviews in control* (vol. 20, pp. 179–195). Oxford, UK: Pergamon.

Zadeh, L. (1965). Fuzzy sets. *Information and Control, 8*, 338–353.

# Chapter 3

# Capturing Attention in the Laboratory and the Real World

*Walter R. Boot, Arthur F. Kramer, and Ensar Becic*

Researchers have long been interested in the forces that control the movement of visual attention. As far back as the writings of William James (1842–1910), psychologists have made the distinction between two types of attention movements: movements that are endogenous, driven by the goals and intentions of the observer, and movements that are exogenous, driven by stimulus properties in the visual environment. The allocation of attention to different regions of the visual environment is widely assumed to be an interaction between these two forces. Sometimes these forces work in concert to allow the correct allocation of attention, but other times stimulus-driven and goal-directed forces may be at odds. When an exogenous shift of attention is made despite the fact that the stimulus property evoking this shift is unrelated to or at odds with the current goal of the observer, it is said that attention has been *captured*. In many instances, drawing the attention of an individual away from his or her primary task can be detrimental. This distraction may interrupt an important task requiring focused attention.

However, in other instances, as in the case of an alarm, drawing attention away from the primary task at a particular instant may have crucial importance.

Basic attention research has used a number of different paradigms to reveal the stimulus properties that will capture an observer's attention while he or she is engaged in some other task (in most cases, a visual search task). Based on these findings, applied attention researchers have used these stimulus properties in displays with the hopes of directing operators' attention to important information. However, it has become increasingly clear that laboratory findings regarding attention capture may not always scale up to more complex, real-world situations. This chapter has three purposes: (1) to review the basic attention capture literature and the important findings of various attention capture paradigms, (2) to point out examples within the basic attention capture literature that suggest instances in which attention capture might fail to scale up, and lastly (3) to highlight some examples in the applied research domain that illustrate failures and successes of the application of attention capture principles to real-world problems. Additionally, we report the results of a series of studies examining whether basic attention capture effects will manifest in a complex and dynamic display modeled on a real-world task.

## BASIC ATTENTION FINDINGS

Basic attention researchers have used a number of paradigms to study the phenomenon of attention capture (Fig. 3.1). These include the additional singleton, oculomotor capture, irrelevant singleton, and contingent capture paradigms. These paradigms, based on simple visual search tasks, aim to measure the influence of an irrelevant or antipredictive stimulus feature (e.g., unique color singleton) on the allocation of attention to a target item. The two features examined most in the attention capture literature are onset (the sudden appearance of an object) and color. Here we provide a brief review of attention capture paradigms commonly used by basic attention researchers and the relevant findings of each.

In the additional singleton paradigm (Fig. 3.1A), observers search for a target location defined by a unique feature (e.g., a circle among square distractors) and indicate the identity of a target at that location. During some trials, another location is made unique on a separate feature dimension (e.g., a red item among green items). More important, this additional singleton is never associated with the target location. Critical to the claim of attention capture, observers have no incentive to attend to the additional singleton and are informed regarding its antipredictive nature. However, a typical finding in this paradigm is that when the additional antipredictive singleton is present, response times to the target item are slowed (e.g., Bacon & Egeth, 1994; Theeuwes, 1994; Theeuwes & Burger, 1998). This finding implies that during some trials attention is first allocated to the irrelevant singleton and then to the target location. In other words, an additional feature that slows response to the target is assumed to capture attention. Both color singletons and onset singletons are found to capture attention in this paradigm.

An oculomotor variant of the additional singleton paradigm, the oculomotor capture paradigm, uses eye movements rather than response times to measure attention capture. In the oculomotor capture task, the search items are arranged around fixation. Initially, all items are the same color, but after a brief period of time all search items change color except for one. The task of the observer is to move his or her eyes from the center of the screen to the item that did not change color and determine the identity of a target at that location. On some trials a new search item is added to the display at the same time as this color change. This new object is never the target item and is the same color as the distractors in the search display. However, the typical finding in this paradigm is that the onset of a new object "captures" the eyes (e.g., Irwin, Colcombe, Kramer, & Hahn, 2000; Theeuwes, Kramer, Hahn, Irwin, & Zelinsky, 1999). That is, during 30 to 40% of trials, even though observers know the target of their search is a color singleton, they first move their eyes to the onset item and then to the correct location. In addition to capturing covert attention, the oculomotor capture task shows that the sudden onset of a new object can capture overt attention.

The irrelevant singleton paradigm (Fig. 3.1B), developed by Yantis and colleagues (e.g., Jonides & Yantis, 1988; Yantis & Jonides, 1984), involves randomly assigning a unique feature to a search item that may or may not be the target of search. Because this unique feature is no more likely to be associated with the target item than it is to be associated with a distractor item, observers have no reason to prioritize search items with this feature. For example, observers might search for an H or U in a display containing several distractor letters. Initially these items are masked by figure-eight premasks. Line segments are removed from these masks to reveal the search items. However, one search item on each trial appears as an onset; it is not preceded by a mask. This item has a 1/n probability (n being the number of items in the search display) of being the target item. Search slopes in this task are used to measure attention capture. The typical finding in this paradigm is that when the target is the onset item, search time is relatively invariant to the number of items in the display (i.e., flat search slopes), indicating that the onset item is always one of the first items to be processed. However, when the target is a nononset item, search time increases linearly with the number of items in the search display. This suggests that after the onset item is processed and determined not to be the target, a serial search of the remaining search elements takes place. The onset is irrelevant to the primary task.

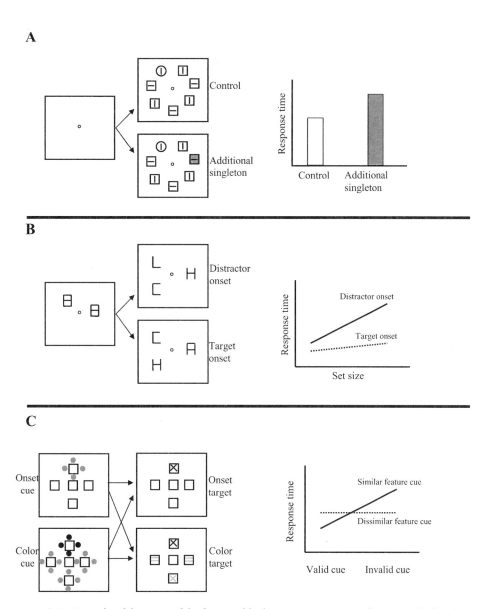

FIGURE 3.1. Example of the types of displays used by basic attention researchers to study the phenomenon of attention capture. (A) In the additional singleton paradigm, observers search for a singleton (in this case, a circle among square distractors). During some trials, an additional singleton (in this case, a dark shape among light shapes) is present. Attention capture is reflected in prolonged response times when the additional singleton is present. (B) In the irrelevant singleton paradigm, observers search for a target letter (in this case, an H or a U). The target may appear as an onset or may appear through the removal of line segments from an already existing item. Attention capture is reflected in relatively flat search slopes when the target appears as an onset. (C) In the contingent capture paradigm, the target screen is preceded by a cue screen. If the cue matches the properties of the target (e.g., an onset cue and an onset target), a response time benefit is observed when the target is in the same location as the cue, and a response time cost is observed when the cue occurs at a nontarget location. When the target and cue are dissimilar (e.g., a color cue and an onset target), no cuing effects are observed.

Even though the onset does not predict the target location, it captures the observers' attention.

Up until now, the paradigms described what has been termed *bottom-up* or *stimulus-driven* attention capture. This type of capture does not depend on the intention or goals of the observer, but instead is driven by the visual properties of a stimulus (although this is an area of active debate). The contingent capture paradigm (Fig. 3.1C), on the other hand, measures *top-down* or *goal-driven* attention capture. Contingent capture refers to the fact that with some tasks, a feature will only capture attention if that feature shares some property consistent with the current goal of the observer (e.g., Folk, Remington, & Johnston, 1992; Folk, Remington, & Wright, 1994). For example, an observer might be asked to search for a red target among white distractor letters. In this instance, a red cue will capture attention, but an onset cue will not. Conversely, if observers are asked to search for an onsetting target, an onset cue will capture attention, but a color singleton cue will not. This distinction between top-down and bottom-up capture is an important one and is discussed in greater detail later.

In general, both the onset of a new object and a uniquely colored item have been found to capture attention. However, these results are not consistent across the paradigms described earlier. For example, in the additional singleton, oculomotor capture, and irrelevant singleton paradigms, onsets reliably capture attention. However, color singletons consistently capture attention only in the additional singleton paradigm (and the contingent capture paradigm when the observer has an attentional set for color). This has led some researchers to suggest that special neural mechanisms might exist to prioritize onsets when they occur. It is speculated that these mechanisms have evolved, because the onset of a new object in the visual environment (such as the appearance of a predator) is more biologically relevant than other changes that might occur.

The majority of these paradigms suggest that onset alarms should be a reliable means to direct attention. However, do these basic research findings scale up? Even within the basic attention literature there is evidence that onsets might not always be effective in capturing attention. The next section describes instances in the basic attention literature in which context determines whether an onset will capture attention.

## THE CASE FOR AND AGAINST ONSET ALARMS

In the visual search literature, onsets appear to be the most effective way of drawing attention to a region of space (e.g., Boot, Kramer, & Peterson, 2005b; Cole, Kentridge, & Heywood, 2005; Enns, Austen, Di Lollo, Rauschenberger, & Yantis, 2001; Irwin et al., 2000; Jonides & Yantis, 1988). From this literature, the obvious (but possibly premature) recommendation to display designers would be to capitalize upon the neural mechanisms involved in the prioritization of newly appearing objects by using onsets to direct attention to important information and events. Evidence from basic attention paradigms suggests that onset cues are detected quickly and accurately, and require few resources to process. For example, Jonides (1981) compared the ability of peripheral onset cues and central arrow cues to direct attention to a search target. Simultaneously, participants also had to maintain a series of digits in memory. The power of a predictive central cue to direct attention decreased when observers also had to maintain digits in memory. This was not the case for peripheral onset cues. The cuing effect for onset cues was invariant to memory load. These findings suggest that the processing of onset cues is automatic. Further evidence of automaticity is suggested by the fact that even when an onset is known to be antipredictive of the target location, onsets still capture attention and the eyes. This would make onset cuing appear to be the perfect means to direct attention in complex displays.

Despite this large body of evidence suggesting that onsets capture attention, it is unclear whether onset capture is an effective means of directing attention in other contexts. Four important issues must be addressed in making the leap from laboratory findings to real-world application when it comes to attention capture: display complexity, onset eccentricity, dual-task load, and attentional set.

The paradigms typically used to measure attention capture involve simple search displays containing anywhere from two to a dozen discrete search items placed in the context of a blank background (Fig. 3.1). These items might vary slightly in terms of shape or color, but for the most part these search displays are relatively homogenous. With some exceptions, the only change occurring in the display is the onset of the new item. An important question is whether the findings obtained using these simple search displays will scale up to real-world complex displays. Martin-Emerson and Kramer (1997) addressed an issue related to display complexity using the irrelevant singleton paradigm. With the irrelevant singleton paradigm, line segments are removed (offset) from figure-eight premasks to reveal search items simultaneously with the onset of a new letter. Martin Emerson and Kramer (1997) manipulated the complexity of the figure-eight premasks so that the number of line segments that had to offset to reveal the search letters varied. This led to more or less display change occurring at the instant the onset occurred. The critical finding of this series of experiments is that as the number of offsetting line segments in the display increased, the power of the onset to capture attention decreased. These findings support an *interrupt threshold* account of attention capture in which an onset will only capture attention if the total display change created by the onset exceeds the total change at nononset locations. These results highlight the role display complexity might have on the ability of an operator to detect an onset alarm. Given that in a complex visual display many display elements might be changing at the same time, the interrupt threshold theory of attention capture may play an important role in our understanding of when onset alarms will succeed or fail to capture attention.

Eccentricity may play another important role in determining whether an onset alarm will capture attention. The majority of visual search paradigms described here have used stimulus eccentricities of anywhere between 5 deg and 15 deg, and displays no larger than a typical computer monitor. However, actual displays used by operators in a number of real-world tasks may encompass a much larger area. Take, for example, the visual display a driver is confronted with, which includes the view outside the windshield, the front and side mirrors, and the instruments on the dashboard. To date, no study has systematically investigated the effect of onset eccentricity on attention capture in the major attention capture paradigms. Such a study would be useful in determining the effective range of an onset's ability to capture attention.

In addition to the visual properties of a display, it may also be important to consider issues such as workload in determining whether an onset alarm will be effective in capturing an operator's attention. Jonides (1981) found that peripheral onset cues remained effective as a means of directing attention when observers were given an additional memory load. However, in this case the onset cues were highly predictive of the target location, signaling the target

location on 80% of trials. It is uncertain whether the same results would be obtained if the onset were less frequent and less related to the primary search task. Relatively little research has been done examining attention capture in dual-task situations. Boot, Brockmole, and Simons (2005a) added an auditory secondary task to the irrelevant singleton search paradigm. In addition to the search task, observers also completed an auditory one-back task. This auditory task required observers to listen to a string of digits and count the number of times two sequentially read numbers were the same. This counting task required both attention and working memory to complete. The search task was imbedded within this counting task such that observers had to do both tasks simultaneously. Critically, onsets lost their ability to capture attention under this dual-task condition. No prioritization of the onset item was observed during the irrelevant singleton task when observers had to attend to the auditory task. This finding may have important implications for display design, given that onset alarms occur in the context of some primary task that usually taxes attention and working memory. Note that this reduction in visual attention capture occurred despite the secondary task being auditory in nature. A visual secondary task may be even more detrimental to onset detection because both the visual secondary task and the visual onset detection task may rely more on common resources (Wickens, 1984).

Finally, the research of Folk and colleagues shows that the "attentional set" of the observer, determined by the nature of the primary task, will constrain the types of features that will capture attention. The contingent capture paradigm illustrates a situation during which an onset will fail to capture attention (e.g., Folk, Remington, & Johnston, 1992; Folk, Remington, & Wright, 1994). For example, if an observer is looking for a color singleton, an onset cue will not effectively capture attention. Therefore, it may be important to analyze the nature of the primary task to evaluate whether an alarm (onset or otherwise) is consistent with the attentional set induced by the task.

In summary, although the basic attention capture literature strongly emphasizes the ability of onset cues to capture attention, this literature also hints at limitations of this method in directing attention to a region of space. Display complexity, onset eccentricity, primary task complexity, and task-induced sets may all play important roles in determining whether an onset alarm will capture the observer's attention in a particular context.

## ONSET ALARMS

Many complex visual displays use onset cues to direct attention to important information based on the assumption that onsets are effective in capturing attention. Numerous examples of such cues exist in applied contexts, including driving, aviating, and air traffic control. Examples of the use of onset cues within these three domains are explored further in this section.

In an automated cockpit, the flight mode annunciator (FMA) conveys to the pilot the mode of automation that is currently active. Awareness of the current operating mode is important; certain actions in one mode of operation may be inappropriate in others. Thus, inadequate mode awareness can lead to safety-critical errors (Degani, Shafto, & Kirlik, 1999). Mode changes are signaled by the FMA with the onset of a green box, with the purpose of drawing the pilot's attention to the mode change. Based on some of the basic attention research reviewed here, one might expect pilots to fixate the FMA soon after the onset accompanying the mode change. However, eye-tracking data from pilots in a Boeing 747 flight simulator showed that this is not the case. Mumaw, Sarter, and Wickens (2001) found that pilots failed to fixate the FMA after a mode change 40% of the time and that many of the times when the FMA was fixated these fixations occurred only after a number of seconds had elapsed. A number of factors, such as display complexity and eccentricity, might have led to pilots failing to detect this important change (Fig. 3.2). Nikolic and colleagues (2001) examined these issues in displays meant to simulate the highly complex display within which the FMA is embedded. Observers focused attention on a puzzle task while also detecting peripheral green onset targets 35 deg or 45 deg away. These targets were imbedded within displays that varied in complexity. Displays were varied in terms of motion (static vs. moving dials) and color (monochrome vs. color). Nikolic and colleagues (2001) found that as the display complexity increased, accuracy of detection decreased and response time increased. Furthermore, accuracy of detection was significantly worse for more eccentric targets. These findings support the

FIGURE 3.2. Example of a complex display—in this case, the cockpit of a Boeing 747 aircraft.

idea that display complexity and eccentricity are factors that lead to pilots missing mode changes. However, other important factors, such as workload, might also play a role. During flight, the important tasks of aviating, navigating, and communicating require both attention and working memory. Under these dual-task conditions, the power of an onset to capture attention is most likely diminished.

Brake lamps in the domain of driving are another important onset meant to capture a driver's attention quickly and reliably. The salient red onset of these lamps alerts the driver that the vehicle in front of them is braking and that he or she needs to act accordingly (e.g., slow down, change lanes). If brake lamps fail to capture the driver's attention, the consequences can be disastrous. Approximately 40% of all traffic accidents are rear-end collisions, presumably because the brake lamps of the leading vehicle were either not attended or attended too late to prevent an accident (McKnight, Shiner, & Reizes, 1989). In some instances eccentricity may be partly responsible for this failure. Summala and coworkers (1998) tested the ability of brake lamps to capture attention at various eccentricities. As observers were driving, they had to complete a secondary task presented on an in-vehicle display either directly above the dashboard, at the speedometer level, or on the mid console of the car. Eccentricity had a profound impact on braking performance. Summala and colleagues (1998) found that brake lamp detection was substantially impaired when drivers were focusing on the in-vehicle display at the speedometer level. Surprisingly, when participants were focusing on the mid-console (most eccentric) display, breaking time to the onset of the brake lamps was no different than for the same condition in which the lead car had no break lamps. In other words, there was no advantage to break lamps when the break lamps were very eccentric. This result would appear to demonstrate a complete failure of onsets to capture attention. These findings have important implications for the design of in-vehicle technologies, and for any system in which onset alarms may be distant from the current fixation, as well.

Similarly, a secondary task might affect the ability of brake lamps to capture attention much in the same way that an auditory secondary task affected the ability of onsets to capture attention in the study of Boot, Brockmole, and Simons (2005a). Using a simulated driving task, Cosiglio and associates (2003) had observers respond to the onset of a red brake lamp. Observers either had to do this task alone or in addition to listening to the radio, having a conversation with a passenger, or having a conversation on a hand-held or hands-free cell phone. All conversation conditions led to slower reaction times, regardless of whether the conversation was with someone present or on a cell phone, and regardless of whether the cell phone was hand-held or hands-free. That is, these effects seem to be specific to dual-task situations involving speech production. Furthermore, Strayer and Drews (this volume) report that the P300 (an event-related potential component related to attention and memory) showed a decreased amplitude to the onset of break lights while participants had a simulated cell phone conversation. These findings have important safety implications. Even small amounts of interference caused by a secondary task can make the difference between stopping in time and a rear-end collision.

Finally, Thackray and Touchstone (1991) examined the use of color singleton and onset (flashing) cues in directing attention to potential conflicts in an air traffic control simulation. Observers had a number of tasks to perform in this type of simulation. First, observers had to detect transponder failures in which the altitude of a given aircraft was replaced by a series of Xs. Second, observers had to detect potential conflicts between aircraft (aircraft with the same altitude and intersecting flight paths). Observers had the additional task of detecting untracked aircraft intruding into the observer's airspace. These items were shape singletons (triangles among circles) that could either be accompanied by a color singleton cue (red among green), a continuous onset (flashing) cue, or both. The findings obtained illustrate the successful application of onset cues in a complex real-world display. Detection of intruding aircraft was most successful when these aircraft were accompanied by a redundant onset cue, although some improvement was also observed with color cues. When onset cues were used, detection performance was relatively unaffected by workload and time on task, whereas detection of color cues suffered under high workload conditions and as time on task increased. Another important finding appears to be that onset cues eliminated any "edge effect." Onset cues were detected just as well in the periphery as they were when they occurred at the center of the screen. In this particular instance, onset cues appear to be an effective means of directing attention to important information in a complex visual display.

The examples described here illustrate both successes and failures of onset capture in complex displays. Display complexity, onset eccentricity, and dual-task load appear to be plausible explanations for why onsets might not always capture attention, and the applied examples cited here appear to support this speculation. They are also likely to be the reasons why onsets capture attention in some applied domains (e.g., the onset cues used by Thackray and Touchstone [1991]) and not others (e.g., the FMA studied by Mumaw and associates [2001]). For example, Thackray and Touchstone (1991) found that onset cues effectively directed attention regardless of eccentricity. However, this was limited to a range of eccentricities defined by the air traffic control display, whereas the eccentricities of brake lamps in a driving task or the FMA in aviation could be much larger. Additionally, the nature of the onset cue might also be important. The onset cue used by Thackray and Touchstone (1991) was a *continuous* onset that blinked on and off. This is likely to be an important factor in determining whether an onset cue will capture attention. A single continuously blinking item is always unique, whereas a single onset is unique only at the moment it onsets, and then may be no different than any other element in the search display. Indeed, this was the explanation

Boot, Brockmole, and Simons (2005a) suggested for why onsets lost their ability to capture attention in their dual-task study. If the secondary task reduces an observer's ability to detect the onset at the moment it appears (i.e., the transient it creates), the onset may not be any more salient than other distractor items.

### EXPERIMENT OVERVIEW

Our lab has been investigating questions of stimulus-driven and goal-contingent orienting using a dynamic change detection paradigm in which numerous objects of different color move across a gray circular display. This paradigm differs from most basic attention paradigms in that the display is cluttered (up to 24 objects can appear in the display) and that there are multiple transients occurring within the display as the objects move (Fig. 3.3). Two types of changes can occur within this display; either a new object can onset or an already existing item can change color. These changes create the same amount of display change and psychophysical luminance change; however, only one involves the creation of a new object. A trial consists of an 8-second viewing of this dynamic display. Either a color change or an onset can occur

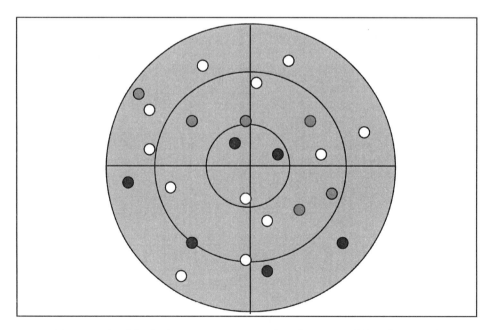

FIGURE 3.3. Example of the displays participants viewed. Red, green, and blue dots moved across a gray background.

within this 8-second period, and participants are instructed to push a button as soon as they detect a change. Additionally, there are control trials during which no change occurs. Set size is manipulated so that the set size was either small (eight or nine objects) or large (23 or 24 objects).

Using this paradigm, Boot and colleagues (in press) found that even in this cluttered and dynamic display onset changes were detected more accurately, and in the large set size more quickly, compared with color changes. These results are consistent with the results of the basic attention literature. Thus, we illustrate a successful scaling up of attention capture findings in that onset changes can more reliably alert operators of important information.

However, within the same paradigm we also notice failures of onsets to capture attention (or even to be detected at all). We noted large individual differences in scan strategy, with some participants choosing to move their eyes frequently while searching for the change (in some instances, making as many as 25 eye movements within an 8-second period) whereas other participants chose to adopt a "sit and wait" strategy in which they fixated the center of the screen and searched for the change covertly. We used the average number of eye movements made during control (no change) trials to quantify scan strategy. Participants who actively searched for the change with many eye movements performed worst whereas participants who searched for the change with few eye movements performed best. In fact, 60 to 70% of the variance in change detection performance could be accounted for by the number of eye movements participants made during control (no change) trials. To investigate this result further, we examined the accuracy of onset detection conditional upon when the change occurred relative to an eye movement and found a sharp decline in accuracy starting 45 msec presaccade, with a rapid recovery starting immediately after the end of a saccade to about 30 msec postsaccade. When the change occurred while the eyes were in flight, participants were practically blind to the change (less than a 10% detection rate). Thus, assuming a saccade duration of 30 msec, visual thresholds are elevated for more than 100 msec for every saccade made. Some participants made as many as 20 or more saccades per trial, resulting in their visual thresholds being elevated for a whole 2 seconds or more out of an 8-second-long trial. In addition to factors such as eccentricity, dual-task load, and display complexity, it appears that scan

strategy also needs to be taken into account when evaluating the potential effectiveness of using an onset to alert operators of important display changes. If the onset occurs while the eyes are in flight, or shortly before or after a saccade, participants may not notice the transient signal associated with the onset at all. If the transient signal is not processed at the time the item onsets, the onset item may look no different from any other item in the display, making it extremely difficult to detect that a new object has been added. An obvious display recommendation would be to use continuous onset (blinking) cues that persist for a duration that is longer than the visual suppression associated with making an eye movement.

Two experiments reported here examine the notion that participants can adopt an attentional set for a particular type of event, leading this type of event to be prioritized over other events. Folk and colleagues (1992, 1994) argue that this is indeed possible and provide evidence that when participants are set or motivated to detect a particular type of feature, the same or similar features will capture attention. First, we asked participants to prioritize color changes over onset changes to determine if, with instruction, color changes can be detected as well or even better than onset changes. Additionally, we asked whether participants can adopt specific sets, including only a subset of color changes (e.g., a color change to red).

## Experiment 1

An experiment was conducted to determine whether participants could improve color change detection performance in a dynamic display by adopting an attentional set for color change. This was accomplished through an instructional manipulation in which participants were told that color changes were more important than onset changes. A point system was implemented and participants were encouraged to earn as many points as possible. Correct detection of a color change resulted in 1000 points, whereas correct detection of an onset change resulted in only 100 points. It was stressed that the goal of the experiment was to earn as many points as possible, and participants were told to pay particular attention to color changes because they were more valuable. Participants were given feedback (hit, miss, false alarm) after every trial in addition to a running total of points earned. Participants completed two sessions on separate days and were encouraged during session 2 to beat their previous session 1 score. If participants are able to adopt an attentional set for color changes successfully, color change detection should be equal or better than onset change detection.

## Method

**Participants**   Sixteen participants from the University of Illinois were paid $20 for their participation in 2-hour-long experimental sessions on separate days. All participants demonstrated normal color vision as measured by the Ishihara Color Blindness Test and normal visual acuity as measured by Snellen charts.

**Stimuli**   Displays consisted of red, blue, and green dots traveling across a gray background at a rate of 0.82 deg/second. Dots measured 0.48 deg and the circular background on which they traveled measured 25 deg. All colors, including the background, were psychophysically matched for luminance in a pilot experiment. Dots were randomly assigned a linear path to travel, with the constraint that no dot was assigned a path that would take it out of the gray circular background. Two changes could occur in the display. An onset change involved a new dot appearing in the display. A color change involved an already existing dot changing color. Set size was manipulated so that a change could occur within a small set (eight or nine objects) or a large set (23 or 24 objects). One third of trials were color change trials, one third were onset change trials, and one third of trials were control trials in which no change occurred. The change could occur 1, 2, 3, or 5 seconds from the start of each 8-second-long trial.

**Procedure**   Participants were instructed to push a button if they detected a change within the display. It was emphasized that color changes were more important than onset changes, and participants were encouraged to gain as many points as possible. Participants completed two blocks of 288 trials on separate days.

## Results and Discussion

**Accuracy of Detection**   Average hit rate and false alarm rate for each condition are depicted in Figure 3.4. A three-way repeated-measures analysis of variance (ANOVA), with change type (onset or color), set size (small or large), and day (day 1 or 2) as factors, was conducted on accuracy data. This analysis revealed no effect of day ($F(1, 15) = 1.07, P = .32$), a main effect of set size ($F(1, 15) = 45.49, P < .001$), and a main effect of change type ($F(1, 15) = 47.76, P < .001$). Day and change type reliably interacted ($F(1, 15) = 10.72, P < .01$) as well as change type and set size ($F(1, 15) = 7.89, P < .05$). Despite instructions to prioritize color changes, onsets still received priority over color changes. This was more apparent for day 1 than day 2. Additionally, onsets were detected better than color changes, and this difference was larger for larger set sizes. These results suggest that participants were unable to prioritize color changes over onset changes even when given incentive to do so.

**Response Time**   Correct response times are depicted in Figure 3.5. An identical analysis was performed on response time data as was performed on accuracy data. This analysis revealed a main effect of day ($F(1, 15) = 11.78, P < .001$), a main effect of change type ($F(1, 15) = 4.82, P < .05$), and no effect of set size ($F(1, 15) = 0.64, P = .45$). There was a trend for day and set size to interact ($F(1, 15) = 3.32, P = .09$), with participants showing more of an improvement in response time on day 2 for the large set size condition. No other interactions were close to reaching significance (all, $P > .32$). Overall, participants were faster at detecting onset changes compared with color changes, again suggesting that they were unable to prioritize color changes.

Both the accuracy and response time data suggest that onset prioritization is difficult to overcome. Even when instructed to prioritize color change events, participants still detected onset events faster and more accurately. This may not be at all unexpected. Folk and colleagues (1994) have suggested that attentional control settings can only be tuned broadly. Participants might be able to prioritize a static singleton or a transient singleton, but may not be able to prioritize one transient event over another. These results provide support for this notion.

## Experiment 2

Although participants could not prioritize one transient change over another in experiment 1, in experiment 2 we sought to determine whether participants could prioritize a specific color change over an onset or other types of color change. That is, participants were told to prioritize events in which an existing object changed to a specific color (e.g., when an

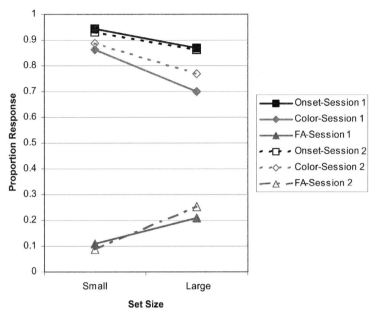

FIGURE 3.4. Mean hit rate and false alarm (FA) rate for onset and color changes in sessions 1 and 2 of experiment 1. Session 1 performance is depicted in solid lines and session 2 performance is depicted in dotted lines.

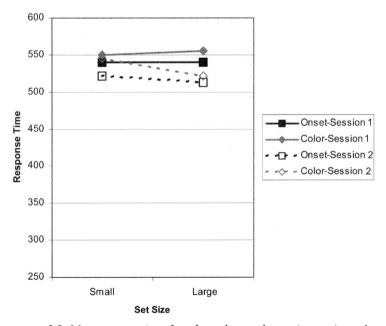

FIGURE 3.5. Mean response times for color and onset changes in experiment 1.

object turned red). As in experiment 1, a point system was implemented in which participants were rewarded with more points for detecting one type of change over others. Twenty-four participants completed 288 trials. One third of the participants were instructed to prioritize color changes to red, one third to prioritize color changes to blue, and one third to prioritize color changes to green. All other aspects of the experiment were identical to experiment 1.

### Results and Discussion

**Accuracy of Detection**    Table 3.1 lists the accuracy of detection for each group and each change type. Change type is broken down by color. That is, onsets were broken down by the color of the object that onset, and color changes were broken down by the color to which the object changed. If participants are able to prioritize successfully one type of color change over another, it is expected that the pattern of detection performance for each color change should differ depending on the instructions they were given. More specifically, if participants are able only to prioritize *color changes* to a specific color, then the color of the onset should not interact with the instructions they were given. However, it is plausible that participants may not be able to adopt an attention set for a particular color change without also prioritizing onsets of the same color. This would suggest that there

are limits to the complexity of what can be specified in an attentional set.

To explore first the effect of instructions, an ANOVA was performed on accuracy data with change type (color or onset), set size (small or large), and change color (red, blue, or green) as within-participant factors, and instruction (prioritize change to red, blue, or green) as a between-participant factor. Critically, there was a significant interaction between change color and instruction ($F(4, 42) = 2.65$, $P < .05$), suggesting that the given instructions were successful in modulating performance of certain color changes. Figure 3.6 suggests the source of this interaction. It appears that during most conditions, participants who were asked to prioritize a certain color were more accurate at detecting changes involving that color compared with participants who were asked to prioritize a different color. Note, however, that there was no interaction between instruction, color change, and change type ($F(4, 42) = 0.05$, $P = .99$), suggesting that participants could only adopt a set for a particular color, not a particular type of change (i.e., color vs. onset) involving a particular type of color. For further statistical evidence that participants were indeed prioritizing the color assigned to them, we focus on those participants who were instructed to prioritize either red or green color changes. Difference scores were calculated for these participants based on their accuracy in detecting changes involving green and red colors

TABLE 3.1. Accuracy and Response Time for Each Change Broken down by Change Color and Priority Instruction.

| | Proportion of Hits | | | | | |
| | Onset | | | Color Change | | |
| Prioritization Instruction | Red | Green | Blue | Red | Green | Blue |
|---|---|---|---|---|---|---|
| Prioritize red | 0.99 | 0.84 | 0.97 | 0.87 | 0.79 | 0.82 |
| Prioritize green | 0.92 | 0.89 | 0.97 | 0.80 | 0.85 | 0.84 |
| Prioritize blue | 0.96 | 0.84 | 0.97 | 0.88 | 0.83 | 0.85 |
| | RT, ms | | | | | |
| | Onset | | | Color Change | | |
| | Red | Green | Blue | Red | Green | Blue |
| Prioritize red | 449 | 535 | 470 | 494 | 510 | 516 |
| Prioritize green | 500 | 538 | 515 | 543 | 553 | 532 |
| Prioritize blue | 461 | 535 | 477 | 509 | 543 | 513 |

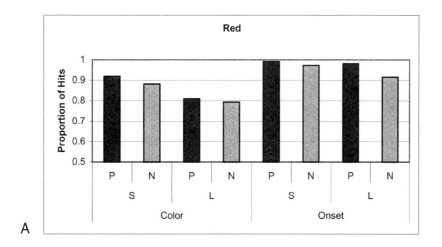

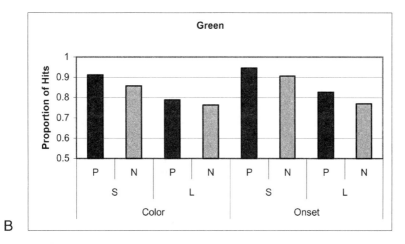

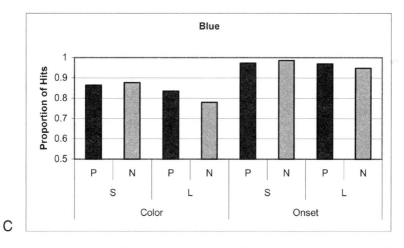

FIGURE 3.6. (A–C) Mean hit rate for changes of each color (red [A], green [B], or blue [C]). Data are broken down by set size (small [S] or large [L]) and change type (color or onset), and whether participants were asked to prioritize that color (P) or prioritize another color (N).

(green minus red). Although there may be some baseline differences in the detection of each color (green appears to be harder to detect than other colors), this score should provide an indication of whether participants can overcome these baseline differences. Figure 3.7 depicts difference scores for participants who prioritized either red or green color changes. Modulation based on instructions can be clearly observed. As expected, an ANOVA of these data revealed a main effect of instruction ($F(1, 14) = 8.00$, $P < .01$). Instruction did not interact with change type ($F(1, 14) = 0.10, P = .76$). Thus, although it is clear that attentional sets can influence change detection performance, it does not appear that this set is specific to color changes, but can influence the detection of other transient events.

**Response Time**   Response times were analyzed in an identical manner as accuracy. An ANOVA was performed of response time data with change type (color or onset), set size (small or large), and change color (red, blue, or green) as within-participant factors, and instruction (prioritize change to red, blue, or green) as a between-participant factor. Of critical importance, there was a significant interaction between change color and instruction ($F(4, 42) = 3.70, P < .05$), suggesting that the given instructions were successful in modulating response times for certain color changes.

However, the prioritization effect is less clear in the response time data than in the accuracy data, with clear prioritization only appearing to take place when participants were asked to prioritize red (Fig. 3.8). For further statistical evidence that participants were indeed prioritizing the color assigned to them, we focus on those participants who were instructed to prioritize either red or green color changes. Difference scores were calculated for these participants based on their response times for detecting changes involving green and red colors (green minus red) (Fig. 3.9). As expected, an ANOVA of these data indicated an effect of instruction ($F(1, 14) = 8.00, P < .01$). Again, instruction did not interact with change type ($F(1, 14) = 1.66, P = .22$). However, from the data it looks like there exists a trend for a larger instruction effect for onset changes compared with color changes, despite participants being told specifically to pay attention to color changes of a certain type.

### SUMMARY AND CONCLUSIONS

The results of the two experiments reported here are consistent with previous research focusing on stimulus-driven and goal-directed shifts of attention. Onsets, by default, appear to be prioritized by the visual system. This research suggests that this prioritization occurs

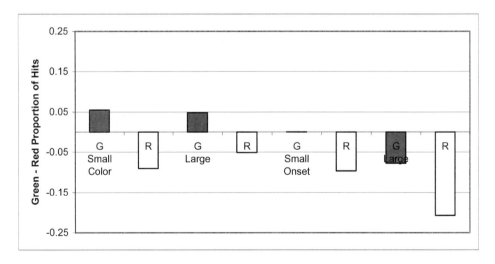

FIGURE 3.7. To calculate a measure of prioritization, red accuracy was subtracted from green accuracy for participants who were asked to prioritize either red (R) or green (G) color changes. Clear modulation can be observed during each condition depending on whether participants were asked to prioritize red or green color changes. "Small" and "Large" refer to set sizes.

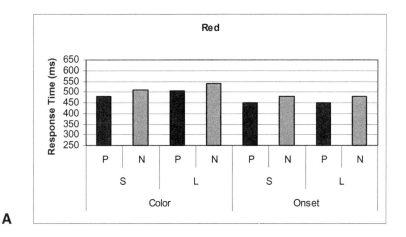

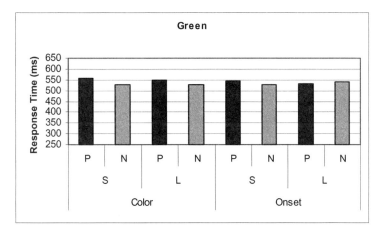

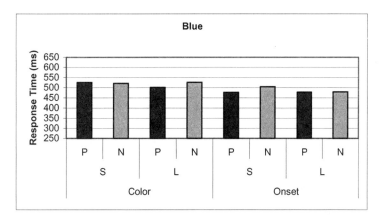

FIGURE 3.8. (A–C) Mean response times for changes of each color (red [A], green [B], or blue [C]). Data are broken down by set size (small [S] or large [L]) and change type (color or onset), and whether participants were asked to prioritize that color (P) or prioritize another color (N).

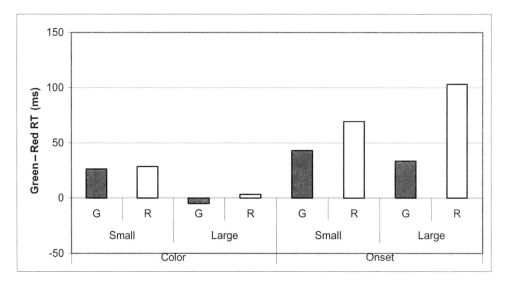

FIGURE 3.9. To calculate a measure of prioritization, red response times were subtracted from green response times for participants who were asked to prioritize either red (R) or green (G) color changes. Although it appears that red changes were generally detected faster than green changes, a main effect of instruction was significant. Although the interaction was not significant, it appears that this modulation was more pronounced during onset conditions.

even within the context of a dynamic and cluttered display. Additionally, observers have the ability to adopt attentional sets that can modulate performance. However, both experiments suggest important limitations regarding what can be specified within an attention set. These limitations are largely consistent with the work of Folk and colleagues (1994), who suggest that attention can only be set to prioritize very broad categories of change. For example, they suggest that attention can be set for either static discontinuities (e.g., color) or dynamic discontinuities (e.g., onset), but not for specific features within each of these categories. Participants may have been unable to adopt an attention set for color change because both color change and onset change are dynamic discontinuities. Similarly, participants were able to prioritize a specific color but appear to be unable to prioritize that color only in the context of one transient change type (i.e., color change).

These findings may have important design implications. For example, if an observer's task were to monitor a display for transient changes such as onsets, if the display also contained unimportant elements of a transient nature these unimportant elements might hinder performance by capturing the observer's attention and drawing attention away from the primary task.

That is, observers may be unable to limit their attention set to include only the important transient changes. Similarly, by analyzing a task, designers might predict what is included in an observer's attention set and use this to design alarms consistent with this set. For example, if in the current display a color change to red signaled an important event, other critical alarms in the display might also include red because observers are already set to detect this color. In fact, that nature of the alarm could be changed to be consistent with whatever attention set an observer might have at a particular phase of the task.

It is important to note that although onsets were detected quickly and more reliably, it is somewhat difficult to make claims regarding *capture* as defined by a stimulus-driven shift of attention because the onset that occurred was always relevant. This is a distinction that is likely to be an important one. For example, Jonides (1981) found that relevant onset cues were invariant to a memory load, whereas Boot and colleagues (2005a) found that an irrelevant onset lost its ability to capture attention under a working memory load. Although this may be the result of the nature of the secondary task, the relevance of the cue probably plays an important role as well. A strong attentional set may be immune to various attentional and working memory manipulations whereas stimulus-driven shifts of attention may suffer. Similarly, Martin–Emerson and Kramer (1997) found that multiple irrelevant transients reduced attention capture by an irrelevant onset, but these transients had little effect when the onset was predictive of the target. Thus, when determining whether an onset will be an effective cue in the real world, it is important to take into consideration the relation of the onset alarm to the primary task. This may determine whether a secondary task or other irrelevant transients will reduce onset prioritization.

## FUTURE DIRECTIONS

The data reviewed here suggest that sometimes the findings in the basic attention capture literature scale up to more complex tasks and sometimes they do not. Thus, it is important that context be taken into account. Assuming that an onset alarm will be an effective means of capturing attention may sometimes be a false assumption. Both the basic and applied literature suggest that there are factors that may decrease or eliminate attention capture effects, including working memory load, eccentricity, and irrelevant transients. It is our belief that attention researchers should think about not only what features capture attention, but when (in what contexts) these same features fail to capture. Research should focus on finding the boundary conditions of attention capture. For example, to our knowledge no research has been conducted that has systematically varied the eccentricity of the onset in most attention capture paradigms. We believe that both basic and applied attention researchers have much to contribute to this area, and a dialogue between these groups is important in furthering our understanding of the phenomenon of attention capture.

## References

Bacon, W. F., & Egeth, H. E. (1994). Overriding stimulus-driven attentional capture. *Perception & Psychophysics, 55*, 485–496.

Boot, W. R., Brockmole, J. R., & Simons, D. J. (2005a). Modulation of attention capture in a dual-task situation: Why capture cannot be stimulus-driven. *Psychonomic Bulletin and Review.*

———, Kramer, A. F., & Peterson, M. S. (2005b). Oculomotor consequences of abrupt object onsets and offsets: Onsets dominate oculomotor capture. *Perception and Psychophysics.*

———, Kramer, A. F., Becic, E., Wiegmann, D. A., & Kubose, T. (In press). Detecting transient changes in dynamic displays: The more you look, the less you see. *Human Factors.*

Cole, G. G., Kentridge, R. W., & Heywood, C. A. (2005). Object onset and parvocellular guidance of attentional allocation. *Psychological Science, 16*, 270–274.

Cosiglio, W., Driscoll, M. W., & Berg, W. P. (2003). Effects of cellular telephone conversation and other potential interference on reaction time in braking response. *Accident Analysis and Prevention, 35*, 495–500.

Degani, A., Shafto, M., & Kirlik, A. (1999). Modes in human–machine systems: Review, classification, and application. *International Journal of Aviation Psychology, 9*, 125–138.

Enns, J. T., Austen, E. L., Di Lollo, V., Rauschenberger, R., & Yantis, S. (2001). New objects dominate luminance transients in setting attentional priority. *Journal of Experimental Psychology: Human Perception & Performance, 27*, 1287–1302.

Folk, C. L., Remington, R. W., & Johnston, J. C. (1992). Involuntary covert orienting is contingent on attention control settings. *Journal of Experimental Psychology: Human Perception & Performance, 18*, 1030–1044.

———, Remington, R. W., & Wright, J. H. (1994). Selectivity in distraction by irrelevant featural singletons: Evidence for two forms of attentional capture. *Journal of Experimental Psychology: Human Perception and Performance, 24*, 847–858.

Irwin, D. E., Colcombe, A. M., Kramer, A. F., & Hahn, S. (2000). Attention and oculomotor capture by onset luminance and color singletons. *Vision Research, 40*, 1443–1458.

Jonides, J. (1981). Voluntary vs. automatic control over the mind's eye's movement. In J. B. Long & A. D. Baddeley (Eds.), *Attention and performance IX* (pp. 185–203). Hillsdale, N.J.: Lawrence Erlbaum Associates.

Jonides, J., & Yantis, S. (1988). Uniqueness of abrupt visual onset in capturing attention. *Perception & Psychophysics, 43*, 346–354.

Martin-Emerson, R., & Kramer, A. F. (1997). Offset transients modulate attentional capture by sudden-onsets. *Perception and Psychophysics, 59*, 739–751.

McNight, A. J., Shiner, D., & Reizes, A. (1989). *The Effect of Center High-Mounted Stop Lamp on Vans and Trucks.* Washington, DC: National Highway Traffic Safety Administration. Report DOT HS 807 506.

Mumaw, R. J., Sarter, N. B., & Wickens, C. D. (2001). Analysis of pilots' monitoring and performance on an automated flight deck. In R. S. Jensen (Ed.), *Proceedings of the 11th International Symposium on Aviation.* Columbus, Ohio: The Ohio State University Press.

Nikolic, M. I., Orr, J., & Sarter, N. B. (2001). Why onsets don't always capture attention: The importance of context in display design. In R. S. Jensen (Ed.),

*Proceedings of the 11th International Symposium on Aviation.* Columbus, Ohio: The Ohio State University Press.

Summala, H., Lamble, D., & Laakso, M. (1998). Driving experience and perception of the lead car's braking when looking at in-car targets. *Accident Analysis and Prevention, 30,* 401–407.

Thackray, R. I., & Touchstone, R. M. (1991). Effects of monitoring under high and low taskload on detection of flashing and coloured radar. *Ergonomics, 34,* 1065–1081.

Theeuwes, J. (1994). Stimulus-driven capture and attentional set: Selective search for color and visual abrupt onsets. *Journal of Experimental Psychology: Human Perception and Performance, 20,* 799–806.

———, & Burger, R. (1998). Attentional control during visual search: The effect of irrelevant singletons. *Journal of Experimental Psychology: Human Perception and Performance, 24,* 1342–1353.

———, Kramer, A. F., Hahn, S., Irwin, D. E., & Zelinsky, G. J. (1999). Influence of attentional capture on oculomotor control. *Journal of Experimental Psychology: Human Perception & Performance, 25,* 1595–1608.

Wickens, C. D. (1984). Processing resources in attention. In R. Parasuraman & R. Davies (Eds.), *Varieties of attention* (pp. 63–101). New York: Academic Press.

Yantis, S., & Jonides, J. (1984). Abrupt visual onsets and selective attention: Evidence from visual search. *Journal of Experimental Psychology: Human Perception & Performance, 10,* 601–621.

# Chapter 4

# Elaborations of the Multiple-Resource Theory of Attention

## *Peter A. Hancock, Tal Oron-Gilad, and James L. Szalma*

The multiple attentional resource theory represents a construct that, in its time, served to unify two fundamentally disparate views of human performance capacity (Wickens, 1980). Subsequently, the theory has had a particularly strong influence on the practice of human factors, especially in system development, where it arguably remains the strongest behavioral heuristic for interface design. This confluence of contribution to both fundamental theory and practical application served to facilitate the impact of multiple resources and Wickens's influence on the domains of both human factors and experimental psychology (and see Carswell [2005]). Here we provide elaborations on the original theory. In doing so, we seek to generate a wider vista of discourse with respect to the notion of separable components of human attention and, potentially, the individual experience of consciousness and reality itself.

## THE HISTORIC CONTEXT

To a large degree, science proceeds in fits and starts. Most often there is an original, observation-driven theory that encourages structured experimental investigation and then slowly, as the empirical database assembles, inconsistencies between prediction and recorded behavior begin to emerge. With respect to the original theory, it is often the case that an almost intolerable dissonance arises that acts to goad subsequent theorists to propose new formulations to straddle the more extensive behavioral landscape revealed by preceding experimental evaluations. In this sense, virtually all good theories contain—as part of their intrinsic structure—the seeds of their own destruction. Those theories that do not contain this characteristic often prove essentially untestable and, although they may be ubiquitous, such theories are most often also fundamentally vacuous (for a more extensive discussion of a particular example, see Hancock and Ganey [2003]). Thus, although new and sweeping insights permit a general brisance of understanding, they can only be accomplished effectively by those steeped in the problem and intimately familiar with the nuances and inconsistencies of the current state of knowledge. In a true sense, such individuals are always in debt to their forebears and this is the veridical meaning of Newton's observation that, "if I have seen further, it is by standing on the shoulders of giants" (Andrews, Riggs, Seidel, et al., 1996). In essence, one has to know one's problem to generate solutions to one's problem.

It was thus in the latter part of the 1970s that Wickens, among others, approached the conundrum of human attention that was then interpreted in terms of two major theoretical perspectives. The first perspective was derived from the early, linear information processing models (e.g., Broadbent, 1958) whereas the more recent "resource" conception emphasized an energetic, fluid formulation (e.g., Kahneman, 1973; and see Freeman, 1948). Wickens's thorough understanding of the attention literature at this juncture allowed him to encapsulate this vast sweep of issues and findings, and so provide a structured synthesis that subsequently dominated the literature for many years. The added benefit of his formulation was that it also represented a strong design heuristic that amplified the impact of the theory well beyond the literature in experimental psychology alone. However, like all true theories, it did not remain static and unchanging, but sought to encapsulate new findings as the structure and tenets of the theory itself also evolved (Wickens, 2002). By introducing differing and extended interpretations of the various multiple-resource model axes, we hope to indicate some avenues of possible future progress through which to enlarge this useful framework.

## PAYING ATTENTION

Single-channel approaches to information processing were identified largely during the late 1940s and early 1950s, when the first blush of formal information theory penetrated into the psychological sciences (Fitts, 1954; Miller, 1956; Shannon & Weaver, 1949). Attention, as an issue, was somewhat of a problem for these early-stage models (Broadbent, 1958; Welford, 1967). The solution to this problem was to link the concept of attention to a filter, a bottleneck, or some form of "rate-limiting" element somewhere in the progressive processing chain. Unfortunately, contradictory experimental findings led to much dispute about the nature of this bottleneck and its relative location in the identified sequence (Moray, 1967; Treisman, 1969; Wachtel, 1967). These issues, although leading to a series of ingenious experiments, never really reached a definitive conclusion, and it was during this time that an alternative conception arose. In contrast to the processing filter approaches, the resource notion of Kahneman (1973) presented an energetic perspective on attention. In this conception, degrees of processing resources could be directed to a task, compared with an all-or-none allocation that a completely pristine stage model implied. These processing resources have been conceived as either "pools" of energy or as "processing units." (For a review, see Szalma and Hancock [2002].) After its initial formulation, debate continued over whether there was only one such attentional resource (Kantowitz & Knight, 1976) or several such resources (Navon & Gopher, 1979). The protestation of a single resource pool is supported, if by nothing else than the general principle of parsimony (Kantowitz, 1987). So, if predictions from a single resource model could be shown to emulate the empirical data satisfactorily, then multiple-resource models would be overelaborative and thus redundant (although see Bronowski [1966] on the potential fallacy of parsimony).

One can, for example, cope with many of the potential problems that appear to face single-resource conceptions by use of switching strategies and thus finesse the issues of limitations by transferring the problems of attention expressed in the spatial domain to an alternative "answer" expressed in the temporal domain. In short, if a single-resource pool model is formulated that can switch sufficiently quickly and effectively between the tasks, it can emulate the output from most forms of multiple-resource models. It remains an open question, and one very relevant to Wickens's conception, regarding whether the current "landscape" of empirical data can still be accounted for by a single-resource model as originally conceived by Kahneman. Of perhaps even greater importance is Kantowitz's (1987) further observation that multiple-resource approaches are simply *too* powerful. That is, they have sufficient explanatory degrees of freedom open so that almost any pattern of data may be encapsulated by the appropriate manipulation of the variables proposed. We return to this observation later in our discussion because it is directly relevant to our own proposed extensions.

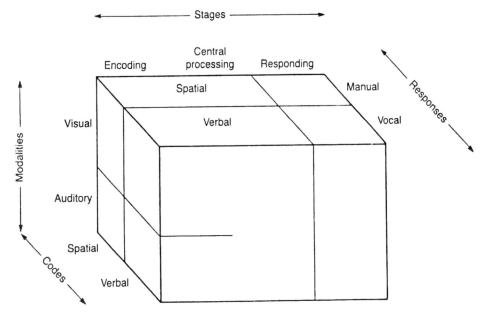

FIGURE 4.1. The classic Wickensian "box model" of human attention, and design heuristic for information and response distribution for the human operator. After Wickens (1980).

The modal multiple-resource approach is crystallized in Wickens's conception, rendered colloquially as the "box model" (Wickens, 1980). From this conception, shown in Figure 4.1, multiple attentional resources were identified upon the basis of three fundamental dimensions. The first dimension was that of *processing stage*. This is essentially a temporal axis reflecting the concern for the sequence of encoding, decision making, and response, which is made seriatim in traditional stage models (even though the potential for parallel processing was considered by Wickens). A second identified axis was that of *processing code*, consisting of the verbal and spatial components of a task. The final axis was that of *processing modality*, which was separated into the visual and the auditory senses. These respective differentiations were made essentially from post hoc interpretations of experimental data derived largely from procedures using a dual-task paradigm. In noticing occasions when two tasks failed to interfere with each other's performance, a prediction that, by the way, is impossible from a strict unitary resource formulation, Wickens used the concept of *difficulty insensitivity* to help distinguish the resource structures given in Figure 4.1 (and see Wickens et al., 1981).

Together with the concept of functional cerebral space (Kinsbourne & Hicks, 1978) and the differentiation of resources as advocated by Navon and Gopher (1979), Wickens (1980, 1987) was able to define a hybrid model that solved many of the contemporary questions and impasses that largely concerned the division of attention. Theoretically, it remains an unresolved question regarding whether this new formulation was able to account for the range of then-existing experimental data because of its more close affiliation with actuality (which would be what all good theorists would try to achieve), or whether a major degree of its power came from the greater number of explanatory degrees of freedom intrinsic to a formulation that advocates a multiple-factor versus a single-factor construct. This, of course, is intrinsic to all such elaborations of a unitary factor theory, as has been seen in developments in the concepts of IQ (Sternberg, 1982), arousal (Eysenck, 1967), fatigue (Hancock & Desmond, 2001), and other similar energetic constructs in human behavior. Independent of these meta-theoretical considerations, Wickens's formulation proved to have a substantial and long-lasting impact in the realm of human factors and system design.

There have been a number of critiques and commentaries on the theoretical, methodological, and existential characteristics of the multiple resource model. (See Damos and Lyall [1986], Navon [1984], and Sarter [this volume], among others.) Numerous concerns remain unresolved. For example, in multiple task situations, who or what decides on the priority between tasks that do have some degree of resource overlap? If no such mechanism can be illustrated in the model, then it becomes purely reactive, lacking purposiveness and intentionality. How could such a passive formulation represent the personally active process of attention? Speaking of attention, the multiple-resource model is, strictly speaking, only an architecture. It does not tell us what attention actually is. Are these supposed resources only a metaphor, or do they represent some actual form of "brain" fuel? And given this, to what degree does neurophysiological evidence inform what this fuel might be? Furthermore, Wickens (2002) himself noted that the visual channel is not a simple unitary one, but now is better suited to a bifid division between focal and ambient modes. Very recent evidence also suggests that the auditory channel can be divided into two elements, as well. Wherefore multiple resources if the resources simply keep proliferating? These are important questions, but we do not have space to address each one. Rather, what we wish to achieve is an examination of certain specific elaborations of the model that allow us to extend its generality and consider the impact of these elaborations, mostly in the theoretical realm, but partly in terms of practical issues, as well.

### ROTATING THE BOXES

We have shown the classic representation of the Wickens formulation in Figure 4.1, but the first question we can ask is whether it need necessarily be expressed in this specific orientation, form, and structure. Can we take Wickens's original architecture and make small initial changes to provide a somewhat differing perspective? We suggest that indeed we can do so.

#### Processing Codes

When Wickens presented his original model, he elaborated upon the nature of the end axes of Figure 4.1 and expressed these in the form we have shown in Figure 4.2. The examples shown within each box represent specific cases of the combination of the vertical and horizontal axes shown. As we will continue to emphasize, it is these sort of exemplars that subsequently allowed usability and human factors professionals to use this conception as a design heuristic. However, let us take one step back to see this compartmentalization from another perspective.

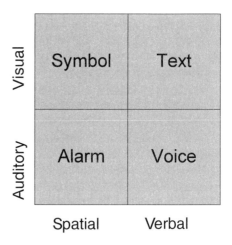

FIGURE 4.2. Examples of members in the four end cells of the box model. A simple auditory alarm tone in the spatial code is expanded into a voice stimulus in the verbal realm. Similarly, a visual symbol is transmuted to text as the change is made from a spatial code to a verbal code.

Considering the processing code axis in greater detail, in the original formulation it lay on the base and was divided between spatial and verbal components. However, this horizontal differentiation implies a qualitative distinction between the two. But is this qualitative distinction justified as being necessarily so? We suggest perhaps not. In fact, it can be easily argued that any verbal representation can be given as an abstraction of the spatial dimension. Let us consider this in a little more detail. With respect to speech (voice), this is considered a form of verbal code. However, in reality, speech is actually the complex distribution of energy in space–time, and because we shall deal with time later as a vital element of one of the other dimensions, we might be justified in treating verbal representations as special forms of temporarily enduring spatial codes. Similarly, if the verbal code is expressed in the visual dimension, it is viewed as letters, words, sentences, and the like (or more generally, text). However, a passage of text, such as this sentence, is only a particular, convention-based form of geometric ordering of marks in a particular spatial configuration. Therefore, text is also actually a particular form of abstraction of graphic markings. Thus, if each form of the verbal code is viewed as particular, high-level abstractions of spatial codes (in reality spatiotemporal codes), then we can rotate the boxes so that this is now graphically represented as a hierarchy of such abstraction. This rotation

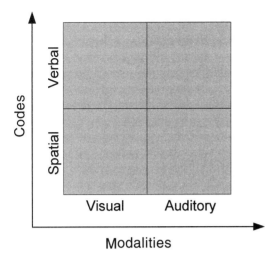

FIGURE 4.3. The box model rotated 90° to emphasize the emergent relationship between the respective codes.

(only for the left-facing "end" axes of the multiple-resource model) now appear as shown in Figure 4.3. There is, however, a secondary advantage to this rotation. The new base axis is now modality, and although it is true that different sensory systems transduce different ranges and forms of stimulus energy, their parsing into the classic sensory systems is probably more logical because there is no necessary abstraction from vision to audition and so on. The hierarchical abstraction of codes now fits appropriately on the vertical axis.

However, we have not yet reached the end of the issue of processing code. We suggest that if the verbal level is actually an abstraction of the spatiotemporal level, then there are other possible abstractions beyond the verbal. We see at least three other levels: the informational level, the symbolic level, and the meta-abstract level. Perhaps an example will be useful in differentiating these levels. Consider the United States Declaration of Independence. When approaching the document in the National Archives in Washington, DC (although the document is now, unfortunately, very faded and, as a consequence, almost illegible), it is evident that there are spatiotemporal graphic markings on the physical document itself. Furthermore, it is also evident that these graphic images are arranged in the form of (English) words. These observations are evident to *anyone* who sees the document, regardless of their ability to read or write English. However, to a non-English speaker, the words themselves, when expressed either in the visual or the aural form, are essentially meaningless.

There are examples of this beyond the visual sense—for example, the tactile–kinesthetically expressed dot patterns of Braille to the uninitiated. In contrast to the non-English speaker, the individual familiar with English will find a vast amount of information contained in the document. Thus, information, which is always a combinational property of individuals and the environment in which they find themselves (Hancock, Szalma, & Oron-Gilad, 2005), is a level beyond verbal expression alone. Therefore, we now have an abstractional sequence from spatial, to verbal, to an informational level.

However, the extrapolation of codes extends even further. Continuing with our specific example, the Declaration itself is much more than simply another bit of paper. For the people of the United States, and arguably for many others around the world beyond the borders of America, the Declaration has great symbolic significance—*as an object in and of itself*. Indeed, as good designers know, items in the world created by human beings most often have symbolic value as well as spatiotemporal continuity, verbal appellation, and informational content. Thus we can add to the spatial, verbal, and informational levels an additional symbolic level. Lest anyone believe that we are absolutists about this, we do not see an exclusive requirement to attach symbology to every possible material item. In this respect, we are not equating this level of extraction to Aristotle's material form of cause. However, having ascended this far, can we go higher?

We believe that, indeed, we can go one level higher still. This level is the one we have labeled the *meta-abstract* and it is the apex of the abstraction process. Although representative of all the levels we have been discussing, the Declaration itself goes one step beyond this. It is symbolic *beyond itself as an entity*. Thus, although the physical document itself is of great (monetary) value, its true value goes well beyond any financial valuation. People can, and do, see in this document intangibles such as freedom, liberty, and hope made manifest. The exact antithesis of this meta-level representation may be seen, for example, in a German document of the Second World War authorizing transportation of Jewish individuals to concentration camps. This latter document would also have all the attributes at each abstraction level appropriate to those fluent in German. However, at the meta-level, the moral attribution is evidently very distinct from the former example, as is the origin of the motivation in its earlier conceptual form. This is crucial to understand, because it means the implications for cognition and, subsequently, reality can vary according to interpretations derived at each level.[1] The problem, of course, is to perceive and be able to attend to these abstraction levels in the context of the natural ambient environment and not simply to restrict this idea to human manufacturing alone (Hancock, 1997). Thus, in the ways we have indicated, and of course potentially in ways we have not, processing codes go well beyond the simple "spatial" and "verbal" differentiation given in Wickens's original formulation (Wickens, 1980, 1987).

At this juncture, we should acknowledge two caveats. The first is that there is no necessary reason for all objects, entities, or creations in the environment to have attributes at each of these levels of abstraction. As Freud is once alleged to have remarked, "Sometimes a cigar is just a cigar." Second, it remains unresolved as to what degree upper levels of representation are contingent upon the sensory channel through which they are first assimilated. We suspect that this sensory dependence grows progressively weaker the higher up the code hierarchy one progresses. At the highest level we suspect there is very little degree of resource differentiation, if any division exists at all. This is certainly an area that future work can address. That we can then comprehend and incorporate these new levels of code abstraction into the design of technology is a crucial insight. Through this elaboration, we can now see that the act of creation embodied from the first conceptions of design to the ultimate manifestation in actual manufacture are not "neutral" events that simply act to make an object, item, or thing (Illich, 1973). Rather, they are part of a collective enterprise in which this multiple layering of meaning and apperception play a central role in creating what we see and understand our world to be (Hancock, 1997).

With respect to the "pools" of attentional resources as Wickens conceived them, whether there is a differentiated pool of visual attention for each of these levels, separated from an auditory attentional resource pool, is a debatable issue. In our view, this issue (e.g., can one differentiate between seeing and hearing a conception such as hope?) is one that remains to be explored in much greater detail in future considerations of the nature of attention and its relation to consciousness. Hopefully, these issues will form a greater focus of a more detailed discussion relating theories of human behavior to the wider vistas of human action. We note, in passing, that our elaborations are no criticism of Wickens himself, because as a theorist he could only work with the data then at hand. And indeed, Wickens (2002) himself has indicated that his

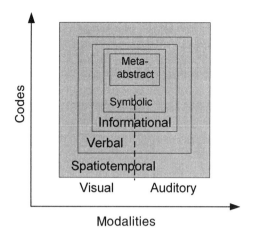

FIGURE 4.4. The processing codes revised. The codes are now presented as an abstraction hierarchy.

1980 model was based on "a sort of meta analysis of a wide variety of multiple task experiments in which structural changes between task pairs had been compared, and found strong evidence that certain structural 'dichotomies' . . . behaved like separate resources" (p. 162). Proliferation of the putative number of "resources" at the time that Wickens first published his model may well have discouraged then-contemporary scientists from subsequent experimental evaluation. Hopefully, future advances will explore our code extensions of the model in the way that Wickens's original postulation triggered empirical enquiry. Thus, the addition of these hierarchical code extraction levels now provide us with an adjustment to Figure 4.3 that we now show in Figure 4.4. This representation implies that not all code levels are necessarily of equivalent importance and that there is a necessary nesting of levels involved, as well.

One interesting speculation that comes from this hierarchy of abstractions concerns the notion of human language development itself. Although pictographs and orthographic symbology represent our earliest recorded history (e.g., Lascaux, and so on), speculation about early human language must, perforce, be more tentative. However, it is possible to propose that both picture symbology and subsequently print, together with spoken language, resulted from the ability to expand into the functional "space" available. This notion of "space" is somewhat different than the much more spatially and neurally constrained idea of functional cerebral space (e.g., Kinsbourne & Hicks, 1978), but the notion of a general ecological niche representing room for expansion is fundamentally relevant to both ideas. It implies that as the state of understanding grows and the pressure to increase the precision of

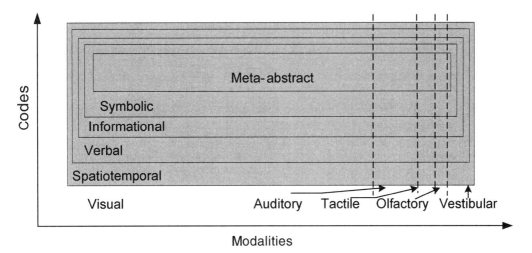

FIGURE 4.5. The elaboration of the now base modality axis combined with the processing codes' abstraction hierarchy.

communication increases, another level of the hierarchy is exploited and/or created. It is feasible, then, to suggest that human–machine interaction forms the basis for the next level of abstraction, and that human factors can be the language to interpret that next emergent abstraction (Hancock, 1997).

Coding levels are never completely crossed, in a factorial sense, with modality. In Wickens's original formulation (Fig. 4.1) the separation between the modalities was maintained only for the earliest stage of processing. Thus, one would expect the spatiotemporal, verbal, and perhaps informational levels to be used predominantly in the encoding stage, where the input data are frequently differentiated by modality. However, the symbolic and meta-abstract levels would be likely to be engaged largely at the central processing stage. One would therefore not necessarily expect to encode "hope" along different modalities, but encoding of the letters or sounds would be differentiated at that level. An area in need of both theoretical and empirical exploration within the multiple-resource model is how data from each modality is integrated into information for central processing. Such theorizing is underway (Hancock et al., 2005), but integration within the Wickens conception is needed to clarify the process of transition between the "boxes," especially those represented on the processing stage axis.

### Processing Modalities

Having considered processing code, let us now consider the new base axis, which is processing modality. In identifying the visual and auditory modalities,

Wickens specified the two major avenues through which individuals assimilate sensory information. However, this does not exhaust the number of possible modalities. There are obvious extrapolations to the tactile, olfactory, and kinesthetic senses, whereas others such as thermal sensation and pain can also be identified. It is important to note that the processing modality axis is *not* subject to the potential for an infinite regress, but rather is limited to the known array of sensory transduction systems. In human beings, vision dominates (Sivak, 1996). Thus the size of the boxes should be adjusted to reflect this dominance of, and contribution of, each particular modality. This adjustment for importance is illustrated in Figure 4.5. Clearly for different organisms, the relative contribution of each modality changes—the ascendancy of olfaction in tracker dogs being perhaps a pertinent example (Budiansky, 2000). Because we eventually seek to conclude here that the derived universe of extended Wickens boxes actually composes the model from which any organism derives its own personal "reality," it is important to understand that there are significant cross-species differentiations with respect to how these resources are assembled. That reality therefore also varies between individuals within any single species, as well as across species, has not escaped our notice. More could certainly be said about the ordering, the impact, and the integration of the respective sensory systems, and the neuroscience of these capacities would well inform a "corticotropic," rather than box, representation. Again, this opens a fruitful vista of opportunities through which to seek an integration of the elaborated resource model with the ongoing efforts in neuroscience to try to plot the geography of consciousness.

## Processing Sequence

Initially it may appear that the temporal axis that subsumes the processing sequence is somewhat less contentious and less amenable to expansive discourse than either processing code or processing modality. However, this is not so. Indeed, such is the complexity of the way in which the temporal nature of processing occurs that we can provide only a brief commentary on this issue here, but see Hancock and colleagues (2005). It is necessary to divide this sequence into preprocessing, processing, and postprocessing stages. Initially during the preprocessing stage, data are simply embedded in the range of distributed environmental energy. This range extends across the electromagnetic continuum and is a priori independent of any particular transducer (observer). The energetic representation ascends to *information* only within the sensory transduction range of the exposed individual. It is among these *latter* expressions that a stimulus array is available to be selected (Gibson, 1979). The principles by which individuals select among a number of possibilities are still being distinguished; however, it is clear that attention is the key process in such selection. Attention is implicated not only in information selection, but with modulating feedback effects from response. It has been suggested that information flow rate needs to be modulated in the same manner that other physiological systems require stable rates of stimulation (Hancock & Chignell, 1987). This form of sensory balancing requires the "narrowing of attention" when in overloaded situations and the "broadening of attention" when experiencing comparable levels of underload. Wickens (2002) himself acknowledged that his model only accounts for overload and that underload is not included in the original formulation. This is a crucial omission because, by logic, half of the picture is left out if underload is neglected.

For most applied contexts, it is likely that the original Wickens model, which consisted of verbal and spatial coding, is sufficient, and therefore this matrix is still effective in the majority of applications. However, the formulation fails when higher levels of abstraction are required. The operators need both *to acquire these higher levels of abstraction* (via training and experience) and *to find value in using them*. Under stress, operators choose to process information via the lowest code level (spatiotemporal and verbal) and therefore are faster in processing but also more error prone in response (Hancock & Szalma, 2003). The extended model can account for underload and variations in workload. For instance, underload may tax the lower levels via the lack of stimulation. The operator adopts a top-down strategy to self-regulate. This observation implies that operators actively seek to regulate resource levels, not merely have them just react passively to external demand. Attending to higher levels in the abstraction hierarchy implies more attention to internal processes, and operators are again more likely to miss the more fundamental spatiotemporal and verbal cues.

It therefore seems unlikely that optimal real-world design requires visual processing to occur in complete silence, or optimal auditory processing to occur in the dark. Indeed, redundancy and cross-talk between channels appears to be an important design aspect and implies crucial permeability between Wickens's mode differentiations to generate a full reality. Postprocessing and feed-forward and feedback loops provide control on the whole sequence and imply the future selection of stimuli and decisions to be made can be largely predicated on past actions because, as noted elsewhere, memory is primarily for the future (Hancock et al., 2005). The responding component of the processing stage may also be presented in a hierarchical way. We currently propose the two lower spatiotemporal and verbal levels; however, higher levels such as self-regulation and effort can also be suggested. Further research is required to determine the abstraction levels of responding. As this discussion progresses, the box model appears to become more of a streaming matrix from perception to action, rather than a tank-like repository of "pools" of attention (Fig. 4.6).

## Response Modes

Minsky (1986) opined that the model of reality that connected consciousness was actually an emergent property of what he called a "society of mind." By this he meant that the unity of consciousness was a functional illusion that only retained a phenomenological wholeness as the byproduct of the consensus of multiple contributory processes. If we accept this conception, it is not too much to see the current extensions of Wickens's boxes as the psychological expression of these respective mind's "citizens." True, one can have the same functional description of this interaction via cortical areas at the neurophysiological level, but it is our

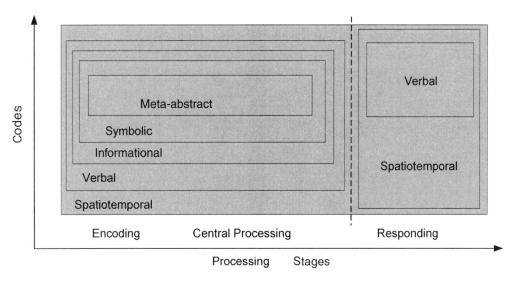

FIGURE 4.6.  The general elaboration of the side of the rectangular box model, omitting the dimension of the processing mode for the sake of illustrative convenience.

contention that the box model is the foundation of its psychologically expressed companion. In the same way that Penfield and Rasmussen (1950) distinguished a *sensory homunculus*, we believe that the elaborated Wickens model becomes an *attentional homunculus* (but does not bear the philosophical burden of the naive interpretation of a homunculus). The sensory homunculus differentiates various parts of the body on the basis of innervation level, yet retains the idea of the body as a single, "whole" entity, so we believe the "attentional" homunculus performs the same function, but in this case the phenomenological whole that is experienced represents the fundamental sense of "reality." In this way, the elaboration of the original Wickens model is much more than a mere extension to a notion of attention, but might be more fully appreciated as a significant foundation of consciousness. The issue of time remains very central to this elaboration (Hancock & Szalma, 2005).

### The Issue of Explanatory Degrees of Freedom

Earlier in the chapter we promised to return to the issue of explanation and the degrees of theoretical freedom problem. With n + 1 degrees of freedom, one can easily explain any system with only n degrees of freedom. This hardly constitutes an "explanation," because all one has done is to introduce a slightly more complex description of the same system, merely expressed in another language. All of the great discoveries of science have been those that accounted for large swaths of the Universe with expressions of breath-taking simplicity and very few (if any) degrees of freedom. Achievements beyond this become the realm of genius. With respect to the multiple-resource notion, it is evident that the addition of an increased number of resource pools constitutes greater explanatory degrees of freedom. The question one has to ask is whether the larger range of findings that can now be accounted for is worth the trade that has been made. This issue lies not merely at the heart of theory itself; it has a direct impact on the way in which theory is used in real-world situations. There are some advocates of the "wrong and strong" school in application areas. That is, such individuals acknowledge that a theory is not right (and they may well be justified in this in that no theory is ever right, and even scientific laws are sometimes flawed) (Hancock & Ganey, 2003), but it contains sufficient specificity so that effective approximations of behavior can be derived and used. This is also very much an engineering staple in that engineers do not seek to explain the whole world, just sufficient amounts of it to be able to effect the change they desire safely and efficiently. From this perspective, the inflation of resources from one to many is only justified if an unequivocal benefit is evident. It is our opinion that Wickens's conception justified this expansion and thus did not illegitimately cut Occam's Razor. We are far less sanguine about our own formulations. We have suggested here several extensions to the resource conception, the prime effect of which is to expand the number of potential resource pools enormously. Although these may be intuitively reasonable proposals, we also begin to deal in conceptions such as the symbolic and the meta-abstract that will prove much harder to define and quantify. Such recommendations act to blur the precision of the original notion and we are very aware of this concern. However, resolution to such issues will certainly be forthcoming from future inspired theorists and experimentalists.

## SUMMARY AND CONCLUSIONS

Despite valiant efforts, the conundrum of attention as posed initially by James (1890) still remains to be resolved. In some ways, the show has now moved on from the original Wickensian notion of the late '70s and early '80s. Now, new, largely neuropsychological conceptions have been promulgated and popularized. However, in many ways, what seems to represent progress is often simply the same ignorance expressed in another jargon or, more properly, another paradigmatic language (this being the fate of most human knowledge, of course). Wickens's elaboration of attention was actually another in a long and tried tradition in psychology (especially the energetic aspects of psychology) in which a unitary concept (e.g., attention, IQ, arousal, fatigue, memory, and so on) has been broken into component elements that better explain the nuances of the empirical landscape, but often only at the expense of proliferating explanatory degrees of freedom. Eventually, this leads to a fractionation and balkanization that leaves theorists unhappy and experimenters confused and frustrated.

Attention is not all of consciousness. The recent pragmatic expression of the operational face of consciousness—situation awareness—has been defined as the external face of consciousness directed beyond the self (Smith & Hancock, 1995). We know consciousness is more than attention, because evidently stimuli find their way into long-term memory without attention necessarily being directed to them. These characteristics of memory cause surprise when attention is drawn to their subtle penetration (Schacter, 2001). However, much of what the individual recognizes as reality has to be conveyed through the refined portals of attention, and much as attention can be divided

between the different elements of the external and internal landscape. Fortunately, we do not experience these divisions as separate phenomenological realities, except in the case of evident mental illness (Gardner, 1976).

That the sensory homunculus describes innervations of various parts of the sensory cortex does not negate the experience of the body as a unified whole. Similarly, that stimulus perception by different sensory modalities in different parts of the sensory environment occurs also does not negate attention or reality as a unified phenomenon. As Gibson (1966) rightly noted, one can erect a theory of perception based upon the exceptions or the illusions, but such a theory would make a very poor heuristic for any organisms' survival or its prosperity in any environment. Similarly, one can believe in diverse attentional pools and the nonconscious processing of stimuli, because the data support such contentions, at least to some degree. However, reliance on them would make a poor guide for designing any practical technical system with which an attentive human could have to interact. In the end, the Wickens box model has served to guide us toward a greater enlightenment on the issue of attention. In recognizing his unique contribution, we now need to proceed more vigorously toward theory and design based upon what humans *should* do, rather toward a future based upon economically driven, efficiency-inspired mandates about what human beings *can* do. If this transition can be realized, then our science will have truly served its ultimate purpose and attention, fractionated or not, will have been directed appropriately.

## ACKNOWLEDGMENTS

The views expressed in this work are those of the authors and do not necessarily reflect official US Army policy. This work was facilitated by the Department of Defense Multidisciplinary University Research Initiative program administered by the Army Research Office under Grant no. DAAD19-01-1-0621, P. A. Hancock, Principal Investigator.

### Note

1. Parenthetically, it introduces a very important but complex argument concerning the nature of entropy. For the physicist, the transformation of both documents,

if someone burned them, would be exactly equivalent. As is evident from our discussion, for the psychologist, for the sociologist, in fact for the everyday individual, these respective acts would be regarded very differently indeed.

# References

Andrews, R., Biggs, M., Seidel, M., et al. (Eds.). (1996). *The Columbia world of quotations*. New York: Columbia University Press.

Broadbent, D. E. (1958). *Perception and communication*. London: Pergamon Press.

Bronowski, J. (1966). *The common sense of science*. Cambridge, Mass.: Harvard University Press.

Budiansky, S. (2000). *The truth about dogs*. Penguin: New York.

Carswell, C. M. (2005). Editorial. *Ergonomics in Design, 13*(3), 3.

Damos, D. L., & Lyall, E. A. (1986). The effect of varying stimulus and response modes and asymmetric transfer on the dual-task performance of discrete tasks. *Ergonomics, 29*, 519–533.

Eysenck, H. J. (1967). *The biological basis of personality*. Springfield: Ill., Charles C. Thomas.

Fitts, P. M. (1954). The information capacity of the human motor system in controlling the amplitude of movement. *Journal of Experimental Psychology, 47*, 381–391.

Freeman, G. L. (1948). *The energetics of human behavior*. Ithaca, N.Y.: Cornell University Press.

Gardner, H. (1976). *The shattered mind*. New York: Vintage Books.

Gibson, J. J. (1966). *The senses considered as perceptual systems*. Boston, Mass.: Houghton Mifflin.

———. (1979). *The ecological approach to visual perception*. Boston, Mass.: Houghton Mifflin.

Hancock, P. A. (1997). *Essays on the future of human–machine systems*. Eden Prairie, Minn.: Banta.

———, & Chignell, M. H. (1987). Adaptive control in human–machine systems. In P. A. Hancock (Ed.), *Human factors psychology* (pp. 305–345). Amsterdam: North-Holland.

———, & Desmond, P. A. (Eds.). (2001). *Stress, workload, and fatigue*. Mahwah, N.J.: Erlbaum.

———, & Ganey, H. C. N. (2003). From the inverted-U to the extended-U: The evolution of a law of psychology. *Journal of Human Performance in Extreme Environments, 7*(1), 5–14.

———, & Szalma, J. L. (2003). Operator stress and display design. *Ergonomics in Design, 11*(2), 13–18.

———, & Szalma, J. L. (August 2005). *The marriage of mind and machine: Advanced human–machine interaction*. Presented at the 113th annual convention of the American Psychological Association. Washington, DC.

———, Szalma, J. L., & Oron–Gilad, T. (2005). Time, emotion and the limits to human information processing.

In D. McBride & D. Schmorrow (Eds.). *Quantifying human information processing* (pp. 157–175). Lanham, Md.: Lexington Books.

Illich, I. (1973). *Tools for conviviality*. New York: Harper & Row.

James, W. (1890). *Principles of psychology*. New York: Holt.

Kahneman, D. (1973). *Attention and effort*. Englewood Cliffs, N.J.: Prentice-Hall.

Kantowitz, B. H. (1987). Mental workload. In P. A. Hancock (Ed.), *Human factors psychology* (pp. 81–121). North Holland: Amsterdam.

———, & Knight, J. L. (1976). On experimenter limited processes. *Psychological Review, 83*, 502–507.

Kinsbourne, M., & Hicks, R. E. (1978). Functional cerebral space: A model for overflow, transfer, and interference effects in human performance: A tutorial review. In R. Nickerson (Ed.), *Attention and performance VII* (pp. 345–362). Hillsdale, N.J.: Erlbaum.

Miller, G. A. (1956). The magical number seven, plus or minus two: Some limits on our capacity for processing information. *Psychological Review, 63*, 81–97.

Minsky, M. (1986). *The society of the mind*. New York: Simon and Schuster.

Moray, N. (1967). Where is capacity limited? A survey and a model. *Acta Psychologica, 27*, 8492.

Navon, D. (1984). Resources: A theoretical soupstone? *Psychological Review, 91*, 216–234.

———, & Gopher, D. (1979). On the economy of the human information processing system. *Psychological Review, 86*, 214–255.

Penfield, W., & Rasmussen, T. L. (1950). *The cerebral cortex of man: A clinical study of localization of function*. New York: MacMillan.

Schacter, D. L. (2001). *The seven sins of memory: How the mind forgets and remembers*. New York: Houghton Mifflin Company.

Shannon, C. E., & Weaver, W. (1949). *The mathematical theory of communication*. Urbana, Ill.: University of Illinois Press.

Sivak, M. (1996). The information that drivers use: Is it indeed 90% visual? *Perception, 25*, 1081–1089.

Smith, K., & Hancock, P. A. (1995). Situation awareness is adaptive, externally-directed consciousness. *Human Factors, 37*, 137–148.

Sternberg, R. (1982). *Handbook of human intelligence*. New York: Cambridge University Press.

Szalma, J. L., & Hancock, P. A. (2002). *On mental resources and performance under stress*. White paper. MIT$^2$ Laboratory, University of Central Florida. [Online]. Available: www.mit.ucf.edu

Treisman, A. (1969). Strategies and models of selective attention. *Psychological Review, 76*, 282–299.

Wachtel, P. L. (1967). Conceptions of broad and narrow attention, *Psychological Bulletin, 68*, 417–429.

Welford, A. T. (1967). Single channel operation in the brain. *Acta Psychologica, 27*, 5–21.

———. (1980). The structure of attentional resources. In R. S. Nickerson (Ed.), *Attention and performance VIII* (pp. 239–257). Hillsdale, N.J.: Lawrence Erlbaum Associates.

———. (1987). Attention. In P. A. Hancock (Ed.), *Human factors psychology* (pp. 29–80). North Holland: Amsterdam.

———. (2002). Multiple resources and performance prediction. *Theoretical Issues in Ergonomic Science*, 3(2), 159–177.

———. Mountford, S. J., & Schreiner, W. A. (1981). Multiple resources, task–hemispheric integrity, and individual differences in time sharing, *Human Factors*, 23(2), 211–229.

# Part II

# Emerging Issues in Applied Attention Theory

# Chapter 5

# Individual Differences in Attention and Working Memory: A Molecular Genetic Approach

## *Raja Parasuraman and Pamela Greenwood*

Textbooks in cognitive psychology (e.g., Anderson, 2000) typically describe various characteristics of human behavior in terms of general rules and laws that apply to people as a whole. Some of these different aspects of perception, cognition, and action can be described quantitatively. Well-established quantitative models include Weber's Law, information theory, Hick's Law, signal detection theory, Fitts's Law, decision theory, and several others (Card, Moran, & Newell, 1983; Sheridan & Ferrell, 1974).

In addition to these theoretical functions and models, empirically defined functions can also provide good quantitative descriptions of other aspects of human performance. For example, consider vigilance—the ability to sustain attention over a prolonged period of time to detect an infrequently and unpredictably occurring signal (Davies & Parasuraman, 1982). A two-term exponential function closely fits the profile of decline in the mean signal detection rate over a 40-minute period—the vigilance decrement (Giambra & Quilter, 1987), whereas a one-term hyperbolic function captures

well the acquisition of vigilance skill over 20 sessions of performance (Parasuraman & Giambra, 1991). As Figure 5.1 shows, however, any such attempt at fitting functions to the vigilance performance of *individual* participants does not do so well. Figure 5.1A shows the vigilance decrement function for a group of 20 participants. The group decrement function shows the typical initial rapid drop in the detection rate of critical signals followed by a slower decline—a decrement that could be fitted well with an exponential function, as indicated. Figure 5.1B plots the time-on-task profiles of all 20 participants, ordered from the best overall (S7) to the worst overall performer (S14). As Figure 5.1B shows, however, the average decrement function is not true of all participants. Some exhibit the typical decrement over time on task, whereas others show stable or even perfect (S7) performance over time. Figure 5.2, which displays data from a functional magnetic resonance imaging (fMRI) study of working memory, indicates that a similar issue arises when one considers task-related changes in neural measures.

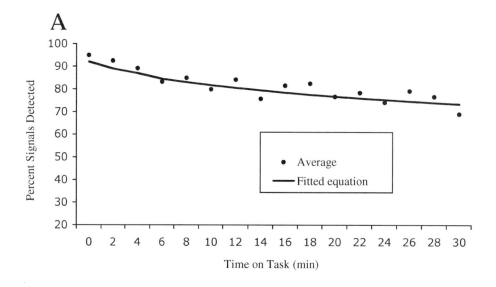

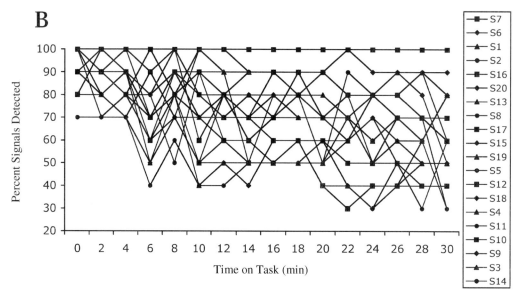

FIGURE 5.1. (A) Mean changes in detection performance as a function of time on task for a sample of 20 participants in a 30-minute vigilance task (solid circles). The solid line shows a fitted function to the data using a two-term exponential of the type suggested by Giambra and Quilter (1987). (B) Individual time-on-task functions for each of the 20 participants.

The mean percentage activation (over baseline) in a specific region of the prefrontal cortex increases systematically with increased working memory load—a monotonic relationship that can be fitted well with a simple linear function, as indicated by the median subject profile in Figure 5.2. However, although this func-tion captures the changes in prefrontal activation of the median participant, others require linear functions with different slopes or curvilinear functions (e.g., those between the 25th–75th percentiles), and some (the "odd man out") do not exhibit a monotonic increase. How can we account for these individual differences?

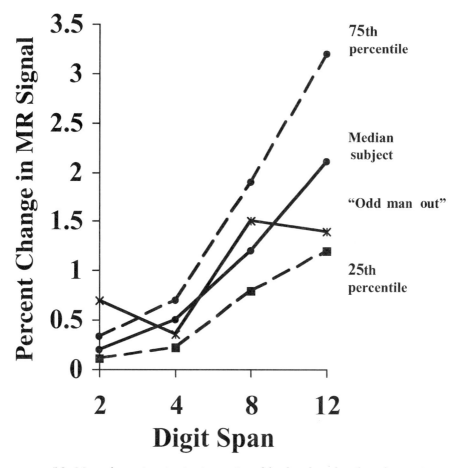

FIGURE 5.2. Mean change inactivation in a region of the dorsolateral prefrontal cortex in a functional magnetic resonance imaging study of working memory, as a function of digit span. Functions are shown for the median, 25th percentile, and 75th percentile participants.

In contrast to cognitive psychology and human factors, which typically focus on the characteristics of the "average" person, psychometrics is concerned with explaining differences between people. With some exceptions (e.g., Matthews, Davies, Westerman, & Stammers, 2000), these two traditions of investigation have rarely interacted. In a sense, one investigator's "noise" is the other's "signal." But rather than treating differences in effects between study participants as noise masking the signal of interest, new developments in molecular genetics and bioinformatics now make it possible to supplement the psychometric approach to identify sources of individual differences in human performance. In this chapter we describe such developments with reference to the domains of attention and working memory.

The program of research we describe in this chapter is a basic one. The initial goal is to be able to identify single genes that are associated with individual differences in elementary cognitive operations underlying attention and working memory. As such, this work does not have immediate applications to practical issues involving individual differences in human performance, such as selection and training, but may do so in the future as more such research is conducted on complex cognitive functions. We hope to show, nevertheless, that the work has relevance to the "applied attention" theme of this book by pointing out the routes toward application, much in the spirit of Christopher Wickens's research, which epitomizes theory-based application (Wickens & Hollands, 2000).

## NEUROERGONOMICS

The approach to individual differences in cognition that we describe in this chapter draws not only from molecular genetics but also from neuroscience. As such, this research falls within the emerging field of *neuroergonomics* (Kramer & Parasuraman, in press; Parasuraman, 2003; Parasuraman & Rizzo, 2007), which is concerned with the study of brain mechanisms in relation to the use of technology at work and in everyday life. The goal is to harness the power of neuroscience to the engineering of human–machine systems for safety and efficiency. Individual differences in cognitive functions relevant to operator performance have typically been evaluated in the framework of the idiographic approach, using self-assessments of intelligence and personality. This chapter describes a new, complementary approach that capitalizes on the breakthroughs provided by the success of the Human Genome Project. The goal is to increase knowledge of individual variation in cognitive functions by parsing genetic and environmental contributions and to identify specific genes that are related to these functions. By examining the expression of these genes in the brain, genetic and neural information can be combined to yield a more robust understanding of the neural correlates of normal cognitive variation. This, in turn, can inform practical issues concerning cognitive functioning in real-world settings.

## GENETICS AND INDIVIDUAL DIFFERENCES IN COGNITION

Progress in understanding the genetic sources of individual differences in human behavior took a major step forward in the late 19th and early 20th centuries, following the belated acceptance of the laws of inheritance proposed by Gregor Mendel. Francis Galton, Charles Spearman, and others showed that a number of human characteristics, including intelligence and personality, were highly heritable. This early work led to the development of the field of behavioral genetics (Plomin, DeFries, McClearn, & McGuffin, 2001), which has been largely concerned with quantifying the relative influence of heritability and environment in determining individual variation in various psychological characteristics.

Much of what we know about the genetics of cognition has come from behavioral genetic studies in which identical and fraternal twins are compared to assess the heritability of a trait. This paradigm has been widely used by behavioral geneticists for more than a century and has been used, for example, to show that general intelligence, or g, is highly heritable (Plomin & Crabbe, 2000). The basic technique has also been used to assess the heritability of specific cognitive functions. Fan and colleagues (2001), for example, used the twin method to show that attention control was heritable in a Chinese population. In addition, g has also been correlated with this aspect of attention (Duncan, Seitz, Kolodny, Bor, Herzog, Ahmed, Newell, & Emslie, 2000). However, in general, the association between g and specific cognitive functions is modest. More important, heritability studies have not addressed the issue of the *specific* genes associated with individual differences in cognitive functions.

Recent advances in molecular genetics now provide a different, complementary approach to the twin method—that of *allelic* association. A proportion of genes in the human genome show small variations (called *alleles*) between unrelated individuals in a part of the DNA sequence of base pairs of nucleotides that defines the gene. Such allelic differences between individuals can then be associated with differences in cognitive functions in the same people. The allelic association method has been recently applied to the study of individual differences in cognition in healthy individuals and revealed increasingly compelling evidence of modulation of cognitive task performance by specific neurotransmitter and neurotrophic genes (Egan, Goldberg, Kolachana, Callicott, Mazzanti, Straub, Goldman, & Weinberger, 2001; Fan et al., 2003; Goldberg & Weinberger, 2004; Greenwood, Sunderland, Friz, & Parasuraman, 2000; Parasuraman, Greenwood, Kumar, & Fossella, 2005).

## THE ALLELIC ASSOCIATION METHOD

The general outline of the allelic association approach to the assessment of individual differences in cognition is as follows (for more details, see Greenwood and Parasuraman [2003] and Parasuraman and Greenwood [2004]). The first step involves the identification of candidate genes—genes deemed likely to influence a given cognitive ability or trait as a result of the functional role of each gene's protein product in the brain. At first glance, this might seem a daunting task because there are 30,000 to 35,000 genes in the human genome. However, the search through the genome need not be exhaustive, because when investigating normal individual differences, only genes that occur in different forms—alleles—need be examined. More than 99% of individual DNA sequences in the human genome do not differ between individuals and hence are not of much interest in investigating individual differences in normal cognition. However, a small proportion of DNA base pairs occur in different forms or alleles. The search for variants of genes that might be associated with normal individual differences in cognition can then be restricted to these regions of the genome.

Variations in the DNA sequence that define a gene occur in different ways. Many variations are the result of substitution of *one* of the four nucleotides in the DNA "alphabet"—adenine (A), guanine (G), cytosine (C), and thymine (T), where A and G form a complementary base pair (A/G), and C and T another (C/T)—with its complement. Such substitutions are referred to as single nucleotide polymorphisms (SNPs). For example, a gene having as part of its complete DNA sequence the series ACATAGA could have a variant in which the T is substituted for a C, resulting in ACACAGA. Other polymorphic variations in DNA gene sequences include insertions, deletions, and repetitions of nucleotides.

Even though only about 1% of the human genome need be examined to uncover potential associations with cognition, there are still so many DNA base pairs (1% of 3 billion base pairs [bp] = 30 million bp) and so many potential variations (SNPs are estimated to number 2–3 million), that some constraints on a search through the SNP databases is necessary. As a first cut, the SNPs should be selected that are likely to influence neurotransmitter function or to have effects on neurotrophic activity. Second, existing cognitive neuroscience research on the cognitive function in question (e.g., working memory) should be reviewed to identify the brain networks that mediate that function. Third, examining pharmacological and neurophysiological studies in animals can identify the neurotransmitter innervation of these networks. Finally, SNPs that influence neurotransmitter or neurotrophic function can be identified for potential association with the cognitive function. These multiple levels of analysis can be combined into a joint bottom-up and top-down approach (see Fig. 5.3). Bottom-up, one can use bioinformatics methods and a search of

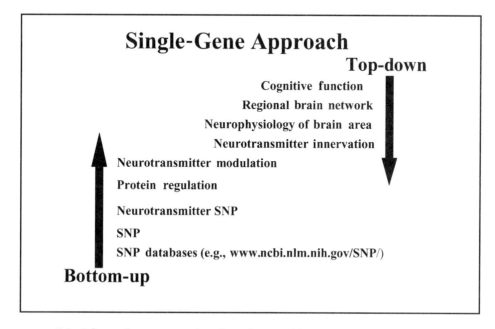

FIGURE 5.3. Schema showing a combined top-down and bottom-up approach to the identification of single candidate genes in molecular genetic studies of cognition. SNP, single nucleotide polymorphism.

SNP databases to identify potential candidate genes. There are several Web sites that list currently known human SNPs, with the databases being updated regularly. At this level of analysis, SNPs with known influences on neurotransmitter function are of special interest. At the same time, a top-down approach can be used, beginning with the cognitive function in question. By identifying the neural networks known to mediate the function and the neurotransmitters that innervate those networks, the top-down and bottom-up approaches can converge on a few genes that may be potential candidates for an association study.

There are some limitations in this allelic association approach to the molecular genetics of cognition. No component of cognition, no matter how microscopic, is likely to be modified by only one gene, and the interpretation of individual differences in a particular cognitive function will ultimately involve specification of the role of many genes as well as environmental factors (Plomin & Crabbe, 2000). It is also important that SNPs or other candidate genes are chosen in a theory-based manner for their functional significance for cognition, to minimize the probability of type I error in finding gene–cognition links.

We illustrate the use of the allelic association method by describing recent studies from our laboratory. We focus on two aspects of cognitive function: visuospatial attention and working memory. In these studies, samples of normal healthy adults were genotyped for naturally occurring variations in neurotransmitter genes and were administered cognitive tasks selected on a theoretical basis for potential associations with these genes.

## VISUOSPATIAL ATTENTION

We chose first to examine genetic contributions to individual differences in attention because the brain networks mediating different attentional functions are increasingly well understood. For example, Posner has proposed an influential "attentional network" theory in which three separate attentional functions—orienting, alerting, and executive—are linked to the activation of separate but overlapping cortical and subcortical networks (Posner & Petersen, 1990). Of these, we examined visuospatial attention, which is associated with the orienting network, using two different tasks: a simple, cued letter discrimination task and a more complex, cued visual search task. Neuroimaging studies have

pointed to the intraparietal cortex as a major focus of cortical activity associated with spatial attention (Corbetta, Kincade, Ollinger, McAvoy, & Shulman, 2000; Yantis, Schwarzbach, Serences, Carlson, Steinmetz, Pekar, & Courtney, 2002). Anticholinergic agents such as scopolamine, when administered directly to the intraparietal cortex in monkeys, impair the speed of reorienting visuospatial attention (Davidson & Marrocco, 2000). Patients with Alzheimer disease with dysfunction of the posterior parietal cortex, as revealed by positron emission tomography (PET), are similarly slowed in disengaging attention from a cued spatial location (Parasuraman, Greenwood, Haxby, & Grady, 1992). The parietal cortex is known to have cholinergic receptors that modulate neuronal function there (Xiang, Huguenard, & Prince, 1998). Attentional orienting is also modulated by nicotine administration in rats (Phillips, McAlonan, Robb, & Brown, 2000) and in humans who smoke (Murphy & Klein, 1998). Other pharmacological studies in animals also point to an important role for nicotinic receptors in attention (Levin & Simon, 1998; Nordberg, 2001).

All these lines of evidence indicate that genes that modulate nicotinic receptors might be good potential candidate genes. Nicotinic acetylcholine receptors are composed of subunits that assemble together to form the receptor itself. There are seven α-like subunits (α-2–7 and α-9) and three β-like subunits (β-2, β-3, and β-4). The most widely distributed nicotinic receptor in the central nervous system is composed of α-4 and β-2 subunits assembled together (Flores, DeCamp, Kilo, Rogers, & Hargreaves, 1996). Using our combined bottom-up/top-down approach, we chose to examine polymorphisms in the gene controlling the most frequent receptor subunit, alpha-4, a gene named CHRNA4. One polymorphism in this subunit receptor gene, involving a common C-to-T substitution at position 1545 (CHRNA4 C1545T) is of interest because of its potential role in both smoking quantity and nicotine addiction (Li, Beuten, Ma, Payne, Lou, Garcia, Duenes, Crews, & Elston, 2005). As discussed previously, nicotine has been shown to modulate visuospatial attention in both animals and humans, suggesting that this nicotinic receptor gene might be linked to visuospatial attention.

### Shifting Visuospatial Attention

In our first study, a sample of 89 healthy adults with a mean age of 35 years was genotyped for the CHRNA4

C1545T polymorphism (Parasuraman et al., 2005). Approximately 0.5 to 3 μg DNA was extracted from buccal (cheek) samples obtained by cell brush and was prepared for polymerase chain reaction. Forward and backward primers were used to identify the T-to-C polymorphism (Steinlein, Deckert, Nothen, Franke, Maier, Beckmann, et al., 1997), which is associated with 152-bp and 138-bp bands for the T allele; and 152-bp, 105-bp, and 33-bp bands for the C allele. Using these methods, the sample of 89 participants was subdivided into three groups based on the number of C alleles: 0 (TT genotype, n = 46), 1 (TC genotype, n = 4), or 2 (CC genotype, n = 19).

The participants were administered a cued letter discrimination task modeled after the orienting task introduced by Posner (1980). An arrow cue indicated which of two locations to the left or right of fixation would contain a letter target. Following a cue target delay of 200 to 2000 msec, the target letter appeared. Participants were required to make a speeded decision regarding whether the target was a consonant or vowel. Cue validity (valid, invalid, neutral) was varied so that both benefits (neutral cue response time [RT] – valid cue RT) and costs (invalid cue RT – neutral cue RT) of cueing could be obtained.

Both RT benefits of valid cues and RT costs of invalid cues on letter discrimination varied in a systematic manner with CHRNA4 genotype. With an increased "gene dose" of the C allele (from 0 to 1 to 2 C alleles) RT benefits increased progressively (Fig. 5.4A), whereas RT costs decreased, also in a similarly progressive manner (Fig. 5.4B). These systematic results provided the first evidence for an association between a nicotinic receptor gene, CHRNA4, and individual differences in the efficiency of shifting spatial attention in response to location cues.

Several important aspects of these results should be noted. First, the effect sizes of the associations we observed were moderate to large (Cohen, 1988), which is often not the case in allelic association studies of disease (Ioannidis, Ntzani, Trikalinos, & Contopoulos-Ioannidis, 2001). Effect size was .45 for RT benefits and .3 for RT costs. Second, the genetic associations we observed involved *component* cognitive operations of visuospatial attention. Normal allelic variation in the CHRNA4 gene was associated only with individual differences in the efficiency of shifting attention in response to valid and invalid location cues. Overall participant accuracy or speed of performance on this attention task was unrelated to

CHRNA4 genotype. Third, and perhaps most important, a gene–cognition association was not found for another cognitive operation. This sample of participants was also administered a working memory task, described more fully later. No association was found between CHRNA4 genotype and any aspect of performance on the working memory task. With the sample of 89 participants used in this study, the power to detect a moderate size (.25) effect of CHRNA4 C1545T on working memory was greater than 88%. Thus, in sum, we observed a strong association between a common nicotinic receptor gene and component operations underlying visuospatial attention, and at the same time observed a dissociation between CHNRA4 and working memory.

## Scaling Visuospatial Attention

To examine further the specificity of the association between the nicotinic receptor polymorphism and visuospatial attention, we conducted another study of CHRNA4 using a cued visual search task (Greenwood, Fossella, & Parasuraman, 2005). We hypothesized that a link between CHRNA4 and visuospatial attention shifting would be strengthened if an association could be found for another task in which this component operation could be isolated.

We genotyped a sample of 104 healthy participants using the same methods described previously. The 104 participants were subdivided into three groups based on the number of C alleles of CHRNA4 C1545T: 0 (TT genotype, n = 61), 1 (TC genotype, n = 25), or 2 (CC genotype, n = 18). Participants were administered a cued visual search task designed to induce changes in the scale of spatial attention (Greenwood & Parasuraman, 1999), the so-called zooming in and zooming out of spatial attention (Eriksen & St. James, 1986), The use of such a task also allowed us to conduct a more rigorous test of the dissociation between CHRNA4 and working memory reported by Parasuraman and colleagues (2005). This dissociation was not in accord with the view that visuospatial attention represents the rehearsal mechanism for spatial working memory (Awh, Jonides, & Reuter-Lorenz, 1998). That view would suggest an association between a gene linked to spatial attention and individual differences in spatial working memory. However, the task used by Parasuraman and colleagues (2005) required participants only to shift attention to a single item in the visual field, as

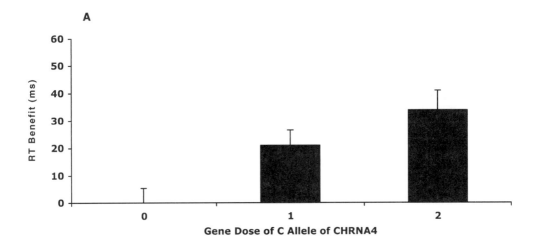

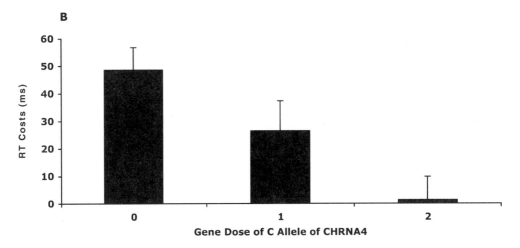

FIGURE 5.4. Effects of allelic variation in the CHRNA4 gene on visuospatial attention in a cued letter discrimination task. (A) Reaction time (RT) benefits of valid location cues (neutral RT–valid RT). (B) RT costs of invalid location cues in the same task (invalid RT–neutral RT). The three genotypes TT, TC, and CC correspond to increasing gene dose (0, 1, and 2) of the C allele of the CHRNA4 gene.

opposed to a variable number of items within the attentional focus, which would presumably be more likely to be the mechanism postulated to be the same as the rehearsal mechanism among items held in spatial working memory. The cued visual search task used by Greenwood and associates (2005) required participants to search an array of 15 letters for a specific target letter defined either by both form and color (conjunction search) or uniquely by color (feature search) (Treisman & Gelade, 1980). Target location was precued with a rectangle of increasing size that enclosed 1, 3, 9, or all 15 letters. On a minority of

catch trials the target was absent. In previous research with this task (Greenwood & Parasuraman, 1999), RTs to detect both feature and conjunction targets have been shown to increase monotonically with increased cue size, presumably because the spatial scale of attention is expanded or zoomed out, therefore making the search less efficient.

Target detection RT was faster for feature than for conjunction search and increased with cue size, as expected. RT also increased with gene dose of the CHRNA4 C allele, and this effect interacted with task type (feature/conjunction search) and cue size.

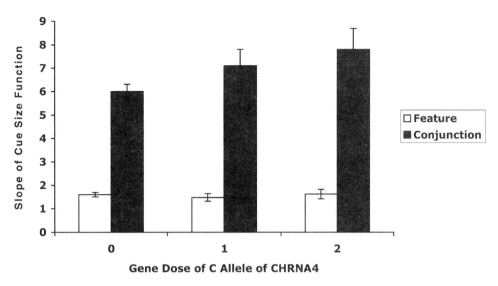

FIGURE 5.5. Effects of allelic variation in the CHRNA4 gene on visuospatial attention in a cued visual search task. The change in response time with cue size, as indicated by slope, is shown for both feature and conjunction search, and for increasing gene dose (0, 1, and 2) of the C allele of the CHRNA4 gene.

The interaction can be better appreciated by examining the slope of the RT/cue size function, which summarizes the change in search speed as spatial attention is scaled from small to large. This analysis showed that search slope was larger for conjunction search than for feature search. In addition, search slope increased progressively with increased C allele dose for conjunction search but not for feature search (Fig. 5.5). The effect size of the CHRNA4 genotype for conjunction search was .25 (a moderate size effect). There were no effects of genotype on accuracy in either the feature or conjunction search task.

These results indicate that the association between CHRNA4 and attention shifting found in the previous study by Parasuraman and colleagues (2005) is also found for a conjunction search task (Greenwood et al., 2005). This association considerably bolsters the view that this nicotinic receptor gene is specifically associated with component operations of visuospatial attention, including attentional shifting and attention scaling.

## WORKING MEMORY

The molecular genetic studies of visuospatial attention show, in two fairly large samples of healthy adults, a strong pattern of association between a nicotinic receptor polymorphism, CHRNA4 C1545T, and component attentional operations. At the same time, this gene was not associated with individual differences in working memory. A pattern of association and dissociation, respectively, between a gene and two cognitive functions naturally invites the question of whether the dissociated cognitive function can be associated with another gene. Furthermore, can a *double* dissociation be demonstrated?

To examine these issues, we focused on identifying potential candidate genes for working memory, the cognitive function that was contrasted to visuospatial attention in the previous studies. Dopaminergic receptor genes are likely candidates for genetic effects on working memory because of the importance of dopaminergic innervation for prefrontal cortical areas involved in working memory. Dopamine agents have been shown to modulate working memory and prefrontal cortex function in monkeys (Sawaguchi & Goldman-Rakic, 1991) and humans (Muller, von Cramon, & Pollmann, 1998). Dopamine plays an important role not only in prefrontal cortex-mediated processes of working memory, but also in hippocampal inputs to that region (Gurden, Takita, & Jay, 2000). Candidate genes include the COMT gene, which is involved in the dopaminergic degradation pathway (Egan et al., 2001). Another candidate is the DBH gene, which is involved in converting dopamine to norepinephrine in adrenergic vesicles (Cubells, van Kammen, Kelley, Anderson, O'Connor, Price, Malison, Rao, Kobayashi, Nagatsu, & Gelernter, 1998). An SNP in the DBH gene involving a G-to-A substitution at 444, exon 2 (G444A) on chromosome 9q34 has been linked to changes in the dopamine-to-noradrenaline ratio in brain (Cubells & Zabetian, 2004) and to attention deficits in children (Daly, Hawi, Fitzerald, & Gill, 1999). DBH is a functional polymorphism, because the A allele is associated with lower plasma dopamine β-hydroxylase (DBH) levels, and the G allele is associated with higher DBH levels (Cubells et al., 1998). We therefore examined its role in mediating individual differences in working memory (Parasuraman et al., 2005).

A group of 103 healthy individuals were genotyped for the G444A polymorphism of the DBH gene. Genomic material was obtained via buccal cell brush and prepared as described previously. After genotyping, the sample of 103 participants was subdivided into three groups based on the number of G alleles: 0 (AA genotype, n = 17), 1 (AG genotype, n = 39), or 2 (GG genotype, n = 47).

The working memory task was a variant of the delayed match-to-sample paradigm and involved maintaining a representation of up to three spatial locations over a period of 3 seconds. After a fixation period, participants were shown target circles at one to three locations for 500 msec. Simultaneous with the

offset of the dot display, the fixation cross reappeared for a 3-second delay, at the end of which a single red test dot appeared alone, either at the same location as one of the target dots (match) or at a different location (nonmatch). Participants had 2 seconds to decide whether the test dot location matched one of the target dots.

We first assessed the sensitivity and reliability of the working memory task. As Figure 5.6 shows, matching accuracy decreased as the number of locations to be maintained in working memory increased, demonstrating the sensitivity of the task to variations in memory load. In follow-up studies with other samples of subjects, we have found this task to provide a well-specified memory load function across a range of memory set sizes and delays. Furthermore, inter- and intraindividual differences on the task are relatively stable. The test–retest reliability at the highest three-location memory load was .75. These findings indicate that individual differences on the working memory task were reliable and stable. We then examined to what extent differences between individuals could be associated with the gene dose of the G allele of the DBH gene. Accuracy was equivalent for all three genotypes at the lowest memory load, but increased with higher gene dose of the G allele, particularly for the highest (three-target) load, as confirmed by a simple effects analysis (Fig. 5.6). Memory accuracy for the GG allele (G gene dose = 2) was

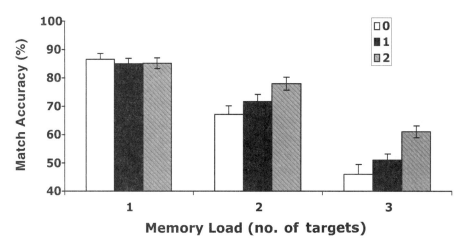

FIGURE 5.6. Effects of allelic variation in the dopamine β-hydroxylase (DBH) gene on match accuracy in the working memory task as a function of the number of spatial locations to be maintained in working memory. The three genotypes AA, AG, and GG correspond to increasing gene dose (0, 1, and 2) of the G allele of the DBH gene.

significantly greater than that for both the AG (G gene dose = 1) and AA alleles (G gene dose = 0). The effect size of the G allele on working memory accuracy at the highest memory load was moderate to high (.25). In sum, these findings point to a substantial association between the DBH gene and working memory performance.

Increasing gene dose of the G allele of the DBH gene was associated with better working memory performance. This effect was most apparent when the number of target locations to be retained was high. Thus, the association between the DBH gene and working memory was particularly marked under conditions that most taxed the working memory system. Cubells and coworkers (1998) reported that the G444A polymorphism of the DBH gene influences levels of the DBH enzyme in plasma, and there is evidence for high concentrations of DBH-labeled fibers in several prefrontal cortical sites (Gaspar, Berger, Febvret, Vigny, & Henry, 1989). Although the precise relationship between the enzymatic activity of DBH and human brain dopamine levels is not known, the association we found between DBH genotype and working memory is consistent with the well-known role of dopaminergic agents in prefrontal cortex and its dopaminergic mediation of working memory (Abi-Dargham, Mawlawi, Lombardo, Gil, Martinez, Huang, Hwang, Keilp, Kochan, van Heertum, Gorman, & Laruelle, 2002).

The results described to date thus point to an association between the CHRNA4 gene and visuospatial attention, a dissociation between CHRNA4 and working memory, and an association between the DBH gene and working memory. Can the pattern sequence be completed by a dissociation between DBH and visuospatial attention? The answer is yes. The sample of participants genotyped for the DBH gene was also administered the visuospatial attention task described previously. Neither the RT benefits of a valid location cue, nor RT costs resulting from an invalid cue, were significantly associated with the DBH genotype. With the sample size of 103, power to detect a moderate-size (.25) association between DBH and visuospatial attention was greater than 94%, suggesting that the dissociation was real.

In summary, these results indicate that the CHRNA4 gene is strongly associated with individual differences in the efficiency of visuospatial attention. The association was demonstrated for two different tasks in which this cognitive operation is used. CHRNA4 was not associated with spatial working memory, which is associated with the DBH gene. At the same time, DBH was not associated with visuospatial attention. Thus these findings are consistent with a double dissociation between the effects of CHRNA4 and DBH on attention and working memory.

## FUTURE DIRECTIONS

The new field of the molecular genetics of cognition is barely a few years old and can be considered to be in its infancy. Despite this, the results obtained to date are very promising with respect to the ultimate goal of providing a neural and genetic basis for characterizing individual differences in various cognitive functions. In this chapter we described our efforts to identify genes that modulate component cognitive operations in visuospatial attention and working memory. Other groups are conducting similar studies examining different subcomponents of human executive function (Diamond, Briand, Fossella, & Gehlbach, 2004; Egan et al., 2001; Fossella, Sommer, Fan, Wu, Swanson, Pfaff, & Posner, 2002). Progress is also being made in understanding the genetic underpinnings of the effects of aging on various cognitive functions (Greenwood & Parasuraman, 2003; Parasuraman, Greenwood, & Sunderland, 2002).

The foundational work that has been done so far needs to be supplemented by several new directions for research. For example, cognitive (behavioral) phenotypes will need to be supplemented by those derived from electrophysiological (e.g., event-related potential [ERP]) and both structural and functional neuroimaging measures (e.g., fMRI) to exploit further the power of cognitive neuroscience research on the neural networks and the neurochemical basis of different cognitive functions. This will be challenging given the high cost of neuroimaging studies with large samples of participants, but recent studies using ERPs (Reinvang, Espeseth, & Gjerstad, 2005), structural MRI (Espeseth, Greenwood, Reinvang, Fjell, Walhovd, Westlye, Wehling, Lundervold, Rootwelt, & Parasuraman, 2006), and functional MRI (Fan et al., 2003) suggest that the payoff could be considerable.

Furthermore, to date, single-gene associations between SNPs and specific cognitive functions have been identified. It will be important to determine whether these genes act independently of each other, or, as is more likely, interact with each other.

For example, Espeseth and associates (2006) recently reported that the CHRNA4 gene described previously interacts with a neuronal repair gene, APOE, in its effects on individual differences in the same visuospatial attention task used by Parasuraman and colleagues (2005). Additional analyses also need to be conducted to examine whether the polymorphisms that have been associated with cognitive functions are inherited together with other SNPs or DNA loci that are in close proximity to the polymorphism in question. Such so-called *haplotypes* may provide for a better understanding of the functional relationships between genotype and cognitive and neural phenotypes. Finally, PET studies using neurotransmitter ligands may also permit genetic associations to be investigated in real time in participants performing cognitive tasks while being imaged. The coming decade is likely to witness an explosion in these and other types of molecular genetic research that could well revolutionize our understanding of individual differences in cognition.

### ACKNOWLEDGMENT

The research described in this chapter was supported in part by the National Institute on Aging (grant no. AG19653).

### References

Abi-Dargham, A., Mawlawi, O., Lombardo, I., Gil, R., Martinez, D., Huang, Y., Hwang, D. R., Keilp, J., Kochan, L., van Heertum, R., Gorman, J. M., & Laruelle, M. (2002). Prefrontal dopamine D1 receptors and working memory in schizophrenia. *Journal of Neuroscience 22*, 3708–3719.

Anderson, J. R. (2000). *Cognitive psychology and its implications.* New York: Worth.

Awh, E., Jonides, J., & Reuter-Lorenz, P. A. (1998). Rehearsal in spatial working memory. *Journal of Experimental Psychology: Human Perception and Performance, 24*, 780–790.

Card, S., Moran, R., & Newell, A. (1983). *The psychology of human–computer interaction.* Hillsdale, N.J.: Erlbaum.

Cohen, J. (1988). *Statistical power analysis for the behavioral sciences* (2nd ed.). Hillsdale, N.J.: Lawrence Erlbaum.

Corbetta, M., Kincade, J. M., Ollinger, J. M., McAvoy, [M. P.,] & Shulman, G. L. (2000). Voluntary attention is dissociated from target detection in the human posterior parietal cortex. *Nature Neuroscience, 3*(3), 292–297.

Cubells, J. F., van Kammen, D. P., Kelley, M. E., Anderson, G. M., O'Connor, D. T., Price, L. H., Malison, R., Rao, P. A., Kobayashi, K., Nagatsu, T., & Gelernter, J. (1998). Dopamine beta-hydroxylase: Two polymorphisms in linkage disequilibrium at the structural gene DBH associate with biochemical phenotypic variation. *Human Genetics, 102*(5), 533–540.

———, & Zabetian, C. P. (2004). Human genetics of plasma dopamine ß-hydroxylase activity: Applications to research in psychiatry and neurology. *Psychopharmacology, 174*, 463–476.

Daly, G., Hawi, Z., Fitzerald, M., & Gill, M. (1999). Mapping susceptibility loci in attention deficit hyperactivity disorder: Preferential transmission of parental alleles at DAT1, DBH, and DRD5 to affected children. *Molecular Psychiatry, 4*, 192–196.

Davidson, M. C., & Marrocco, R. T. (2000). Local infusion of scopolamine into intraparietal cortex alters covert orienting in rhesus monkeys. *Journal of Neurophysiology, 83*, 1536–1549.

Davies, D. R., & Parasuraman, R. (1982). *The psychology of vigilance.* London: Academic Press.

Diamond, A., Briand, L., Fossella, J., & Gehlbach, L. (2004). Genetic and neurochemical modulation of prefrontal cognitive functions in children. *American Journal of Psychiatry, 161*, 125–132.

Duncan, J., Seitz, R. J., Kolodny, J., Bor, D., Herzog, H., Ahmed, A., Newell, F. N., & Emslie, H. (2000). A neural basis for general intelligence. *Science, 289*, 457–460.

Egan, M. F., Goldberg, T. E., Kolachana, B. S., Callicott, J. H., Mazzanti, C. M., Straub, R. E., Goldman, D., & Weinberger, D. R. (2001). Effect of COMT Val108/158 Met genotype on frontal lobe function and risk for schizophrenia. *Proceedings of the National Academy of Sciences U S A, 98*(12), 6917–6922.

Eriksen, C. W., & St. James, J. D. (1986). Visual attention within and around the field of focal attention: A zoom lens model. *Perception & Psychophysics, 40*, 225–240.

Espeseth, T., Greenwood, P. M., Reinvang, I., Fjell, A. M., Walhovd, K. B., Westlye, L. T., Wehling, E., Lundervold, E., Rootwelt, H., & Parasuraman, R. (2006). Interactive effects of APOE and CHRNA4 on attention and white matter volume in healthy middle-aged and older adults. *Cognitive, Affective, and Behavioral Neuroscience, 6*, 31–43.

Fan, J., Fossella, J. A., Sommer, T., Wu, Y., & Posner, M. I. (2003). Mapping the genetic variation of attention onto brain activity. *Proceedings of the National Academy of Sciences U S A, 100*(12), 7406–7411.

Flores, C. M., DeCamp, R. M., Kilo, S., Rogers, S. W., & Hargreaves, K. M. (1996). Neuronal nicotinic receptor expression in sensory neurons of the rat trigeminal ganglion: Demonstration of alpha3beta4, a novel subtype in the mammalian nervous system. *Journal of Neuroscience, 16*, 7892–7901.

Fossella, J., Sommer, T., Fan, J., Wu, Y., Swanson, J. M., Pfaff, D. W., & Posner, M. I. (2002). Assessing the molecular genetics of attention networks. *BMC Neuroscience, 3*, 14–19.

Gaspar, P., Berger, B., Febvret, A., Vigny, A., & Henry, J. P. (1989). Catecholamine innervation of the human cerebral cortex as revealed by comparative immunohistochemistry of tyrosine hydroxylase and dopamine-beta-hydroxylase. *Journal of Comparative Neurology, 279*, 249–271.

Giambra, L. M., & Quilter, R. E. (1987). A two-term exponential functional description of the time course of sustained attention. *Human Factors, 29*, 635–643.

Goldberg, T. E., & Weinberger, D. R. (2004). Genes and the parsing of cognitive processes. *Trends in Cognitive Sciences, 8*, 325–335.

Greenwood, P. M., Fossella, J. A., & Parasuraman, R. (2005). Specificity of the effect of a nicotinic receptor polymorphism on individual differences in visuospatial attention. *Journal of Cognitive Neuroscience, 17*, 1611–1620.

Greenwood, P. M., & Parasuraman, R. (1999). Scale of attentional focus in visual search. *Perception & Psychophysics, 61*, 837–859.

Greenwood, P., & Parasuraman, R. (2003). Normal genetic variation, cognition, and aging. *Behavioral and Cognitive Neuroscience Reviews, 2*(4), 278–306.

Greenwood, P. M., Sunderland, T., Friz, J. L., & Parasuraman, R. (2000). Genetics and visual attention: Selective deficits in healthy adult carriers of the varepsilon 4 allele of the apolipoprotein E gene. *Proceedings of the National Academy of Sciences USA, 97*(21), 11661–11666.

Gurden, H., Takita, M., & Jay, T. M. (2000). Essential role of D1 but not D2 receptors in the NMDA receptor-dependent long-term potentiation at hippocampal-prefrontal cortex synapses in vivo. *Journal of Neuroscience, 20*(22), RC10, 1–5.

Ioannidis, J. P., Ntzani, E. E., Trikalinos, T. A., & Contopoulos-Ioannidis, D. G. (2001). Replication validity of genetic association studies. *Nature Genetics, 29*, 306–309.

Kramer, A., & Parasuraman, R. (In press). Neuroergonomics —Application of neuroscience to human factors. In J. Caccioppo, L. Tassinary, & G. Berntson (Eds.), *Handbook of psychophysiology* (2nd ed.). New York: Cambridge University Press.

Levin, E. D., & Simon, B. B. (1998). Nicotinic acetylcholine involvement in cognitive function in animals. *Psychopharmacology (Berlin), 13*, 217–230.

Li, M. D., Beuten, J., Ma, J. Z., Payne, T. J., Lou, X. Y., Garcia, V., Duenes, A. S., Crews, K. M., & Elston, R. C. (2005). Ethnic- and gender-specific association of the nicotinic acetylcholine receptor alpha4 subunit gene (CHRNA4) with nicotine

dependence. *Human Molecular Genetics 14*, 1211–1219.

Matthews, G., Davies, D. R., Westerman, S., & Stammers, R. (2000). *Human performance: Cognition, stress and individual differences.* Hove, UK: Psychology Press.

Muller, U., von Cramon, D. Y., & Pollmann, S. (1998). D1- versus D2-receptor modulation of visuospatial working memory in humans. *Journal of Neuroscience, 18*(7), 2720–2728.

Murphy, F. C., & Klein, R. M. (1998). The effects of nicotine on spatial and non-spatial expectancies in a covert orienting task. *Neuropsychologia, 36*, 1103–1114.

Nordberg, A. (2001). Nicotinic receptor abnormalities of Alzheimer's disease: Therapeutic implications. *Biological Psychiatry, 49*, 200–210.

Parasuraman, R. (2003). Neuroergonomics: Research and practice. *Theoretical Issues in Ergonomics Science, 4*, 5–20.

——, & Giambra, L. (1991). Skill development in vigilance: Effects of event rate and age. *Psychology and Aging, 6*, 155–169.

——, & Greenwood, P. M. (2004). Molecular genetics of visuospatial attention and working memory. In M. I. Posner (Ed.), *Cognitive neuroscience of attention* (pp. 245–259). New York: Guilford.

——, Greenwood, P. M., Haxby, J. V., & Grady, C. L. (1992). Visuospatial attention in dementia of the Alzheimer type. *Brain, 115*, 711–733.

——, Greenwood, P. M., Kumar, R., & Fossella, J. (2005). Beyond heritability: Neurotransmitter genes differentially modulate visuospatial attention and working memory. *Psychological Science, 16*(3), 200–207.

——, Greenwood, P. M., & Sunderland, T. (2002). The apolipoprotein E gene, attention, and brain function. *Neuropsychology, 16*, 254–274.

——, & Rizzo, R. (2007). *Neuroergonomics: The brain at work.* New York: Oxford University Press.

Phillips, J. M., McAlonan, K., Robb, W. G., & Brown, V. J. (2000). Cholinergic neurotransmission influences covert orientation of visuospatial attention in the rat. *Psychopharmacology (Berlin), 150*, 112–116.

Plomin, R., & Crabbe, J. (2000). DNA. *Psychological Bulletin, 126*, 806–828.

——, DeFries, J. C., McClearn, G. E., & McGuffin, P. (2001). *Behavioral genetics* (4th ed.). New York: Worth Publishers.

Posner, M. I. (1980). Orienting of attention. *Quarterly Journal of Experimental Psychology, 32*, 3–25.

——, & Petersen, S. E. (1990). The attention system of the human brain. *Annual Review of Neuroscience, 13*, 25–42.

Reinvang, I., Espeseth, T., & Gjerstad, L. (2005). Cognitive ERPs are related to ApoE allelic variation in mildly cognitively impaired patients. *Neuroscience Letters, 382*(3), 346–351.

Sawaguchi, T., & Goldman-Rakic, P. S. (1991). D1 dopamine receptors in prefrontal cortex: Involvement in working memory. *Science, 251*(4996), 947–950.

Sheridan, T. B., & Ferrell, W. R. (1974). *Man–machine systems.* Cambridge, Mass.: MIT Press.

Steinlein, O. K., Deckert, J., Nothen, M. M., Franke, P., Maier, W., Beckmann, H., et al. (1997). Neuronal nicotinic acetylcholine receptor alpha 4 subunit (CHRNA4) and panic disorder: An association study. *American Journal of Medical Genetics, 74,* 199–201.

Treisman, A., & Gelade, G. (1980). A feature integration theory of attention. *Cognitive Psychology, 12,* 97–136.

Wickens, C. D., & Hollands, J. G. (2000). *Engineering psychology and human performance* (3rd ed.) New York: Longman.

Yantis, S., Schwarzbach, J., Serences, J. T., Carlson, R. L., Steinmetz, M. A., Pekar, J. J., & Courtney, S. M. (2002). Transient neural activity in human parietal cortex during spatial attention shifts. *Nature Neuroscience, 5,* 995–1002.

Xiang, Z., Huguenard, J. R., & Prince, D. A. (1998). Cholinergic switching within neocortical inhibitory networks. *Science, 281,* 985–988.

# Chapter 6

# Affect, Attention, and Automation

## John D. Lee

*Feelings are the Germ and Starting Point of Cognition, Thoughts the Developed Tree.*
—W. James (1890, p. 222)

The landmark book *Engineering Psychology and Human Performance* (Wickens, 1984a) brought together the seemingly unrelated fields of cognitive psychology and engineering. This book and the two subsequent editions (Wickens, 1992; Wickens & Hollands, 2000) have had an enormous impact on engineering design and have garnered more than 780 citations in the scientific literature as of June 2005. One important contribution of this book was to relate the substantial theoretical and empirical results of psychology to engineering problems associated with human–technology interaction. Another important contribution was to demonstrate the important theoretical contributions of engineering to basic research. Engineering is not just an applied science. Engineering design challenges identify theoretical issues that might go unaddressed if theory is not forced to confront a broader reality. Applying psychology to design challenges identifies important theoretical gaps.

These theoretical gaps sometimes emerge because the field of psychology often severs important connections

in its efforts to address the daunting complexity of human behavior. One particularly important set of connections has to do with the influence of technology on behavior. Arguably, technology is what makes human cognition unique. Broadly considered, technology has coevolved with humans and it continues to define fundamental characteristics of human cognition. In the context of maritime navigation, Hutchins (1995) showed that cognition depends on tools, such as annotations on charts that help mariners determine the ship's position. Such instances of distributed cognition increasingly govern the performance of complex sociotechnical systems (Hollan, Hutchins, & Kirsh, 2000). Engineering psychology demonstrates that understanding cognition requires an understanding of the connections between cognition and technology.

As systems become increasingly complex, people are confronted with more dynamic, interconnected, and uncertain situations in which various forms of automation play an ever more central role (Parasuraman & Riley, 1997; Woods, 1988). Often people must address interleaved and concurrent tasks in collaboration with a distributed team of humans and automation (Sarter & Woods, 2000; Skitka, Mosier, Burdick, & Rosenblatt, 2000; and Gao & Lee, 2006). Such complexity, ambiguity, and indeterminacy define situations in which affect and emotion can have a strong influence on cognition (Forgas, 1995, 2002), particularly as it relates to human reliance on automation (Lee & See, 2004). Early conceptions of attention and cognition viewed cognition and affect as integral to human behavior (James, 1890; Titchener, 1908). However, the behavioral and information processing traditions tend to sever the relationship between affect and cognition. Only recently have researchers begun to identify the theoretical importance of connecting cognition and affect (Damasio, 1994). For engineering psychology to address emerging design challenges, it may also need to consider the connections between affect and cognition.

Several recent books and reviews suggest affect plays a critical role in cognition and in human interaction with technology (Gladwell, 2005; Hancock, Pepe, & Murphy, 2005; Lee & See, 2004; Norman, 2004; Picard, 1997). A special issue of the *International Journal of Human–Computer Studies* (Hudlicka, 2003) titled "Applications of Affective Computing in Human–Computer Interaction," and a special issue of *Ergonomics* titled "Hedonomics: Affective Human Factors Design" (Helander & Tham, 2003), reinforce this view. These publications reflect a growing realization that addressing the design challenges of complex sociotechnical systems may need to include affect in the description of cognition.

## AFFECT: EMOTION, FEELINGS, AND MOOD

Affect describes several related constructs that are distinct, but frequently treated as interchangeable, including emotion, feelings, and mood. Emotion refers to the physiological response of the brain and body, whereas feelings are the mental representation of that response (Damasio, 2001). Feelings follow emotions evolutionarily and experientially. Emotions represent an automatic adaptive response that prepares organisms to respond to threats and opportunities, whereas feelings represent the conscious perception of that bodily response. Although emotions are the physiological response to emotional stimuli, either real or imagined, feelings reflect the interpretation of

the physiological response (Damasio, 1994; James, 1890). Emotions are relatively intense, have a salient cause, and both occur and diminish quickly. In contrast, moods are less intense, more diffuse, and more enduring. Although moods are more subtle, they often exert a more enduring effect on behavior (Forgas, 2002).

Researchers often characterize emotions and feelings in terms of valence and arousal. Figure 6.1 shows examples of pictures that range from negative to positive valence and from high to low arousal. Valence describes feelings as generally positive or negative, but the more refined distinction of appetitive and aversive feelings may account for behavior more precisely. Appetitive or approach-related emotions are concerned with positive feelings associated with goal attainment, such enthusiasm and pride, and aversive or withdrawal-related emotions are concerned with negative feelings that threaten goal attainment, such as fear and disgust (Davidson, Jackson, & Kalin, 2000).

Arousal and valence are useful descriptions of emotions in that they account for many effects of emotion on behavior and brain activity; however, qualitatively different types of emotions influence behavior in ways that cannot be explained by valence and arousal alone. For example, fear and anger influence behavior in ways not predicted by valence or arousal whereas fear leads to pessimistic judgments, anger tends to produce optimistic judgments (Lerner & Keltner, 2000).

Many different emotions contribute to behavior. Damasio (1999) describes a spectrum that ranges from background emotions, common to microorganisms and mammals, to basic emotions that are universally experienced by all people, to social emotions that depend on social norms. Background emotions reflect the internal state of the organism and typically include energy level and feeling of well-being. Basic emotions include fear, anger, sadness, happiness, disgust, and surprise (Ekman, 1992; Johnson-Laird & Oately, 1992). Basic emotions occur in all cultures and display universal physiological and facial response characteristics. Although the specific triggering conditions are not universal, mammals seem genetically predisposed to respond with certain basic emotions to certain events. For example, the sight of a snake reliably elicits a fear response in monkeys, even after a single exposure to another monkey showing fear toward a snake (Cook, Mineka, Wolkenstein, & Laitsch, 1985; Mineka, Davidson, Cook, & Keir, 1984). Social emotions help

FIGURE 6.1.  Emotional space defined by arousal and valence (Maljkovic & Martini, 2005).

guide interactions between people and include sympathy, jealousy, envy, gratitude, admiration, indignation, and trust (Adolphs, Tranel, & Damasio, 1998; Damasio, 1999). The triggering conditions and specific manifestation of social emotions depend on cultural norms. Although background, basic, and social emotions all influence human interaction with technology, social emotions and attitudes such as trust may be most critical as automation becomes more animate, complex, and unpredictable (Lee & See, 2004).

### AFFECT AND INFORMATION PROCESSING

The information processing perspective has proved to be a useful description of a wide range of behavior (Broadbent, 1958; Fitts & Posner, 1969; Wickens & Hollands, 2000). Within this context, the multiple-resource theory (MRT) provides a useful tool for assessing the cost to performance of concurrent activity

that is typical of complex, dynamic systems (Wickens, 1984b, 2002). MRT predicts performance decrements when two tasks demand the same attentional resources, defined by processing modes, codes and stages. SEEV (salience, effort, expectancy, and value) describes a complementary set of factors that have been recently combined to describe how people guide their attention to events in the world (Wickens, Goh, Helleberg, Horrey, & Talleur, 2003). In some circumstances, affect may play a critical role in extending the predictions of MRT and SEEV. Figure 6.2 shows how affect influences human information processing. Affective stimuli capture attention and are processed in parallel with nonaffective stimuli. Affect also has selective influences on each stage of information processing. It primes perception, memory, and response, as well as modulates the availability of attentional resources. Affect also influences overall information processing style, such as the relative weight given to top-down and bottom-up processing. With these pervasive

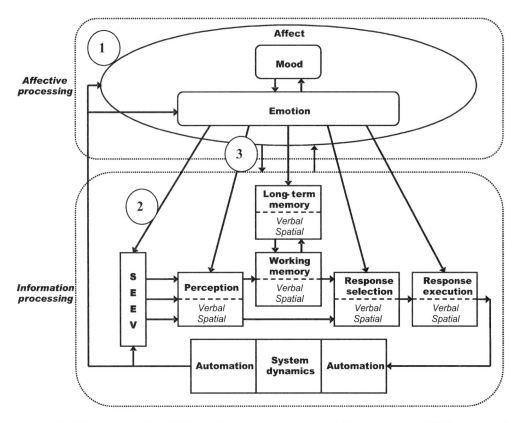

FIGURE 6.2. Emotion, mood, and information processing stages, and their interactions. (1) Processing of emotionally charged stimuli. (2) Effects of affect on information processing stages. (3) Effect of affect on information processing style. SEEV = salience, effort, expectancy, and value.

effects on cognition, affect may represent a distinction as fundamental in guiding attention and information processing as the visual and spatial codes of MRT (Lang, Bradley, & Cuthbert, 1990).

The influence of affect outlined in Figure 6.2 increases in importance as automation becomes more prevalent and complex. Affect can influence the ability of a person to perform a task manually and it can also alter how a person manages automation. The following sections describe how affect influences attention paid to automation, the processing of automation-related information, and the overall cognitive style engaged in managing automation.

### PROCESSING OF AFFECTIVE STIMULI

All stimuli are affectively evaluated and certain stimuli stimulate emotional responses (Cacioppo, Gardner, & Berntson, 1999). Such affective or "emotionally

competent stimuli" reach this status through experience and genetic predisposition (Damasio, 1999). Angry faces, spiders, and snakes all seem predisposed to elicit fear through humans' evolutionary heritage (Ohman & Mineka, 2001). Emotional stimuli are processed in parallel—but separate—pathways, unlike stimuli that lack an affective association (Ohman & Mineka, 2001). The specific brain structures engaged in processing affective stimuli depend on the type of affect (e.g., arousal, valence, and the specific basic or social emotion), but differ from those structures used to process emotionally neutral stimuli.

### CAPTURING ATTENTION: SNAKES, SPIDERS, AND ANGRY FACES

Simon (1967) suggested that affect might play an important role in guiding attention to critical events and interrupting ongoing tasks, but most research has only addressed this possibility relatively recently. Early research addressing auditory selective attention provided some confirmatory evidence. In a dichotic listening task, different auditory streams are presented in each ear. When shadowing one stream, people are not able to recall the content of the other. However, affective stimuli, such as one's own name, can sometimes break through to conscious awareness (Moray, 1959). More recently, Hansen and Hansen (1988) found that angry faces break through to conscious awareness particularly easily. The time to detect an angry face in a crowd of happy faces does not depend on the number of happy faces, suggesting that the characteristics that define an angry face can be processed preattentively, similar to low-level stimuli that produce the pop-out effect in visual search tasks (Treisman & Gormican, 1988).

Although Hansen and Hansen's original study (1988) confounded perceptual features of the stimuli with expression of anger (Purcell, Stewart, & Skov, 1996), subsequent studies have controlled for a range of physical features and possible confounding effects and have found that angry, but not happy, faces support very efficient, if not automatic, visual search (Ohman, Lundqvist, & Esteves, 2001). These results suggest that attention is preferentially oriented to threats, with specific facial features of eyebrows, mouth, and eyes having the greatest effect on attention and perception of anger (Lundqvist & Ohman, 2005). Specific features convey emotional information particularly strongly. The combination of eyebrows and mouth convey threat almost as effectively as the entire face (Lundqvist, Esteves, & Ohman, 2004). Similarly, low and high spatial frequency features differentially influence face identification and perception of emotional content—in other words, perception of emotional expressions depends on low-frequency information (Vuilleumier, Armony, Driver, & Dolan, 2003). Similarly, interpretation of emotional scenes can occur with parafoveal vision in advance of foveal fixation (Calvo & Lang, 2005). Overall, different cues and visual resources influence face recognition and perception of emotional expressions.

Beyond faces, other threatening stimuli show a similar pattern. Using a visual search paradigm, Ohman, Flykt, and Esteves (2001) found that people detected fear-relevant targets (snakes and spiders) faster than fear-irrelevant targets (mushrooms and flowers). Moreover, the latency to detect fear-relevant stimuli did not depend on the number of stimuli,

whereas fear-irrelevant stimuli did, suggesting fear-relevant stimuli generate an automatic emotional response that captures attention. The effect of fear-relevant targets was enhanced for fearful participants (Ohman, Flykt, & Esteves, 2001). Similar results emerge using a spatial orientation paradigm: People respond faster to targets that appear on the same side of the display as an emotional cue and slower when the targets are on the opposite side of the emotional cue (Dolan, 2002). Convergent evidence from many studies, several experimental paradigms, and brain imaging suggest that certain emotionally charged stimuli capture attention (Dolan, 2002).

The human tendency to give preferential attention to emotionally charged stimuli has important implications for how people attend to automation. Information regarding the status of automation may be processed differently when conveyed in an emotionally competent form. As an example, the Chernoff face is a graphical technique in which data are mapped to a schematic face. One variable might influence the angle of the eyebrows and another the angle of the mouth. Mapping complex, multidimensional data to a Chernov face helps people understand the data and could help people understand the state of automation (Chernoff, 1973; Desoete & Decorte, 1985). However, the influence of affect suggests that data mapped to eyebrows and mouth might influence people's perception of automation more dramatically than the information processing model of cognition may predict.

## Processing without Attention

Unattended stimuli escape awareness, but emotional stimuli are processed without attention and thereby increase the likelihood that they will attract attention and influence behavior regardless of whether they attract attention. Emotional stimuli are processed in situations in which neutral stimuli are not. As an example, emotional stimuli conditioned with an electric shock induced an emotional response of increased skin conductance even when rendered invisible through backward masking; neutral stimuli did not produce a response (Ohman, Esteves, & Soares, 1995). Similarly, another study had people perform a demanding matching task in which they compared stimuli at prespecified locations while task-irrelevant pictures were shown in other locations. In this situation, people processed fearful expressions even when attention was directed elsewhere (Vuilleumier, Armony, Driver, & Dolan, 2001). Functional magnetic resonance imaging (fMRI) data showed that faces activate regions of the visual cortex fusiform gyri when attended to, but not when ignored. In contrast, faces with fearful expressions activate the amygdala independent of whether they are the focus of attention. Results show that the amygdalar response is not driven by face processing, but seems to reflect an automatic and somewhat separate processing of threat-related stimuli (Vuilleumier et al., 2001). Although faces with fearful expressions were processed, they did not reach conscious awareness: People could not describe the faces or their expressions (Vuilleumier et al., 2001). Some emotional stimuli, such as fearful expressions, bypass the primary visual cortex and follow a different neural pathway in which they are directly processed by the amygdala.

In addition to some basic emotions, some social emotions are also processed without attention. When people judged the age and trustworthiness of faces, event-related fMRI data showed that judgments of trustworthiness were associated with distinct brain activation including the amygdala, orbitofrontal cortex, and superior temporal sulcus that differed from the activation associated with expressions of anger, sadness, or fear (Winston, Henson, Fine-Goulden, & Dolan, 2004). Even when participants were not explicitly judging trustworthiness, untrustworthy faces generated activity in the amygdala and right insula (Winston, Strange, O'Doherty, & Dolan, 2002). Viewing people who appear untrustworthy may produce emotional responses, and the feelings associated with these responses could contribute to subsequent judgments of the people (Adolphs, 2002).

These results are supported by studies of brain-damaged patients, who show impairments in recognizing emotion, but can recognize facial features (Anderson & Phelps, 2000b). Specifically, people suffering from damage to the amygdala also suffer from an inability to recognize fearful expressions (Anderson & Phelps, 2000a). Similarly, patients with amygdalar lesions and patients who are autistic make normal judgments of trustworthiness with lexical cues, but fail with visual cues, even though they are able to make visual discriminations (Adolphs, Sears, & Piven, 2001). Behavioral, lesional, and brain imaging studies provide converging evidence for a parallel pathway for processing social cues that bypasses the visual cortex.

## Advantageous Decisions without Awareness

The neurological pathways that process emotionally charged stimuli not only affect attention and perception, but also influence decision making. Damasio and associates (1990) showed that although people with brain lesions in the ventromedial sector of the prefrontal cortices retain reasoning and other cognitive abilities, their emotions and decision-making ability are critically impaired. A series of studies have demonstrated that this decision-making deficit stems from a lack of affect and not from deficits of working memory, declarative knowledge, or reasoning, as might be expected (Bechara, Damasio, Tranel, & Anderson, 1998; Bechara, Damasio, Tranel, & Damasio, 1997).

The somatic marker hypothesis describes one way affect can influence decision making. According to this hypothesis, marker signals from the physiological response to the emotional aspects attached to decision situations influence the processing of information and subsequent responses to similar decision situations. In a simple gambling decision-making task, patients with prefrontal lesions performed much worse than a control group of healthy people. In this task, people drew a series of cards from one of four decks. Two decks provided high payoffs and high losses and were biased to lose. The other decks provided low payoffs and losses, but were biased to win. The patients tended to select from the decks with high payoffs, responding to immediate prospects and failing to accommodate long-term consequences (Bechara, Damasio, Damasio, & Anderson, 1994).

In a subsequent study, healthy subjects showed a substantial emotional response to a large loss, as measured by skin conductance response (SCR), whereas patients with prefrontal lesions did not (Bechara, Damasio, Tranel, & Damasio, 1997). Interestingly, healthy subjects also began to avoid risky choices *before* they explicitly recognized the alternative as being risky. Eventually, most normal subjects and patients could describe why certain decks of cards were risky, but the patients still failed to make advantageous decisions. The somatic markers, such as the SCR, helped healthy subjects to make advantageous decisions. The somatic marker hypothesis also accounts for an interesting result in which visceral awareness, as measured by the ability of people to detect their own heartbeat, was associated with increased sensitivity to predictive cues of mild electric shocks (Katkin, Wiens, & Ohman, 2001). These results provide converging evidence from a range of experimental paradigms that unconscious signals associated with affective stimuli act as covert biases to overt reasoning and evaluation of options (Bechara, Damasio, Tranel, & Damasio, 1997). They suggest that engineering psychology should go beyond studies of situation awareness to consider situation responsiveness without awareness.

The ability of an operator to anticipate the behavior of automation declines as the automation increases in complexity, authority, and autonomy (Sarter & Woods, 1997). When this occurs, the role of emotional pathways in processing and acting on information regarding the performance of automation will likely increase as people struggle to make sense of the situation. A novel approach to supporting more effective automation management may be to make visible the relatively invisible emotional responses that have been observed to support advantageous decision making. Sensing and displaying operators' SCR might enhance their ability to identify relevant cues needed to manage automation. As in the gambling task, the decision to rely on complex automation may be guided as much by the covert influence of emotions and attitudes as by the overt influence of rational judgment (Lee & See, 2004). Making the covert process more visible could help people capitalize on the strengths of both the affective and analytic contributions to decision making.

## Remembering the Emotional

Consolidation of memories for affective stimuli tends to be more efficient than for neutral stimuli. Flashbulb memory describes instances of this in naturalistic settings. Flashbulb memories are the vivid memories one has of important events, such as an assassination (Brown & Kulik, 1977). Unlike other memories, flashbulb memories include details of the event, where one was when one heard the news, and even what one was doing at the time. Although such memories are not perfect photographic records of the event, they often include more detail than is normally retained for less emotionally charged events (Brown & Kulik, 1977). Most commonly, research on flashbulb memories focuses on events with negative affect, or bad news, but events with positive affect also display characteristics of flashbulb memories (Scott & Ponsoda, 1996). Most models of flashbulb memory acknowledge the influence of emotion, but whether

emotion facilitates both initial imprinting and subsequent rehearsal is not clear. Recent analysis using structural equation modeling of the factors contributing to flashbulb memories suggests the primary mechanism may be its effect on rehearsal (Finkenauer, Luminet, Gisle, El-Ahmadi, van der Linden, & Philippot, 1998).

A brain imaging study that compared brain activity for remembered and forgotten words investigated the possible mechanisms underlying memory for emotional events, such as flashbulb memories (Kensinger & Corkin, 2004). Brain imaging for both high-arousal words and neutral words showed a clear pattern of activation in the amygdalar–hippocampal network, whereas negative-valence words showed activation in the prefrontal cortex–hippocampal network (Kensinger & Corkin, 2004). Comparing memory performance for high-arousal, neutral, and negative-valence words in a divided attention paradigm showed that with no concurrent task, both high arousal and negative valence enhanced memory, but a concurrent auditory discrimination task eliminated the superior memory for negative-valence words. High-arousal words, on the other hand, remained highly memorable (Kensinger & Corkin, 2004). These results suggest that two distinct mechanisms support the superior memory associated with emotional stimuli (Kensinger, 2004). High-arousal stimuli are more memorable in cognitively demanding situations, and both high-arousal and negative-valence stimuli are more memorable in low-demand situations.

Retrospective judgments of painful situations also suggest somewhat different mechanisms for affective memory. Such judgments depend on peak affect intensity and final experience, with the duration of the event having little influence. Retrospective ratings of overall discomfort for colonoscopy and lithotripsy were predicted by peak and discomfort during the last 3 minutes of the procedure. The duration of the procedure, which ranged from 4 to 67 minutes, did not influence the ratings (Redelmeier & Kahneman, 1996). In a more controlled experiment, pain was administered by having people immerse a hand in cold water. In one condition, participants held one hand under 14°C water for 1 minute. In another condition, they immersed the hand in 14°C water for 1 minute and then kept it in the water for an additional 30 seconds as the water was warmed slightly to 15°C. Surprisingly, when people chose which experience they would repeat, they preferred the longer, more objectively painful situation (Kahneman, Fredrickson, Schreiber, & Redelmeier, 1993). Affective judgments of pleasant situations showed a similar effect. Ratings of both pleasant and unpleasant films showed no systematic effect of duration. People recognized differences in duration, but did not include it in their judgment (Fredrickson & Kahneman, 1993). Duration does not influence affective judgments as an analytic calculation might suggest.

These findings suggest that people may recall their experiences with automation in a way that is substantially different from the typical information processing predictions. Memory for the performance in highly arousing situations may be stronger than expected. More important, perceived reliability of automation may not follow the rational calculus that defines expected reliability as the time-weighted average of the experienced reliability. Instead, perceived reliability may be influenced by affective calculus that depends on the most recent experience and the worst experience.

## AFFECTIVE STATE INFLUENCES THE INFORMATION PROCESSING STAGES

The previous section demonstrates that affective stimuli, such as angry faces, are processed differently than neutral stimuli. Affect can also influence the cognitive process, changing the way emotionally neutral stimuli are detected, interpreted, and remembered. Surprisingly, the influence of affect can be quite specific to stages and modes of information processing affecting, for example, sensory consolidation, working memory, and judgment.

### Consolidation and Working Memory

Sensory inputs require attention to be consolidated and made available to conscious awareness. The attentional blink phenomenon demonstrates failures of this process. A rapid serial presentation of stimuli, in which a second stimulus follows a first within 500 msec, causes the second stimulus to be neglected as a result of an attentional blink (Broadbent & Broadbent, 1987). The attentional blink phenomenon reflects a limited-capacity perceptual encoding process that consolidates perceptual information into working memory (Luck, Vogel, & Shapiro, 1996). In the serial presentation of words, the magnitude of the neglect depends on the emotional characteristics of the words. Specifically, the degree of arousal reduces the attentional blink, but the valence of words does not (Anderson, 2005). Highly arousing negative and positive words tend to evade the attentional blink. Arousal enhances perceptual encoding and promotes entry into awareness.

The availability of attentional resources also depends on affective state. When participants' affective state was manipulated using films that induced either a withdrawal state (e.g., fearful) or an approach state (e.g., amused), the withdrawal state enhanced spatial working memory capacity, but reduced verbal working memory capacity. In the extreme, such an effect might leave people scared speechless. Conversely, the approach state enhanced verbal working memory capacity, but reduced spatial working memory capacity. This double dissociation was enhanced by individual differences regarding the tendency for withdrawal and approach states (Gray, 2001).

These results directly influence the predictions of MRT and suggest that the resource capacity for encoding information expands as arousal increases. More interesting, affect can have a differential effect on people's spatial and verbal resources. The influence on working memory suggests that information regarding the state of automation may need to be formatted in a graphical rather than textual format during situations in which people are fearful and in a textual format in situations in which people are amused.

### Categorization and Judgment

Task situation and mood have long been known to influence even simple perceptual judgments (Bruner, 1957). Mood also contributes to judgments through what has been termed *the mood congruence effect*—positive moods lead to positive judgments. In one study, people in positive moods (induced by watching a short video) watched a video of their own behavior and tended to identify more positive, skilled behaviors, whereas a negative mood caused people to identify more negative, unskilled behaviors. When judging the behavior of others, a positive mood had a similar effect, but a negative mood induced fewer negative observations about the behavior of others compared with judgments of participants' own behavior (Forgas, Bower, & Krantz, 1984; as cited in Forgas, 1995). Positive and negative moods had a similar effect on the interpretation of written information about people.

People in a positive mood made many more positive judgments and fewer negative judgments compared with people in a negative mood. Mood also affected memory, with those in a positive mood recalling and recognizing more positive than negative items and those in a negative mood recalling and recognizing more negative than positive items (Forgas, Bower, & Krantz, 1984). Mood primes judgments consistent with the valence of the current mood.

Affective response is also strongly linked to risk judgments. In general, objective risk and benefit are positively correlated (higher risk associated with greater benefit), but subjective judgments of risk and benefits tend to be negatively correlated (Finucane, Alhakami, Slovic, & Johnson, 2000). Affect explains this paradox. Substantial evidence suggests that the affective response is primary, and that people derive risk and benefit judgments from their affective response (Slovic, 1999). Events judged positively, such as car travel, tend to lead to lower perceived risk and higher perceived benefit compared with events judged negatively, such as nuclear power. Time pressure enhances the relationship between affective evaluation and risk, and emphasizing benefits reduces perceived risk (Finucane, Alhakami, Slovic, & Johnson, 2000). Affect plays a critical role in judgments because affective response to risk often differs from cognitive assessments. In certain situations, a risk-as-feelings heuristic tends to guide behavior (Loewenstein, Weber, Hsee, & Welch, 2001). The general affect heuristic or affect-as-information model has important implications not only for judgment, but also for response selection (Schwarz & Clore, 2003; Slovic, Finucane, Peters, & MacGregor, 2004).

Beyond judgment, mood also influences recall of information from long-term memory, with people being more likely to recall information that is congruent rather than incongruent with their current mood (Bower, 1981; Schwarz & Clore, 1983). Mood also influences consolidation of information into long-term memory, with a positive mood increasing the tendency for people to incorporate false information, suggested by questions, into eyewitness memories (Forgas, 2002). Most generally, affect primes each stage of information processing to induce mood-congruent responses.

The examples described here focus on the influence of mood on information processing. The reality is a complex, dynamic interaction in which mood influences information processing and the results of that activity influence mood, which in turn influences the response to subsequent experiences.

These findings directly apply to understanding how people respond to automation in that judgments of automation capability and memory of automation performance depend on a person's mood. Positive moods may lead to excessive trust and negative moods may lead to insufficient trust. The influence of mood can be particularly insidious when the mood induced by the performance of some elements of automation exerts a disproportionate effect on the trust people feel for the other elements of it.

## AFFECTIVE STATE AND OVERALL INFORMATION PROCESSING STYLE

Affect influences people's overall information processing style. To put it simply, positive moods tend to promote top-down processing and negative moods promote bottom-up processing. More specifically, positive mood induces more heuristic processing and greater schema-based reliance on preexisting knowledge. Compared with negative moods, positive moods involve paying relatively little attention to the details of the current situation, more superficial processing, faster responses, and a tendency to avoid systematic thinking (Bless & Fiedler, 1995). In contrast, negative moods tend to induce externally focused, systematic processing, with little reliance on preexisting knowledge (Schwarz, 2000; Schwarz & Clore, 2003).

A very important distinction between positive and negative moods concerns how they influence information selected from the environment. Negative moods tend to induce a more accommodative process in which attention is focused on one attribute at a time. Positive moods tend to induce a more assimilative process in which a broader array of information is considered and the information is interpreted in broader categories (Fiedler, Nickel, Asbeck, & Pagel, 2003). One purpose of mood may be to tune cognitive processing to the demands of the situation. When things are going well, as signaled by a positive mood, a more top-down, effort-conserving process is adopted, whereas a negative mood signals the need for a more systematic consideration of the details of the ongoing behavior.

The demands of problem solving illustrate the subtle, but important, influence of mood. Dunker's classic study of problem solving engaged people in a range of tasks that required innovative thinking (Duncker, 1945). One such problem involved fixing a candle to the wall and lighting it using only the following materials: matches, matchbox filled with thumbtacks, and a candle. In recent studies examining the role of affect on problem solving, several studies found the time it took to find a solution depended on mood (Isen, Daubman, & Nowicki, 1987). Those in a positive mood were much more likely to reach the innovative solution in which the empty matchbox is affixed to the wall with a thumbtack to act as a platform for the candle. Negative affect may contribute to cognitive tunneling and functional fixation in which seemingly obvious solutions go undetected (Moray, Lootsteen, & Pajak, 1986). Mood guides an adaptive response to environmental demands that balances between focused attention and the tendency toward perseveration and integrative thinking and the tendency be distracted.

Cooperation also depends on affect. As might be expected, positive affect promotes greater altruism and cooperation (George & Brief, 1992; Rosenhan, Salovey, & Hargis, 1981). Forgas (2002) found that happy people were more cooperative, and that bargaining produced better outcomes for happy people. Positive mood primes positive attributions and negative mood primes negative attributions. The reality is more complex than a simple relationship between happy people and improved cooperation. In one experiment, happy and sad people engaged in a chicken dilemma game in which each person can defect and achieve a better outcome independent of the other person's decision; however, if both choose to defect, the outcome is worse for both (Hertel, Neuhof, Theuer, & Kerr, 2000). Those in a happy mood engaged in a more heuristic mode of interaction and tended to mimic the behavior of the other, cooperating when the other cooperated and defecting when the other defected. In contrast, those in a sad mood engaged in a more analytic mode of interaction and tended to cooperate when the other defected and defect when the other cooperated. This pattern of results clearly shows that effect of mood on cooperation depends on more than the general tendency to cooperate when feeling happy (Hertel, Neuhof, Theuer, & Kerr, 2000). Positive moods promote heuristic responses and integrative processing, whereas negative moods promote more analytic and less integrative strategies.

These findings suggest that emotional state can strongly influence performance in managing automation, particularly when people must troubleshoot complex problems and when automation mediates relationships between people. Successful management of automation depends on a delicate balance between the heuristic, assimilative process associated with positive moods and the more systematic, focused interpretation of new information associated with negative moods. Extremely positive moods may lead to uncritical reliance on automation, whereas extremely negative moods may lead to micromanagement of one element of automation and neglect of other elements.

## BOUNDARY CONDITIONS: WHEN IS IT USEFUL TO INCLUDE AFFECT?

Affect clearly has the potential to influence cognition in ways that researchers and designers should consider. Emotionally charged stimuli are processed differently than neutral stimuli. Emotions and moods also have selective effects for each stage of the processing of neutral stimuli, as well as on overall processing style. Experimental data show these effects have important consequences for human behavior in some circumstances. A critical question is when does affect account for 3% of the variance in behavior and when does it account for 93%?

In many situations, particularly in carefully controlled laboratory settings, affect exerts little influence on behavior. As an example, the mood congruence effect diminishes with simple stimuli, such as judgments of word lists (Forgas, 2002). In contrast, phobias amplify the preferential processing of more naturalistic emotionally charged stimuli, such as snakes and spiders (Ohman & Mineka, 2001).

### Degrees of Affective Influence

The distinctions of skill-, rule-, and knowledge-based (SRK) behavior have served as a useful taxonomy to guide system design (Rasmussen, 1983; Vicente & Rasmussen, 1992). The SRK taxonomy defines qualitatively different information processing modes, each with its own characteristics and requirements. Skill-based behavior represents well-learned responses guided by sensorimotor patterns. Rule-based behavior occurs when people respond to familiar situations with a previously compiled response. Knowledge-based

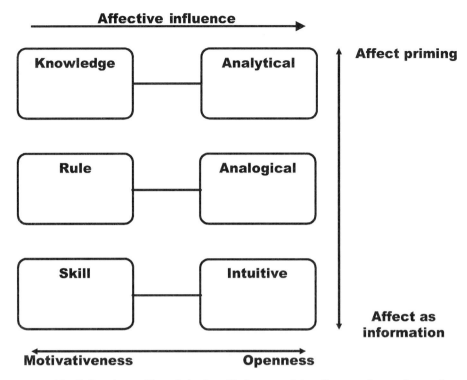

FIGURE 6.3.   Skill-, rule-, and knowledge-based behavior and the affective-influenced equivalents.

behavior occurs when people confront unusual situations that require effortful cognition to develop novel responses. These distinctions are shown on the left of Figure 6.3. The contribution of SRK performance to an ongoing task depends on the task representation, time available, importance, and experience. Experts responding to routine situations through direct interaction tend to rely on skill-based behavior.

Figure 6.3 shows three processes that represent the influence of affect on SRK behavior. A high degree of affective influence leads to analytic, analogical, and intuitive behavior. Analytic behavior corresponds to knowledge-based behavior with a high degree of affective influence. Likewise, analogical thinking corresponds to rule-based behavior, but with a strong affective influence. Finally, intuitive behavior corresponds to skill-based behavior under the influence of affect. The factors that govern the influence of affect are different for each type of behavior.

Forgas (1995, 2002) has developed the affect infusion model to describe the factors that influence the role of affect on cognition. This model describes multiple judgment processes similar to those in Figure 6.3. According to the affect infusion model, judgments

made in unfamiliar situations are particularly prone to affective influence. Situations involving ambiguity and the need for open, constructive, elaborative thinking, which require people to select, encode, and interpret novel information and then to relate this interpretation to preexisting knowledge, increase the influence of affect (Forgas, 2002). Mood congruence effects are most likely in situations that require constructive processing—in other words, active elaboration and transformation of stimulus information and the use of previous knowledge structures to create new knowledge from a combination of stored and new information (Forgas, 1995). The impact of such effects may be greatest when rare failures in complex automation require troubleshooting activities. Decision making that cannot draw upon well-defined cue–action pairings and that requires people to engage in mental simulation of potential outcomes seems prone to affective influence (Klein, 1989, 1993).

Affect has less influence during highly selective and targeted thinking that is dominated by a particular objective that precludes an open information search (Forgas, 2002). Affect also has less influence during the application of a well-defined knowledge structure to achieve a specific goal, such as applying control theory principles to optimize an algorithm. Moreover, mood congruency effects depend on awareness: The effects of mood are diminished or reversed when people are aware that their mood is not related to their judgments (Schwarz, 2000). More generally, the format and presentation of information may influence the degree of affective influence. Numeric representations, many cues, high redundancy among cues, and no available organizing formula all favor a more intuitive response (Hammond, 1996; Hammond, Hamm, Grassia, & Pearson, 1987).

Rule-based behavior governs familiar situations, and affect has little effect if people can rely on direct retrieval of preexisting responses. In highly familiar situations in which previous solutions can be directly paired with current situations, there is little need for constructive processing and affect has little influence (Forgas, 2002). The ambiguity and complexity of many systems make pairing solutions to situations difficult and increase the influence of affect in the interpretation of the situation and identification of an appropriate response.

At the level of both rule- and skill-based behavior, affect can influence behavior by acting as a direct cue to guide decisions. In such situations, affect acts as information and supports heuristic strategies that dominate when time and processing resources do not permit other responses or when the decision involves low personal cost and does not merit substantial cognitive effort (Finucane, Alhakami, Slovic, & Johnson, 2000; Schwarz & Clore, 1983, 2003). In such situations, people tend to select options that "feel right." Reliance on automation, such as software agents that gather information and support buying decisions on the Internet, may be governed by affect-based heuristics and the attitudes of trust and self-confidence (Rathnam, 2005). More important, affect-as-information may play a prominent role in influencing macrocognition and the adaptation of decision-making strategies to the demands of the situation (Gigerenzer & Goldstein, 1996; Klein, Ross, Moon, Klein, Hoffman, & Hollnagel, 2003). Macrocognition involves problem detection, attention management, uncertainty management, and development of mental models. These processes and the transitions between them seem likely to be influenced by affect-as-information in which attention is directed to situations that "don't feel right."

## Factors Mediating the Social Response to Technology

Affect may have a particularly strong influence on automation management because interaction with automation may engage social emotions. Substantial research has demonstrated that people often respond socially to technology (Reeves & Nass, 1996). The degree of this influence is surprising, occurring in situations in which the technology embodies very few "human" characteristics. Although social response to technology is common, it is not universal, and its boundary conditions are poorly defined.

Basic research on human development identifies characteristics that govern social interaction (Tomasello, 1999), and may provide some clues regarding what characteristics of automation are likely to engage a social response. According to Tomasello (1999), as children develop, they make increasingly sophisticated distinctions regarding the agents with which they interact. Initially children distinguish animate agents (e.g., a toy car), then intentional agents (e.g., a dog), and final mental agents (e.g., a person). Tomasello (1999) argues that this development in children is central to linguistic, social, and moral development. The factors that lead children to identify other people as intentional and mental agents may be similar to those factors that lead people to respond socially to technology.

Considering when people might view automation as an animate, intentional, or mental agent might indicate those situations that engage social emotions. Table 6.1 shows how people might come to understand the behavior of automation. The agent will be viewed differently depending on the characteristics of its input (perceptions), output (actions), and goal state. For example, the behavior of simple animate agents is well described by a one-to-one mapping between environmental cues and the agent's response. In contrast, understanding intentional agents requires knowledge of their attention and strategies because a many-to-many mapping links cues and behavior. Although automation may not actually have characteristics of intentional and mental agents, people may endow them with such characteristics to help explain complex behavior. Increasingly, some types of automation may actually embody characteristics of intentional and mental agents—for example, robots that include social learning concepts to learn from their interactions with people (Steels & Kaplan, 2001).

TABLE 6.1.  Factors Influencing the Social Response to Technology (Tomasello, 1999).

|  | Agent's Input | Agent's Output | Agent's Goal State |
|---|---|---|---|
| Animate | Cues | Behavior | Direction |
| Intentional | Attention | Strategies | Goals |
| Mental | Desires | Plans | Beliefs |

The factors described in Table 6.1 correspond to the characteristics that define software agents. First, agents exhibit some degree of *autonomy*, by which agents operate without the direct intervention of humans, and have some control over their actions and internal state. Second, they exhibit *social ability*, by which agents interact with other agents. Third, they are *reactive*, so that agents perceive their environment and respond to changes. Fourth, agents are *proactive* in that they do not simply act in response to their environment, but exhibit goal-directed behavior (Wooldbridge & Jennings, 1995). These characteristics all tend to induce people to consider software agents and similar sophisticated automation as an intentional agent.

Seemingly inconsequential features of technology amplify the factors affecting perception of agency and intentionality. Some have even created robots that capitalize on these features to engage a social response (Breazeal, 2003). Not surprisingly, many of these relate to human characteristics embedded in the computer interface. Facial features are particularly powerful, with even iconic representation of faces and eyes influencing emotional response and visual attention (Driver, Davis, Ricciardelli, Kidd, Maxwell, & Baron-Cohen, 1999; Langton & Bruce, 1999). Voices represent another powerful influence. In one study, the emotional quality of the voice in an in-vehicle device interacted with the mood of the driver such that when the voice matched the driver state (subdued for negative, enthused for positive) drivers drove more safely (Nass, Jonsson, Harris, Reaves, Endo, Brave, et al., 2005). Etiquette, the conventions that govern politeness and social interactions, have a surprisingly strong effect on human perception of technology (Miller & Funk, 2001). In a study in which automation had no overt human characteristics other than displaying "good" etiquette (e.g., being noninterruptive and patient), people performed better and trusted the automation more (Parasuraman & Miller, 2004). Automation or other technological agents will likely engage social responses from people to the degree that they incorporate facial features and voice interaction, and abide by social conventions and etiquette. However, little research has explicitly defined the boundary conditions for when social emotions influence response to technology.

## CONCLUSION

The emergence of engineering psychology reflected the realization that effective designs must consider not just the physical characteristics of people, but also their cognitive characteristics. Thus far, cognitive psychology and engineering psychology have tended to ignore emotions. However, the increasing complexity, uncertainty, time pressure, and pervasiveness of interactive technology all create an environment in which affect tends to influence behavior. These trends suggest engineering psychology should consider the influence of affect on behavior and provide engineers with guidance on how to address affective factors.

MRT, SEEV, and the information processing model of cognitive psychology have proved useful constructs for engineering design as critical design considerations have evolved from being primarily physical to include cognitive constraints. Augmenting these constructs with affective considerations may be a useful first step in supporting design. Affect may become particularly important as system performance comes to depend more on operators' ability to manage increasingly complex automation (Lee, 2001; Lee & See, 2004).

## ACKNOWLEDGMENT

The comments of Kristi Schmidt, Bobbie Seppelt, Zach Crittendon, Richard Backs, and Alex Kirlik were critical in clarifying the thoughts presented in this chapter.

## References

Adolphs, R. (2002). Trust in the brain. *Nature Neuroscience, 5*(3), 192–193.

——, Sears, L., & Piven, J. (2001). Abnormal processing of social information from faces in autism. *Journal of Cognitive Neuroscience, 13*(2), 232–240.

——, Tranel, D., & Damasio, A. R. (1998). The human amygdala in social judgment. *Nature, 393*(6684), 470–474.

Anderson, A. K. (2005). Affective influences on the attentional dynamics supporting awareness. *Journal of Experimental Psychology—General, 134*(2), 258–281.

——, & Phelps, E. A. (2000a). Expression without recognition: Contributions of the human amygdala to emotional communication. *Psychological Science, 11*(2), 106–111.

Anderson, A. K., & Phelps, E. A. (2000b). Perceiving emotion: There's more than meets the eye. *Current Biology, 10*(15), R551–R554.

Bechara, A., Damasio, A. R., Damasio, H., & Anderson, S. W. (1994). Insensitivity to future consequences following damage to human prefrontal cortex. *Cognition, 50*(1–3), 7–15.

——, Damasio, H., Tranel, D., & Anderson, S. W. (1998). Dissociation of working memory from decision making within the human prefrontal cortex. *Journal of Neuroscience, 18*(1), 428–437.

——, Damasio, H., Tranel, D., & Damasio, A. R. (1997). Deciding advantageously before knowing the advantageous strategy. *Science, 275*(5304), 1293–1295.

Bless, H., & Fiedler, K. (1995). Affective states and the influence of activated general knowledge. *Personality and Social Psychology Bulletin, 21*(7), 766–778.

Bower, G. H. (1981). Mood and memory. *American Psychologist, 36*(2), 129–148.

Breazeal, C. (2003). Toward sociable robots. *Robots and Autonomous Systems, 42,* 167–175.

Broadbent, D. E. (1958). *Perception and communication.* London: Pergamon.

——, & Broadbent, M. H. (1987). From detection to identification: Response to multiple targets in rapid serial visual presentation. *Perception and Psychophysics, 42,* 105–113.

Brown, R., & Kulik, J. (1977). Flashbulb memories. *Cognition, 5,* 73–99.

Bruner, J. S. (1957). On perceptual readiness. *Psychological Review, 64,* 123–152.

Cacioppo, J. T., Gardner, W. L., & Berntson, G. G. (1999). The affect system has parallel and integrative processing components: Form follows function. *Journal of Personality and Social Psychology, 76*(5), 839–855.

Calvo, M. G., & Lang, P. J. (2005). Parafoveal semantic processing of emotional visual scenes. *Journal of Experimental Psychology—Human Perception and Performance, 31*(3), 502–519.

Chernoff, H. (1973). The use of faces to represent points in k-dimensional space graphically. *Journal of the Statistical Association, 68*(342), 361–368.

Cook, M., Mineka, S., Wolkenstein, B., & Laitsch, K. (1985). Observational conditioning of snake fear in unrelated rhesus monkeys. *Journal of Abnormal Psychology, 94*(4), 591–610.

Damasio, A. (1994). *Descartes' error: Emotion, reason, and the human brain.* New York: G.P. Putnam's.

——. (1999). *The feeling of what happens: Body and emotion in the making of consciousness.* New York: Harcourt.

——. (2001). Fundamental feelings. *Nature, 413*(6858), 781.

Damasio, A. R., Tranel, D., & Damasio, H. (1990). Individuals with sociopathic behavior caused by frontal damage fail to respond autonomically to social stimuli. *Behavioural Brain Research, 41*(2), 81–94.

Davidson, R. J., Jackson, D. C., & Kalin, N. H. (2000). Emotion, plasticity, context, and regulation: Perspectives from affective neuroscience. *Psychological Bulletin, 126*(6), 890–909.

Desoete, G., & Decorte, W. (1985). On the perceptual salience of features of Chernoff faces for representing multivariate data. *Applied Psychological Measurement, 9*(3), 275–280.

Dolan, R. J. (2002). Emotion, cognition, and behavior. *Science, 298*(5596), 1191–1194.

Driver, J., Davis, G., Ricciardelli, P., Kidd, P., Maxwell, E., & Baron-Cohen, S. (1999). Gaze perception triggers reflexive visuospatial orienting. *Visual Cognition, 6*(5), 509–540.

Duncker, K. (1945). On problem-solving. *Psychological Monographs series, 58*(5).

Ekman, P. (1992). Are there basic emotions? *Psychological Review, 99*(1), 550–553.

Fiedler, K., Nickel, S., Asbeck, J., & Pagel, U. (2003). Mood and the generation effect. *Cognition & Emotion, 17*(4), 585–608.

Finkenauer, C., Luminet, O., Gisle, L., El-Ahmadi, A., van der Linden, M., & Philippot, P. (1998). Flashbulb memories and the underlying mechanisms of their formation: Toward an emotional–integrative model. *Memory & Cognition, 26*(3), 516–531.

Finucane, M. L., Alhakami, A., Slovic, P., & Johnson, S. M. (2000). The affect heuristic in judgments of risks and benefits. *Journal of Behavioral Decision Making, 13*(1), 1–17.

Fitts, P. M., & Posner, M. I. (1969). *Human performance.* Belmont, Calif.: Brooks/Cole.

Forgas, J. P. (1995). Mood and judgment: The affect infusion model (AIM). *Psychological Bulletin, 117*(1), 39–66.

——. (2002). Feeling and doing: Affective influences on interpersonal behavior. *Psychological Inquiry, 13*(1), 1–28.

——, Bower, G. H., & Krantz, S. E. (1984). The influence of mood on perceptions of social interactions. *Journal of Experimental Social Psychology, 20*(6), 497–513.

Fredrickson, B. L., & Kahneman, D. (1993). Duration neglect in retrospective evaluations of affective episodes. *Journal of Personality and Social Psychology, 65*(1), 45–55.

Gao, J., & Lee, J. D. (2006). A dynamic model of interaction between reliance on automation and cooperation in multi-operator multi-automation situations. *International Journal of Industrial Ergonomics, 36*(5), 512–526.

George, J. M., & Brief, A. P. (1992). Feeling good doing good: A conceptual analysis of the mood at work organizational spontaneity relationship. *Psychological Bulletin, 112*(2), 310–329.

Gigerenzer, G., & Goldstein, D. G. (1996). Reasoning the fast and frugal way: Models of bounded rationality. *Psychological Review, 103*(4), 650–669.

Gladwell, M. (2005). *Blink: The power of thinking without thinking*. New York: Little, Brown.

Gray, J. R. (2001). Emotional modulation of cognitive control: Approach–withdrawal states double-dissociate spatial from verbal two-back task performance. *Journal of Experimental Psychology—General, 130*(3), 436–452.

Hammond, K. R. (1996). *Human judgment and social policy: Irreducible uncertainty, inevitable error, unavoidable injustice*. New York: Oxford University Press.

———, Hamm, R. M., Grassia, J., & Pearson, T. (1987). Direct comparison of the efficacy of intuitive and analytical cognition in expert judgment. *IEEE Transactions on Systems, Man, and Cybernetics, SMC-17*(5), 753–770.

Hancock, P. A., Pepe, A., & Murphy, L. L. (2005). Hedonomics: The power of positive and pleasurable ergonomics. *Ergonomics in Design, 13*(1), 8–14.

Hansen, C. H., & Hansen, R. D. (1988). Finding a face in the crowd: An anger superiority effect. *Journal of Personal and Social Psychology, 54*(6), 917–924.

Helander, M. G., & Tham, M. P. (2003). Hedonomics: Affective human factors design. *Ergonomics, 46*(13–14), 1269–1272.

Hertel, G., Neuhof, J., Theuer, T., & Kerr, N. L. (2000). Mood effects on cooperation in small groups: Does positive mood simply lead to more cooperation? *Cognition & Emotion, 14*(4), 441–472.

Hollan, J., Hutchins, E., & Kirsh, D. (2000). Distributed cognition: Toward a new foundation for human–computer interaction research. *ACM Transactions on Computer–Human Interaction, 7*(2), 174–196.

Hudlicka, E. (2003). To feel or not to feel: The role of affect in human–computer interaction. *International Journal of Human–Computer Studies, 59*(1–2), 1–32.

Hutchins, E. (1995). *Cognition in the wild*. Cambridge, Mass.: MIT Press.

Isen, A. M., Daubman, K. A., & Nowicki, G. P. (1987). Positive affect facilitates creative problem solving. *Journal of Personal and Social Psychology, 52*(6), 1122–1131.

James, W. (1890). *The principles of psychology*. New York: Holt.

Johnson-Laird, P. N., & Oately, K. (1992). Basic emotions, rationality, and folk theory. *Cognition and Emotion, 6*, 201–223.

Kahneman, D., Fredrickson, B. L., Schreiber, C. A., & Redelmeier, D. A. (1993). When more pain is preferred to less: Adding a better end. *Psychological Science, 4*(6), 401–405.

Katkin, E. S., Wiens, S., & Ohman, A. (2001). Nonconscious fear conditioning, visceral perception, and the development of gut feelings. *Psychological Science, 12*(5), 366–370.

Kensinger, E. A. (2004). Remembering emotional experiences: The contribution of valence and arousal. *Reviews in the Neurosciences, 15*(4), 241–251.

———, & Corkin, S. (2004). Two routes to emotional memory: Distinct neural processes for valence and arousal. *Proceedings of the National Academy of Sciences USA, 101*(9), 3310–3315.

Klein, G. A. (1989). Recognition-primed decisions. In W. B. Rouse (Ed.), *Advances in man–machine system research* (vol. 5, pp. 47–92). Greenwich, Conn.: JAI Press.

———. (1993). A recognition-primed decision (RPD) model of rapid decision making. In G. A. Klein, J. Orasanu, R. Calderwood, & C. E. Zsambok (Eds.), *Decision making in action: Models and methods* (pp. 21–35). Norwood, N.J.: Ablex.

Klein, G., Ross, K. G., Moon, B. M., Klein, D. E., Hoffman, R. R., & Hollnagel, E. (2003). Macrocognition. *IEEE Intelligent Systems, 18*(3), 81–85.

Lang, P. J., Bradley, M. M., & Cuthbert, B. N. (1990). Emotion, attention, and the startle reflex. *Psychological Review, 97*(3), 377–395.

Langton, S. R. H., & Bruce, V. (1999). Reflexive visual orienting in response to social attention of others. *Visual Cognition, 6*(5), 541–567.

Lee, J. D. (2001). Emerging challenges in cognitive ergonomics: Managing swarms of self-organizing agent-based automation. *Theoretical Issues in Ergonomics Science, 2*(3), 238–250.

———, & See, K. A. (2004). Trust in technology: Designing for appropriate reliance. *Human Factors, 46*(1), 50–80.

Lerner, J. S., & Keltner, D. (2000). Beyond valence: Toward a model of emotion-specific influences on judgment and choice. *Cognition & Emotion, 14*(4), 473–493.

Loewenstein, G. F., Weber, E. U., Hsee, C. K., & Welch, N. (2001). Risk as feelings. *Psychological Bulletin, 127*(2), 267–286.

Luck, S. J., Vogel, E. K., & Shapiro, K. L. (1996). Word meanings can be accessed but not reported during the attentional blink. *Nature, 383*(6601), 616–618.

Lundqvist, D., Esteves, F., & Ohman, A. (2004). The face of wrath: The role of features and configurations in conveying social threat. *Cognition & Emotion, 18*(2), 161–182.

Lundqvist, D., & Ohman, A. (2005). Emotion regulates attention: The relation between facial configurations, facial emotion, and visual attention. *Visual Cognition*, 12(1), 51–84.

Maljkovic, V., & Martini, P. (2005). Short-term memory for scenes with affective content. *Journal of Vision*, 5(3), 215–229.

Miller, C. A., & Funk, H. B. (2001). Associates with etiquette: Communication to make human–automation interaction more natural, productive and polite. In *Proceedings of the 8th European Conference on Cognitive Science Approaches to Process Control* (pp. 329–338). Munich, September 24–26.

Mineka, S., Davidson, M., Cook, M., & Keir, R. (1984). Observational conditioning of snake fear in rhesus monkeys. *Journal of Abnormal Psychology*, 93(4), 355–372.

Moray, N. (1959). Attention in dichotic listening: Affective cues and the influence of instructions. *Quarterly Journal of Experimental Psychology*, 11, 56–60.

———, Lootsteen, P., & Pajak, J. (1986). Acquisition of process control skills. *IEEE Transactions on Systems, Man and Cybernetics*, 16, 497–504.

Nass, C., Jonsson, I. M., Harris, H., Reaves, B., Endo, J., Brave, S., et al. (2005). Improving automotive safety by pairing driver emotion and care voice emotion. In *Conference on Human Factors in Computing Systems*, 1973–1976. Portland, Ore.: ACM.

Norman, D. A. (2004). *Emotional design*. New York: Basic Books.

Ohman, A., Esteves, F., & Soares, J. J. F. (1995). Preparedness and preattentive associative learning: Electrodermal conditioning to masked stimuli. *Journal of Psychophysiology*, 9(2), 99–108.

———, Flykt, A., & Esteves, F. (2001). Emotion drives attention: Detecting the snake in the grass. *Journal of Experimental Psychology—General*, 130(3), 466–478.

———, Lundqvist, D., & Esteves, F. (2001). The face in the crowd revisited: A threat advantage with schematic stimuli. *Journal of Personality and Social Psychology*, 80(3), 381–396.

———, & Mineka, S. (2001). Fears, phobias, and preparedness: Toward an evolved module of fear and fear learning. *Psychological Review*, 108(3), 483–522.

Parasuraman, R., & Miller, C. A. (2004). Trust and etiquette in high-criticality automated systems. *Communications of the ACM*, 47(4), 51–55.

———, & Riley, V. (1997). Humans and automation: Use, misuse, disuse, abuse. *Human Factors*, 39(2), 230–253.

Picard, R. W. (1997). *Affective computing*. Cambridge, Mass.: MIT Press.

Purcell, D. G., Stewart, A. L., & Skov, R. B. (1996). It takes a confounded face to pop out of a crowd. *Perception*, 25(9), 1091–1108.

Rasmussen, J. (1983). Skills, rules, and knowledge: Signals, signs, and symbols, and other distinctions in human performance models. *IEEE Transactions on Systems, Man and Cybernetics*, SMC-13(3), 257–266.

Rathnam, G. (2005). Interaction effects of consumers' product class knowledge and agent search strategy on consumer decision making in electronic commerce. *IEEE Systems, Man, and Cybernetics—Part A: Systems and Humans*, 35(4), 556–572.

Redelmeier, D. A., & Kahneman, D. (1996). Patients' memories of painful medical treatments: Real-time and retrospective evaluations of two minimally invasive procedures. *Pain*, 66(1), 3–8.

Reeves, B., & Nass, C. (1996). *The media equation: How people treat computers, television, and new media like real people and places*. New York: Cambridge University Press.

Rosenhan, D. L., Salovey, P., & Hargis, K. (1981). The joys of helping: Focus of attention mediates the impact of positive affect on altruism. *Journal of Personality and Social Psychology*, 40(5), 899–905.

Sarter, N. B., & Woods, D. D. (1997). Team play with a powerful and independent agent: Operational experiences and automation surprises on the Airbus A-320. *Human Factors*, 39(4), 553–569.

———, & Woods, D. D. (2000). Team play with a powerful and independent agent: A full-mission simulation study. *Human Factors*, 42(3), 390–402.

Schwarz, N. (2000). Emotion, cognition, and decision making. *Cognition & Emotion*, 14(4), 433–440.

———, & Clore, G. L. (1983). Mood, misattribution, and judgments of well-being: Informative and directive functions of affective states. *Journal of Personality and Social Psychology*, 45(3), 513–523.

———, & Clore, G. L. (2003). Mood as information: 20 years later. *Psychological Inquiry*, 14(3–4), 296–303.

Scott, D., & Ponsoda, V. (1996). The role of positive and negative affect in flashbulb memory. *Psychological Reports*, 79(2), 467–473.

Simon, H. (1967). Motivational and emotional controls of cognition. *Psychological Review*, 74, 29–39.

Skitka, L. J., Mosier, K. L., Burdick, M., & Rosenblatt, B. (2000). Automation bias and errors: Are crews better than individuals? *International Journal of Aviation Psychology*, 10(1), 85–97.

Slovic, P. (1999). Trust, emotion, sex, politics, and science: Surveying the risk-assessment battlefield. *Risk Analysis*, 19(4), 689–701. [Originally printed 1997.]

———, Finucane, M. L., Peters, E., & MacGregor, D. G. (2004). Risk as analysis and risk as feelings: Some thoughts about affect, reason, risk, and rationality. *Risk Analysis*, 24(2), 311–322.

Steels, L., & Kaplan, F. (2001). AIBO's first words: The social learning of language and meaning. *Evolution of Communication*, 4(1), 3–32.

Titchener, E. B. (1908). *Lectures on the elementary psychology of feeling and attention*. New York: Macmillan.

Tomasello, M. (1999). *The cultural origins of human cognition*. Cambridge, Mass.: Harvard University Press.

Treisman, A., & Gormican, S. (1988). Feature analysis in early vision: Evidence from search asymmetries. *Psychological Review, 95*(1), 15–48.

Vicente, K. J., & Rasmussen, J. (1992). Ecological interface design: Theoretical foundations. *IEEE Transactions on Systems, Man, and Cybernetics, SCM-22*(4), 589–606.

Vuilleumier, P., Armony, J. L., Driver, J., & Dolan, R. J. (2001). Effects of attention and emotion on face processing in the human brain: An event-related fMRI study. *Neuron, 30*(3), 829–841.

———, Armony, J. L., Driver, J., & Dolan, R. J. (2003). Distinct spatial frequency sensitivities for processing faces and emotional expressions. *Nature Neuroscience, 6*(6), 624–631.

Wickens, C. D. (1984a). *Engineering psychology and human performance*. Columbus, Ohio: Charles Merrill.

———. (1984b). Processing resources and attention. In R. Parasuraman & R. Davies (Eds.), *Varieties of attention* (pp. 63–102). New York: Academic Press.

———. (1992). *Engineering psychology and human performance*. New York: Harper Collins.

———. (2002). Multiple resources and performance prediction. *Theoretical Issues in Ergonomics Science, 3*(2), 159–177.

———, Goh, J., Helleberg, J., Horrey, W. J., & Talleur, D. A. (2003). Attentional models of multitask pilot performance using advanced display technology. *Human Factors, 45*(3), 360–380.

———, & Hollands, J. G. (2000). *Engineering psychology and human performance* (3rd ed.). Upper Saddle River, N.J.: Prentice Hall.

Winston, J. S., Henson, R. N. A., Fine-Goulden, M. R., & Dolan, R. J. (2004). fMRI-adaptation reveals dissociable neural representations of identity and expression in face perception. *Journal of Neurophysiology, 92*(3), 1830–1839.

———, Strange, B. A., O'Doherty, J., & Dolan, R. J. (2002). Automatic and intentional brain responses during evaluation of trustworthiness of faces. *Nature Neuroscience, 5*(3), 277–283.

Woods, D. D. (1988). Coping with complexity: The psychology of human behavior in complex systems. In L. P. Goodstein, H. B. Anderson, & S. E. Olsen (Eds.), *Mental models, tasks, and errors* (pp. 128–148). London: Taylor & Francis.

Wooldbridge, M., & Jennings, N. R. (1995). Intelligent agents: Theory and practice. *The Knowledge Engineering Review, 10*(2), 115–152.

# Chapter 7

# Monitoring a Nuclear Power Plant

## *Kim J. Vicente*

A Canadian nuclear power plant (NPP) operator is in the process of refueling the reactor, a task that will take much of his morning. At the same time, he has to monitor thousands of indicators on the control room panels for signs of an abnormality—perhaps even a rare but potentially catastrophic event. Fortunately, he has visual and auditory alarms to notify him that something is wrong in case he overlooks a crucial indicator. However, the act of refueling the reactor causes several variables to deviate from their normal state, which, in turn, generates alarms. These nuisance alarms are "normal" in the sense that they should be expected when refueling. However, they distract the operator from monitoring the many other indicators and alarms he is responsible for.

Midway through refueling, a maintenance technician comes to the operator's desk to ask permission to perform a routine job. The operator asks several clarifying questions, but the most important one of all is: "Will performing this job generate more nuisance alarms?" The answer is yes. If the operator approves

the maintenance job, then he will be left with the unenviable job of monitoring thousands of indicators while also monitoring the alarms. If an alarm comes in, which it inevitably will, the operator has to decide if it is being caused by the refueling job, the maintenance job, or something else entirely—something potentially far more severe.

As this real-world scenario shows, monitoring an NPP—even under normal operations—seems like an impossibly difficult attention task. Given that "the limitations of human attention represent one of the formidable bottlenecks in human information processing" (Wickens, 1992, p. 74), how can anyone possibly perform such a task reliably, day in and day out, as most NPP operators do? In this chapter, I will summarize some of the work that I conducted with Randy Mumaw, Emilie Roth, and Catherine Burns that bears on this question (Mumaw, Roth, Vicente, & Burns, 2000). The goals of our research were to understand NPP operator monitoring during normal operations, the factors that make monitoring difficult,

FIGURE 7.1. A single unit in the control room of plant A.

and the strategies that operators have developed to cope with these demands.

All three forms of attention can seemingly play an important role in monitoring. The need to maintain *focused* attention on a particular task may be critical, especially if there are less important tasks competing for the operator's attention. The need for *selective* attention is clearly relevant because there are literally thousands of sources of information to choose from in the control room. And finally, divided attention is also important because monitoring is interwoven with other ongoing day-to-day tasks, such as the maintenance request described in the previous scenario. All these forms of attention are relevant to the task of monitoring an NPP. But even though monitoring has sometimes been equated with attention (Moray, 1986), our results showed that attentional resources are not enough to turn what seems like an impossible task into an activity that is routinely performed in a safe and effective manner.

### RESEARCH APPROACH

#### Overview

We conducted three field studies to observe and interview 27 operators in two different control rooms for a total of 209 hours. For each data collection session, we sat on most of the 12-hour shift with a single operator (or pair of operators) to experience the various activities that occur during the course of the day (or night). Interviews were used to obtain general information about operator practice, to follow up on monitoring actions we observed, and to test the representativeness of the monitoring strategies we observed, or were told about, from other operators. For a more detailed description of the methodology, see Mumaw and colleagues (2000).

#### Description of NPP Control Rooms

Our research sponsor provided access to two Canadian NPPs. The control room for plant A has four control units (each controlling its own reactor). Figure 7.1 shows the panels on a single unit. A single operator runs each unit, although there are other personnel serving support roles. Each control unit occupies a "corner" of a single, large room that is completely open (i.e., no barriers to visibility). Therefore, the operator on each unit can see the panels and alarms of all other units. This allows operators to monitor activity on other units and maintain an overall awareness of plant activity.

Each unit consists of stand-up control panels, an operator desk, several printers, and bookshelves for procedures and other operations documents. The control panels are made up of traditional hard-wired meters, strip chart recorders, and control devices. Alarms (primarily those that are safety related) are presented as a series of tiles at the top of the control panels that light up and provide an audio tone if an alarm condition occurs. There are also several cathode ray tubes (CRTs) on each unit. Two CRTs are embedded in the control panels. These are dedicated to presenting textual alarm messages as a chronologically ordered list. In addition, there are several CRTs located next to the operator desk for display of plant state information. This plant had a limited number of plant parameters that were available for display, and limited display capabilities (i.e., some physical schematics, trend displays, and bar chart displays). Some instrumentation is located outside the main control room in a separate room behind the unit control panels. These panels are accessed through a doorway next to the unit.

The second plant, plant B, had a slightly more technologically advanced control room interface. The control room at plant B is similar in layout to the plant A control room. Again, four control units are located in a single, large control room. The operating practices are also similar. The primary differences between the control rooms is in their level of computerization. At plant B many more plant parameters are accessible via the plant computer. There are eight CRTs on each unit for display of plant parameter information. Seven are embedded in the control panels and one is located next to the operator desk. As at plant A, the alarm system consists of a chronologically organized alarm list presented on the dedicated CRT embedded in a control panel, as well as a series of tiles distributed at the top of the control panels.

## HOW OPERATORS MONITOR DURING NORMAL OPERATIONS

In this section, I review the sources of information for monitoring, the reasons why monitoring is difficult, and the strategies operators have developed to make monitoring easier.

### Sources of Information for Monitoring

We expected that the control room instruments and alarms would be the primary sources of information for monitoring. However, the studies revealed that operators rely on a much broader and more diverse set of information sources.

### Shift Turnover

An operator arrives in the control room approximately 15 to 30 minutes before his 12-hour shift begins and conducts a shift turnover with the operator being relieved so that the new operator gets a clear and accurate understanding of the plant state.

### Log

The log is a hand-written, chronological record of significant activities (not necessarily abnormal) that have occurred during a shift (e.g., tests completed). This is a short-term record of the history of a unit, as opposed to the longer term events logged in the long-term status binder.

### Testing

Usually, a number of routine equipment tests are scheduled on every shift to ensure that backup systems and safety systems are in an acceptable state, should they be required. These tests provide operators with a reason to monitor the status of these systems (e.g., which safety systems are working properly, how quickly they are responding, which meters are working).

### Alarm Screens

The CRT screens used to display alarms are a salient and frequently used source of information for monitoring. Because the onset and offset of an alarm is accompanied by auditory signals, the alarm screen frequently captures the operator's attention.

### Control Room Panels/CRT Displays

The control room panels (including the alarm tiles) are an important source of information, as are the computer displays that are available for monitoring. Several displays were found to be monitored on a regular basis by virtually all the operators observed.

### Field Operators

Some parameters and components cannot be monitored from the control room, and control room operators rely on field operators to monitor these parameters and components.

### Field Tour

Periodically, operators take some time to take a walk through their unit out in the plant. This enables them to maintain a "process feel" by directly observing plant components (e.g., turbine, hydrogen panel, oil purifier panel, boiler feed pumps).

### Other Units

Other units and other redundant channels on the same unit provide a relatively easy and reliable way of obtaining a referent against which to compare the parameter operators wish to evaluate.

### Summary

Operators have at their disposal diverse and comprehensive sources of information that they can draw upon when monitoring an NPP. This is both a blessing and a curse. The good news is that there is a great deal of feedback to determine the plant state, but the bad news is that there is so much data to weed through before finding the small subset of interest at any particular moment. Are there any other factors that make monitoring a challenge?

## What Makes Monitoring Difficult?

### System Complexity and Reliability

Each unit consists of thousands of components and instruments. Even though the reliability of each individual component or sensor may be high, equipment failures are bound to occur on a regular basis when there are so many components. Furthermore, some failures can only be effectively repaired when a unit is shut down. Failures of this type—in other words, not essential to the safe and efficient operation of the unit—may persist for a long time before being repaired. For all these reasons, there are *always* components, instruments, or subsystems that are missing, broken, working imperfectly, or being worked on. Nevertheless, the unit can still function safely as a result of redundancy.

However, small failures or imperfections have important implications for monitoring because they change the way in which information should be interpreted. Whether an indicator or set of indicators is normal or abnormal depends strongly on which

components are broken, being repaired, or working imperfectly. The same set of indicators can be perfectly acceptable in one context and safety threatening in another. Thus, the operational status of the unit's components provides a background, or context, for monitoring. Consequently, effective monitoring depends very heavily on an accurate and comprehensive understanding of the current status of plant components and instrumentation. This understanding can then be used to derive expectations about what is normal/abnormal, given the current state of the unit. These expectations then serve as referents for monitoring.

There are two additional aspects of the environment that complicate an operator's ability to establish what is normal. First, because there are so many interactions between components, subsystems, and instrumentation, it is difficult to derive the full implications of the current failures to determine what state any particular parameter should be in. Second, this context changes frequently. It is important that operators be able to track changes effectively so they have an understanding of the current context and are able to derive accurate expectations about the alarms and parameter values displayed on the control room panels.

### Alarm System Design

Operators rely extensively on the alarm system, especially the chronologically organized alarm list presented on the CRTs dedicated to alarm messages, and operators work to keep the number of alarm messages low. There are, however, a number of weaknesses of the alarm system that compromise the ability of operators to use it effectively.

Many of these weaknesses arise from the fact that most alarm set points are not context sensitive. As a result, nuisance (i.e., nonmeaningful) alarms of various types abound. For example, some alarms are always active because the plant is not currently operated the way it was originally intended to be (because of the equipment upgrades and so forth). Others appear because a certain component is being repaired, maintained, or not working perfectly. Nuisance alarms also appear because of a lack of filtering. For example, multiple alarms can appear for the same event and thereby make interpretation more difficult (low-priority alarms only get automatically blocked during a severe abnormal event). Also, equipment status messages are presented on the alarm monitors even though they do not have the same safety implication.

Perhaps the most frustrating source of nuisance alarms arises from the interaction between sensor variability and rigid alarm limits. Alarms emit one auditory signal at onset and another at offset. If a particular parameter is rapidly cycling above and below the alarm set point, an almost continuous stream of auditory signals is generated.

For all these reasons, the vast majority of alarm messages on the alarm CRTs do not require operator action. Estimates and actual counts at both plants revealed a high percentage of alarms (often more than 50%) that were not meaningful. Clearly, the prevalence of nuisance alarms greatly reduces the informativeness of the alarm system and puts a great burden on operators to distinguish the infrequent alarms requiring actions from those that do not.

### Displays and Controls Design

In both plants, we also observed weaknesses in the design of panels, indicators, displays, and controls. The following are general categories of these issues.

**Unreliable Indicators**  There are numerous problems with elements of the interface that provide unreliable indicators too often, which introduces uncertainty for operators. First, at plant A, indicators about status (e.g., flow paths, pump state) are provided by electromechanical indicators (EMIs). We found that these devices sometimes got stuck in the wrong position, and operators were likely not to trust these indicators. Similarly, at plant B, light-emitting diodes (LEDs) are used to indicate that a variable is in an alarm state. Because these LEDs are difficult to replace, operators usually do not change the burned-out LEDs and lose the information provided by the LED. Also, at plant A, operators cannot test the light bulbs on the control panel (unlike those in the alarm windows) to see which ones are burned out. Because there are so many bulbs, it is not uncommon for some to burn out. This can create misleading feedback, making it difficult for operators to determine whether an observed anomaly is being caused by a burned-out light or by an actual problem in the unit.

**Failed Meters**  The older, hard-wired meters used at both plants are poor at showing a failed state. One class of analog meters is motor driven, and when these meters fail, the needle remains in the same position—that is, these meters fail as is, making detection of the failure difficult. Other instruments are designed so that their failed (irrational) value is the same as the low value on the scale. As a result, it is difficult to distinguish a failed sensor signal from a veridical one.

**Few Emergent Features**  Because the control panels have so many different types of objects (meters, controls, EMIs, and so on), it would be valuable to have an emergent feature that is easily perceived that indicates that an abnormal indicator is present and needs to be located. In general, the control panels do not provide an emergent feature for scanning (e.g., the needles or control handles do not all line up when they are all in the normal state). As a result, the status of these instruments and controls cannot be easily and quickly monitored at a glance or from a distance. Instead, operators must monitor them serially and effortfully, having to recall what the normal position or value of each is and then determine whether the control or instrument is in that state.

**Clear Referent Values Are Not Always Available**  Some computer displays (e.g., some bar chart displays) do not show upper or lower referents for determining whether the current values of the displayed parameters are normal. Consequently, these displays require experience, knowledge, and memory to interpret. (Even though these displays may indicate when a value has exceeded the set point, the set point is not available to the operator to allow him to see the approach to set point.) We found this also to be true for meters located in areas of the plant outside the control room. There were few meters that did not require the operator to recall from memory (or a separate document) the referent values.

### Design of Automation

There are two types of automated systems: analog and digital. Analog automated systems are governed by individual controllers and their status is displayed by an analog meter on the control room panels. Digital automated systems are governed by the computer and their status is displayed on computer displays that can be brought up on a CRT.

The status of each analog controller is represented by a linear, vertical analog meter. There is a green band indicating the set point region for the controller, and a red bar indicating the current status. If the red bar is in the green area, then the goal is being satisfied.

Although it may seem like a relatively straightforward task to monitor such controllers, there are several reasons why the monitoring task is more complex than it seems. First, some controllers are backups and therefore are not controlling. In these cases, the red bar is not in the green area, even if everything is normal. Therefore, operators must know which controllers are supposed to be in bounds and which are not. To do this, operators need to be aware of what is being done to the plant, what is down, and what should be active, given the current state. As mentioned earlier, this is quite a bit of information to keep in mind. Second, it is important to distinguish between the actions of an automated system (e.g., trimming valves) and the effects that those actions have on plant parameters (e.g., increased level). From our observations, it seems that there is no direct way of monitoring the former because that information is not displayed. Thus, operators seem to focus on monitoring the effects of the automation on plant parameters instead. This is an important distinction, because if a controller is successfully compensating for a fault (e.g., a leak), no visible signal can be observed in the controller meter because the parameter remains in the goal area. Thus, it is possible that the effects of a fault could be masked. In some cases, indirect cues can be used to detect a problem (e.g., decrease in storage tank level). However, this is not possible in all situations (e.g., when makeup water comes from the lake).

In some ways, monitoring of the digital automation is similar to that of the analog automation. The focus is again on monitoring the effects of the automation on plant parameters. Also, alarms go off when the error signal exceeds the threshold, but this alone makes it very difficult to perform an effective diagnosis. In addition, however, CRT screens are available to summarize the current status of the various control loops. The problem is that there are more control loops than there are CRTs. Consequently, operators can only monitor the effects of the most important loops (e.g., reactor regulating status). This makes it difficult to monitor, and stay in touch with, the status of all of the digital control loops.

## Summary

The list of reasons that make monitoring an NPP difficult is long, and each reason on that list is daunting. When taken together and combined with the frailties of human cognition in general and attention in particular,

we cannot help but wonder: How can operators possibly do this safety-critical job well?

## STRATEGIES OPERATORS USE TO FACILITATE MONITORING

### Strategies That Maximize Information Extraction from Available Data

Operators have developed strategies that can be used to maximize the information they extract from the plant data available to them.

#### Reduce Noise

Operators displayed a variety of alarm management activities designed to remove "noise" so that meaningful changes could be more readily observed. The following are examples of these activities:

1. Clear alarm printer. At shift turnover, operators clear the printer of all alarms generated on the previous shift. Then, an operator can be sure that alarms appearing in the printer happened on his shift, thereby facilitating the search for and organization of information.
2. "Cursor" alarms when they are considered to be unimportant (i.e., delete them off the screen before the alarm actually clears, but do not disable it). This strategy keeps the alarm screen uncluttered to make new alarm messages stand out.
3. Disable nuisance program alarms in software. The set points of software-based alarms cannot be changed easily by the operator. Therefore, if a parameter is bouncing in and out of tolerance, a continuous stream of alarms is generated. This defeats the purpose of the alarm and causes the operator to ignore the nuisance alarm (and, understandably, get extremely frustrated). When this continues for an extended period, the operator may disable that alarm and document this on a Post-It note that is kept on the side of the CRT. If the alarm is still disabled at the end of the shift, the operator either reconnects it or tells the new operator about it.

#### Enhance Signal

This action increases the salience or visibility of an indicator or piece of information. As an example, we observed operators at one of the plants expand the y-axis (the parameter value scale) on a trend plot on the CRT to monitor better the small changes in a particular parameter.

### Document Baseline or Trend

This action documents a baseline condition (e.g., at the beginning of the shift) or establishes a trend over a period of time to provide a referent for comparison at a later time. The most common example of this facilitating activity is making hard copies of several CRT displays (more than is required by formal procedures) at the start of a shift. This produces a hard-copy referent of the history of the unit's status so that if unexpected events occur later in the shift, the operator can see (rather than remember) if there was a change from the previous state, and if so, in what way. This historical record thereby provides a valuable context for interpreting subsequent information.

### Use Other Reactor Units as Referents

Operators mentioned the ability to check equipment and tests with the other three reactor units in the control room as a way of cross-checking information. Operators take full advantage of redundancy throughout the plant using redundant indicators, other channels, and other reactor units to extract the maximum amount of information. This provides them with a means of generating a referent that can be used to determine whether a given value is normal.

### Exploit Knowledge of the Plant and the Current Context to Guide Monitoring

Operators know that certain types of plant changes (e.g., raising power, refueling) are more likely to cause problems, so they proactively monitor certain parameters more closely (e.g., boiler levels, storage tank level) during those times. Again, this allows them to anticipate problems and catch them at a very early stage.

Operators also know what jobs/tests have had problems in the past, either by experience or by looking in the long-term status binder. Based on this knowledge, they are prepared to do more careful proactive monitoring of specific parameters that can reveal problems before they become serious.

During the execution of testing procedures, operators always try to understand the intent of a test and not merely follow the procedures in a rote fashion. As a result, they proactively monitor certain parameters to confirm that the test is going as planned. This knowledge-driven monitoring strategy serves several purposes. First, it generates information that can be used to detect errors as soon as they occur. Second, it can also help compensate for the limitations in the procedures.

Finally, to interpret instruments properly, it is important to know how they can fail. This knowledge can take two forms: knowledge of the internal structure of the instruments and knowledge of where or when they have failed in the past. Operators use both types when monitoring instruments and interpreting anomalies.

### Exploit Unmediated Indications

Operators may also exploit what we have called *unmediated indications*—labeled this way because there is no sensor–indicator link between the event and the operator. For example, when certain plant components fail open, a low rumbling noise can be heard in the control room. Experienced operators use this noise to interpret the state of the reactor unit. Second, the motor-driven meters mentioned earlier make a noise when they move. Therefore, when there is a severe abnormal event, many of them change simultaneously, thereby providing a salient auditory signal to the operator that something severe has happened (in addition to whatever alarms might come on). Third, sometimes the flicker of the lights in the control room is a precursor to problems with the power supply. Experienced operators know this, and thus monitor certain parameters more closely if they notice a flicker.

Operators may also take full advantage of direct observation of components in the plant. For example, field operators once had to go out in the plant to find a heavy water leak of 50 kg/hour (the shutdown limit). Before they went out, they and the operator went to the sink with a cup of known volume and a watch and adjusted the tap flow rate until they created a flow rate of 50 kg/hour. As the operator observed, "You might think that 50 kg/hour sounds big, that it might be a gusher, but it's not. It was just a trickle." By performing this little experiment, operators acquired a perceptual (rather than symbolic) referent that they could then effectively use for monitoring in the plant (for a fuller discussion, see Vicente and Burns [1996]).

## Seek More Information

When an anomalous indicator is observed, operators avoid reacting right away. As one experienced operator put it, "Don't jump in with both feet first." Instead, they consult redundant panel information and/or talk to field operators to establish whether the observed anomaly is being caused by a faulty instrument or by an actual change in plant status. This independent confirmation allows operators to keep from reacting to false indicators that could lead to problems or trips. Sometimes, the problem goes away after a few minutes. Because of the control room hardware reliability issue discussed earlier, many anomalous indicators turn out to be caused by instrumentation problems. This strategy is a way of accommodating this fact.

## Strategies That Create Information

Operators have also developed strategies for creating information not normally provided by the existing interface.

### Create a New Indicator or Alarm

We found several instances when operators modified the interface to create indicators or alarms that did not exist before. Examples include the following:

1. Operators may change the set points of an alarm after an alarm trips. Because an alarm does not trip again after the value exceeds the set point, operators increase the set point after the initial trip to get a "second chance." In this way, if the parameter continues to increase, the alarm trips again. Detecting this subsequent auditory signal is much easier than continually having to check on the parameter to see if it has increased even more.
2. Operators may change an alarm set point on a particular parameter to a temporary value so that an auditory signal occurs when it is time to perform an action (e.g., close a tank valve when the tank has drained to a specified level). Otherwise, they would have to remember to check the meter periodically until its value reached the point when action was required.
3. Operators may manipulate alarm set points in ways not intended by alarm designers to compensate for the lack of direct information needed for a particular problem. At plant A, we were told that in some cases operators manipulate alarm set points on some parameters to

compensate for the lack of alarms on others. They do this by changing the set point on a parameter that is correlated with the one they actually want to monitor. Thus, the set point on the parameter with the alarm is set at a value that indicates that the parameter of interest (the one without an alarm) has reached an undesirable state. This creates an auditory signal. Without this manipulation, no signal would be given because the first parameter was not instrumented with an alarm. By creating this new information, operators create an early warning of trouble or signal an important event. Interestingly, this strategy was not observed or reported at plant B, which was better instrumented.

### Determine the Validity of an Indicator

In some cases, there may be questions about whether an important indicator is valid (e.g., because it may conflict with some other information) or a need to determine which indicator to trust. A method used to determine an indicator's validity is to begin to manipulate plant systems or equipment to determine whether the indicator responds as expected. We found operators also using alarms to determine the validity of a field operator's report. For certain tasks, field operators need to enter restricted areas that are alarmed. Thus, when they enter and exit, the control room operator gets an alarm. Because control room operators know how long it should take to complete a test or maintenance activity accurately, they can monitor field operators. In one case we observed, the control room operator determine that the field operator could not have completed the assigned work in the time he was in the restricted area.

## Strategies to Off-load Cognitive Demands

We observed operators off-loading memory and attentional demands onto the interface or onto other people.

### Create an External Reminder for Monitoring

Operators may leave the door open on a particular strip chart recorder to make it stand out from others when it is important to monitor that parameter more closely than usual. When several parameters need to be monitored, several strip chart doors are open, but the chart that is the most critical to monitor is pulled out to distinguish it from the others. This very simple action has enormous information value. First, it provides an external cue for monitoring. If an operator forgets the need to monitor and then sees an open door, he is prompted that there must be a reason to monitor that particular parameter more closely. Second, this practice also serves as a cue for others. For instance, when the shift supervisor does his rounds, he looks at strip charts with open doors. Otherwise, he just passes by them.

### Create External Cues for Action or Inaction

External cues are also created to remind an operator about unusual configurations requiring modification in action. As one example, operators may put Post-It notes on the control room panel to flag unusual indicators. Usually, operators would respond right away to correct such indicators. Thus, the Post-It note serves as a visual reminder not to react as usual to the observed signals—that is, the unusual indicator is already known. As a second example, at plant B there is a set of analog automatic control devices in a row on one of the control panels. These controllers are normally set on automatic mode. If an operator temporarily changes one to manual, he slides the controller out of the panel an inch to indicate that it was intentionally placed in the manual mode.

### Employ Additional Operators

In some cases, what is needed to support monitoring is another set of eyes. The operator may be required to monitor an indicator closely and may be unable to dedicate himself to that task. Several operators mentioned that when workload gets high, and there are too many monitoring demands, another operator can be dedicated to a small set of indicators or to the alarm screen.

### DISCUSSION

Monitoring an NPP can be viewed as an attention task that requires focus, selection, and division of scarce cognitive resources. But our findings, summarized in Table 7.1, show that the sheer number of information sources and the many difficulties associated with monitoring an NPP greatly exceed the capacity of human attention. It is simply not possible to monitor an NPP using attentional resources alone.

TABLE 7.1. Summary of Field Study Findings.

*Sources of Information for Monitoring*

| | |
|---|---|
| Shift turnover | Log |
| Testing | Alarm screens |
| Control room panels | CRT displays |
| Field operators | Field tour |
| Other units | |

*Factors That Make Monitoring Difficult*

| | |
|---|---|
| System complexity and reliability | Alarm system design |
| Displays and controls design | Design of automation |

*Strategies That Operators Use to Facilitate Monitoring*

*Strategies That Enhance Information Extraction from Available Data*

Reduce noise

Enhance signal

Document baseline or trend

Use other reactor units as referents

Exploit knowledge of the plant and the current context to guide monitoring

Exploit unmediated indications

Seek more information

*Strategies That Create Information*

Create a new indicator or alarm

Determine the validity of an indicator

*Strategies to Off-load Cognitive Demands*

Create an external reminder for monitoring

Create external cues for action or inaction

Employ additional operators

Our results show that operators have developed an intricate and clever set of strategies to turn a seemingly impossible job into something that can be done reliably on a daily basis. These strategies include enhancing information extraction from available data sources, creating new sources of information, and off-loading cognitive demands either to external representations or to other people. These strategies allow operators to make up the distance between the strong limitations of attention and the complex demands of their job.

These results have important implications. For basic research, it is important to realize that experiments that study attention in isolation may not generalize to applied settings and will shed little theoretical light on the skilled coordination of attention with other cognitive skills (like the ones we have documented here). For applied research, our findings show that formal training programs do not capture many of the strategies that we have documented. Facilitative strategies are largely developed and disseminated informally, so it would be useful to capture and implement them in a more systematic way.

Finally, we found that good operators rely extensively on knowledge-driven monitoring instead of rote procedural compliance. This practice allows operators to detect problems before they become significant, to compensate for poor design of procedures, to distinguish instrumentation failures from component failures, and to become better aware (in a deep sense) of the unit's current state. However, current training and licensing programs are based more on a philosophy of procedural compliance than of knowledge-based understanding. Moreover, the trend in many complex sociotechnical systems is to increase the degree and stringency of proceduralization, frequently as a result of organizational accountability and legal liability. But if we want to make the most of the vast array of skills that unencumbered human beings have at their disposal, then we must provide them with more freedom and flexibility to engage in discretionary decision making and problem solving (Vicente, 1999). Balancing the competing need for accountability on the one hand and flexibility on the other remains an important topic of research.

## ACKNOWLEDGMENTS

This work was sponsored by the Atomic Energy Control Board of Canada. The author thanks Les Innes, Felicity Harrison, Francis Sarmiento, Mel Grandame, and Rick Manners of Ontario Hydro for their help in coordinating the field study. Randy Mumaw, Emilie Roth, and Catherine Burns were involved in conducting the studies.

This research would not have been possible without the cooperation of the operators who patiently answered questions and generously shared their insights regarding the demands and skills associated with their jobs.

### References

Moray, N. (1986). Monitoring behavior and supervisory control. In K. Boff, L. Kaufman, & J. Thomas (Eds.), *Handbook of human perception and performance* (pp. 40-1–40-51). New York: Wiley.

Mumaw, R. J., Roth, E. M., Vicente, K. J., & Burns, C. M. (2000). There is more to monitoring a nuclear power plant than meets the eye. *Human Factors, 42*, 36–55.

Vicente, K. J. (1999). *Cognitive work analysis: Toward safe, productive, and healthy computer-based work.* Mahwah, N.J.: Erlbaum.

Vicente, K. J., & Burns, C. M. (1996). Evidence for direct perception from cognition in the wild. *Ecological Psychology, 8*, 269–280.

Wickens, C. D. (1992). *Engineering psychology and human performance* (2nd ed.). New York: Harper-Collins.

# Chapter 8

# The Functional Task Environment

## Wayne D. Gray, Hansjörg Neth, and Michael J. Schoelles

Although human thought may be possible in those floatation tanks that are used to encourage meditative states, in by far the majority of instances thought occurs in the context of some physical task environment. The physical environment can be as simple as a light and book. It can be as complex as the face of a mountain and the equipment of the climber. It may be as dynamic as the cockpit of an F-16 in supersonic flight and as reactive as a firefight in Iraq or as heated as an argument between lovers.

An emphasis on the environment in cognitive science research is not new. The environment was of prime concern to Simon in his famous "Ant on the Beach" parable (Simon, 1996), in which he warned of the perils of mistaking limits imposed by the environment for limits inherent to human cognition. However, the environment can include an infinity of detail. To be at all useful to understanding human cognition requires a focus on the environment from the perspective of the to-be-accomplished task; that is, it is the task that "allows an environment to be delimited" (Newell & Simon, 1972, p. 55).

The task delimited environment, or more simply the *task environment*, forms the first blade in Newell and Simon's (1972) oft-quoted scissors analogy:

> Just as a scissors cannot cut paper without two blades, a theory of thinking and problem solving cannot predict behavior unless it encompasses both an analysis of the structure of task environments and an analysis of the limits of rational adaptation to task requirements. (p. 55)

Although the importance of the task environment has been recognized by cognitive science for at least 50 years, it seems fair to say that for most cognitive scientists (especially those working within the experimental psychology tradition), the task environment is something to be rigidly controlled and factored so as to shed light on just one aspect of cognition or one aspect of perception or one aspect of action. Indeed, to dampen further the extent of change during task performance, the other blade of the scissors—human cognition—is also carefully controlled. Many cognitive

100

studies of both complex (e.g., chess, reading, and so on) as well as very simple tasks (e.g., rapid serial visual presentation, visual search, task switching, and so forth) use expert subjects or train subjects and discard the training trials so that the trial-to-trial operations of the human element remain largely constant.

Unlike critics of contemporary cognitive science research, we do not see these limits on past and current research as an indictment of the failure of cognitive science as a discipline. Rather, we see these limits as a necessary requirement for making advances in our field. Just as it would be unreasonable to ask particle physicists to eschew linear accelerators to pursue their research by studying billiard balls slamming against each other in an actual game of pool, it is also unreasonable to ask cognitive scientists to eschew experimental designs that allow them to isolate and identify the elements and laws of functional cognition.[1] Indeed, these limits on past and some current research have enabled the advances needed for a more integrative approach to cognitive systems.

This chapter introduces the concept of the *functional task environment* (a brief definition is provided in the next section). This concept integrates disparate findings that show important differences between the physical task environment and the ways in which humans perceive, think about, and act on the physical world. The productivity of this concept will be judged by its success at motivating research that leads to the building of integrated models of cognitive systems (Gray, in press). The functional task environment encompasses both blades of Newell and Simon's scissors. Indeed, rather than the metaphor of the scissors, which suggests two structurally independent blades that are used to cut the mental world into small pieces, a metaphor for the functional task environment might be a laser beam that combines "an analysis of the structure of task environments" with "an analysis of the limits of rational adaptation" to provide a strong and focused light onto the operation of a cognitive system that is integrated with the world as well as with perception and action.

The functional task environment is closely related to the main theme of this book: applied attention. Attention operates within the functional task environment and, at the same time, shapes it. As we discuss in the next section, the functional task environment is defined over three time spans: evolutionary, life span, and individual tasks. Attention operates both within and on the constraints imposed by each of these time spans. Indeed, the locus of attention, the cost of shifting attention, and the cost of maintaining attention need to be understood within the context of the functional task environment.

For this chapter to be successful, by the end its reader will understand the functional task environment to be a concept that draws on and unifies much contemporary cognitive theory. Our further goal is to provide the reader with a new appreciation of the, at times exquisite, adaptation of the functional task environment to the demands of interactive behavior. These adaptations run in both directions: adaptations of the cognitive system to meet the demands of the physical task environment, as well as adaptations of the physical task environment to minimize demands on the cognitive system.

## DEFINING THE FUNCTIONAL TASK ENVIRONMENT

The functional task environment emerges from the moment-to-moment intersection of a cognitive agent (human operator) pursuing a particular goal in a particular physical environment. Thus, the functional task environment is mutually constrained by the physical characteristics of the task environment and the functional characteristics of the agent's cognitive system.

It is easy but a mistake to see the contrast as between an objective physical environment and a subjective functional one. The reality is more complex and more interesting. As a first abstraction, the physical task environment is not the same as the complete and objective physical environment in which the task takes place. For example, infrared wavelengths form a part of the objective physical environment. However, because humans are not equipped to perceive these wavelengths, we cannot interact with them and hence they do not form part of our physical task environment.

As a second abstraction, it is clear that many relevant features of the physical task environment are defined for us by the size and shape of our bodies, our strength, and other physiological characteristics. Hence, a pleasant morning swim for a dolphin may be an impossible obstacle for a person. Likewise, a short climb over an overhanging cliff may be an imposing obstacle for a mountaineer.

Finally, as a third abstraction, our physical task environment is defined not simply by reference to the physical environment and our limitations, but by other people, human society, cultural artifacts, and inventions. Hence, our buildings, artifacts, infrared detectors, jet skis, and so on change the nature of our physical task environment.

The physical task environment differs considerably from the natural environment, but that is not the topic of this chapter. In this chapter we assume a physical task environment and focus our discussion on the factors that control our moment-by-moment interactions within that environment. These factors reflect adaptations to the physical task environment as well as adaptations to the limits of bounded cognition. This division of emphasis between the world and the mind was laid out long ago by Simon (1956, 1992) and has been embraced by thinkers as diverse as Todd (Todd & Gigerenzer, 2000; Todd & Schooler, in press), Anderson (1990, 1991), and Shepard (1990). During the last 15 years, evidence has been amassed that shows just how different our experience of the world—the functional task environment—is from the physical task environment.

As Figure 8.1 is meant to suggest, the functional task environment overlies the physical task environment and the mental system. As such, it is meant as a different level of description than either the physical task environment or the raw properties of the mental system.[2] The functional task environment encompasses both less and more than the physical task environment. It may not include the objective physical properties of the infrared spectrum, but it does include human inventions such as language and culture that for most of us, most of the time, seem more

real and objective than the infrared spectrum. However, as important as language and culture are to the human experience, we exclude them from the current chapter to focus more clearly on the process of mutual adaptation that governs our immediate interactive behavior.

Within the limits just discussed, we examine the functional adaptations to the physical task environment that have emerged over three very different periods of time:

1. Evolutionary (multiple generations): centuries, millennia
2. Individual life span (learning and development): days, months, years, decades
3. Individual tasks (problem solving, interactive behavior): milliseconds, seconds, minutes, hours

This order of intervals also reflects different parts of Figure 8.1. The next section, "Adaptations over Evolutionary Time," is illustrated by the bottom of the figure that shows the functional task environment overlaying a subset of the physical task environment. "Adaptations during the Individual Life Span" (a later section) illustrates the top of the figure, which suggests that different tasks and different physical task environments recruit different resources from the mental system. Indeed, this section goes further than this in suggesting that different physical task environments call forth mental resources such as enhanced memory and retrieval resources that are created just for those environments. "Adaptations that Support

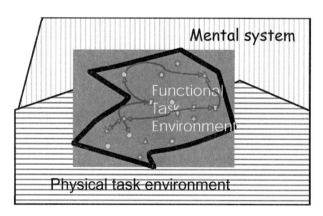

FIGURE 8.1. A notional diagram of the functional task environment as a different level of description that overlays a subset of the physical task environment and the mental system.

Interactive Behavior" shows how interactive behavior stitches together the possible elements in the functional task environment into a temporary network of cognition, perception, and action required to do the current task.

The fascination of experimental psychology with perceptual illusions and cognitive illusions (e.g., the "heuristics and biases" research program of Tversky and Kahneman [1974]) has been denounced by critics throughout the decades (Brunswik, 2001/1957; Gigerenzer, 1996) for focusing on the few cases in which humans make faulty judgments rather than the many cases in which human judgments are correct. However, properly regarded, these illusions can be seen as clues to the limits on our experience of the physical world. In this section we discuss three areas — perception, memory, and attention — in which attending to limits has provided a profoundly interesting perspective on the differences between the physical and the functional task environments.

## Implications of Perceptual Illusions for the Functional Task Environment

Purves and associates (2002) point out: "What we see — whether considered in terms of the brightness of objects, their colors or their arrangement in space — is often at odds with the underlying reality measured with photometers, spectrophotometers or rulers" (p. 236). The fundamental phenomenon is that retinal information is inherently ambiguous. As an example, a small object nearby or a large object far away may generate a line of the same length on the retinal image. Similarly, the same object under the exact same illumination will appear to be a different color depending on its surrounding colors.

Given that our perception of the physical task environment is inherently noisy and ambiguous, what is a mental system to do? The resounding answer from Purves and associates is that the system plays the odds. In a series of fascinating studies (Howe & Purves, 2005a, b; Purves & Lotto, 2003; Purves, Lotto, Williams, Nundy, & Yang, 2001; Purves, Williams, Nundy, & Lotto, 2004; Yang & Purves, 2003), Purves and colleagues show how the wrong answers given to visual illusions tend to reflect the normative answer given

the statistical structure of the physical task environment. For purposes of this chapter, the conclusion we draw is that at a very low level of analysis, the functional task environment has already diverged from the physical task environment.

## Simple Heuristics That Reflect the Environment in Memory

From a naive perspective it might seem as if a memory system should store and be able to retrieve any experience that we might later want to remember. However, our modern experience with the increasingly large storage requirements of electronic media suggests that even if it were possible to store everything forever, retrieving the right memory when needed would constitute a major problem for any retrieval system. In their article, "Reflections of the Environment in Memory," Anderson and Schooler (1991) pose what they considered a very basic, but ignored question: "How does a system behave optimally when it is faced with a huge database of items and cannot make all of them instantaneously available?" (p. 396). Their answer — "It would be behaving optimally if it made most available those items that were most likely to be needed" — begot an innovative attempt to define "most likely to be needed" and to determine whether human memory served this function. In this section we briefly review their evidence and arguments and then introduce a recent study by Schooler and others (Schooler & Hertwig, 2005; Todd & Schooler, in press) that shows how this adaptation of memory to its environment can account for one of Gigerenzer and Todd's "simple heuristics that make us smart" (Gigerenzer & Todd, 1999; Todd & Gigerenzer, 2000).

### Characterizing the Demands That the Environment Makes on Memory

Anderson and Schooler (1991) began by trying to define the demands made on memory by the natural environment. They used three sets of data. First were the words that appeared in the *New York Times* headlines for a period of 730 days. They reasoned that headlines posed a demand on the "potential reader of the article to retrieve information about the referent of that word to decide whether this is an article that the reader might want to read" (p. 401). Second were words from a data set of children's verbal interactions with adults. "Every time someone says a word to a child, this is a demand on the child to retrieve the word's meaning" (p. 401). Third was an analysis of senders of e-mail messages to John Anderson over 3.5 years. "The assumption here is that every time Anderson receives a message from a certain person, that is another demand to retrieve some information from Anderson's memory about the sender" (p. 401).

For each data set they looked at the frequency of occurrence of items for periods of 100 days and asked themselves several questions about day 101. First was the *practice question*: Would the future probability of a word on day 101 reflect its past use in the data set? Second was the *retention question*: Would more remote items occur less likely on day 101? Both questions were confirmed by their analysis. The third question concerned the *spacing effect* for words that appeared twice within a 100-day period: Would their future probability of appearing on day 101 reflect the number of days (space) between the two appearance and the number of days (space) between the second occurrence and day 101? Again, the answer was yes. The data mirrored the human data for studies of massed versus distributed practice. For short lags between the second occurrence and day 101, shorter lags between the first and second occurrences increased the likelihood that the word would occur on day 101. However, for longer lags, use on day 101 increased with the length of the lags between the two occurrences.

Anderson and Schooler (1991) then showed that mathematical functions fitted to the environmental data predicted human data on the effect of practice, forgetting as a function of retention interval, and the spacing effect. They concluded: "This is not a particularly obscure model of the environmental properties of memories. Nonetheless, it turns out these simple assumptions have led to memory characteristics that have confounded psychologists since Ebbinghaus" (p. 408).

### Memory as a Tool in the Adaptive Toolbox: The Case of the Recognition Heuristic

US students have been shown to do surprisingly well when asked which of two German cities has the larger population (Gigerenzer & Todd, 1999). Because the US students could only recognize half the German cities in the data set, this success must be based on "ignorance-based reasoning" (Todd & Schooler, in press). Despite its simplicity, this "recognition heuristic" has been shown to be successful across a wide variety of tasks (Todd & Schooler, in press).

Schooler and others (Schooler & Hertwig, 2005; Todd & Schooler, in press) took the original list of German cities (Goldstein & Gigerenzer, 1999) and determined the probability with which each city was mentioned in the *Chicago Tribune* over a 4,767-day period. In their simulation, based on the probability of encountering the city name on each of those 4,767 days, the declarative memory element that encoded that city strengthened and decayed according to its frequency and recency of use. The success of this relatively simple model at duplicating the empirical results showed that the recognition heuristic follows from a memory system that reflects the expected utility of information in the environment.

Schooler and Hertwig (2005) did not stop here. They asked the further question of whether forgetting enhanced the accuracy of the recognition heuristic. They studied this by varying ACT-Rs decay parameter and determined that the recognition heuristic worked best with intermediate levels of decay. With too little or too much forgetting, performance declined. An intermediate level maintained a distribution of recognition rates that were highly correlated with the criteria of frequency of mention in the *Chicago Tribune*.

For the purposes of this chapter, this picture of memory reflects an interesting broadening of the functional task environment. In the case of the perceptual phenomena discussed by Purves and associates, although each new physical stimulus is in some sense new, it is also indistinguishable from thousands or millions of physical stimuli that the cognitive agent has encountered in the past. The perception of an individual stimuli is treated as the perception of a member of a category defined by some physical characteristic.

In contrast, in the case of memory, the function of memory is to recall a particular and, in some sense, distinct item. Hence, the functional task environment for memory reflects an adaptation to a pattern of stimulus occurrences, not to the occurrence of a given stimulus. What is important for memory is the pattern defined by the frequency and recency of an individual item. It is this pattern that predicts whether an individual item will be remembered or forgotten. It is this pattern that enables ignorance-based heuristics to work so well.

## Peering through the Knothole:
## Our Functional Representation of
## Even Static Physical Task Environments
## Is Partial and Dynamic

The naive view of perception is that we store a high-resolution, surround-sound representation of the physical task environment in our heads. Attending to one part of this representation rather than another seems a simple matter of shifting internal attention. Indeed, when something in the external world changes, it should be a simple matter to compare the new high-resolution representation with the old to detect what has changed.

This caricature of the naive view is unmasked by data (Levin, Momen, Drivdahl, & Simons, 2000) that shows that people consistently and drastically overestimate their ability to detect large changes in visual scenes. Indeed, Findlay and Gilchrist (2003) argue that until recently the view that our representation of our physical task environment is high resolution has dominated, at least implicitly, research on visual perception.

Rensink (2002) shows that the study of *change blindness* emerged out of research on change detection and has now come to define that area. In the mid '90s, researchers (see Findlay and Gilchrist [2003] and Rensink [2002] for a more detailed discussion) studying change detection adopted a paradigm in which changes were made to a visual scene during saccades (we are blind during saccades). They were surprised to discover that in a large number of cases people did not notice the change even when the change consisted of replacing one object for another at the saccade's end point. These changes were in no way subtle. A representative example would be swapping out a picture of a cow for a picture of a motorcycle.

As the work progressed, the changes made by researchers became more and more blatant, yet their subjects still did not notice. In a very dramatic study, Simons and Levin (1998) randomly stopped people on campus to ask for directions. As the victim was gesturing to the questioner, two confederates dressed as workmen and carrying a large door, rudely walked between the questioner and victim. With the door temporarily concealing the questioner from the victim, one workman swapped places with the questioner and continued the conversation as if nothing had happened. Across two replications, only about half the victims noticed the change.

Rensink's work in the laboratory (Rensink, 2000, in press) is almost as blatant and may be more dramatic. Subjects are told to look for changes and for each trial are shown two alternating still shots of the same scene with one major difference. For example, in a scene of Canadian military personnel boarding a transport plane, in one of the two pictures the large engine under one wing is edited out (Fig. 8.2). The engine is fairly large and is toward the center of the picture. The flicker paradigm (Rensink, Oregan, & Clark, 1997) is used in which these pictures alternate continuously until subjects respond that there is or is not a change. Between each of the two pictures, a gray screen is presented that serves to mask the transient abrupt-onset effect. Under these circumstances, although subjects (and large audiences at conference presentations of this work) are staring at the screen, trying to find a change, the change is frustratingly difficult to find. To be clear, the frustration is not the result of the change being small and subtle, but precisely because it is so large and blatant that it is hard to imagine failing to notice it.

The failure to notice a change in the visual display "means that particular piece of information is not part of the internal visual representation" (Hayhoe, 2000, p. 44). The implications of change blindness for understanding the nature of the functional task environment are profound. In terms of representing the external world, the functional task environment contains less information than the physical task environment. Furthermore, the functional representation of even static physical task environments is partial and dynamic as it "varies from moment to moment in concert with the requirements of the ongoing visual tasks" (Hayhoe, 2000, p. 44).

## Conclusions of Evolutionary Adaptations:
## Perception, Memory, and Attention

The three cases covered in this section tell three different but complementary stories about the relationship of the functional task environment to the physical task environment. Rather than beginning with the assumption that an optimal perceptual system should recognize all angles it encounters without fail, Howe and Purves (2005a) began with the obvious fact that two-dimensional stimuli striking the retina can never fully disambiguate a three-dimensional world. They proceeded to ask about the distribution of angles in the environment and pursued the implications of

FIGURE 8.2. Example of the flicker paradigm. Two still pictures are separated by a gray mask. The pictures alternate until the subject finds the change or concludes that there is no change. See www.psych.ubc.ca/~viscoglab/ for online demonstrations. Printed with permission of R. Rensink.

the assumption that the perceptual system was adapted to that distribution. Similarly, rather than assuming that an ideal memory would never forget and that all memories are of equal importance, Anderson and Schooler (1991) began by asking how the demands on memory changed with an item's frequency and recency of occurrence. For both perception and memory, in face of uncertainty in the physical task environment, the functional task environment plays the odds.

In the context of the three phenomena discussed in this section, change blindness is the odd man out. Unlike the problems posed by visual illusions and fallible memory, the problem posed by change blindness is a new discovery. Both common sense and common theories of visual attention implicitly assumed that much more of the external world was represented than is actually the case. Indeed, the puzzle here has shifted from explaining what were assumed to be the few cases in which change is not detected, to an accounting of the many cases in which we are functionally blind to changes taking place before our eyes. At least in this regard, theories of visual attention are lagging far behind theories of memory and perception.

## ADAPTATIONS DURING THE INDIVIDUAL LIFE SPAN

The functional task environment, as Figure 8.1 suggests, includes portions of the mental system (broadly defined to encompass cognition, perception, and action). Different physical task environments require different mixes of mental processes. Hence, in a very straightforward sense, different physical task environments recruit different mental resources, with the result that the functional task environment differs as a function of the task being performed.

The picture becomes more complicated because with experience in a given physical task environment, people improve at performing the same task. This statement may be the most uncontroversial statement in cognitive science. However, the reasons for this acceleration are not as well understood. Fitts and Posner (1967) talked about three stages of skill acquisition that they called *the cognitive, associative, and autonomous stages.* Anderson (2000) writes of these stages as a transition in knowledge from largely declarative (factual) knowledge that is operated on or interpreted by general-purpose procedures, to a transition stage in which special-purpose procedures begin to encapsulate the knowledge needed for the task, to an autonomous stage where the set of specialized procedures is complete and can execute the task with little reliance on declarative knowledge and general-purpose, interpretive procedures. Hence, by this standard accounting of skill acquisition, the operators available to the human problem solver change from the slow and error-prone process of acquiring and interpreting declarative knowledge, to the use of specialized routines or procedures.

This sketch of skill acquisition has been generally accepted for the last 40 years. Although modern research has changed our understanding of how these mechanisms work, the story that these are normal changes that use normal mechanisms of cognition holds.

Recently, evidence has accumulated that in addition to these normal changes during skill acquisition, more specialized changes may take place. Some of these changes serve to bypass accepted limits on the time needed to store items in long-term memory, allowing skilled performers to store more information faster. Other changes serve to bypass limits in the number of items that can be retrieved from the canonical $7 \pm 2$ (Miller, 1956) to 10 or 20 times that amount. Furthermore, neurological evidence is accumulating that, with massive amounts of experience, the brain may change so that different regions become specialized to process different types of material. In this section we discuss life span adaptations of the cognitive system that produce skilled performance in particular functional task environments.

## Long-Term Working Memory

Ericsson and Kintsch (Ericsson, 2003; Ericsson & Kintsch, 1995) argue that some types of skilled performance require the use of long-term memory as a type of permanent auxiliary to working memory. They referred to this phenomenon as *long-term working memory* (LTWM) and they argue that their proposal is consistent with all major assumptions regarding long-term and short-term memory. Their disagreement with the standard view focuses on "auxiliary assumptions" regarding the speed of storage and retrieval in long-term memory.

Newell and Simon (1972) presented evidence that it takes between 5 to 10 seconds to store a new and retrievable memory trace, and about 1 second to retrieve an item from long-term memory. Such time scales cannot account for the digit-span experts who can learn and repeat 50 or more digits (Ericsson & Chase, 1982; Ericsson, Chase, & Faloon, 1980) when read to them at the usual digit-span rate of 1 second per item. Similarly, the best of these experts can memorize and repeat back multiple lists in apparent suspension of the laws of proactive and retroactive interference.

Ericsson and Kintsch (1995) are quite restrained in their claims for the generality of LTWM and are careful to point out that the use of long-term memory as working memory only occurs in the expert's domain of expertise, where it is "closely tailored to the demands of a specific activity and is an integrated, inseparable part of the skill in performing the activity" (p. 239). They walk through the use of LTWM for the mundane expertise of text comprehension and then provide a quick tour of its use by mental abacus experts, mental calculators (those able to multiple large numbers in their heads), expert waiters (who never write down an order, but always get it right), medical diagnosis, and chess experts. They conclude: "The new contribution we hope to explicate is that reliance on acquired memory skills enables individuals to use [long-term memory] as an efficient extension of [short-term working memory] in particular domains and activities after sufficient practice and training" (p. 211).

## Functional Neural Specialization

Individual English letters and Hindu–Arabic numerals have much in common. They are small sets of artificial symbols that share many features and denote abstract entities no one is born knowing. Because of these similarities, Polk and colleagues (Polk & Farah, 1995; Polk, Stallcup, Aguirre, Alsop, D'Esposito, Detre, & Farah, 2002) have become fascinated with the differences between these categories of symbols. In studies of visual search, a pop-out effect occurs when a target and its distracters differ on primitive features such as color. For example, a single red L hidden among multiple green Ts is quickly found. Treisman and Gelade (1980) proposed that such primitive features are processed in specialized modules, and this hypothesis is generally consistent with neuroscientific evidence for spatially segregated cortical areas that process such features (Polk & Farah, 1995). However, the fact that the pop-out effect for red Ls hidden among green Ts may have a neuroscientific basis does not explain why a similar pop-out effect occurs when a given letter is hidden among numbers (but not when the same letter is hidden among other letters) and vice versa.

Polk and Farah (1995) point out that letters tend to occur with other letters, and numbers tend to occur with other numbers. Hence, if the functional architecture of cognition makes a distinction between letters and numbers, then perhaps the statistical probability of letters co-occurring more with letters than with numbers (and vice versa) interacts with correlation-based learning to lead to maps for letter and digit recognition. They test this hypothesis in two ways.

First, Polk and Farah (1995) found a population of adult subjects for whom the co-occurrence of letters and numbers is much greater than for the population at large. This population was foreign mail sorters at the Philadelphia air mail facility who spend 4 hours each day sorting "Canadian zip codes in which letters and digits occur together (for example, M5S 1A4)" (p. 648). Testing this population on search time for letters among numbers or vice versa yields a greatly reduced pop-out effect (and longer search times) compared with the control groups. From this they conclude that, "environmental statistics can influence the functional architecture of vision, even in adulthood" (p. 649).

Second, Polk and colleagues (2002) used functional magnetic resonance imaging and found an area of the brain that responds more to letters than to digits. Unlike other areas specialized for visual processing, letters versus digits do not exist in the natural world and can have no evolutionary history. They conclude: "The present finding implies that school-age learning can lead to the creation of new functionally defined brain areas" (p. 154).

## Conclusions of Adaptations in Support of Skilled Performance

During the acquisition of skilled performance, repeated experience in a stable physical task environment leads to changes in the functional task environment, which serve to enhance skilled performance. This enhancement includes the recruitment of general-purpose mechanisms that convert declarative knowledge to procedural knowledge. However, it goes beyond such general-purpose mechanisms in that it changes the way the cognitive system processes information and, apparently, changes the neurological architecture of the brain itself.

## ADAPTATIONS THAT SUPPORT INTERACTIVE BEHAVIOR

People make adjustments in how they do a task while they are doing it. This statement may seem so obvious that it does not require a demonstration. A light rain on the highway suddenly becomes a torrential downpour. We may quickly turn on our headlights, turn up the speed of the windshield wipers, and reduce our speed. As we do so we may become more attentive to traffic around us, the feel of the road, and so on.

Agre and Shrager (1990) present a detailed analysis of the spontaneous changes one person made while using a photocopier for 4 minutes to make three copies of 17 pages from a book. Their subject came to their study with prior experience using a copying machine but not necessarily prior experience with the particular copying machine used in the study and, almost certainly, no prior experience copying the particular pages from the particular book.

Measuring the time it took the subject to copy each even-odd page pair (e.g., pages 2 and 3, 4 and 5, and so on) they found that work sped up from about 53 seconds for the first pair of pages to around 22 seconds for the final pair. Their analysis makes it clear that this acceleration is not simply the quantitative acceleration of a fixed set of actions such as might be expected by the Fitts and Posner (1967) three-stage analysis of skill acquisition discussed earlier. Rather, qualitative change occurs: As the subject became adapted to the machine, she changed how she handled the book and the machine. Different handling left her hands, body, and the machine in different states with respect to each other. These different states engendered further adaptation and so on.

How these adjustments occur, the role of top-down strategies, tradeoffs between cognitive versus perceptual–motor processes, and so on, is less clear. However, studies that have been done have demonstrated such adjustments over a wide range of tasks that involve a wide range of cognitive, perceptual, and action operations.

In this section we focus on by minute, by second, and by hundred millisecond adjustments to our functional task environment. Some of these adjustments reflect changes in the allocation of mental resources and processes that better adapt us to the physical task environment. Other adjustments reflect changes in the physical task environment to adapt it better to our mental resources and processes. To complicate matters, these changes occur amid all the differences between the functional and physical task environments that we discussed in the first two sections. Our perceptual system is playing the odds. Our memory system is biased either toward very immediate experiences or toward past experiences that recur with some regularity. Our visual attention does not veridically record the visual environment and may be blind to huge changes. This has the effect of turning stable and static physical task environments into dynamic functional ones. A further complication is that the cognitive resources we can recruit change as we use them and change because we use them. What's a mental system to do? Viewed from this perspective, it may seem to be a miracle that we are able to clothe ourselves and get out the door each morning, let alone productively pursue our careers, lives, and loves.

Fortunately, the mental system is very robust and seems to excel at making adaptations to the physical task environment. In this section we first review the concept of the unit task (Card, Moran, & Newell, 1983) and introduce the concept of interactive routines. In the second section we review a series of studies that show that small manipulations of the physical task environment result in stable and predictable differences in performance and outcomes.

### The Unit Task Level

Unit tasks (Card et al., 1983) are subtasks of a larger task that take about 3 to 30 seconds to perform. By definition, "the unit task is fundamentally a control construct, not a task construct" (Card et al., 1983, p. 386). As a control construct, unit tasks are not given by the physical task environment, but result from the interaction of the physical task environment with the control problems faced by the mental system.

The prototypical example of a unit task is the structure imposed by a typist on transcription typing. The physical task environment for transcription typing consists of the dictated speech, a word processor, plus a foot pedal that controls how much of a recording is played back. As speech is typically much faster than skilled typing, the basic problem faced by the typist is how much of the recording to listen to before shutting it off. The efficient typist listens while typing, and the longer he or she listens, the greater the lag between what they are hearing and what they are typing. At some point the typist shuts off the recording and continues to type until she or he can remember no more

of the recording with certainty. With some experience with the particular speaker and maybe with the particular topic, a skilled transcription typist will minimize the amount of rewind and replay, and maximize the amount typed per unit task. This chopping up of the physical task environment into unit tasks reflects a control process that adjusts performance to the characteristics of the task (the speed of dictation and clarity of speech), to the typist's general typing skill (number of words per minute), as well as to the typist's cognitive, perceptual, and motor limits.

The realm of traditional task analysis (Kirwan & Ainsworth, 1992) lies above the unit task level. As the level of analysis increases from minutes to days, our typist's job may be analyzed into a succession of talks that need transcribing ("transcribe Prof. Wickens' talk, transcribe Prof. Moray's talk") or even higher level activities that need to be completed (transcribe symposium talks, proofread transcription, send copy of each transcription to the speaker for review). Below the unit task level we would analyze the unit task into a series of interactive routines (Fig. 8.3)—that is, into an activity network of cognitive, perceptual, and action operators (Gray & Boehm-Davis, 2000; Schweickert, Fisher, & Proctor, 2003).

Figure 8.3 provides an example of an interactive routine for moving the cursor to a target location (e.g., menu item, icon, sentence, word, and so forth). The center row shows activities of central cognition that initiate or harvest the activities of other modules. For example, the "initiate move cursor" item initiates a motor command to "move cursor" to a target location. Below the line of central cognitive operators are the motor operators for manual and eye movements. Above the line are visual perceptual operators. Above all these operators is the one box—"new cursor location"—that indicates that a change has been made in the physical task environment.

There are several noteworthy things about interactive routines and their elements for our analysis of the functional task environment. First, interactive routines occur over a time span of 0.333 to 1 second. This level of analysis has been identified by Ballard as the embodiment level (Ballard, Hayhoe, Pook, & Rao, 1997). It is the level at which interactive routines bring together the elements of embodied cognition— namely, cognition, perception, and action.

Second, there is something very fluid about the notion of an interactive routine. The template shown in Figure 8.3 can be instantiated in a number

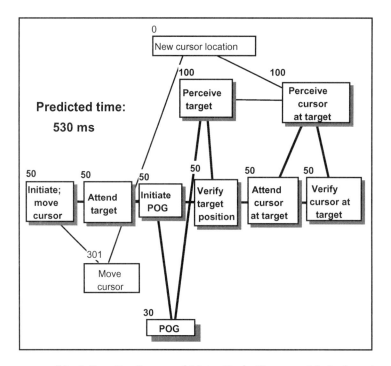

FIGURE 8.3. A Cognitive Perceptual Motor-Goals, Operators, Methods, and Selection Rules (CPM-GOMS) model of the interactive routine required to move a mouse to a predetermined location on a computer screen. Total predicted time is 530 ms. CPM-GOMS is a network modeling technique. In the middle row are cognitive operators with a default execution time of 50 ms each. Above that line are the perceptual operators and below it are the motor operators. The flow of operators is from left to right, with connecting lines indicating dependencies. Within an operator type the dependencies are sequential. However, between operator types the dependencies may be parallel. The numbers above each operator indicate the time, in milliseconds, for that operator to execute. Time is accumulated from left to right along the critical path. The critical path is indicated by bold lines connecting shadowed boxes. loc, location; POG, point of gaze. See Gray and Boehm-Davis (2000) for more detailed information.

of different ways. The beginning cursor position, the distance moved, and the size, color, shape of the target all may vary, but the interactive routine would be the same. The operators of an interactive routine seem to encapsulate a low-level control structure that can be used, as in the example provided by Figure 8.3, to move any given cursor, any given distance, to any given object within the physical task environment defined by a computer display.

### Adaptations below the Unit Task Level

The development of Goals, Operators, Methods, and Selection Rules (GOMS) (Card et al., 1983) as a tool for cognitive task analysis at the unit task level coincided with and contributed to the rise of the cognitive engineering movement (Newell & Card, 1985; Norman, 1982, 1986, 1989). This movement strongly implied that because of how changes in design interacted with human cognitive, perceptual, and action resources, small changes in artifacts or task environments could affect both the efficiency and effectiveness of human performance. Given this background, it is perhaps not surprising that some of the first work in this area was done by researchers with strong ties to applied research communities (e.g., Gray & Anderson, 1987; Gray & Orasanu, 1987; John, 1990; John, Rosenbloom, & Newell, 1985; Lohse, 1993; Payne &

Green, 1986; Payne, Squibb, & Howes, 1990), who then turned toward more basic research issues as their work evolved.

In this section we review some of the key studies from the last 15 years that substantiate the claims of the cognitive engineering movement and that have helped to establish basic research in embodied cognition. The reviewed research explores the types of changes that produce effects, as well as the scope of these effects. Speculations about the control mechanisms responsible for these changes are outside the scope of the current chapter. However, such issues have formed the focus of much recent work (Fu & Gray, 2004, 2006; Gray & Fu, 2004; Gray, Schoelles, & Sims, 2005; Maloney, Trommershäuser, & Landy, in press; Mozer, Kinoshita, & Shettel, in press).

### Do Imposed Changes in the Structuring and Sequencing of Interactive Routines Affect Unit Task Performance?

The utility of analysis below the unit task level for cognitive engineering was shown in the unlikely domain of telephone company Toll and Assistance Operators (TAOs). The study was initiated by a telephone company that was considering replacing its current workstations for TAOs with a proposed new workstation at the cost of approximately $70 million (in 1990 dollars), but with a projected savings in operating costs of $12 million per year.

Using CPM-GOMS (see Fig. 8.3 for an example of this type of analysis), Gray and coworkers (1993) built two models for each of 15 different call types—one for executing the call on the old workstation and one for the proposed workstation. The models tended to predict that the proposed workstation would take expert users longer to operate than the old workstation. Using the phone company's basis for calculating operating costs, this increase in predicted time translated into an increase in annual operating costs of approximately $2 million per year (rather than the expected savings of $12 million per year). A 4-month field trial with "live traffic" (i.e., real customers placing real calls) confirmed the predictions of the model both in terms of direction (i.e., proposed workstation slower than old workstation) and magnitude (approximately 1 second per average call slower rather than the expected 4 seconds per call faster).

Although the proposed workstation was in fact faster than the old workstation by all the metrics its

designers had touted (e.g., speed to display text on screen, time to move to and press the most frequently used keys, and so on), the design of the old workstation supported more efficient ordering and interleaving of interactive routines. For example, the old workstation enabled an ordering of operations that tended to put listening to the customer, not operations by the human operator, on the critical path, thereby permitting the TAO to press critical keys and initiate queries to external databases while the customer spoke. Likewise, the old workstation enabled more efficient use of two hands. The proposed workstation required one hand to move between common sequences of two keys, but the old workstation enabled the TAO to move, say, the left hand into position while pressing the first key using the right hand. Although the workstation component of the physical task environment was slower for the old than the proposed workstation, the functional task environment was faster in that it permitted a more efficient coordination of human cognitive, perceptual, and action resources.

### Increasing the Cost of Taking an Action and of Accessing Information in the World

Although the study by Gray and coworkers (1993) emphasized the importance of effective interleaving of cognition, perception, and action within a dynamic environment, other studies highlighted the importance of interaction costs to tasks that are often considered more deliberative. For example, Lohse and Johnson (1996) noted changes in the type of decision-making strategies used as the cost of information access changed from a mouse movement and click to an eye movement. Similarly, in what might be the smallest factor manipulated, Ballard and associates (1995) varied the costs of information acquisition from a simple eye movement to a head movement and noted that the shift decreased the number of times that external information was accessed by presumably increasing subjects' reliance on memory.

Other experimenters documented similar trade-offs. For example, across a series of studies, O'Hara and Payne (1998, 1999) varied the cost of making a move in simple tasks such as the "eight puzzle." As costs increased from a simple click on the object to be moved to typing in a string of simple commands, they found that the number of moves made decreased whereas the overall quality of the moves increased. Hence, in the low-cost interface subjects made many moves before reaching a solution whereas in the high-cost interface a solution was reached in fewer moves.

### Imposing a Change in Mental Workload and Cognitive Control

In a series of interesting studies, Carlson and Sohn (Carlson & Sohn, 2000; Sohn & Carlson, 1998) manipulated the control and storage requirements for a series of simple tasks each of which had the same abstract structure. Each task was a four-step task in which the result of each step had to be used as an operand for the next step. For example, if step A yielded 4 as its result and step B was "add (X, 3)," the result of step B would be 7, and 7 would be an operand for step C.

To manipulate cognitive control, Carlson and Sohn varied whether for each step subjects received the operator first (e.g., "add") or the missing operand first (e.g., "3"). In a series of studies they consistently found that steps in which the operator was received first were about 200 msec faster than steps in which the operand was received first.

To manipulate mental workload, they varied the storage requirements of their tasks. For example, in Sohn and Carlson's (1998) spatial navigation task, people might be given the list of all four operators (e.g., left, right, right, up) and required to hold these in memory as they accessed the operands (e.g., 3, 4, 1, 2) one by one to apply each in-the-head operator to an in-the-world operand (i.e., left-3, right-4, right-1, and up-2). The reverse case was also used in which people were required to hold the operands in memory while they accessed the operators one by one. Holding either operands or operators in memory added approximately 600 to 700 msec per step to task performance; however, it did not change the basic finding that people were faster when they accessed operators first than operands first.

Carlson and Sohn's results are consistent with those of Gray and colleagues (Gray et al., 1993), which suggested that TAOs could rearrange and interleave interactive routines to shave off several seconds from a 25-second (approximate average) phone call. Both sets of results are consistent with an interpretation of the studies by Lohse and Johnson (1996) and O'Hara and Payne (1998, 1999) that suggest that in the different conditions of their studies, the same set of unit tasks were implemented by different sets of interactive routines. The interactive routines chosen worked to optimize the cognitive, perceptual, and action resources brought to bear on the physical task environment. When conditions for their application exist, the interactive routine that saves milliseconds is selected and applied—"milliseconds matter" (Gray & Boehm-Davis, 2000)!

### Top-down Control of the Sequencing of Cognitive Operations

Because the emphasis in this section is on interactive behavior, most of the examples have an in-the-world component as well as in-the-head ones. However, the concept of interactive routines and of functional task environments extends to the mostly mental world as well. An important question here is whether the selection and operation of mental interactive routines is purely task driven or whether selection can be under conscious or top-down control.

A compelling study of mental interactive routines was provided by Ehrenstein and associates (1997), who required subjects to do two concurrent memory tasks. The memory search task required subjects to hold in memory a set of four, five, or six digits and to indicate after a short delay whether the probe digit was a member of the target set. The arithmetic task presented subjects with a number from four to nine and required them to subtract either a one or two from this number. The search set was presented first, but the probe digit and the arithmetic digit were presented simultaneously. They manipulated top-down cognitive control by instructing subjects to respond to the arithmetic task and then the search task or vice versa.

The analyses were as interesting as they were intricate. Their critical path analysis ruled out alternative interpretations of the data to reveal that subjects were doing one task and then the other, and that the order in which the tasks were performed varied with the instructions that the subjects were given. This study has interesting implications for theories of working memory as well as for theories of cognitive control. For working memory the authors conclude: "Searching a memory set for a displayed item, performing mental arithmetic, and preparing responses to either task all require access to limited working memory processes and appear to be executed sequentially" (Ehrenstein et al., p. 795).

For control of cognition, the authors pit their findings (that the order of processing may be under the top-down or conscious control of the subjects) against a position that would argue that task-driven or bottom-up processes determine the order of processing. We, however, draw a more general conclusion; namely, that the order of low-level cognitive processes, even those that use the same cognitive resource, is not strictly determined by the physical task environment, but can be influenced by the functional one.

### Coordinating and Optimizing the Use of Mental and Motor Operations

Most of the research reviewed in this section has a strong mental or cognitive processing perspective. When motor movements or actions are considered at all, they are viewed primarily as a means of manipulating the cost of a cognitive process. In contrast, a primarily motor movement perspective is provided by Shin and Rosenbaum (2002) who constructed a "nested" aiming arithmetic task that required both perceptual–motor and cognitive processing. They argue that maximum performance in their task required that cognitive processes be coordinated with perceptual–motor ones. Their task required subjects to move a cursor to a small circle (about the size of a typical radio button) on one side of the screen that made task information pop up in an adjacent box. Subjects then were required to move the cursor to the other side of the screen into another small circle to access the next piece of information (which appeared in a box adjacent to that circle). On the first access, subjects saw a single digit. After the first access they saw an operand–operator pair that had to be summed with the current running total. For example, 6, − 2, + 4, −5, +1 would equal 4.

Subjects in this study might perform the task by accessing all information before doing any mental calculations. Shin and Rosenbaum (2002) demonstrated that this was not the case. They then argued that to minimize interference, subjects needed to compute a partial sum using the latest operator–operand pair before accessing the next operator–operand pair. However, subjects could meet this constraint in one of two major ways. They could complete all calculations at each step and then move in a strictly serial order (a calculate–aim strategy) or they could let the two processes run on in parallel. They demonstrated that subjects did not do these tasks in serial order, but did the two in parallel.

After concluding that (1) all information is not collected prior to any calculations and (2) the two tasks of calculate and aim are performed in parallel, Shin and

Rosenbaum (2002) then demonstrated that calculation took longer than aiming. This finding suggested that subjects must have adjusted the two processes so that both completed before the cursor entered the next small circle to access the next operator–operand pair. They then ruled out alternative explanations to show that in the nested aiming arithmetic task, movement times slowed down to accommodate the speed of calculations. This is an interesting finding because it once again suggests that low-level processes are being adjusted to meet the demands of a given task environment. Shin and Rosenbaum (2002) instructed their subjects on the basic procedures for doing the task but, unlike Ehrenstein and associates (1997), did not instruct subjects on how to order the subtasks (i.e., how to coordinate aiming and arithmetic). Hence, although it is not clear to what extent consciously adopted top-down strategies contributed to these results, it is clear that these adaptations show an exquisite sensitivity to the demands of the functional task environment.

### If Provided the Opportunity to Reduce Memory Load or to Control Scheduling, Can People Take It?

A difficulty in predicting goal-directed behavior is that, although mental processing can flexibly adapt to the physical task environment, when given a chance, humans will alter the physical task environment to reduce the amount of mental processing required. In the studies reviewed in this section, we see an active (if not necessarily deliberate or conscious) adaptation of the physical task environment to enable the use of interactive routines that minimize mental processing. In both directions, the adaptation of the mental to the physical task environment and the adaptation of the physical task environment to resource constraints, the adaptive processes that create the functional task environment act as if milliseconds matter.

An interesting example of this is provided by Kirlik's (in press) naturalistic investigation of short-order cooks, which found that experienced cooks utilized the two-dimensional layout of a grill to create a functional task environment that minimizes cognitive workload. The physical position and ordering of a steak on the grill provides the cooks with easy assessment and control of the hard-to-observe variable of doneness.

A similar example is provided by the investigation by Neth and others (Neth & Payne, 2001; Neth, 2004)

of people's spontaneous use of interactive routines and organizing activities for a mental arithmetic task. Neth (2004) first showed that adults are faster and more reliable when mentally adding numbers involving round results (such as 10, 20, 30) than numbers that do not add up to round sums. For example, if given the three-term problem $4 + 7 + 6$, efficient adders would ignore the serial order and add $4 + 6$ to produce 10 (the round intermediary sum), and then $10 + 7$ to produce the final sum of 17. Those trials during which round intermediate sums were used were generally faster and more accurate than those for which this strategy was not used.

In related work, Neth and Payne (2001) and Neth (2004) gave subjects long lists of single- and double-digit numbers to sum. Some groups were given access to simple tools like pointers (fingers or cursor) and pens. In general, people who could point at, mark, or move addends (on paper or on a computer screen) adapted their task environment in a variety of ways that increased their performance. Interestingly, the ways in which people used these simple tools varied as a function of their arithmetic expertise. Less expert adders used the paper and pencil to externalize memory for intermediate results and as an aid for performing calculations. In contrast, the better adders made fewer notes but marked off numbers as they were added to facilitate a nonserial adding strategy.

In a similar vein, Cary and Carlson (2001) studied the distribution of working memory demands over internal and external resources. Participants performed a multistep arithmetic task (unlike Neth's task 2004, the order of these steps was controlled by the experimenter) in which intermediate results were used as operands for subsequent operations. Subjects were encouraged to take notes as needed.

People's distribution and coordination of knowledge in the world versus knowledge in the head varied with experimental conditions. Conditions with a consistent goal structure presumably allowed for more reliable internal strategies and, as predicted by the experimenters, resulted in fewer notes. Likewise, increasing the perceptual–motor costs of note taking also reduced the number of notes—presumably reflecting a willingness to increase mental effort to avoid physical effort. Likewise, note taking decreased when the physical layout of the notes did not correspond to their temporal layout. In this case, keeping track of which note corresponded to which step seems

to have required an increase in mental effort (e.g., memory and visual attention) that offset the utility of note taking and increased the likelihood of in-the-head strategies. Finally, Cary and Carlson (2001) found that as people became more expert at the task, they labeled fewer intermediate steps and took fewer notes.

## Summary and Conclusions of Interactive Behavior Adaptations

Viewed as a whole, the studies in this section paint a consistent picture: People make adjustments in what they do as they do it. The statement that people tend to distribute working memory resources over internal and external resources seems almost trivially true. This makes it even more surprising how little we currently know about the exact principles and processes by which people spontaneously interact with their physical task environments and spontaneously adapt to situational cost–benefit constraints.

The demands that the functional task environment makes on human cognitive, perceptual, and action operations causes these operations to adapt to each other and to the functional task environment in ways that are defined by various interactive routines. Sometimes these adaptations result in a readjustment that is limited to cognition, perception, and action; other times these adaptations result in changes in the pattern of use of mental versus environmental resources; and sometimes an operator's actions adapt the environment itself, which then may lead to additional adaptations and changes.

Viewed at or below the unit task level, these adaptations do not resemble incremental increases in the speed with which a limited set of processes are executed, but constitute qualitative shifts in the interactive routines used to implement a given unit task. These qualitative shifts sometimes work in direct opposition to simple notions of "speed up with practice" as, for example, in the nested aiming arithmetic task (Shin & Rosenbaum, 2002) in which motor movements slow down to accommodate cognition operations. Likewise, although the swapping often recruits resources from in the world to replace those in the head, these swaps may be temporary. As Cary and Carlson (2001) showed, as experience with a task (especially one with a consistent goal structure) increases, the use of external resources (note taking) may decrease. In this case it seems as if external resources provide the mental equivalent of "water wings" that support the novice swimmer but, as skill increases, become a hindrance that is removed.

This close look at changes in interactive behavior at or below the unit task level has served to reveal a wide range of adaptations that seem to influence a wide range of higher level goals from serving telephone customers more efficiently (Gray et al., 1993), to the strategies selected for decision making (Lohse & Johnson, 1996), to influencing the nature of planning (O'Hara & Payne, 1998, 1999), to more efficient methods for doing simple arithmetic (Carlson & Sohn, 2000; Cary & Carlson, 2001; Shin & Rosenbaum, 2002; Sohn & Carlson, 1998), to simply following the experimenter's instructions (Ehrenstein et al., 1997). What has not emerged is any simple and consistent theory for predicting how the physical task environment affects the functional one or vice versa. Unlike the phenomena discussed in earlier sections (with the exception of the change blindness discussion), clear principles have not emerged that can guide us in identifying the key features in the functional task environment to which embodied cognition is adapting. (Although see Gray [in press] for some discussion of the emerging issues on this topic.)

## SUMMARY AND CONCLUSIONS

The determinants of human behavior are complex and are often obscured by naive or ill-informed assumptions about the nature of the task environment. It is insufficient to maintain that human behavior is governed by characteristics of the human organism and characteristics of the physical task environment. Instead, we must understand the functional task environment within which the human organism operates.

The twists and turns of the story presented in this chapter may seem very subtle. After offering a broad definition of the functional task environment in the section titled "Defining the Functional Task Environment," in "Adaptations over Time" we discussed the bottom half of Figure 8.1, which shows the functional task environment overlaying a subset of the physical one. This part of the figure represents adaptations to the physical task environment over evolutionary time. We reviewed recent evidence that suggests that perception was adapted to strike an optimal balance between the realities of using receptors that distinguish between two

dimensions in a three-dimensional world. We also considered evidence that suggested that the memory system functions to provide us with the fastest and most reliable access to those memories that we are most likely to need. We then reviewed evidence that shows that, contrary to our naive experience as well as to older theories of visual perception, we do not have access to a high-resolution representation of all that the eye perceives. Rather, we perceive the world through the knothole of the visual saccade and fixation. Representing an aspect of the visual world is not an automatic consequence of holding our eyes open, but requires moving the knothole to attend to that aspect.

These adaptations result in functional task environments that are so profoundly different from their physical task environments and so seamless that it has literally taken centuries for researchers to notice the discrepancies and provide explanations for how the functional task environment differs from the physical one. Indeed, change blindness is the most recent and arguably most profound discrepancy to be discovered between the physical and functional task environments. Although its pervasiveness has now been well documented, a satisfactory explanation for the factors controlling change blindness has not yet emerged.

As discussed in "Adaptations during the Individual Life Span," the top half of Figure 8.1 represents the contribution to the functional task environment by the cognitive, perceptual, and action elements of embodied cognition. Much of this part of the functional task environment is defined by normal processes with bounds that experimental psychology has been exploring for more than 100 years. However, modern research is showing that specializations of functional cognition emerge during an individual's life span throughout the months and years in which skilled practice takes place. Indeed, as the research by Polk and colleagues (2002) shows, these adaptations may result in specialization of the neural architecture.

The nodes and links in Figure 8.1 span the entire functional task environment: the part that overlies the physical task environment as well as the one that overlies the mental system. These nodes and links represent dynamic and temporary adjustments in the structure and performance of individual tasks. Certainly, much of interactive behavior requires the learning of new skills, such as when we learn how to drive a car, touch type, or rappel down a mountainside. However, although the scope of the changes discussed in the section titled "Adaptations That Support Interactive Behavior" was wide ranging, none of them seem to involve learning a new skill. Rather, all seemed to involve qualitative changes in how a unit task was implemented or how the physical task environment itself was structured. These qualitative adjustments seem exquisitely sensitive to the cost structure of the functional task environment or to the instructions of the experimenters.

The functional task environment is the playground of immediate behavior. Immediate behavior, when extended in time, is interactive behavior. Interactive behavior presumes a task environment within which behavior interacts. Behavior within a task environment is assumed to be goal directed. In a system with limited resources, it is necessary to use these resources efficiently to accomplish the goal at hand. An efficient use of resources may require restructuring the physical task environment to bring into play more efficient interactive routines.

## ACKNOWLEDGMENT

The writing of this chapter was supported by grants from the Air Force Office of Scientific Research (grant no. F49620-03-1-0143) as well as the Office of Naval Research (grant no. N000140310046).

## Notes

1. On the subject of making progress by avoiding environmental considerations, we refer the reader to the interesting discussion by Margaret Wilson (2002) on the discovery of the laws governing the properties of hydrogen.

2. We thank Alex Kirlik for pointing out various too-literal interpretations of our earlier descriptions of the functional task environment.

## References

Agre, P. E., & Shrager, J. (1990). Routine evolution as the microgenetic basis of skill acquisition. In *Twelfth annual conference of the Cognitive Science Society* (pp. 694–701). Hillsdale, N.J.: Lawrence Erlbaum Associates.

Anderson, J. R. (1990). *The adaptive character of thought.* Hillsdale, N.J.: Lawrence Erlbaum Associates.

———. (1991). Is human cognition adaptive? *Behavioral and Brain Sciences, 14*(3), 471–517.

———. (2000). *Cognitive psychology and its implications* (5th ed.). New York: Worth Publishers.

———, & Schooler, L. J. (1991). Reflections of the environment in memory. *Psychological Science, 2,* 396–408.

Ballard, D. H., Hayhoe, M. M., & Pelz, J. B. (1995). Memory representations in natural tasks. *Journal of Cognitive Neuroscience, 7*(1), 66–80.

———, Hayhoe, M. M., Pook, P. K., & Rao, R. P. N. (1997). Deictic codes for the embodiment of cognition. *Behavioral and Brain Sciences, 20*(4), 723–742.

Brunswik, E. (2001/1957). Scope and aspects of the cognitive problem. In K. R. Hammond & T. R. Stewart (Eds.), *The essential Brunswik: Beginnings, explications, applications* (pp. 300–312). New York: Oxford University Press.

Card, S. K., Moran, T. P., & Newell, A. (1983). *The psychology of human–computer interaction.* Hillsdale, N.J.: Lawrence Erlbaum Associates.

Carlson, R. A., & Sohn, M.-H. (2000). Cognitive control of multiple-step routines: Information processing and conscious intentions. In S. Monsell & J. Driver (Eds.), *Control of cognitive processes: Attention and performance XVIII* (pp. 443–464). Cambridge, Mass.: MIT Press.

Cary, M., & Carlson, R. A. (2001). Distributing working memory resources during problem solving. *Journal of Experimental Psychology — Learning Memory and Cognition, 27*(3), 836–848.

Ehrenstein, A., Schweickert, R., Choi, S., & Proctor, R. W. (1997). Scheduling processes in working memory: Instructions control the order of memory search and mental arithmetic. *Quarterly Journal of Experimental Psychology Section A—Human Experimental Psychology, 50*(4), 766–802.

Ericsson, K. A. (2003). Exceptional memorizers: Made, not born. *Trends in Cognitive Sciences, 7*(6), 233–235.

———, & Chase, W. G. (1982). Exceptional memory. *American Scientist, 70*(6), 607–615.

———, Chase, W. G., & Faloon, S. (1980). Acquisi-tion of a memory skill. *Science, 208*(4448), 1181–1182.

———, & Kintsch, W. (1995). Long-term working memory. *Psychological Review, 102*(2), 211–245.

Findlay, J. M., & Gilchrist, I. D. (2003). *Active vision: The psychology of looking and series.* New York: Oxford University Press.

Fitts, P. M., & Posner, M. I. (1967). *Human performance.* Belmont, CA: Brooks Cole.

Fu, W.-T., & Gray, W. D. (2004). Resolving the paradox of the active user: Stable suboptimal performance in interactive tasks. *Cognitive Science, 28*(6), 901–935.

———, & Gray, W. D. (2006). Suboptimal tradeoffs in information seeking. *Cognitive Psychology, 52*(3), 195–242.

Gigerenzer, G. (1996). On narrow norms and vague heuristics: Reply. *Psychological Review, 103*(3), 592–596.

———, & Todd, P. M. (Eds.). (1999). *Simple heuristics that make us smart.* New York: Oxford University Press.

Goldstein, D. G., & Gigerenzer, G. (1999). The recognition heuristic: How ignorance makes us smart. In G. Gigerenzer & P. M. Todd (Eds.), *Simple heuristics that make us smart*. New York: Oxford University Press.

Gray, W. D. (Ed.). (In press). *Integrated models of cognitive systems*. New York: Oxford University Press.

———, & Anderson, J. R. (1987). Change-episodes in coding: When and how do programmers change their code? In G. M. Olson, S. Sheppard, & E. Soloway (Eds.), *Empirical studies of programmers: Second workshop* (pp. 185–197). Norwood, N.J.: Ablex.

———, & Boehm-Davis, D. A. (2000). Milliseconds matter: An introduction to microstrategies and to their use in describing and predicting interactive behavior. *Journal of Experimental Psychology—Applied*, 6(4), 322–335.

———, & Fu, W. -T. (2004). Soft constraints in interactive behavior: The case of ignoring perfect knowledge in-the-world for imperfect knowledge in-the-head. *Cognitive Science*, 28(3), 359–382.

———, John, B. E., & Atwood, M. E. (1993). Project Ernestine: Validating a GOMS analysis for predicting and explaining real-world performance. *Human–Computer Interaction*, 8(3), 237–309.

———, & Orasanu, J. (1987). Transfer of learning: Contemporary research and applications. In: S. Cormier & J. Hagman (Eds.), *Transfer of training* (pp. 183–215). San Diego, Calif.: Academic Press.

———, Schoelles, M. J., & Sims, C. R. (2005). Adapting to the task environment: Explorations in expected value. *Cognitive Systems Research*, 6(1), 27–40.

Hayhoe, M. (2000). Vision using routines: A functional account of vision. *Visual Cognition*, 7(1–3), 43–64.

Howe, C. Q., & Purves, D. (2005a). Natural-scene geometry predicts the perception of angles and line orientation. *PNAS*, 102(4), 1228–1233.

———, & Purves, D. (2005b). The Muller–Lyer illusion explained by the statistics of image–source relationships. *PNAS*, 102(4), 1234–1239.

John, B. E. (1990). Extensions of GOMS analyses to expert performance requiring perception of dynamic visual and auditory information. In J. C. Chew & J. Whiteside (Eds.), *ACM CHI'90 conference on human factors in computing systems* (pp. 107–115). New York: ACM Press.

———, Rosenbloom, P. S., & Newell, A. (1985). A theory of stimulus–response compatibility applied to human–computer interaction. In L. Borman & B. Curtis (Eds.), *ACM CHI'85 conference on human factors in computing systems* (pp. 213–219). New York: ACM Press.

Kirlik, A. (In press). Ecological resources for modeling interactive cognition and behavior. In W. D. Gray (Ed.), *Integrated models of cognitive systems*. New York: Oxford University Press.

Kirwan, B., & Ainsworth, L. K. (Eds.). (1992). *A guide to task analysis*. Washington, D.C.: Taylor & Francis.

Levin, D. T., Momen, N., Drivdahl, S. B., & Simons, D. J. (2000). Change blindness blindness: The metacognitive error of overestimating change-detection ability. *Visual Cognition*, 7(1–3), 397–412.

Lohse, G. L. (1993). A cognitive model for understanding graphical perception. *Human–Computer Interaction*, 8(4), 353–388.

———, & Johnson, E. J. (1996). A comparison of two process tracing methods for choice tasks. *Organizational Behavior and Human Decision Processes*, 68(1), 28–43.

Maloney, L. T., Trommershäuser, J., & Landy, M. S. (In press). Questions without words: A comparison between decision making under risk and movement planning under risk. In W. D. Gray (Ed.), *Integrated models of cognitive systems*. New York: Oxford University Press.

Miller, G. A. (1956). The magical number 7, plus or minus 2: Some limits on our capacity for processing information. *Psychological Review*, 63(2), 81–97.

Mozer, M. C., Kinoshita, S., & Shettel, M. (In press). Sequential dependencies in human behavior offer insights into cognitive control. In W. D. Gray (Ed.), *Integrated models of cognitive systems*. New York: Oxford University Press.

Neth, H. (2004). *Thinking by doing: Interactive problem solving with internal and external representations*. Unpublished doctoral dissertation, Cardiff University, Wales, UK.

———, & Payne, S. J. (2001). Addition as interactive problem solving. In J. D. Moore & K. Stenning (Eds.), *Twenty-third annual conference of the Cognitive Science Society* (pp. 698–703). Hillsdale, N.J.: Lawrence Erlbaum Associates.

Newell, A., & Card, S. K. (1985). The prospects for psychological science in human–computer interaction. *Human–Computer Interaction*, 1(3), 209–242.

———, & Simon, H. A. (1972). *Human problem solving*. Englewood Cliffs, N.J.: Prentice-Hall.

———. (1982). *Steps toward a cognitive engineering: Design rules based on analyses of human error*. Presented at the 1982 conference Human Factors in Computing Systems. Gaithersburg, Md.

———. (1986). Cognitive engineering. In D. A. Norman & S. W. Draper (Eds.). *User centered system design: New perspectives on human–computer interaction* (pp. 31–61). Hillsdale, N.J.: Lawrence Erlbaum Associates.

———. (1989). *The design of everyday things*. New York: DoubleDay.

———, & Payne, S. J. (1998). The effects of operator implementation cost on planfulness of problem solving and learning. *Cognitive Psychology*, 35, 34–70.

O'Hara, K. P., & Payne, S. J. (1999). Planning and the user interface: The effects of lockout time and error recovery cost. *International Journal of Human–Computer Studies*, 50(1), 41–59.

Payne, S. J., & Green, T. R. G. (1986). Task-action grammars: A model of the mental representation of task languages. *Human–Computer Interaction*, 2(2), 93–133.

——, Squibb, H. R., & Howes, A. (1990). The nature of device models: The yoked state space hypothesis and some experiments with text editors. *Human–Computer Interaction, 5*(4), 415–444.

Polk, T. A., & Farah, M. J. (1995). Late experience alters vision. *Nature, 376*(6542), 648–649.

——, Stallcup, M., Aguirre, G. K., Alsop, D. C., D'Esposito, M., Detre, J. A., & Farah, M. J. (2002). Neural specialization for letter recognition. *Journal of Cognitive Neuroscience, 14*(2), 145–159.

Purves, D., & Lotto, R. B. (2003). *Why we see what we do: An empirical theory of vision.* Sunderland, Mass.: Sinauer.

——, Lotto, R. B., & Nundy, S. (2002). Why we see what we do: A probabilistic strategy based on past experience explains the remarkable difference between what we see and physical reality. *American Scientist, 90*(3), 236–243.

——, Lotto, R. B., Williams, S. M., Nundy, S., & Yang, Z. Y. (2001). Why we see things the way we do: Evidence for a wholly empirical strategy of vision. *Philosophical Transactions of the Royal Society of London Series B—Biological Sciences, 356*(1407), 285–297.

——, Williams, S. M., Nundy, S., & Lotto, R. B. (2004). Perceiving the intensity of light. *Psychological Review, 111*(1), 142–158.

Rensink, R. A. (2000). Visual search for change: A probe into the nature of attentional processing. *Visual Cognition, 7*(1–3), 345–376.

——. (2002). Change detection. *Annual Review of Psychology, 53*, 245–277.

——. (In press). The modeling and control of visual perception. In W. D. Gray (Ed.), *Integrated models of cognitive systems.* New York: Oxford University Press.

——, Oregan, J. K., & Clark, J. J. (1997). To see or not to see: The need for attention to perceive changes in scenes. *Psychological Science, 8*(5), 368–373.

Schooler, L. J., & Hertwig, R. (2005). How forgetting aids heuristic inference. *Psychological Review, 112*(3), 610–628.

Schweickert, R., Fisher, D. L., & Proctor, R. W. (2003). Steps toward building mathematical and computer models from cognitive task analyses. *Human Factors, 45*(1), 77–103.

Shepard, R. N. (1990). *Mind sights.* New York: Freeman.

Shin, J. C., & Rosenbaum, D. A. (2002). Reaching while calculating: Scheduling of cognitive and perceptual–motor processes. *Journal of Experimental Psychology-General, 131*(2), 206–219.

Simon, H. A. (1956). Rational choice and the structure of the environment. *Psychological Review, 63*, 129–138.

——. (1992). What is an "explanation" of behavior? *Psychological Science, 3*(3), 150–161.

——. (1996). *The sciences of the artificial* (3rd ed.). Cambridge, Mass.: MIT Press.

Simons, D. J., & Levin, D. T. (1998). Failure to detect changes to people during a real-world interaction. *Psychonomic Bulletin & Review, 5*(4), 644–649.

Sohn, M. H., & Carlson, R. A. (1998). Procedural frameworks for simple arithmetic skills. *Journal of Experimental Psychology—Learning Memory and Cognition, 24*(4), 1052–1067.

Todd, P. M., & Gigerenzer, G. (2000). Precis of simple heuristics that make us smart. *Behavioral & Brain Sciences, 23*(5), 727–780.

——, & Schooler, L. J. (In press). Disintegrated architectures of cognition: The adaptive toolbox for decision making. In: W. D. Gray (Ed.), *Integrated models of cognitive systems.* New York: Oxford University Press.

Treisman, A. M., & Gelade, G. (1980). A feature integration theory of attention. *Cognitive Psychology, 12*, 97–136.

Tversky, A., & Kahneman, D. (1974). Judgment under uncertainty: Heuristics and biases. *Science, 185*(4157), 1124–1131.

Wilson, M. (2002). Six views of embodied cognition. *Psychonomic Bulletin & Review, 9*(4), 625–636.

Yang, Z. Y., & Purves, D. (2003). Image/source statistics of surfaces in natural scenes. *Network-Computation in Neural Systems, 14*(3), 371–390.

# Part III

# Attention and Driving

# Chapter 9

# Multitasking in the Automobile

## *David L. Strayer and Frank A. Drews*

While often being reminded to pay full attention while driving an automobile, people regularly engage in a wide variety of multitasking activities when they are behind the wheel. Indeed, data from the 2000 US census indicates that drivers spend an average of 25.5 minutes each day commuting to work, and there is a growing interest in trying to make the time spent on the roadway more productive (Reschovsky, 2004).

Unfortunately, because of the inherent limited capacity of human attention (e.g., Kahneman, 1973; Navon & Gopher, 1979; Wickens, 1984), engaging in these multitasking activities often comes at a cost of diverting attention away from the primary task of driving. There are a number of more traditional sources of driver distraction. These "old standards" include talking to passengers, eating, drinking, lighting a cigarette, applying makeup, and listening to the radio (cf. Stutts, Feaganes, Rodman, Hamlet, Meadows, Rinfurt, Gish, Mercadante, & Staplin, 2003). However, during the last decade many new electronic devices were developed and are making their way into the vehicle. In many cases, these new technologies are engaging, interactive information delivery systems. For example, drivers can now surf the Internet, send and receive e-mail or faxes, communicate via cellular device, and even watch television. There is good reason to believe that some of these new multitasking activities may be substantially more distracting than the old standards because they are more cognitively engaging and because they are often performed over more sustained periods of time.

This chapter focuses on how driving is impacted by cellular communication, because this is one of the most prevalent exemplars of this new class of multitasking activity. Indeed, the National Highway Transportation Safety Administration estimates that that 8% of drivers on the roadway at any given daylight moment are using their cell phone (Glassbrenner, 2005). Here we summarize research from our laboratory that addresses four interrelated questions related to cell phone use while driving.

First, does cell phone use interfere with driving? There is ample anecdotal evidence suggesting that it does. However, multiple-resource models of dual-task performance (e.g., Wickens, 1984) have been inter-preted as suggesting that an auditory/verbal/vocal cell phone conversation may be performed concurrently with little or no cost with a visual/spatial/manual driving task (e.g., Strayer, Drews, & Johnston, 2003; but see Wickens, 1999). Unfortunately, there is only limited empirical evidence to answer the question definitively (Alm & Nilsson, 1995; Briem & Hedman, 1995; Brookhuis, De Vries, & De Waard, 1991; Brown, Tickner, & Simmonds, 1969; McCarley, Vais, Pringle, Kramer, Irwin, & Strayer, 2004; McKnight & McKnight, 1993; Redelmeier & Tibshirani, 1997; Strayer, Drews, & Johnston, 2003; Strayer & Johnston, 2001).

Second, if using a cell phone does interfere with driving, what are the bases of this interference? For example, how much of this interference can be attrib-uted to manual manipulation of the phone (e.g., dialing, holding the phone) and how much can be attributed to the cognitive demands placed on attention by the cell phone conversation itself? This question is of practical importance because if the interference is primarily the result of manual manipu-lation of the phone, then policies such as those enacted by New York state (chapter 69 of the Laws of 2001, section 1225c for the State of New York) discouraging drivers from using hand-held devices while permitting the use of hands-free units would be well grounded in science. On the other hand, if signif-icant interference is observed even when all the interference from manual manipulation of the cell phone has been eliminated, then these regulatory policies would not be supported by the scientific data.

Third, to the extent that the cell phone conversa-tion itself interferes with driving, what are the mec-hanisms underlying this interference? One possibility that we explore in this chapter is that the cell phone conversation causes a withdrawal of attention from the visual scene, yielding a form of inattention blindness (Rensink, Oregan, & Clark, 1997; Simons & Chabris, 1999). Finally, what is the real-world significance of the interference produced by concurrent cell phone use? That is, when controlling for frequency and duration of use, how do the risks compare with other activities commonly engaged in while driving? The benchmark that we use here is that of the driver who is intoxicated from ethanol at the legal limit (0.08 wt/vol). How do the impairments caused by cell phone conversations compare with this benchmark?

## EXPERIMENT 1

Our first study was an observational one designed to determine the effects of cell phone use on the per-formance of drivers using their own vehicle who were unaware that their behavior was being monitored.[1] By visual inspection, we observed more than 1,700 drivers to determine whether they were conversing on a cell phone and whether each driver came to a complete stop before entering a four-way intersection with stop signs for all directions of traffic. The resulting $2 \times 2$ contingency table permitted an assessment of the effects of cell phone use on real-world driving.

### Method

#### Participants

A total of 1,748 drivers were observed in naturalistic driving situations in the Avenues residential section of the Salt Lake City, Utah. Observations were made on six occasions for 1 hour on each occasion, between the hours of 5:00 PM and 6:00 PM. Two of the data col-lection sessions were on Mondays, two were on Wednesdays, and two were on Fridays. Drivers were not aware that they were being observed.

#### Stimuli and Apparatus

Three four-way intersections with stop signs in all directions of traffic were selected in the Avenues residential section of Salt Lake City, Utah. Each location was used twice in the study. The locations were (1) the intersection of E Street and 11th Avenue, (2) the intersection of I Street and 11th Avenue, and (3) the intersection of I Street and 3rd Avenue. The posted speed limit at all locations was 25 mph. Through-out the observation intervals, the driving conditions were good with normal daytime visibility.

#### Procedures

Observations were made by two research assistants. As each vehicle approached the intersection, the observers recorded whether the driver was using a cell phone. If the driver could be seen using a cell phone (i.e., a cell phone was held to the driver's ear), the driver was classified as using a cell phone. If a cell phone was not visibly in use at the time of observation, the driver was classified as not using a cell phone. In addition, the observers determined whether the driver came to a complete stop at the intersection. Based on definitions provided by the Salt Lake City Police Department, drivers were required to come to a complete stop at the white stop line painted across the intersection to be classified as stopping at the intersection. If the driver failed to stop at or before the white stop line, then the driver was classified as failing to stop at the intersection.

### Results and Discussion

Table 9.1 presents the data arranged in a 2 × 2 contingency table. Approximately 6% of our sample of drivers was using a cell phone at the time that they approached the intersection and approximately 24% of our sample of drivers failed to come to a complete stop at the intersection. However, it is clear that the ratio of drivers failing to stop at the intersection differed depending on whether they were using their cell phone. A logistic regression analysis was used to compare the differential rates of failure to stop at the intersection. For drivers not using a cell phone, the odds ratio for failing to stop at the intersection was 0.27, whereas for cell phone drivers the odds ratio was 2.93, a 10-fold increase in the odds ratio. The difference in odds ratios was significant ($\chi^2(1) = 129.8, P < .01$), providing clear evidence for impaired real-world driving when drivers are using their cell phone (see also Redelmeier & Tibshirani, 1997). Thus, these data provide clear-cut evidence that conversing on a cell phone significantly interferes with driving.

However, there are limitations to this observational study. Most notably, although the study established a strong association between cell phone use and failure to stop at intersections, it did not demonstrate a *causal link* between cell phone use and driving impairment. It is possible that self-selection factors underlie the association. For example, people who use their cell phone may be more likely to engage in risky behavior,

and this increase in risk taking may be the cause of the correlation. To understand better the causal relations between cell phone use and driving impairment, we now turn to a series of controlled laboratory studies using a high-fidelity driving simulator.

### EXPERIMENT 2

Experiment 1 found that cell phone drivers were more likely to fail to stop at a four-way intersection than were drivers who were driving without the distraction caused by cell phone use. One possible interpretation of these findings is that the cell phone conversation reduced the attention paid to information in the external environment. Our second study was designed to examine how cell phone conversations affect the driver's attention to objects that are encountered while driving. We contrasted performance when participants were driving but not conversing (single-task conditions) with that when participants were driving and conversing on a hands-free cell phone (dual-task conditions).

Our second experiment used a two-alternative forced-choice (2AFC) recognition memory paradigm to determine what information in the driving scene participants paid attention to while driving.[2] The procedure required participants to perform a simulated driving task without the foreknowledge that their memory for objects in the driving scene would be subsequently tested. Later, participants were given a surprise 2AFC recognition memory task in which they were shown objects that were encountered while they were driving and were asked to discriminate these objects from foils that were not in the driving scene. The difference between driving (i.e., single task) and the driving while conversing on a cell phone condition (i.e., dual task) provides an estimate of the degree to which attention to visual information in the driving environment is distracted by cell phone conversations.

### Method

#### Participants

Sixty-four undergraduates from the University of Utah participated in the experiment. All had normal or corrected-to-normal vision and a valid driver's license.

TABLE 9.1. Cell Frequencies for Experiment 1.

|  | Failed to Stop at Intersection | Stopped Properly at Intersection | Total |
|---|---|---|---|
| On Cell Phone | 82 | 28 | 110 |
| No Cell Phone | 352 | 1286 | 1838 |
| Total | 434 | 1314 | 1748 |

*Stimuli and Apparatus*

A PatrolSim high-fidelity fixed-base driving simulator, manufactured by GE I-Sim and illustrated in Figure 9.1, was used in the study. The simulator incorporates proprietary vehicle dynamics, traffic scenarios, and road surface software to provide realistic scenes and traffic conditions. The dashboard instrumentation, steering wheel, and gas and brake pedals were taken from a Ford Crown Victoria sedan with an automatic transmission.

The key manipulation in the study was the placement of 30 objects (e.g., cars, trucks, pedestrians, traffic signs, billboards, and so forth) along the roadway in the driving scene. Another 30 objects were not presented in the driving scene and served as foils in the 2AFC recognition memory task. The objects were counterbalanced across participants so that each was used equally often as a target and as a foil. Objects in the driving scene were positioned so that they were clearly in view as participants drove past them.

Eye movement data were recorded from 32 of the participants using an Applied Science Laboratories (ASL) eye and head tracker (model 501). The ASL mobile 501 eye tracker is a video-based unit that allows free range of head and eye movements, thereby affording naturalistic viewing conditions for the participants as they negotiated the driving environment.

*Procedure*

When participants arrived for the experiment, they completed a questionnaire that assessed their interest in potential topics of cell phone conversation. Participants were then familiarized with the driving simulator using a standardized 20-minute adaptation sequence. The experiment involved driving two 7-mile sections of an urban highway. One of the scenarios was used in the single-task (i.e., driving-only) condition and the other was used in the dual-task (i.e., driving and conversing on a cell phone) condition. The order of single-task and dual-task conditions and driving scenarios were counterbalanced across participants. The participant's task was to drive through each scenario following all the rules of the road.

FIGURE 9.1. A participant talking on a cell phone while driving in the GE I-SIM driving simulator.

The dual-task condition involved conversing on a cell phone with a research assistant. The participant and the research assistant discussed topics that were identified in the preexperimental questionnaire as being of interest to the participant. To avoid any possible interference from manual components of cell phone use, participants used a hands-free cell phone that was positioned and adjusted before driving began. Additionally, the call was initiated before participants began the dual-task scenarios. Thus, any dual-task interference that we observe must be the result of the cell phone conversation itself, because there was no manual manipulation of the cell phone during the dual-task portions of the study.

Immediately after the driving portion of the study, participants performed a 2AFC recognition memory task in which they attempted to identify which objects had been presented in the driving scenario. During each trial, two objects were presented on a computer display and remained in view until participants made their judgment (i.e., which of the two objects did they see while driving in the simulator?). After the forced-choice judgment, participants were also asked to rate the two objects in terms of their relevance to safe driving using a 10-point scale (participants were given an example in which a child playing near the road might receive a rating of 9 or 10 points, whereas a sign documenting that a volunteer group cleans a particular section of the highway might receive a rating of 1 point). There was no relationship between the order of presentation of the objects in the driving task and the order of presentation in the 2AFC recognition memory task. Participants were not informed about the memory test until after they had completed the driving portions of the experiment.

### Analysis

Eye-tracking data from 32 participants were analyzed to determine whether the participant fixated on each object. To ensure that the image had stabilized on the participants' retinas, we required the eyes to be directed at the center of the object for at least 100 msec for the object to be classified as having been fixated.

### Results and Discussion

Objects encountered during single-task conditions were correctly recognized more often than objects from dual-task conditions ($F(1,63) = 5.80$, $P < .05$). Corrected-for-guessing mean recognition probability for the single-task conditions was 0.21 (standard deviation [SD] $= 0.14$) and for the dual-task condition was 0.16 (SD $= 0.11$). These data are consistent with the hypothesis that the cell phone conversation disrupts performance by diverting attention from the external environment associated with the driving task to an engaging internal context associated with the cell phone conversation.

We next assessed whether the differences in recognition memory may be the result of differences in eye fixations on objects in the driving scene. The eye-tracking data indicated that participants fixated on approximately 61% of the objects in the driving scene. The difference in the probability of fixating on objects from single- to dual-task conditions was not significant ($F(1,31) = 0.78$, $P > .40$). Thus, the contribution of fixation probability on recognition memory performance would appear to be minimal. We also measured fixation duration during single- and dual-task conditions to ensure that the observed differences in recognition memory were not the result of longer fixation times during single-task conditions. There was a tendency for recognition probability to increase with fixation duration ($r = .14$); however, the difference in fixation duration between single- and dual-task conditions was not significant ($F(1, 31) = 1.63$, $P > .16$). As noted earlier, the differences in recognition memory performance that we observed in single- and dual-task conditions do not appear to be the result of alterations in visual scanning of the driving environment.

We also computed the conditional probability of recognizing an object given that participants fixated on it while driving. This analysis is important because it specifically tests for memory of objects that were presented where the driver's eyes were directed. The corrected-for-guessing conditional probability analysis revealed that participants were more likely to recognize objects encountered during the single-task condition (mean, 0.25; SD, 0.15) than in the dual-task condition (mean, 0.15; SD, 0.19; $F(1,31) = 5.28$, $P < .05$). Note that dual-task performance was 60% of that obtained during single-task conditions. Estimates of effect size (Cohen's d $= 0.58$) indicate that this is a medium-size effect. Thus, when we ensured that participants fixated on an object, we found significant differences in recognition memory between single- and dual-task conditions.

Our final analysis focused on participants' rating of each item's relevance in the driving scene in terms of traffic safety. Item relevance ratings ranged from 1.5 to 8 points and the overall rating of traffic relevance was $4.1 \pm 1.0$ points. As would be expected given the counterbalancing procedures, the difference in the rating of traffic relevance from single- to dual-task conditions was not significant $(F(1,31) = 0.93, P > .37)$. We conducted a series of regression analyses to determine the extent to which driving relevance affected recognition memory performance in single- and dual-task conditions. The correlation between recognition memory performance and traffic relevance was not significant $(r = .03)$ and remained unchanged when the variance associated with single- and dual-task conditions was partialed out. That is, traffic relevance had absolutely no effect on the difference in recognition memory between single- and dual-task conditions. This analysis is important because it demonstrates that participants did not strategically reallocate attention from the processing of less relevant information in the driving scene to the cell phone conversation while continuing to give highest priority to the processing of task-relevant information in the driving scene. In fact, the contribution of an object's perceived relevance to safe driving on recognition memory performance would appear to be negligible.

The results indicate that conversing on a cellular phone disrupts the driver's attention to the visual environment. Even when participants looked directly at objects in the driving scene, they were less likely to create a durable memory of those objects if they were conversing on a cell phone. Moreover, this pattern was obtained for objects of both high and low relevance, suggesting that very little semantic analysis of the objects occurs outside the focus of attention. McCarley and colleagues (2004) also reported that the cell phone conversations of younger adults disrupt the detection of change in complex driving scenes for items of both high and low relevance. These data provide strong support for the inattention blindness hypothesis in which the disruptive effects of cell phone conversations on driving are due, in large part, to the diversion of attention from driving to the phone conversation. We suggest that even when participants are directing their gaze at objects in the driving environment, that they may fail to "see" them their because attention is directed internally to the phone conversation.

## EXPERIMENT 3

The differences between single- and dual-task recognition memory performance in experiment 2 are consistent with the inattention blindness hypothesis in which cell phone conversations interfere with the initial encoding of the objects in the driving scene. However, an alternative possibility is that there were no differences in the initial encoding, but that there were differences in the retrieval of the information during the recognition memory test. This distinction is more than academic because the former has direct implications for traffic safety whereas the latter does not (i.e., failing to recognize an item at a later point in time does not necessarily imply an impairment in encoding and reaction to an object in the driving environment).

The purpose of experiment 3 was to test further the inattention blindness hypothesis by recording online measures of brain activity elicited by events in the driving environment.[3] Prior research has found that the amplitude of the P300 component of brain event-related potential (ERP) is sensitive to the attention allocated to a task (e.g., Sirevaag, Kramer, Coles, & Donchin, 1989; Wickens, Kramer, Vanasse, & Donchin, 1983) and, furthermore, that memory performance is superior for objects eliciting larger amplitude P300s during encoding (e.g., Fabiani, Karis, & Donchin, 1986; Otton & Donchin, 2000). Moreover, Kramer and associates (1987; see also Sirevaag, Kramer, Wickens, Reisweber, Strayer, & Grenell, 1993) measured ERPs in a flight simulator and found that the P300 component of the ERP discriminated among levels of task difficulty, decreasing as the task demands increased. If the impairments in recognition memory performance observed in experiment 2 are the result of differences in the initial encoding of objects in the driving scene, we predict that P300 amplitude will be smaller during dual-task conditions than single-task conditions. By contrast, if the recognition memory differences observed in experiment 2 are the result of impaired retrieval of information at the time of the recognition memory test but not at the time of encoding, then we would not expect to find differences in P300 amplitude between single- and dual-task conditions.

We used a car-following paradigm (see also Alm & Nilsson, 1995; Strayer et al., 2003) in which participants drove on a multilane freeway in single-task (i.e., driving only) and dual-task (i.e., driving and conversing on a cell phone) conditions. Participants followed a pace car that would brake at random intervals, and ERPs were time locked to the onset of the pace car brake lights during both single- and dual-task conditions. Do cell phone conversations suppress the traffic-related brain activity as predicted by the inattention blindness hypothesis?

## Method

### Participants

Thirty-two undergraduates, recruited as friend dyads from the University of Utah, participated in this study. One participant out of each dyad was randomly selected to be the driver and the other was selected to be the conversing partner. All had normal or corrected-to-normal visual acuity and a valid driver's license.

### Stimuli and Apparatus

The PatrolSim high-fidelity driving simulator used in experiment 2 was also used in the current study. A freeway road database simulated a 24-mile multi-lane beltway with on and off ramps, overpasses, and two- and three-lane traffic in each direction. A pace car, programmed to travel in the right-hand lane, braked intermittently throughout the scenario. Distractor vehicles were programmed to drive between 5% and 10% faster than the pace car in the left lane, providing the impression of a steady flow of traffic. Unique driving scenarios, counterbalanced across participants, were used for each condition in the study.

Electroencephalographic (EEG) activity, time locked to the onset of the pace car brake lights, was recorded from three midline sites (Fz, Cz, and Pz, according to the International 10-20 System) (Jasper, 1958). Bipolar vertical and horizontal electroculo-graphic (EOG) activity was simultaneously recorded to ensure that eye movements did not contaminate the EEG records. MED 10-mm diameter Ag/AgCl biopotential electrodes were used at all electrode sites, and electrode impedance did not exceed 10 k$\Omega$. EEG and EOG signals were amplified with a Grass model 12 Neurodata Acquisition System. Both EEG and EOG data were sampled every 2 msec and the digitized data were stored on disk for subsequent analysis. EOG artifacts were corrected off-line using the procedure described by Gratton and coworkers (1983).

### Procedure

When participants arrived for the experiment, they completed a questionnaire assessing their interest in potential topics of cell phone conversation. Participants were then familiarized with the driving simulator using a standardized 20-minute adaptation sequence. Participants then drove four 10-mile sections on a multilane highway. Half the scenarios were used in the single-task driving condition and half were used in the dual-task (i.e., driving and cell phone conversation) condition. The order of conditions and scenarios was counterbalanced across participants using a Latin square design, with the constraint that both single- and dual-task conditions were performed during the first half of the experiment and both single- and dual-task conditions were performed during the last half of the experiment.

The participant's task was to follow a pace car that was driving in the right-hand lane of the highway. When the participant stepped on the brake pedal in response to the braking pace car, the pace car released its brake and accelerated to normal highway speed. If the participant failed to depress the brake, they would eventually collide with the pace car. That is, like real highway stop-and-go traffic, the participant was required to react in a timely and appropriate manner to vehicles slowing in front of them.

The dual-task condition involved conversing on a cell phone with the driver's friend. The driver and friend discussed topics that were identified during the preexperimental questionnaire as being of interest to both parties (cf. Drews, Pasupathi, & Strayer, 2004). To avoid any possible interference from manual components of cell phone use, participants used a hands-free cell phone that was positioned and adjusted before driving began. Additionally, the call was initiated before participants began the dual-task scenarios. As before, any dual-task interference that we observe must therefore be the result of the cell phone conversation itself, because there was no manual manipulation of the cell phone during the dual-task portions of the study.

## Results and Discussion

The average ERPs recorded at the parietal electrode site are presented in Figure 9.2. In the figure, the solid line represents ERPs recorded during the single-task condition and the dotted line represents the ERPs

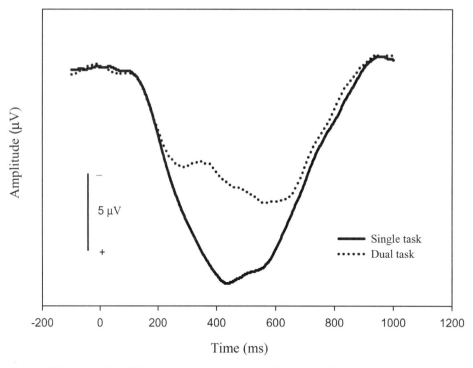

FIGURE 9.2. Event-related brain potentials elicited by the onset of the pace car brake light in experiment 3 (recorded at Pz).

recorded during the dual-task condition. Inspection of the figure reveals a large positive potential between 250 msec and 750 msec (the P300 component of the ERP). It is evident that the P300 component of the ERPs is larger during single- than dual-task conditions. P300 amplitude was quantified by computing the area under the curve between 250 msec and 750 msec poststimulus onset for each subject/condition. A correlated $t$-test indicated that the difference between single- and dual-task conditions was significant ($t(15) = 4.41$, $P < .01$). Estimates of effect size (Cohen's d = 0.46) indicate that this is a medium-size effect.

We also measured the peak latency of the P300 component, because this has been taken as an index of the time for stimulus evaluation processes largely uncontaminated by response mechanisms (e.g., Kutas, McCarthy, & Donchin, 1977; Magliero, Bashore, Coles, & Donchin, 1984; McCarthy & Donchin, 1981). The peak latency of the P300, estimated using a single-trial peak picking algorithm (Fabiani, Gratton, Karis, & Donchin, 1988), was greater during dual- than single-task conditions ($t(15) = 6.32$, $P < .01$). Estimates of effect size

(Cohen's d = 0.89) indicate that this is a large-size effect. The delay in P300 latency during dual-task conditions provides good evidence that the initial processing of information necessary for the safe operation of a motor vehicle is impaired when drivers were conversing on a cell phone (i.e., these differences cannot be attributed to differences in response criteria during single- and dual-task conditions).

The reduced P300 amplitude in dual-task conditions provides strong evidence for the inattention blindness hypothesis. In particular, the data support an interpretation in which the initial encoding of information in the driving environment is interfered with by the cell phone conversation. In experiment 2 we suggested that cell phone drivers looked but often failed to see objects in the driving environment. The ERP data further indicate that when drivers converse on a cell phone, the brain activity associated with processing information necessary for the safe operation of a motor vehicle is suppressed. Thus, drivers using a cell phone fail to see information in the driving scene because they do not encode it as well as they do when they are not distracted by the cell phone conversation. In situations when the driver is required to react with alacrity, these data suggest that those using a cell phone will be less able to do so because of the diversion of attention from driving to the phone conversation.

## EXPERIMENT 4

Our fourth study was designed to evaluate the real-world risks associated with conversing on a cell phone while driving.[4] One way to evaluate these risks is by comparison with other activities commonly engaged in while driving (e.g., listening to the radio, talking to a passenger in the car, and so forth). The benchmark that we used in our final study was driving while intoxicated from ethanol at the legal limit (0.08 wt/vol). We selected this benchmark because there are well-established societal norms and laws regarding drinking and driving. Indeed, the World Health Organization recommended that the behavioral effects of an activity should be compared with alcohol under the assumption that performance should be no worse than when operating a motor vehicle at the legal limit (Willette & Walsh, 1983). How does conversing on a cell phone compare with the drunk driving benchmark?

Redelmeier and Tibshirani (1997) used an epidemiological approach and concluded that "the relative risk [of being in a traffic accident while using a cell phone] is similar to the hazard associated with driving with a blood alcohol level at the legal limit" (p. 465). If this finding can be substantiated in a controlled laboratory experiment, then these data would be of immense importance for public safety. Here we directly compared the performance of drivers who were conversing on a cell phone with the performance of drivers who were legally intoxicated with ethanol. We used the car-following paradigm described in experiment 3. Three conditions were studied: single-task driving (baseline condition), driving while conversing on a cell phone (cell phone condition), and driving with a blood alcohol concentration of 0.08 wt/vol (alcohol condition).

## Method

### Participants

Forty adults, recruited via advertisements in local newspapers, participated in the study. All had normal or corrected-to-normal vision and a valid driver's license.

A further requirement for inclusion in the study was that participants were social drinkers, consuming between three to five alcoholic drinks per week. The experiment lasted approximately 10 hours (across the 3 days of the study) and participants were remunerated at a rate of $10 per hour.

### Stimuli and Apparatus

The PatrolSim high-fidelity driving simulator used in experiment 2 was used in the current study. Measures of real-time driving performance, including driving speed, distance from other vehicles, and brake inputs, were sampled at 30 Hz and stored for later analysis. Blood alcohol concentration levels were measured using an Intoxilyzer 5000, manufactured by CMI Inc.

### Procedure

The experiment was conducted in three sessions on different days. The first session familiarized participants with the driving simulator using a standardized adaptation sequence. The order of subsequent alcohol and cell phone sessions was counterbalanced across participants. In these latter sessions, the participant's task was to follow the intermittently braking pace car driving in the right-hand lane of the highway.

During the alcohol session, participants drank a mixture of orange juice and vodka (40% alcohol by volume) calculated to achieve a blood alcohol concentration of 0.08 wt/vol. Blood alcohol concentrations were verified using infrared spectrometry breath analysis immediately before and after the alcohol driving condition. Participants drove in the 15-minute car-following scenario while legally intoxicated. Average blood alcohol concentration before driving was 0.081 wt/vol and after driving was 0.078 wt/vol.

During the cell phone session, three counterbalanced conditions, each 15 minutes in duration, were included: single-task baseline driving, driving while conversing on a hand-held cell phone, and driving while conversing on a hands-free cell phone. During both cell phone conditions, the participant and a research assistant engaged in naturalistic conversations on topics that were identified on the first day as being of interest to the participant. The task of the research assistant in our study was to maintain a dialogue in which the participant listened and spoke in approximately equal proportions. To minimize interference from manual components of cell phone use, the call was initiated before participants began driving.

## Results and Discussion

Table 9.2 presents the nine performance variables that were measured to determine how participants reacted to the vehicle braking in front of them. *Brake reaction time* is the time interval between the onset of the pace car's brake lights and the onset of the participant's braking response (i.e., defined as a minimum of 1% depression of the participant's brake pedal). *Braking force* is the maximum force that the participant applied to the brake pedal in response to the braking pace car (expressed as a percentage of maximum). *Speed* is the average driving speed of the participant's vehicle (expressed in miles per hour). *Mean following distance* is the distance prior to braking between the rear bumper of the pace car and the front bumper of the participant's car. *SD following distance* is the standard deviation of following distance. *Time to collision (TTC)*, measured at the onset of the participant's braking response, is the time that remains until a collision between the participant's vehicle and the pace car if the course and speed were maintained (i.e., had the participant failed to brake). Also reported are the frequency of trials with TTC values less than 4 seconds, a level found to discriminate between cases in which drivers find themselves in dangerous situations from cases in which the driver remains in control of the vehicle (e.g., Hirst & Graham, 1997). *Half recovery time* is the time for participants to recover 50% of the speed that was lost during braking (e.g., if the participant's car was traveling at 60 mph before braking and decelerated to 40 mph after braking, then the half recovery time would be time taken for the participant's vehicle to return to 50 mph). Also shown in Table 9.2 is the total number of collisions in each phase of the study. We used a multivariate analysis of variance (MANOVA) followed by planned contrasts to provide an overall assessment of driver performance during each of the experimental conditions.

We performed an initial comparison of driving while using a hand-held versus hands-free cell phone. Both hand-held and hands-free cell-phone conversations impaired driving. However, there were no significant differences in the impairments caused by these two modes of cellular communication (all, $P > .25$). Therefore, we collapsed across the hand-held and hands-free conditions for all subsequent analyses reported in this chapter. The observed similarity between hand-held and hands-free cell phone conversations is consistent with earlier work (e.g., Mazzae, Ranney, Watson, & Wightman, 2004; Patten, Kircher, Ostlund, & Nilsson, 2004; Redelmeier & Tibshirani, 1997; Strayer & Johnston, 2001) and calls into question driving regulations that prohibit hand-held cell phones and permit hands-free cell phones.

MANOVAs indicated that both cell phone and alcohol conditions differed significantly from baseline ($F(8,32) = 6.26, P < .01$ and $F(8,32) = 2.73, P < .05$, respectively). When drivers were conversing on a cell phone, they were involved in more rear-end collisions, their initial reaction to vehicles braking in front of them was slowed by 9%, and the variability in following distance increased by 24%, relative to baseline. In addition, compared with baseline, it took participants who were talking on a cell phone 19% longer to recover the speed that was lost during braking.

TABLE 9.2. Means and Standard Errors (in parentheses) for the Alcohol, Baseline, and Cell-Phone Conditions of Experiment 4.

|  | Alcohol | Baseline | Cell Phone |
|---|---|---|---|
| Total Accidents | 0 | 0 | 3 |
| Brake Reaction Time, msec | 779 (33) | 777 (33) | 849 (36) |
| Maximum Braking Force | 69.8 (3.7) | 56.7 (2.6) | 55.5 (3.0) |
| Speed, mph | 52.8 (2.0) | 55.5 (0.7) | 53.8 (1.3) |
| Mean Following Distance, m | 26.0 (1.7) | 27.4 (1.3) | 28.4 (1.7) |
| SD Following Distance, m | 10.3 (0.6) | 9.5 (0.5) | 11.8 (0.8) |
| Time to Collision, seconds | 8.0 (0.4) | 8.5 (0.3) | 8.1 (0.4) |
| Time to Collision < 4 seconds | 3.0 (0.7) | 1.5 (0.3) | 1.9 (0.5) |
| Half Recovery Time, seconds | 5.4 (0.3) | 5.3 (0.3) | 6.3 (0.4) |

By contrast, when participants were intoxicated, neither accident rates, nor reaction time to vehicles braking in front of the participant, nor recovery of lost speed after braking differed significantly from baseline. Overall, drivers in the alcohol condition exhibited a more aggressive driving style. They followed closer to the pace vehicle, had twice as many trials with TTC values less than 4 seconds, and braked with 23% more force than in baseline conditions. More important, our study found that accident rates during the alcohol condition did not differ from baseline; however, the increase in hard braking and the increased frequency of TTC values less than 4 seconds are predictive of increased accident rates over the long run (e.g., Brown, Lee, & McGehee, 2001; Hirst & Graham, 1997).

The MANOVA also indicated that the cell phone and alcohol conditions differed significantly from each other ($F(8,32) = 4.06$, $P < .01$). When drivers were conversing on a cell phone, they were involved in more rear-end collisions and took longer to recover the speed that they had lost during braking than when they were intoxicated. Drivers in the alcohol condition also applied greater braking pressure than drivers in the cell phone condition.

Finally, the accident data were analyzed using a nonparametric chi-squared statistical test. The chi-squared analysis indicated that there were significantly more accidents when participants were conversing on a cell phone than during the baseline or alcohol conditions ($\chi^2(2) = 6.15$, $P < .05$).

Taken together, we found that both intoxicated drivers and cell phone drivers performed differently from baseline and that the driving profiles of these two conditions differed. Drivers using a cell phone exhibited a delay in their response to events in the driving scenario and were more likely to be involved in a traffic accident. Drivers in the alcohol condition exhibited a more aggressive driving style, following closer to the vehicle immediately in front of them, necessitating braking with greater force. With respect to traffic safety, the data suggest that the impairments associated with cell phone drivers may be as great as those commonly observed with intoxicated drivers.

## CONCLUSIONS

Cell phone conversations alter how drivers perceive and react to information in the driving environment. We found cell phone drivers were more likely to fail to stop at four-way intersections and more likely to be involved in rear-end collisions than drivers not using a cell phone. In fact, even when cell phone drivers were directing their gaze at objects in the driving environment they often failed to see them because attention was directed elsewhere. Moreover, we found that cell phone conversations suppress the ERPs elicited by traffic-related information. We suggest that talking on a cell phone creates a form of inattention blindness, muting driver's awareness of important information in the driving scene.

We also compared hand-held and hands-free cell phones and found that the impairments to driving are identical for these two modes of communication. There was no evidence that hands-free cell phones were any safer to use while driving than hand-held devices. In fact, we consistently found significant interference even when we removed any possible interference from manual components of cell phone use (e.g., by having drivers place a call on a hands-free cell phone that was positioned and adjusted before driving began). Although there is good evidence that manual manipulation of equipment (e.g., dialing the phone, answering the phone, and so forth) has a negative impact on driving (Mazzae et al., 2004), the distracting effects of cell phone conversation persist even when these manual sources are removed. Moreover, the duration of a typical phone conversation is often significantly greater than the time required to dial or answer the phone. Thus, these data call into question driving regulations that prohibit hand-held cell phones and permit hands-free devices, because no differences were found in the impairments caused by these two modes of cellular communication.

Finally, what is the real-world risk associated with using a cell phone while driving? An important epidemiological study by Redelmeier and Tibshirani (1997) found that cell phone use was associated with a fourfold increase in the likelihood of getting into an accident, and that this increased risk was comparable with that observed when driving with a blood alcohol level at the legal limit. Our simulator-based research controlling for time on task and driving conditions found that driving performance was more impaired when drivers were conversing on a cell phone than when these same drivers were intoxicated at 0.08 wt/vol. Taken together, these observations provide clear-cut evidence indicating that driving while conversing on a either a hand-held or hands-free cell phone poses significant risks both to the driver and to the general public.

## Notes

1. We thank Henrik Burns and Kyle Strayer for collecting the data reported in experiment 1.

2. We acknowledge Joel Cooper's assistance in collecting the data reported in experiment 2.

3. We thank Mandi Martinez for assistance in collecting the data reported in experiment 3.

4. We thank Amy Alleman, Joel Cooper, and Danica Nelson for collecting the data reported in experiment 4.

## References

Alm, H., & Nilsson, L. (1995). The effects of a mobile telephone task on driver behaviour in a car following situation. *Accident Analysis & Prevention*, 27(5), 707–715.

Briem, V., & Hedman, L. R. (1995). Behavioural effects of mobile telephone use during simulated driving. *Ergonomics*, 38(12), 2536–2562.

Brookhuis, K. A., De Vries, G., & De Waard, D. (1991). The effects of mobile telephoning on driving performance. *Accident Analysis & Prevention*, 23, 309–316.

Brown, T. L., Lee, J. D., & McGehee, D. V. (2001). Human performance models and rear-end collision avoidance algorithms. *Human Factors*, 43, 462–482.

Brown, I. D., Tickner, A. H., & Simmonds, D. C. V. (1969). Interference between concurrent tasks of driving and telephoning. *Journal of Applied Psychology*, 53(5), 419–424.

Drews, F. A., Pasupathi, M., & Strayer, D. L. (2004). Passenger and cell-phone conversations in simulated driving. In *Proceedings of the 48th annual meeting of the Human Factors and Ergonomics Society* (pp. 2210–2212). Santa Monica, Calif.: Human Factors and Ergonomics Society.

Fabiani, M., Gratton, G., Karis, D., & Donchin, E. (1988). The definition, identification, and reliability of measurement of the P300 component of the event-related brain potential. In P. K. Ackles, J. R. Jennings, & M. G. Coles (Eds.), *Advances in psychophysiology* (vol. 2, pp. 1–78). Guilford, Conn.: JAI Press.

———, Karis, D., & Donchin, E. (1986). P300 and recall in an incidental memory paradigm. *Psychophysiology*, 23, 298–308.

Glassbrenner, D. (2005). Driver cell phone use in 2004: Overall results. In *Traffic safety facts*. Research note (DOT HS 809 847). Available: http://www-nrd.nhtsa.dot.gov/pdf/nrd-30/NCSA/RNotes/2005/809847.pdf

Gratton, G., Coles, M. G. H., & Donchin, E. (1983). A new method for off-line removal of ocular artifact. *Electroencephalography and Clinical Neurophysiology*, 55, 486–484.

Hirst, S., & Graham, R. (1997). The format and presentation of collision warnings. In Y. I. Noy, (Ed.), *Ergonomics and safety of intelligent driver interfaces* (pp. 202–219). Mahwah, N.J.: Lawrence Erlbaum.

Jasper, H. H. (1958). The ten-twenty electrode system of the international federation. *Electroencephalography and Clinical Neurophysiology*, 10, 371–375.

Kahneman, D. (1973). *Attention and effort*. Englewood Cliffs, N.J.: Prentice Hall.

Kramer, A. F., Sirevaag, E. J., & Braun, R. (1987). A psychophysiological assessment of operator workload during simulated flight missions. *Human Factors*, 29, 145–160.

Kutas, M., McCarthy, G., & Donchin, E. (1977). Augmenting mental chronometry: The P300 as a measure of stimulus evaluation time. *Science*, 197, 792–795.

Magliero, A., Bashore, T. R., Coles, M. G. H., & Donchin, E. (1984). On the dependence of P300 latency on stimulus evaluation processes. *Psychophysiology*, 21, 171–186.

Mazzae, E. N., Ranney, T. A., Watson, G. S., & Wightman, J. A. (2004). Hand-held or hands-free? The effects of wireless phone interface type on phone task performance and driver performance. In *Proceedings of the 48th annual meeting of the Human Factors and Ergonomics Society* (pp. 2218–2221). Santa Monica, Calif.: Human Factors and Ergonomics Society.

McCarley, J. S., Vais, M., Pringle, H., Kramer, A. F., Irwin, D. E., & Strayer, D. L. (2004). Conversation disrupts scanning and change detection in complex visual scenes. *Human Factors*, 46, 424–436.

McCarthy, G., & Donchin, E. (1981). A metric for thought: A comparison of P300 latency and reaction time. *Science*, 211, 77–80.

McKnight, A. J., & McKnight, A. S. (1993). The effect of cellular phone use upon driver attention. *Accident Analysis & Prevention*, 25(3), 259–265.

Navon, D., & Gopher, D. (1979). On the economy of the human processing system. *Psychological Review*, 86, 214–255.

Otton, L. J., & Donchin, E. (2000). Relationship between P300 amplitude and subsequent recall for distinctive events: Dependence on type of distinctiveness attribute. *Psychophysiology*, 37, 644–661.

Patten, C. J. D., Kircher, A., Ostlund, J., & Nilsson, L. (2004). Using mobile telephones: Cognitive workload and attention resource allocation. *Accident Analysis and Prevention*, 36, 341–350.

Redelmeier, D. A., & Tibshirani, R. J. (1997) Association between cellular-telephone calls and motor vehicle collisions. *The New England Journal of Medicine*, 336, 453–458.

Reschovsky, C. (2004). *Journey to work: 2000, census 2000 brief*. Issued March 2004. [Online]. Available: www.census.gov/prod/2004pubs/c2kbr-33.pdf

Rensink, R. A., Oregan, J. K., & Clark, J. J. (1997). To see or not see: The need for attention to perceive changes in scenes. *Psychological Sciences*, 8, 368–373.

Simons, D. J., & Chabris, C. F. (1999). Gorillas in our midst: Sustained inattentional blindness for dynamic events. *Perception, 28,* 1059–1074.

Sirevaag, E. J., Kramer, A. F., Coles, M. G. H., & Donchin, E. (1989). Recourse reciprocity: An event-related brain potential analysis. *Acta Psychologia, 70,* 77–97.

Sirevaag, E. J., Kramer, A. F., Wickens, C. D., Reisweber, M., Strayer, D. L., & Grenell, J. H. (1993). Assessment of pilot performance and mental workload in rotary wing aircraft. *Ergonomics, 9,* 1121–1140.

Strayer, D. L., Drews, F. A., & Johnston, W. A. (2003). Cell phone induced failures of visual attention during simulated driving. *Journal of Experimental Psychology: Applied, 9,* 23–52.

———, & Johnston, W. A. (2001). Driven to distraction: Dual-task studies of simulated driving and conversing on a cellular phone. *Psychological Science, 12,* 462–466.

Stutts, J., Feaganes, J., Rodman, E., Hamlet, C., Meadows, T., Rinfurt, D., Gish, K., Mercadante, M., & Staplin, L. (2003). *Distractions in everyday driving.* AAA Foundation for Traffic Safety. [Online]. Available: www.aaafoundation.org/pdf/Distractions InEverydayDriving.pdf

Wickens, C. D. (1984). Processing resources in attention. In R. Parasuraman & R. Davies (Eds.), *Varieties of attention* (pp. 63–101). New York: Academic Press.

———. (1999). Letter to the editor. *Transportation Human Factors, 1,* 205–206.

———, Kramer, A. F., Vanasse, L., & Donchin, E. (1983). Performance of concurrent tasks: A psychophysiological assessment of the reciprocity of information-processing resources. *Science, 221,* 1080–1082.

Willette, R. E., & Walsh, J. M. (1983). *Drugs, driving, and traffic safety.* Publication no. 78. Geneva: World Health Organization.

# Chapter 10

# Novice Driver Crashes: Failure to Divide Attention or Failure to Recognize Risks

## Donald L. Fisher and Alexander Pollatsek

### THE PROBLEM

The fatality rate per 100 million vehicle miles among 16-year-old novice drivers is almost eight times higher than it is among the safest cohort of drivers, those with their driver's license for 20 years or more (Insurance Institute for Highway Safety, 2002). In 2002, a total of 2,730 16-year-olds died in automobile crashes (National Center for Statistics and Analysis, 2004). Perhaps more disturbing is the fact that the number of 16-year-olds per 100,000 licensed drivers in fatal crashes has remained constant during the last 10 years—the period of time during which the graduated licensing program (typically consisting of three stages: learner's permit, restricted licensure, and full licensure) has been introduced into almost all states. In particular, for 16-year-old licensed drivers, there were 73 fatal crashes per 100,000 drivers in 1993 and 74 fatal crashes per 100,000 drivers in 2003 (Insurance Institute for Highway Safety, 2005).

We asked ourselves whether there was anything that we, as cognitive psychologists interested in attention

and perception, could do to reduce this rate. Clearly, any serious attempt at remediation requires that one understand something about the types of behaviors that lead to crashes and what it is about driving that leads to such behaviors for the novice. A number of studies, both those using crash data in the field and those using eye movement data in the field and in the lab, point to inadequate search for potential risks as a major problem for the novice driver. There are many possible reasons why searching for potential risks might not be a trivial skill. We take as our starting point multiple-resource theory (Wickens, 1984). Perhaps problems occur for novice drivers that do not occur for more experienced drivers because experienced drivers can better divide their attention between the vehicle control task and the search and risk prediction tasks. For example, it may be that more experienced drivers have automated the vehicle control task whereas for novice drivers this remains a more attention-demanding task. There are other variants of what we refer to globally as the *divided attention hypothesis*; which are discussed later.

One possible way to test the divided attention hypothesis would be to give novice drivers training that increases their knowledge of risks, but does not teach them explicitly how to time-share these with vehicle control processes that should be executed in parallel to be maximally effective. If inadequacies in attention management rather than failures of knowledge were entirely responsible for novice drivers' crashes, then there should be no change in their behaviors in risky situations after risk awareness training. Surprisingly, the results from studies on a driving simulator are inconsistent with the divided attention hypothesis (Pollatsek, Narayanaan, Pradhan, & Fisher, 2006; Pradhan, Hammel, DeRamus, Pollatsek, Noyce, & Fisher, 2005b). They suggest that failures of knowledge contribute substantially to crashes among novice drivers (discussed later). The results are consistent with what we refer to as the *knowledge hypothesis*. (Note that we realize that knowledge of the risky elements in a scenario is useless unless the driver attends to those elements. We elaborate more fully on what we consider to be the differences between the knowledge hypothesis and the set of possible attentional hypotheses later in the chapter.)

In these studies examining the knowledge hypothesis, drivers were trained using schematic (top-down) *plan views* of risky scenarios that were displayed on a personal computer (PC; Fig. 10.1). In the training, they were instructed to indicate where potential risks might arise in these plan views, and then were given feedback on where those potential risks might appear (such as a pedestrian emerging from behind a parked truck). Improvement in performance in the simulator

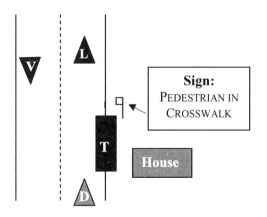

FIGURE 10.1. Truck crosswalk scenario: plan view. (T: truck parked on the side; L: lead vehicle; V: vehicle in opposing lane. D: participant's vehicle.)

resulting from the PC training was not likely to be the result of low-level pattern matching, because the participants only saw schematic and static plan views during training, whereas the tests on the simulator obviously involved an interaction with dynamic perspective views. Thus, it is arguably the case that trained drivers would still need to use as many resources to predict risks as untrained drivers. Knowledge of where potential risks might arise would appear to be the only difference between the PC-trained and -untrained drivers. Still, by giving PC-trained drivers knowledge of the risks, we may have increased the potency of the dynamic stimulus (here conceived as the entire scenario as it unfolds over time near the location where risks need to be predicted) that leads to retrieval of the relevant search behaviors. This, in turn, could have made it easier for the PC-trained drivers to time-share the search and more basic vehicle control tasks. We refer to this as the *retrieval hypothesis*.

It is possible to determine whether the trained and untrained drivers would be equally aware of the risks if the stimuli signaling the risks were more obvious. In particular, it could be that novice drivers are every bit as aware of risks as more experienced drivers when there are cues signaling the presence of the risks, but that they lose awareness of the situation when the indicators of risk are less obvious and require more in-depth processing. This would be consistent with the retrieval hypothesis. For example, novice drivers may not think to look to the left and right for pedestrians when seeing a marked midblock crosswalk in the distance if there are no pedestrians in the crosswalk or on either side of it, but they may look to the left and right if they see a pedestrian in the crosswalk far in advance of their passing over the crosswalk. Studies, however, suggest that novice drivers lack a basic knowledge of the risks presented by the scenario because cueing does not solve the problem and, as such, the results are not consistent with the retrieval hypothesis (discussed later).

Last, one needs to ask the more general, but perhaps more profound, question that is raised by the studies we report: Why are all drivers, not just novice drivers, so unaware of risks? In particular, why is it that experienced drivers, on average, recognize risks only about half the time? We examine again the divided attention, knowledge, and retrieval hypotheses in an attempt to explain this failure in a later section.

We want to admit up front that our program of research did not follow the line of argument presented earlier. We have been interested first and foremost in identifying those behaviors that put novice drivers at risk and then in remediating those behaviors. We did not stop to examine all the different reasons that they might be at risk. Quite simply, we (1) made an educated guess about the cause of the novice drivers' failure to recognize the risks based on the results of several different studies on a driving simulator of novice and experienced drivers (Fisher, 2002; Pradhan et al., 2005b), (2) developed a PC training program for novice drivers based on that guess (Fisher, Narayanaan, Pradhan, & Pollatsek, 2004), and then (3) evaluated the effectiveness of that training program on a driving simulator (Pollatsek et al., 2006). It is only in retrospect that we are trying to piece together what we hope is theoretically a better motivated discussion of the progress of our research.

## THE PROBLEMATIC BEHAVIORS

One's first impression, certainly our first impression, was that the novice driver problem was not one that was in the domain of the cognitive psychologist, but more so that of the social psychologist. We assumed that alcohol, speeding, and generally risky behaviors would explain the bulk of the crashes among novice drivers. However, this turns out not to be the case. In a recent study, McKnight and McKnight (2003) found that in only 0.7% of the crashes in which novice drivers were involved were they traveling 70 mph or more. Speed was sometimes a factor, but only because novice drivers failed to adjust their speed appropriately—to curves, slick surfaces, or other relevant traffic conditions. Alcohol was also not a factor among novice drivers (McKnight & McKnight, 2003).

To understand better those behaviors that do cause problems for novice drivers, one needs to turn to studies using real crash data and studies using eye movement data gathered both in the field (in noncrash settings) and the laboratory (in both crash and non-crash scenarios). The studies using crash data are based on police accident reports. The obvious weakness of police accident reports is that there is no hard record of the vehicle or driver behavior throughout the crash. One can turn to other types of studies that were designed to collect these data. These include both field studies and laboratory studies that monitor drivers' eyes. However, obviously these latter field studies are designed for crashes not to occur.[1] The laboratory studies, in which crashes can occur, are conducted primarily on driving simulators. The obvious weakness of such studies is that the driver is in a simulated world and the behaviors observed there may not be generalized to the open road. Given the relative weaknesses of the two sets of studies, it makes sense to look at both and combine the information as best as possible.

### Crash Data

Consider studies based on actual crash data. The major problem for novice drivers appears largely to be the result of a lack of experience and, in particular, a failure to scan effectively for potential risks. Not only are novice drivers involved in more crashes than experienced drivers, in which failures of search would appear to be the source of the crash, but the great majority of novice drivers crashes are ones in which search seems to be the cause, rather than crashes in which some other factor appears to be involved. Three types of evidence point to this conclusion.

First, police accident reports can be used to infer the reasons for a crash. For example, in a recent study, McKnight and McKnight (2003) reviewed 2,000 police accident reports: 1,000 reports of crashes involving drivers who were 16 and 17 years old, and 1,000 reports of crashes involving drivers who were 18 and 19 years old. The reports were obtained from two states: California and Maryland. The 16- and 17-year-olds were about three times as likely to be involved in a crash as the 18- and 19-year-old drivers who had had their license for 1 to 3 years. (Police reports tend to be sketchy, so one isn't sure whether the reported cause of the accident was from direct eyewitness reports or from plausible inference given the positions of the vehicles.) In absolute terms, inferred failures to search ahead, to the side, or to the rear were implicated in 43.1% of the crashes. Novice drivers were also more likely to drive too fast for the road conditions, especially on curves and slick surfaces. Overall, failure of the driver to adjust the speed of the vehicle was implicated in 20.8% of the crashes. Other, possibly overlapping, causes of crashes among the set of drivers included basic vehicle control (8.0%), traffic control signals (5.6%), attention (23%), driver–vehicle impairment (6.3%), maintaining space (9.8%), turn signaling (1.2%), and emergency vehicle handling (9.4%). McKnight and McKnight (2003) conclude: "The overwhelming majority of non-fatal accidents appears to result from failure to employ routine safe operating practices and failure to recognize the danger in doing so rather than what might be viewed as thrill-seeking or other forms of deliberate risk-taking" (p. 924). Their data indicate that majority of such crashes were the result of failures to search ahead, to the side, or to the rear.

Second, police accident reports can be used to compute what is called the relative accident involvement ratio (RAIR). The RAIR is set equal to the ratio of the percentage of at-fault drivers in a particular crash type to the percentage of not-at-fault drivers in the same crash type. For example, in a recent study of 16-, 17-, 18-, and 19-year-old drivers in Kentucky, Kirk and Stamatiadis (2001) found that 16-year-olds are more likely to be involved in left-turn (RAIR = 1.86), rear-end (RAIR = 1.42), single-vehicle (RAIR = 1.61), and passing crashes (RAIR = 1.48). The overinvolvement of the 16-year-olds in the left-turn and rear-end crashes is consistent with the findings of McKnight and McKnight (2003), assuming that visual search is the cause of the crash; as is the overinvolvement in single-vehicle crashes, assuming that drivers' failure to adjust their speed to the road conditions leads to such crashes. The overinvolvement of the 16-year-olds in the crashes involving passing could be taken as evidence that this cohort is more risky. However, it is also possible that 16-year-olds are simply less experienced at judging how quickly an oncoming car is advancing toward them or that they are not looking ahead as far as they need to in order to determine whether a vehicle might appear from around a curve before they complete their passing maneuver. In any case, it is clear that inadequate search is a plausible factor in left-turn, rear-end, and passing crashes.

Third, one can look at the frequency of crashes of a given type. The numbers in Table 10.1 are for drivers in Massachusetts averaged over 2 years (2002 and 2003) and normalized per licensed driver. Four types of crashes are listed (angle, rear end, head on,

and single vehicle) for drivers age 16 through 19. It is clear that angle, rear-end, and head-on crashes constitute a majority of the crashes, and all arguably involve visual search. It is also clear that novice drivers (defined here as 16-year-olds) are overinvolved in angle, rear-end, head-on, and single-vehicle crashes. Assuming that angle crashes occur primarily during left turns and the head-on crashes occur primarily during passing, the results from Massachusetts mirror those from Kentucky (Kirk & Stamatiadis, 2001).

In summary, the crash data collected in field studies indicate that novice drivers are overinvolved in four types of crashes: left-turn, rear-end, single-vehicle, and passing crashes. Moreover, not only are they overinvolved in these types of crashes, but these types of crashes constitute the large majority of crashes (89% of the crashes for the 16-year-olds in Table 10.1). Finally, analyses of police accident reports suggest that failures of the visual scanning process are primarily responsible for three of these crash types: left turn, rear end, and passing. Single-vehicle crashes are presumably the result primarily of judgment errors, not errors of the visual search process. However, it appears from the field studies that single-vehicle crashes are a little less than one quarter of the total crashes in these four categories. Thus, it is arguably the case that failures of the visual search are responsible for at least 75% of the crashes in the four most frequent crash types.

## Eye Movement Studies

Of course, as McKnight and McKnight (2003) point out, the evidence that novice drivers fail to search as effectively as more experienced drivers is based entirely on inferences from police accident reports. There is no hard evidence available in a typical accident report that failure to search was a problem per se. That is, it could have been that drivers were scanning

TABLE 10.1. Angle, Rear-End, Head-on, and Single-Vehicle Crashes Normalized per 10,000 Licensed Drivers.

| Age of Driver, y | Angle (Left Turn[a]) | Rear End | Head On (Passing[b]) | Single Vehicle | Other |
|---|---|---|---|---|---|
| 16 | 1168 | 954 | 112 | 729 | 374 |
| 17 | 645 | 601 | 62 | 347 | 216 |
| 18 | 482 | 464 | 47 | 247 | 182 |
| 19 | 392 | 383 | 37 | 189 | 154 |

[a]Left-turn crashes are a subset of angle crashes.
[b]Passing crashes are a subset of head-on crashes.

effectively but instead made a misjudgment (e.g., of the speed of the oncoming vehicle in the left-turn and passing crashes, or the closing speed in the case of rear-end crashes [the closing speed is the difference in the velocities of the driver's own vehicle and the vehicle immediately in front of the driver]). To get a better handle on the extent to which failures of the search process per se are involved, direct evidence is needed on the scanning process. Such direct evidence is potentially available from studies in which eye (and/or head) movements are measured throughout a drive, either on the open road or in a simulator.

The earliest work was done by Mourant and Rockwell (1972). Drivers' eyes were tracked on the open road on two different types of roadway: a neighborhood route 2.1 miles long and a freeway route 4.3 miles long. Six novice drivers (16 and 17 years old) and four experienced drivers (31–43 years old) were evaluated. Two measures are relevant here. First, for each of several critical portions of a section of roadway, the horizontal component of each eye movement was measured and the range of the horizontal extent of the eye travel (i.e., the distance between the farthest left movement of the eyes and the farthest right movement of the eyes) was computed for this critical portion of the roadway; these range values were then averaged over participants. (Such large eye movements were undoubtedly combinations of eye movements and head movements.) They found, for example, that experienced drivers changing into the left lane had an average horizontal range of 42 deg whereas novice drivers in this same situation had an average horizontal range of only 15 deg. The size of the difference in the horizontal range varied across critical roadway sections, but the experienced drivers always scanned more broadly. Similar information exists for the vertical component. Here, however, there was a different measure: The median of the vertical component of a participant's fixations in a particular section of roadway was calculated and then the average across participants was computed. Interestingly, in the neighborhood sections (but not the freeway sections), the average median fixation of the novice drivers was 3 deg less than the average median fixation of the more experienced drivers. This is consistent with a failure of visual search for the novice drivers as well. That is, the novice drivers' fixation may have been closer than optimal to the front of the driver's vehicle.

More recently, Crundall and Underwood (1998) ran a larger version of the Mourant and Rockwell

(1972) study. Participants were asked to drive normally through three types of roadway: a rural, single-lane carriageway; a suburban road through a small village with shops, parked cars, and marked crosswalks; and a dual carriageway (i.e., expressway). Sixteen novice drivers (average age, 17.9 years) and 16 experienced drivers (average age, 27.7 years) were evaluated. The variance of the fixation locations along the horizontal axis was computed. Experienced drivers' horizontal eye positions changed more than those of novice drivers on dual carriageways (a standard deviation of about 9 deg vs. a standard deviation of about 7 deg), but there was no difference between the groups on either rural or suburban routes. The finding that there was no effect of experience on the difference in the suburban routes appears to be at odds with the finding of Mourant and Rockwell (1972) that there were differences between groups in the average horizontal range in neighborhood routes; however, the measures were somewhat different. Crundall and Underwood (1998) did not analyze the location of the median vertical fixation, as did Mourant and Rockwell (1972). However, they did analyze the variability along the vertical axis. Novices' vertical variation was greater than experienced drivers in rural sections and suburban sections (about 4.5 deg vs. about 3.5 deg), but there was no difference on the dual carriageways, a finding consistent with earlier work by Renge (1980) and Evans (1991). This is not necessarily at odds with the finding of Mourant and Rockwell (1972), because Crundall and Underwood (1998) were measuring variability in the vertical component rather than the central tendency. Unfortunately, neither study reported both measures (i.e., variability along the vertical axis and median vertical gaze location).

In addition to field studies of drivers' scanning behaviors, there have been more detailed simulator studies. Only one, conducted in our laboratory, will be mentioned here (Pradhan et al., 2005b). We asked 24 novice drivers (16 and 17 years old, who had their license no more than 6 months; average age, 16.3 years[2]), 24 younger drivers (age range, 19–29 years; average age, 21.3 years), and 24 older drivers (age range, 60–75 years; average age, 66.9 years) to negotiate 16 scenarios displayed on three screens located immediately in front of a 1995 Saturn sedan. Figure 10.2 illustrates the display projected on the center screen. The participants operated the controls of the Saturn just as they would those of a normal vehicle, controlling their path through the simulated world the same way they would do so through the real world. All participants were fitted with an ASL 5000

FIGURE 10.2. Truck crosswalk scenario: perspective view.

eye tracker, which also tracked head movements. As output from the eye tracker, we had both real-world coordinates and a digital recreation of where the driver was looking at each point in a scenario (the eye point was indicated by cross-hairs overlaid on the digital recreation).

We were interested in differences in the search behavior of the three groups of drivers, as were Mourant and Rockwell (1972) and Crundall and Underwood (1998). However, unlike them, we were more interested in exactly where drivers were looking at particular strategic points in a scenario, rather than in gross measures such as the variability of the horizontal components of the scan. To illustrate the goals of the experiment, 2 of the 16 scenarios are described. Consider the plan view of the truck crosswalk scenario (Fig. 10.1). The participant driver (gray triangle, D) is approaching a marked midblock crosswalk with a truck (black rectangle, T) parked along the side of the road, perhaps a moving van making a delivery. A vehicle is in the opposing lane coming toward the crosswalk (black triangle, V). A lead vehicle (black triangle, L), which the participant is supposed to follow, is ahead of the driver but is largely irrelevant in this scenario. A driver should be aware of the risks presented by a pedestrian crossing in front of the truck. Such an aware driver would look to the right as he or she passes

immediately in front of the truck to check for potential conflicts with a pedestrian.

The perspective view of the same scenario, presented in Figure 10.2 (grayscale) is a snapshot of what the participant driver sees on the center screen in the simulator. The zebra stripes that indicate the presence of a midblock crosswalk are clearly visible as the driver approaches the back of the truck. A pedestrian who might be starting to cross in front of the truck is obscured from the participant driver's view. The participant driver should clearly look to the right as he or she passes in front of the truck. In this scenario, we find that 10%, 29%, and 57% of the novice, younger, and older drivers, respectively, do so as they pass in front of the crosswalk. The visual angle between the center of the area of risk and focus of expansion in this case was 11.7 deg. Thus, there was never any problem differentiating between participant drivers who looked to the right and those who did not.

A plan view of a second scenario, the truck left-turn scenario, is displayed in Figure 10.3. The participant driver (the gray triangle, D) is traveling through a four-way signal intersection, and a truck (black rectangle triangle, T) is in the adjacent lane and getting ready to take a left turn. The truck blocks the participant driver's view of vehicles in the opposing lane across the intersection (black triangle, V). These vehicles, in

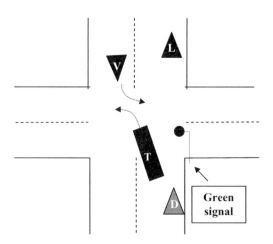

FIGURE 10.3. Truck left turn scenario. (T: truck in left turn lane; L: lead vehicle; V: vehicle in opposing lane. D: participant's vehicle.)

turn, cannot see the driver and may not even see that there is a second lane adjacent to the truck. Thus, these vehicles may turn left in front of the truck. The participant driver should look to the left as he or she passes in front of the truck to make sure there aren't such vehicles about to cross the road.

Two perspective views of the same scenario, which capture something of what the driver sees on the simulator, are displayed in Figure 10.4. What the participant driver sees when relatively distant from the intersection is displayed on the left; what the driver might see as he or she is about to pass the truck is displayed on the right. Note that risks never did materialize in the actual experiment in any of the scenarios; this was done to keep the participants from becoming hypervigilant. We found that 5%, 20%, and 50% of the novice, younger, and experienced drivers, respectively, looked to the left as they passed immediately in front of the truck. Again, it was always clear whether drivers did look to the left because the visual angle between the center of the area of risk and focus of expansion was 27.8 deg.

In summary, both the eye movement data from the field studies and the eye movement data from the laboratory studies are consistent with the hypothesis that novice drivers are scanning risky areas less often. The eye movement data from the field is useful because it shows that, in general, novice drivers are scanning less, but it does not indicate specifically whether they are scanning the critical areas of potential risk less well. The laboratory data confirm that novice drivers are not only scanning less broadly than more experienced drivers (and therefore are less likely to be aware of unpredictable risks), but they are not scanning the specific areas of a scenario where risks can be predicted. The question at this point is why this is the case.

**A**

**B**

FIGURE 10.4. Truck left turn scenarios: perspective views. (A) Distance view. (B) Close-up view. The signal is green.

## DIVIDED ATTENTION

There are many different reasons why novice drivers may be less able to divide their attention between the vehicle control and risk prediction processes than more experienced drivers. We consider only three. First, driving does take some practice, and skills that are automatic for the experienced driver are not necessarily so for the novice driver. Mourant and Rockwell (1972) suggested that one reason the novice drivers may look more closely toward the area to the front and right edge of the car is that they are using information from the curb to "microadjust" the position of their vehicle. This requires more attention than is typical of a more experienced driver performing the same simple task (keeping the vehicle centered in the lane). In turn, this implies that less attention is available for other tasks.

If this is true, and the novice drivers are attending to things that have become automatized for more experienced drivers (Schneider & Shiffrin, 1977), then there is a large amount of literature that can be brought to bear on an understanding of the reasons that novice drivers may have more difficulty predicting potential risks in the roadway ahead. For example, it is well-known that an automatic and controlled task can be more easily time-shared than can two controlled tasks (Schneider & Fisk, 1982). If the elementary driving tasks are automatic ones and the risk prediction tasks are controlled ones for experienced drivers, whereas both tasks are controlled ones for novice drivers, then it follows that (all else being equal) the novice drivers should have more difficulty predicting risks than do more experienced drivers.

The discussion of automatic and controlled processing usually assumes an undifferentiated pool of resources. A related attentional explanation is also worth pursuing, one that assumes that the pool of resources is differentiated. Arguably Wickens (1980, 1984, 1991) has done the most to elaborate a model of differentiated resources, work that builds on earlier models proposed by Kantowitz and Knight (1976) and Navon and Gopher (1979). Briefly, as articulated in Wickens and Hollands (2000), the inputs considered are either auditory or visual (obviously other modalities are possible), and the information is coded either verbally (linguistic coding) or spatially (analog coding). The coded information is then processed, with the processing including perceiving and other cognitive operations involving short- and long-term memory.

Finally, a response is programmed and executed. The actual responses considered are either vocal or manual.

So, what does this have to do with the differences between the novice and the more experienced driver? Imagine that the novice driver is trying to keep the vehicle in the lane as well as predict the risks in the roadway ahead. Much of the relevant information for both tasks is input through the visual modality and is coded spatially. It then needs to be processed cognitively and responded to appropriately. Regardless of the distinction between automatic and controlled processing, it is clear that elementary (lane keeping) and more advanced (risk prediction) driving skills share resources at several stages of processing. The input modality is being shared (visual), a common code is being processed in working memory (spatial), and a common response is required (scanning). If there are limits at each stage and if processing at each stage must be shared between elementary and advanced driving skills, then practice should reduce the demands on the attentional resources that elementary driving skills make. Thus, one would predict that more experienced drivers have more time and resources to predict risks in the roadway ahead and therefore are more likely to do so.

There is one final, related, attentional hypothesis. The optimal allocation of attention may itself be an ability that is learned over time. One could argue that what changes with practice is not the amount of resources needed by the elementary and advanced driving skills, but instead the ability to allocate attention to those tasks that most require it. For example, Schneider and Fisk (1982) found that participants could better time-share an automatic and controlled task if they were taught to allocate their attention almost entirely to the control task. Left to their own devices, the participants paid too much attention to the automatic task. More generally, novice drivers may allocate too much attention to tasks that require relatively few resources. More experienced drivers, through years of experience, probably know better that to which they truly need to attend.

## KNOWLEDGE OF ROADWAY RISKS

We want to consider an alternative to the divided attention hypotheses as an explanation of why novice drivers are less likely to scan risky areas of the roadway than more experienced drivers. This is the knowledge hypothesis that we referred to earlier. It may seem an unlikely hypothesis, given that most novice drivers undertake some form of driver training, and as part of the curriculum they will have 30 hours of classroom training. However, the training that goes on in the classroom typically does not give the novice driver help in visualizing and reasoning spatially about the potential risks that are hidden by the other traffic or the natural or built environment. In addition, the driver training curriculum involves 6 hours in a car with an instructor, three of them as the driver and three of them as a passenger. However, the instruction in the car, almost of necessity, must be focused on the most basic of motor skills because the novice driver cannot be put at risk.

As a test of the knowledge hypothesis, we developed 16 scenarios in which we expected drivers who were aware of potential risks to respond differently than drivers who were not aware of these potential risks (Fisher, Laurie, Glaser, Connerney, Pollatsek, Duffy, & Brock, 2002). These scenarios were displayed on the three screens on the driving simulator described earlier. The truck crosswalk (Fig. 10.2) and the truck left-turn (Fig. 10.3) scenarios discussed earlier were among the 16 scenarios that were presented to participants. We collected information on vehicle and control behaviors (but not eye movement behaviors). Three groups of drivers were run: (1) novice drivers who received no training outside the standard driver education curriculum, (2) novice drivers who received risk awareness training in addition to the standard driver education curriculum, and (3) more experienced drivers. Novice drivers were trained to recognize risks using a PC-based program, Driver ZED, developed by the AAA Foundation for Traffic Safety (Willis, 1998). In this program, drivers were taught to recognize a risk like the one presented in the truck left-turn scenario by seeing filmed versions of actual near crashes. Little explanation was given of why the situation was a risky one, either in particular or more generally. The results were somewhat disappointing. In only 5 of the 16 scenarios did we find clear evidence of vehicle and driver behaviors that differentiated the trained novice drivers from the untrained novice drivers. Two examples of differences that we did find were that significantly more trained novice drivers braked as they passed by the truck in the truck left-turn scenario (Fig. 10.3), and trained novice drivers slowed more than the untrained novice drivers as they approached the crosswalk in the truck crosswalk scenario (Fig. 10.1).

We were surprised to find so few scenarios in which we could identify differences between the trained and untrained novice drivers. So rather than use this experiment as a hat on which to hang our test of the knowledge hypothesis, we thought more deeply about the problem of measuring risk recognition, and it became clear to us that one needed to separate the recognition of a potential risk from the responses produced by the anticipation of that risk. That is, the measures of vehicle and control behavior that we used here were indices of anticipatory response following the recognition of a risk. However, any particular anticipatory response that we assessed was not always necessary to avoid an accident, whereas recognizing that a potential risk could exist in a certain location and attending to that location would certainly be necessary. Moreover, for novice drivers, it was far from clear whether certain driving maneuvers (e.g., swerving away from the parked truck) were actually helpful or dangerous. As a result, we believed that a better measure of whether a driver recognizes the risk in the scenarios we constructed would be whether the driver fixates the area where a risk might materialize. Therefore, we essentially reran the study on untrained novice drivers, younger drivers, and older drivers, only this time using eye behavior. (We were not testing the knowledge hypothesis per se in this experiment, although the results would be consistent with this hypothesis. Rather, we were evaluating whether we could use eye movements and, in particular, where a driver gazed at a particular location in a scenario, to determine whether untrained novice drivers were less likely to recognize risks than more experienced older drivers.[3])

The study to which we refer here is discussed earlier (Pradhan et al., 2005b). As noted in that study, eye behaviors were a much more sensitive and easy-to-interpret measure of risk recognition. Experienced older drivers were about six times as likely to look to the right for a potential pedestrian as they passed in front of the truck stopped just before a marked midblock crosswalk (Fig. 10.1) and were about 10 times as likely to look to the left for a hidden car as they passed a truck in the left turn lane (Fig. 10.3). (We should note here that we are aware that a glance in the area of a potential risk is not proof that a driver actually recognizes that risk. However, it is awkward to refer to the glance as being an inference that the driver recognizes the risk. We return to this point later in the chapter.)

Now that we had what is arguably a good way to measure a driver's recognition of risks and now that we had observed large differences between novice and experienced drivers using this measure, we hoped we could run a more convincing test of the knowledge hypothesis. However, it was clear that such a test required us to construct our own PC-based training risk awareness and perception training program because the existing PC-based programs had relatively few examples of scenarios that contained the sorts of risks that we wanted to train. Moreover, as indicated earlier, many programs like Driver ZED used filmed versions of actual near crashes, so that transfer from the film to what is seen on the driving simulator may be accomplished on the basis of relatively low-level pattern matching between the visual input in training and the visual input at test. Thus, testing the effects of the training when it uses such films is difficult because one wants the drivers to learn something general about the risks in the scenarios.

As a way around this objection we developed a PC-based training program that used only plan (schematic top-down) views of a scenario (Pollatsek et al., 2006). A total of 10 scenarios were included in the training program. The training for each scenario involves three successive screens on the PC, each of which contains a plan view of the scenario. (An example of the three successive screens, and associated plan views, is illustrated in Figure 10.5.) In the first, using the subject response screen, the participant has two tasks. One involves placing yellow ovals on appropriate locations on the screen and the other involves placing red circles appropriately (using click, drag, and drop operations with a mouse). The first task is to move one or more yellow ovals to a location (or locations) on the plan view where an object (vehicle, pedestrian) might be that constitutes a potential threat, but is obscured from view of the driver in the plan view. The second task is to move one or more red circles to a position that is visible to the driver in the plan view and should continuously be monitored because a risk might materialize. On the second screen, the vision obstruction screen, the driver is shown exactly where on the plan view a plausible risk could be that is obstructed from the driver's point of view. In Figure 10.5, it is the area behind the bushes on the left from which a vehicle might emerge. Finally, in the third screen, the answer explanation screen, the driver is shown where the yellow ovals and red circles should be placed. In this case, a yellow oval should be placed behind the bushes on the left because a vehicle is hidden by the bushes and could

potentially pose a threat. A red circle should be placed both on the left where the fork enters the main road and straight ahead of the driver, because both positions need constant monitoring.

The novice drivers were tested before and after training. A total of 24 novice drivers were evaluated. Overall, the novice drivers clearly benefited from training. They placed the red circles correctly 50% of the time on the pretest and 91% of the time on the posttest (t(23) = 12.9, $P < .001$), and they placed the yellow circles correctly 32% of the time on the pretest and 90% on the posttest (t(23) = 19.1, $P < .001$). These benefits occurred not only overall, but for each scenario as well (Fig. 10.6).

The key question, however, is whether the learning generalizes to the recognition of risks on the driving simulator (and ultimately the open road). To evaluate the effectiveness of the training on the driving simulator, the performance of the 24 novice drivers who were trained with the PC-based program was compared with the performance of 24 novice drivers who had not been trained. A total of 16 test scenarios were constructed. Ten of these scenarios were similar to the ones that had been used in the PC-based training program. They could be used to test the near transfer of risk recognition skills (the transfer from a static plan view to a real-time perspective view). The other six scenarios were not similar to what the novice drivers saw on the PC-based training and were used to test far transfer. The test of training was whether the driver fixated an area of potential risk. For example, in the parked truck scenario, drivers were scored as recognizing the risk if they fixated on or near the left edge of the parked truck and then somewhat further to the right just as they passed it. This scoring was made simple because the difference between recognizing and not recognizing a risk was virtually always clear-cut. For example, the drivers who were scored as not recognizing the risk in the parked truck scenario looked straight ahead virtually the whole time they were passing the truck. The effects of training were quite clear. Averaged over the 16 scenarios, the trained drivers recognized risks 57.7% of the time and the untrained drivers recognized risks only 35.4% of the time (F(1, 46) = 21.2, $P < .001$). In addition, the difference in performance between the trained and untrained novice drivers on the near and far transfer scenarios was almost identical, so that the training appeared to be of general concepts. Moreover, as can be seen in Figure 10.7, the training appeared to be effective,

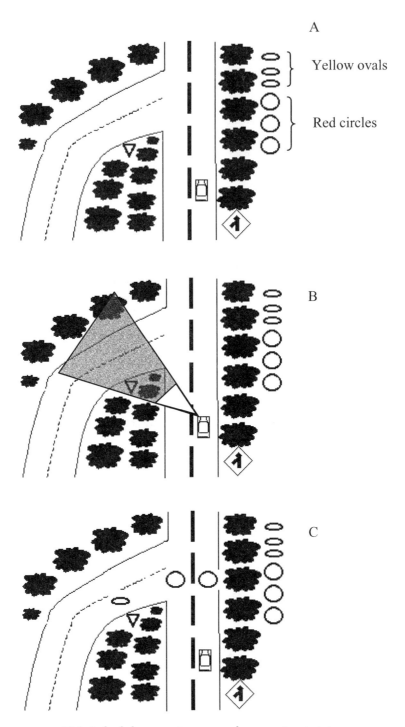

A

Yellow ovals

Red circles

B

C

FIGURE 10.5. Left fork scenario: personal computer training screens. (A) Subject response screen. (B) Vision obstruction screen. (C) Answer explanation screen.

A

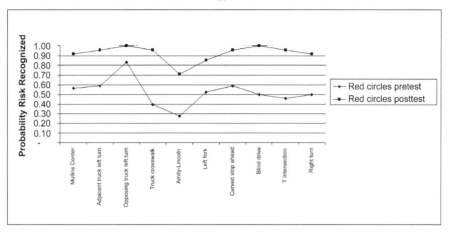

B

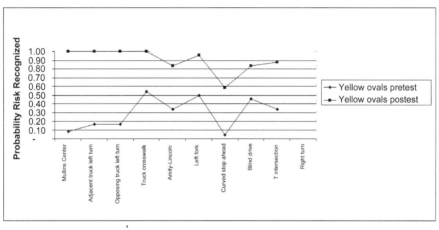

FIGURE 10.6. Personal computer training program test results. (A) Red circles: pre- and posttest. (B) Yellow ovals: pre- and posttest. There were no yellow ovals given in the right turn scenario because there were no hidden risks.

at least for some of the trained drivers, in almost all scenarios. We should add that, in this study, the test was immediately after the training session. Thus, there was the concern that the learning was transient. However, a subsequent study (Pradhan, Fisher, & Pollatsek, 2005a) replicated these findings with delays between the PC training and test on the driving simulator of 2 to 5 days.

We can now ask what implications this study has for an understanding of the role that knowledge plays in the finding that novice drivers recognize risks much less often than experienced drivers. The three divided attention hypotheses need to be considered again here. First, it is clear that the training we used did

nothing that would plausibly create an automatic process the first time the driver encountered a risky situation in the driving simulator. The training of automatic skills can take upward of thousands of trials (Schneider & Shiffrin, 1977); in contrast, our participants had only one trial. Second, it seems implausible that the training decreased the resources that a novice driver would need to recognize a situation as a risky one. Obviously, the PC training did not change the input modality needed to guide the vehicle or recognize risks (the input was visual in both cases), and PC training did not alter the output modality needed to recognize the risks (motor or eye movements).

**A**

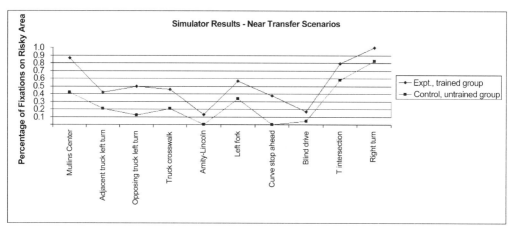

**B**

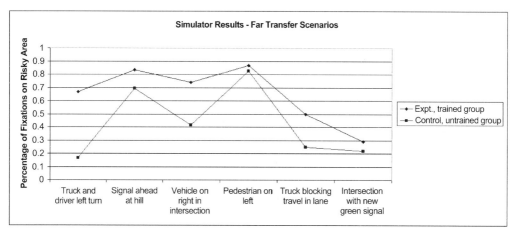

FIGURE 10.7. Driving simulator evaluation. (A) Ten near-transfer scenarios. (B) Six far-transfer scenarios.

Thus, the resources still needed to be shared at input and output. Moreover, it also seems implausible that the PC training would have changed the type of reasoning or central processing that was needed for the elementary and advanced tasks. It was still spatial, either when guiding the vehicle or recognizing a hidden risk. Finally, it is equally clear that we did little that would help drivers divide attention, because they were given only one task (risk prediction) to complete and there was no time limitation imposed on executing the task during training.

In summary, the improvement in risk recognition that was observed could simply be the result of the fact that the novice drivers had no knowledge of the risks inherent in a given risky scenario prior to training, whereas they did have such knowledge after training.

Indeed, given the improvement in risk recognition observed between the pretest and posttest on the PC-based training program, it is difficult to see how it could be otherwise. That is, on the pretest, the novice drivers had all the time they needed to move the yellow ovals and the red circles to the critical regions, so that it is hard to ascribe the increase to improvement in divided attention skills. One might argue that the PC task was so foreign to the participants that, despite the instructions prior to the pretest, they had a poor understanding of where the yellow ovals and red circles were to be positioned, and thus that the improvement that we observed on the posttest was a consequence of learning to place the markers in their appropriate locations. This seems unlikely, because the concept of how to place the circles and ovals should have been clear after seeing the first scenario or two, but the difference between posttest and pretest on the PC was just as large in the later scenarios as it was in the early scenarios. However, assuming that the novice drivers did know the scenarios before training, then any practice they had thinking about the risky scenarios should make it easier for them to recognize the same risks on the driving simulator. This would reduce the resources the risk retrieval process placed on the spatial processing resources and so we might observe an improvement in risk recognition that was not the consequence of drivers having learned to recognize risks after training that they did not recognize before training.

## RETRIEVAL

How might one test the hypothesis that the novice driver is aware abstractly of the risks in a particular scenario but, because of constraints on the processing resources, he or she cannot identify (retrieve) the risk? For example, the novice driver might have the knowledge that a pedestrian may pass in front of the truck stopped just before the crosswalk, but cannot apply this knowledge in the situation because the cognitive processing required to retrieve this knowledge requires more time and resources available. One way to test this *retrieval hypothesis* is to give novice drivers a preview in which a risk materializes far enough in advance to warn the driver of an upcoming danger but does not pose an actual threat. The risky scenario then appears moments later, but without the risky element actually materializing. For example, in the truck crosswalk scenario, a pedestrian (the risky element) might emerge from behind the truck when the driver was far enough upstream of the crosswalk not to be a threat but close enough to see it (Fig. 10.8, top panel). If the novice driver has knowledge of the potential risk, then given a preview (foreshadowing) of a pedestrian, the novice driver in this situation may be as likely as the experienced driver to look to the right in front of the truck for potential pedestrians just as he or she passes over the crosswalk.

We ran an experiment to test this hypothesis on the driving simulator (Garay-Vega & Fisher, 2005). There were 24 novice drivers who were 16 and 17 years old (average age, 16.5 years; age was recorded in whole years) and 24 experienced drivers between the ages of 40 and 50 years old with more than 20 years of driving

experience (average age, 44.7 years). Nine scenarios were used, three with an element that foreshadowed the risk (Fig. 10.8). (The plan views in Figure 10.8 are for illustrative purposes only; participants were not trained and never saw these plan views.) One of these was the truck crosswalk scenario just described and displayed in the top panel of Figure 10.8. The second is displayed in the middle panel. Here the participant driver (green) is approaching a merge with a major street. The lead car (red) is about to enter the merge. A blue motorcycle, the foreshadowing element, can be seen ahead of the participant driver, creating a potential threat for the lead car and also signaling the participant driver that the scenario is a risky one that requires him or her to glance to the left. The third scenario is displayed in the bottom panel. The participant driver (green car) is on the stub of a T intersection, getting ready to take a right turn just after the lead vehicle (red). Across the main street is a row of houses, all with driveways that function as implicit advance cues. Slightly to the left of the lead vehicle is a driveway out of which a yellow car, the foreshadowing element, is taking a left turn, potentially colliding with the lead car. The foreshadowing element should alert the participant driver to the fact that he or she needs to look to the left and into the driveway for cars potentially entering and taking a left turn.

As with previous studies, experienced drivers looked at the risk more often than novice drivers (81.9% vs. 43.0%). However, unlike previous studies, in this study, and in particular in the three scenarios that we used to evaluate the situation awareness hypothesis, we coded both whether the driver looked at the foreshadowing element and whether the driver looked at the area of risk (Table 10.2). Using this information, we could compute the conditional probability that the novice driver looked in the direction of a risk, given that the driver fixated on the foreshadowing element (Table 10.3). The percentage of experienced drivers recognizing the risk, given that they saw the foreshadowing element (85%), was significantly larger than the percentage of novice drivers recognizing the risk, given that they too saw the foreshadowing element (47%). This was particularly true in situations involving pedestrians (Fig. 10.8, scenario 1). A similar trend was observed in situations involving traffic signs and conflicting traffic (scenarios 2 and 3). Performance among the novice drivers was even worse when a foreshadowing element was not fixated. Only 20% of the novice drivers recognized risks in these situations.

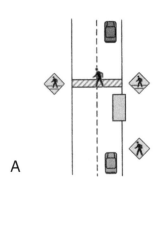

☐  Advance cue: PEDESTRIAN AHEAD sign

☐  Foreshadowing element: pedestrian

A

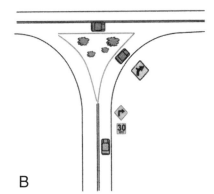

☐  Advance cue: INTERSECTION/CURVE sign

☐  Foreshadowing element: blue motorcycle traveling in major roadway

B

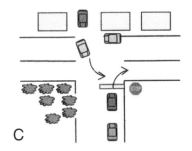

☐  Advance cue:  Opposing driveways

☐  Foreshadowing element: yellow entering vehicle

C

FIGURE 10.8.  Illustrations of scenarios with foreshadowed risks. (A) Scenario 1. Truck in front of crosswalk. (B) Scenario 2. Yield to traffic. (C) Scenario 3. Turning vehicle at T intersection.

Although this rules out the retrieval hypothesis as the sole explanation of why the novice drivers fail to recognize the risks as frequently as more experienced drivers, it does suggest that retrieval may be a problem. The novice drivers were 10 to 20% more likely to recognize the risky area given that they fixated the foreshadowing element than they were to recognize the risky area, given that they failed to fixate the foreshadowing element.

Still, it is difficult to determine whether this increase was the result of the novice drivers becoming aware of a risk for the first time or, instead, was the result of the novice drivers having an easier time retrieving the risky elements of a scenario with a risk with which they were already familiar.

In summary, it appears from the study by Garay-Vega and Fisher (2005), that novice drivers truly do

TABLE 10.2. Joint Probabilities.

| Joint Events | Scenario[a] | | | | | |
| | 1 | 2 | 3 | 1 | 2 | 3 |
| --- | --- | --- | --- | --- | --- | --- |
| | Experienced | | | Novice | | |
| Looked at foreshadowed element and risk | .75 | .792 | .375 | .458 | .458 | .083 |
| Looked at foreshadowed element and did not look at risk | .125 | .000 | .167 | .292 | .250 | .417 |
| Did not look at foreshadowed element but looked at risk | .042 | .208 | .208 | .125 | .125 | .042 |
| Did not look at either foreshadowed element or risk | .083 | .000 | .250 | .125 | .167 | .458 |

[a]Scenario 1, truck in front of crosswalk; scenario 2, yield to Traffic; scenario 3, turning vehicle at two-way stop control intersection.

not know that certain scenarios contain hidden risks. It is difficult to see that there is any other explanation for those occasions when they fixated the foreshadowing element but did not fixate the risky area. Having said this, it is also clear from the results that the retrieval hypothesis explains at least some of novice drivers' failure to recognize risks. When novice drivers did not fixate the foreshadowing element, the probability that they recognized the risk was only 20%, whereas when they did fixate the foreshadowing element, the probability that they recognized the risk was 47%.

## GENERAL DISCUSSION

Here we summarize what we have learned about novice drivers from the studies we presented and we indicate where we think additional research should be focused. We then describe what we believe may be the reasons that more experienced drivers still have the difficulties that they do.

## Novice Drivers

Our experiments indicate that novice drivers do not scan the risky areas of a scenario anywhere near as frequently as do more experienced drivers (Pradhan et al., 2005b). Furthermore, these experiments suggest that it is neither the failure of novice drivers to divide their attention between vehicle control and risk prediction tasks nor the failure of novice drivers to retrieve what they already know that can by themselves explain the increased likelihood that they will miss areas of a scenario containing potential risks (Pollatsek et al., 2006). Rather, we have argued that novice drivers do not have the basic knowledge they need to recognize a situation as a risky one.

As we indicated earlier in the chapter, we do not want to suggest knowledge is all that is required for the novice driver to succeed. Attention is required as well. Obviously, novice drivers who do not pay attention to the task will fail to recognize the risks, regardless of how much they know. However, the failure is not with divided attention, nor for that matter is it with selective

TABLE 10.3.  Conditional Probabilities.

| Conditional Events | Scenario | | | | | |
| | 1<br>Cwk[a] | 2<br>Yld[b] | 3<br>T[c] | 1<br>Cwk | 2<br>Yld | 3<br>T |
| --- | --- | --- | --- | --- | --- | --- |
| | Experienced Drivers | | | Novice Drivers | | |
| Probability driver *looked at risk* given that the driver *looked at foreshadowing element* | 0.86 | 1.00 | 0.69 | 0.61 | 0.65 | 0.17 |
| Probability driver *looked at risk* given that the driver *did not look at foreshadowing element* | 0.34 | 1.00 | 0.45 | 0.50 | 0.43 | 0.08 |

[a]Scenario 1 is the crosswalk scenario (Fig. 10.8).
[b]Scenario 2 is the yield scenario (Fig. 10.8).
[c]Scenario 3 is the T intersection scenario (Fig. 10.8).

attention or focused attention (Wickens, 1984). We have discussed why we believe that the failure is not one of divided attention. We now want to discuss briefly why we believe that the failure is not one of either selective or focused attention.

First, consider selective attention. A failure of selective attention is defined by Wickens and Hollands (2000) as a failure to scan several different locations containing critical information in the sequence that minimizes the time to find a target (or optimizes some more general objective function). If the problem was simply one of selective attention, then novice drivers should have been as likely as experienced drivers to have looked at the risks when those risks were foreshadowed (Garay-Vega & Fisher, 2005), because the risks of not doing so would be apparent. That is, if novice drivers had the basic knowledge of those areas of the roadway to which attention should be paid but were focusing on the wrong areas, then the use of foreshadowing should have signaled the importance of focusing on the areas being foreshadowed. It did increase their probability of attending, but not by much. Additionally, if the problem were only one of selective attention, then during the PC training task novice drivers should have shown relatively little improvement because they were given enough time to respond and because they were told explicitly to pay attention to those areas to which they were given a low priority (assuming that the problem is one with selective attention).

Second, consider focused attention. A failure of focused attention is defined by Wickens and Hollands (2000) as the failure to attend to a central stimulus while ignoring more peripheral stimuli. Thus, the problem, instead, is that the novice driver either ignores or does not understand the significance of the peripheral stimulus. In summary, no amount of attention is sufficient if a driver does not know to what he or she should attend.

As a final caveat, and one relevant to selective attention (i.e., the sequencing of fixations across different spatial locations), we did not attempt to assess how important the novice drivers believed the different areas of potential risks were. Obviously, it is critical to pay attention to the roadway ahead as well as to look around. A recent study suggests that 90% of crashes occur when the driver is distracted from the roadway for at least 3 seconds (Dingus, 2005). However, the issue here is not whether the novice driver pays attention to the roadway ahead (an issue with eating, or dialing a hand-held cell phone); rather, the issue here is

which areas of the roadway deserve at least some attention at some point in the drive. It is difficult to believe that the roadway immediately ahead, which offers a clear view, is of more importance than a glance to an area of risk from which a pedestrian or another vehicle could suddenly emerge in our scenarios.

In summary, we believe that many (certainly not all) novice drivers are unaware of the risks inherent in a scenario, even when those risks are foreshadowed. We further believe, based on our experiments, that much of this knowledge can be trained and observed anywhere between some time immediately after training (Pollatsek et al., 2006) and up to 5 days after training (Pradhan et al., 2005a) on a driving simulator. Whether it can also be observed on the open road is a question that still remains to be answered.

### Experienced Drivers

Our data on the experienced drivers present something of a puzzle. Why, one might ask, would such a relatively large percentage of experienced drivers fail to look at areas of the roadway where potential risks might occur? Endsley's (1995) theory, which posits three different stages of situation awareness, may help to frame this discussion. The three stages defined by Endsley are ones in which (1) the driver (or, more generally, the individual involved in a task) must correctly perceive all the elements, (2) the driver must comprehend what he or she is seeing, and finally (3) the driver must project potential actions based on a comprehension of the perceived situation.

First, consider the results in Table 10.2. In particular, consider the probability that the driver looked neither at the foreshadowing element nor at the risk. This is as high as .25 in the T-intersection scenario and as low as zero in the crosswalk scenario. The simple probability that the driver did not look at the risk was as high as .42 in the T-intersection scenario and, again, as low as zero in the crosswalk scenario. This wide variation from scenario to scenario is reflected in other studies (Pradhan et al., 2005b). In the study by Pradhan and colleagues (2005b), experienced drivers recognized the risk as infrequently as 11% of the time in one scenario and as frequently as 100% of the time in another scenario. Experienced drivers are thus usually failing to scan all the relevant areas of the roadway in some scenarios. It seems highly unlikely that the experienced driver does not have the resources to scan and drive at the same time, given all the multitasking that drivers do now with electronic in-vehicle devices. Rather, it would appear from these data that, at least in some cases, the problem is one associated with selective attention (i.e., the areas to which attention should be given and the order in which those areas should be processed) and, in particular, an appropriate scanning strategy. In terms of the model of situation awareness, this is the initial perception stage that is affected because the awareness of the situation is compromised by a failure to code all the relevant information.

Next consider the results in Table 10.3. Recall that the conditional probability that a driver will fixate a particular risk, given that the driver has or has not fixated the foreshadowing element, is the dependent variable of interest. There we see that when the foreshadowing element is fixated, the likelihood that the risky area is fixated is .86, 1.0, and .69 in the crosswalk, yield, and T-intersection scenarios, respectively. These conditional probabilities decrease to .34, 1.0, and .45, respectively, when the driver fails to fixate the foreshadowing element. This says two things. First, the experienced driver can make use of cues in his or her environment that signal risk and act accordingly. In the crosswalk and T-intersection scenarios, the experienced driver is much more likely to fixate the risky area when the foreshadowing element has been fixated than he or she is to do so when the foreshadowing element has not been fixated (there can be no improvement in the yield scenario because the experienced driver's performance is at ceiling). As with novice drivers, it cannot be determined from the results whether the foreshadowing element alerted the experienced drivers to risks of which they were already aware or, instead, made them aware of risks of which they had no prior knowledge. If we had to guess, it would be that the foreshadowing elements alerted the drivers to the risks inherent in a scenario of which they had prior knowledge.

Second, this still leaves us wondering why 14% of the experienced drivers in the crosswalk scenario and 31% of the drivers in the T-intersection scenario failed to focus on the risky area even when they saw the foreshadowing element. Again, we find it difficult to believe that it is a failure of divided attention. Rather, it would appear to be that experienced drivers simply did not comprehend the risks inherent in the scenario that was being played out before them, even though they do see an element that foreshadows the risks. This would appear clearly to be either a failure of comprehension or of projecting the correct action

(i.e., either Endsley's [1995] second or third stage). The type of failure probably depends on the scenario. In the T-intersection scenario, it may not be obvious that a collision is possible between the vehicle exiting the driveway and the lead car (and then the participant driver). Thus, it seems not unreasonable to infer that because 69% of the participants recognized the risks, given that they saw the foreshadowed element, these 69% of the participants understood the dangers posed by the threat vehicle and the remaining 31% did not.[4] In the crosswalk scenario, the driver presumably cannot fail to understand the possibility of a collision. Perhaps, instead, the driver simply does not project the correct action from that understanding for whatever reason. That is, it is arguably the case that all drivers understood the risks inherent in the scenario, but that the 84% of the drivers who recognized the risks, given that the foreshadowed element was fixated, projected the risks correctly whereas the 16% of the drivers who recognized the risks, given that the foreshadowed element was fixated, failed to project the risks.

In summary, the reasons experienced drivers fail to recognize risks more frequently than they do are complex. For some drivers, it appears that they fail to engage the appropriate scanning strategies, not looking broadly enough to see the potential risks (e.g., 28% of the drivers neither saw the foreshadowing element nor fixated on the potentially risky area in the T-intersection scenario even when they had plenty of opportunity to do such). For other drivers, it appears that they scan effectively, but are not sufficiently sensitive to the risks, perhaps because the scenario is an infrequent one. For example, in the same scenario, the percentage of drivers who fixate the risky area, given that they saw the foreshadowing element, is higher than the percentage of drivers who fixated the risky area, given that they did not fixate the foreshadowing element. The foreshadowing element increases the potency of the risk, and these drivers then fixate the risky area. Finally, it appears that there are those drivers who scan effectively, but either do not comprehend the risks or, if they do comprehend them, fail to project the correct action from those risks. Again, in the same scenario, the percentage of drivers who fixate the risky area, given that they have fixated the foreshadowing element, is considerably less than unity. These alternatives clearly need to be pursued before an effective training program can be developed.

## ACKNOWLEDGMENTS

Various aspects of this research were funded by grants from the Link Foundation for Simulation and Training, the AAA Foundation for Traffic Safety, the Massachusetts Governor's Highway Safety Bureau, the National Center for Injury Prevention and Control, the National Highway Traffic Safety Administration, and the National Science Foundation (equipment grant no. SBR 9413733 for the partial acquisition of the driving simulator).

The authors especially want to thank Robert Glaser, Reddy Kichhanagari, Anuj Pradhan, and Nancy Laurie for all the work that they put into developing the visual databases, running the subjects, and analyzing the results in the experiments reported in this chapter; Robin Riessman for her help with the administration of portions of the contract; Michelle Langone in the Department of Civil and Environmental Engineering for her help with the collection of the Massachusetts data for teen drivers; and Tom Marlow for his help keeping the driving simulator always operating at its fullest potential.

## Notes

1. The preliminary results of a field study using instrumented vehicles reported just this year did include a record of actual vehicle and driver behavior in crashes (Dingus, 2005). However, novice drivers have not yet been included in the sample.

2. Age was recorded in whole years, not years and months.

3. It is possible that the useful field of view expands with experience and thus that the fixation data for experienced drivers underestimates how well they are attending and recognizing risks. However, we doubt it, because the inexperienced drivers are not inexperienced either in viewing the world from a moving vehicle or in driving themselves through the world.

4. There may have been some among the 31% who understood the risks, but did not project them correctly.

## References

Crundall, D. E., & Underwood, G. (1998). Effects of experience and processing demands on visual information acquisition in drivers. *Ergonomics, 41,* 448–458.

Dingus, T. (July 2005). *Naturalistic driving and the Virginia Tech 100 car study.* Presented at Driving Assessment 2005. Rockport, Maine.

Endsley, M. R. (1995). Towards a theory of situation awareness. *Human Factors, 37,* 32–64.

Evans, L. (1991). *Traffic safety and the driver.* New York: Van Nostrand Reinhold.

Fisher, D. L., Laurie, N. E., Glaser, R., Connerney, K., Pollatsek, A., Duffy, S. A., & Brock, J. (2002). The use of an advanced driving simulator to evaluate the effects of training and experience on drivers' behavior in risky traffic scenarios. *Human Factors, 44,* 287–302.

———, Narayanaan, V., Pradhan, A., & Pollatsek, A. (2004). The use of eye movements to evaluate the effect of PC-based risk awareness training on an advanced driving simulator. In *Proceedings of the 48th Human Factors and Ergonomics Society's annual meeting* (p. 2266). Santa Monica, Calif.: Human Factors and Ergonomics Society.

Garay-Vega, L., & Fisher, D. L. (2005). Can novice drivers recognize foreshadowed risks as easily as experienced drivers. *Proceedings of the Third International Driving Symposium on Human Factors in Driver Assessment, Training and Vehicle Design* (pp. 441–447). Iowa City: University of Iowa Public Policy Center.

Insurance Institute for Highway Safety. (2002). *Fatality factors for older people.* [Online]. Accessed September 14, 2004. Available: www.highwaysafety. org/safety_facts/fatality_facts/older_people.htm

Insurance Institute for Highway Safety. (2005, February 24). *Fewer 16 year-olds are getting involved in crashes: Big decline in crash rates of beginning drivers over a decade.* [Online]. Accessed May 24, 2005. Available: www.iihs.org/news_releases/2005/ pr022405.htm

Kantowitz, B. H., & Knight, J. L. (1976). Testing tapping timesharing: I. Auditory secondary task. *Acta Psychologica, 40,* 343–362.

Kirk, A., & Stamatiadis, N. (2001). Crash rates and traffic maneuvers of younger drivers. *Transportation Research Record, 1779,* 68–74.

McKnight, J. A., & McKnight, S. A. (2003). Young novice drivers: Careless or clueless. *Accident Analysis and Prevention, 35,* 921–925.

Mourant, R. R., & Rockwell, T. R. (1972). Strategies of visual search by novice drivers and experienced drivers. *Human Factors, 14,* 325–335.

National Center for Statistics and Analysis. (2004). *Fatality analysis reporting system: Web-base encyclopedia.* [Online]. Available: www-fars.nhtsa. dot.gov

Navon, D., & Gopher, D. (1979). On the economy of human information processing systems. *Psychological Review, 86,* 254–255.

Pollatsek, A., Narayanaan, V., Pradhan, A., & Fisher, D. L. (2006). The use of eye movements to evaluate the effect of PC-based risk awareness training on an advanced driving simulator. *Human Factors, 48,* 447–464.

Pradhan, A, Fisher, D. L., & Pollatsek, A. (June 2005a). The effects of PC-based training on novice drivers' risk awareness in a driving simulator. In *Proceedings of the Third International Driving Symposium on Human Factors in Driving Assessment, Training, and Vehicle Design* (pp. 81–89). Iowa City: University of Iowa Public Policy Center.

Pradhan, A. K., Hammel, K. R., DeRamus, R., Pollatsek, A., Noyce, D. A., & Fisher, D. L. (2005b). The use of eye movements to evaluate the effects of driver age on risk perception in an advanced driving simulator. *Human Factors, 47,* 840–852.

Renge, K. (1980). The effects of driving experience on a driver's visual attention. *International Association of Traffic Safety Sciences Research, 4,* 95–106.

Schneider, W., & Fisk, A. D. (1982). Concurrent automatic and controlled visual search: Can processing occur without cost? *Journal of Experimental Psychology: Learning, Memory and Cognition, 8,* 261–278.

———, & Shiffrin, R. M. (1977). Controlled and automatic human information processing I: Detection, search, and attention. *Psychological Review, 84,* 1–66.

Wickens, C. D. (1980). The structure of attentional resources. In R. Nickerson (Ed.), *Attention and performance VIII* (pp. 63–101). New York: Academic Press.

———. (1984). Processing resources in attention. In R. Parasuraman & R. Davies (Eds.), *Varieties of attention* (pp. 63–102). Orlando: Academic Press.

———. (1991). Processing resources and attention. In D. Damos (Ed.), *Multiple task performance* (pp. 3–34). London: Taylor & Francis.

Wickens, C. D., & Hollands, J. G. (2000). *Engineering psychology and human performance* (3rd ed.). Upper Saddle River, N.J.: Prentice Hall.

Willis, D. K. (1998). The impetus for the development of a new risk management training program for teen drivers. In *Proceedings of the Human Factors and Ergonomics Society 42nd annual meeting* (pp. 1394–1395). Chicago, Ill.: Human Factors and Ergonomics Society.

# Part IV

# Attention and Aging

# Chapter 11

# Attention Goes Home: Support for Aging Adults

## Arthur D. Fisk and Wendy A. Rogers

Older adults, like younger adults, engage in a variety of activities every day. Some of these activities— walking, getting up from a chair, going to the bathroom, eating a meal—are fundamentally important for daily functioning. These activities are referred to as *activities of daily living* (ADLs) (Lawton, 1990). Other activities are more cognitively intense, such as balancing a checkbook, maintaining a medication regimen, or preparing a meal. These activities are referred to as *instrumental activities of daily living* (IADLs) (Lawton, 1990) and are necessary for independent living. Other activities are related more to quality of life, such as pursuing educational opportunities, engaging in hobbies and leisure activities, or communicating with family and friends. These are referred to as *enhanced activities of daily living* (EADLs) (Rogers, Meyer, Walker, & Fisk, 1998).

The psychological processes of attention are involved in the behaviors associated with many of these activities, especially IADLs and EADLs. Consequently, it is important to understand if and how attentional processes change as individuals age. Both of us have studied attention and aging for nearly 20 years. Of course, we are not alone in these pursuits, as evidenced by reviews of the field (McDowd & Shaw, 2000; Rogers & Fisk, 2001; Rogers & Spieler, in press). However, our focus in this chapter is on our journey to understand issues of aging and attention as they relate to everyday activities of older adults. Our overarching goal has been to conduct practically relevant research—that which advances both theory and practice (Fisk & Kirlik, 1996).

### AGING AND ATTENTION: HISTORICAL OVERVIEW

#### The Prevailing Belief

We referred to the psychological *processes* of attention because attention is a multidimensional construct involving selection of information, sustained effort over time, more focus on certain stimuli relative to other stimuli, and a switch between tasks (Parasuraman & Davies, 1984). James (1890) recognized and described these varieties of attention, and present-day studies in neuropsychology have confirmed the differences by showing varying patterns of brain activation for tasks that differ in the nature of their attentional demands (Parasuraman, 1998).

Tasks that are attentionally demanding in some way are presumed to require control processing whereas those tasks that can be initiated without attention are referred to as being performed via automatic processing (Schneider & Shiffrin, 1977; Shiffrin & Schneider, 1977). Most complex tasks require both automatic and control processing. For example, when driving a car, little attention is required for an experienced driver to steer or change gears. However, control processing is required for monitoring the roadway, responding to unexpected events, and route planning.

Based in part on an influential paper published by Hasher and Zacks (1979), the general view in the early 1980s in the cognitive aging literature was that age-related differences should be most evident for control processes but not for automatic processes. These hypotheses were tested using memory and visual search detection tasks wherein consistently mapped (CM) stimuli may lead to automatic processing after practice but variably mapped (VM) stimuli continue to require control processing. During a CM task, stimuli or classes of stimuli are always associated with the same response (e.g., shifting to second gear always requires a downward movement). During a VM task, the same stimulus may be responded to in different ways across trials (e.g., sometimes a highway sign is relevant and results in the driver taking an exit; sometimes it is irrelevant and is ignored).

The consensus of early studies in this area was that age-related differences were minimized for CM tasks, but exacerbated for VM tasks (e.g., Gilmore, Tobias, & Royer, 1985; Madden, 1983; Madden & Nebes, 1980; Plude & Hoyer, 1981; Plude, Kaye, Hoyer, Post, Saynisch, & Hahn, 1983; Puglisi, 1986; Salthouse, & Somberg, 1982). However, Fisk and colleagues (1988) conducted a study in which they provided much more extensive practice than most of the earlier studies and they found the opposite pattern of results. As illustrated in Figure 11.1, younger adults did not show an increase in reaction time (RT) with an increase in memory set size for the CM stimuli, which is one indication of an automatic process. On the contrary, even after 8100 trials of practice, older adults did show a significant slope for the function relating RT to memory

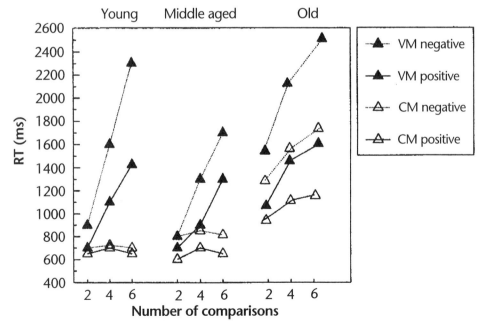

FIGURE 11.1. Consistent mapping (CM) and varied mapping (VM) performance for younger, middle-age, and older adults. From Fisk, McGee, and Giambra (1988). Reprinted with permission.

set size. Thus age-related differences were observed for the CM task. For the VM task, the pattern was quite similar across younger and older adults. That is, at the end of practice, the VM comparison slope estimates were similar across age groups. (Note that the middle-age group did not differ substantially from the younger group for either the CM task or the VM task.)

What was the source of the difference between the results of Fisk and colleagues (1988) and the previously reported findings in the literature? One possibility was the amount of practice provided in the different studies. Figure 11.2 presents a schematic of what age-related differences for CM and VM might be at different points in practice. If the amount of practice were stopped at points 1 or 2, age-related differences would be larger for the VM task relative to the CM task; at point 3, the age-related differences would be similar across the two tasks. However, at point 4, the pattern is reversed, with larger differences for the CM task relative to the VM task. This explanation seemed to represent the trends reported in the literature. It also made clear that patterns of performance observed early in practice could not necessarily be extended to explain performance after extended practice.

Although differential amounts of practice as well as other methodological differences seemed to explain the disparity in patterns of data, this explanation did not provide any real insight into the mechanisms underlying the age-related differences for CM and VM tasks. We spent the 1990s pursuing a theoretical understanding of such mechanisms. The goal was to understand more completely aging and control processes as well as automatic processes.

## Locus of Age-Related Differences in Control versus Automatic Processing

The data described earlier revealed that age-related differences were sometimes observed for CM tasks and sometimes observed for VM tasks. Figure 11.3 provides a road map of our quest to understand the underlying mechanisms of these differences. The first question we asked was whether the source of the differences was the result of encoding, responding, or some central processing difference. The encoding explanation was not very plausible, because in most studies participants were screened to ensure that their vision was sufficient to see the stimuli and the stimulus sizes were large enough to minimize encoding as a source of the age-related differences.

Research suggested that the response component of the task was a likely candidate, because the response requirements (e.g., "respond only yes for target presence" vs. "respond yes for target presence and no for target absence") had been shown to influence performance for both CM tasks (Egeth, Jonides, & Wall, 1972; Fisk & Ackerman, 1988; Kristofferon, 1975) and VM tasks (Strayer, Wickens, & Braune, 1987).

We investigated the role of the response component of the task by requiring participants to respond only when a target was present or only respond when a target was absent (Fisk, Rogers, & Giambra, 1990). The results showed that regardless of the response requirements of the task, age-related differences were observed after extensive practice on the CM search task, with younger adults developing an automatic process, but older adults continuing to perform the task using control processing. Age-related differences in comparison times for the VM task were minimal after practice.

As illustrated in Figure 11.3, we focused next on the central processes involved in search detection tasks to identify the mechanisms underlying age-related performance differences. Many of the tasks reported in the literature had required memory scanning (hold several items in memory and compare with one item in a display), visual search (hold one item in memory and compare it with several items in a display), or a mixed memory/visual search task (hold several items in memory and compare them with several items in a display). The problem was that the role of the memory and visual search components had not been isolated to determine their relative influence on age-related differences in performance.

The goal of the series of studies by Fisk and Rogers (1991) was to investigate memory scanning and visual search for CM and VM tasks for younger and older adults for different levels of task complexity (letter search vs. category search). The general pattern of age-related results was as follows: (1) differences for VM visual search were minimal, (2) differences for VM memory search were evident, (3) differences for CM memory search were minimal, and (4) differences for CM visual search remained even after extensive practice.

The VM memory search differences were assumed to be the result of the continued working memory demands required for a control processing task. Working memory declines with age have been well-documented (for a review, see Zacks and associates [2000]).

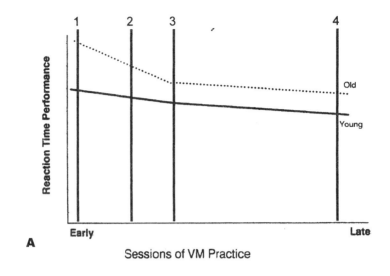

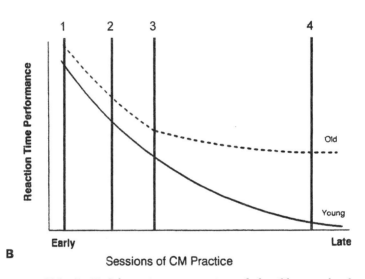

FIGURE 11.2. (A, B) Schematic representations of plausible age-related differences in varied mapping (VM) and consistent mapping (CM) performance as a function of sessions of practice. If the amount of practice were stopped at points 1 or 2, age-related differences would be larger for the VM task relative to the CM task, at point 3 the age-related differences would be similar across the two tasks, and at point 4 the differences would be larger for the CM task relative to the VM task.

Why, then, wouldn't age-related differences be evident for the CM memory task? After extensive practice on a CM memory search task, the memory set items become unitized through a process of associative learning (Schneider & Detweiler, 1987). The fact that both younger and older adults showed evidence of this memory set unitization suggested that the mechanism of associative learning remained intact for older adults.

Older adults were slower to unitize the memory set, and later studies showed that within a given older adult group there are individual differences in associative learning that influence performance on CM memory tasks (Rogers, Hertzog, & Fisk, 2000).

With respect to the visual search tasks, age-related differences in the research of Fisk and Rogers (1991) were more evident for CM, rather than VM tasks. Why?

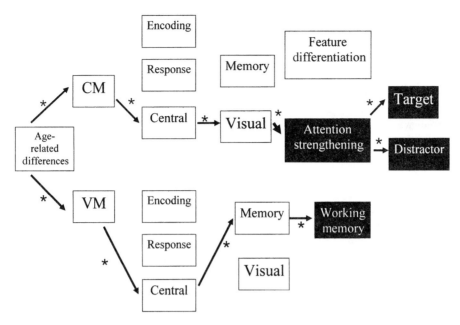

FIGURE 11.3. Identifying the source of age-related differences in attentional learning. CM, consistent mapping; VM, varied mapping.

According to the model by Schneider and Detweiler (1987) (see also Schneider and Chein [2003]), extensive CM practice can lead to the strengthening of target items and the weakening of distractor items. The resultant effect is that of an automatic attention response such that the target item attracts attention without the need for control processing. The analogy is hearing your own name called in a crowded room. Your attention is immediately captured.

Figure 11.3 shows that before we could be certain that age-related differences in CM visual search were the result of attention strengthening, we first had to rule out the possibility of age-related differences in feature differentiation. Fisher and coworkers (e.g., Fisher & Tanner, 1992) argued that practice on visual search tasks enabled participants to attend selectively to relevant features of the stimuli and hence speed their processing. Such feature learning may be necessary but not sufficient for attention strengthening. In Rogers and Fisk (1991), we designed a study to assess separately the role of feature learning and attention strengthening in age-related differences in CM visual search tasks. The results were clear: Both younger and older adults benefited from feature learning, and performance improved with practice, but only the younger adults showed evidence of attention strengthening.

As described earlier, attention strengthening in a visual search task can involve increasing the attention attraction strength of the target items as well as decreasing the attention attraction strength (i.e., weakening) of distractor items. In the study by Rogers (1992), the goal was to determine whether older adults had difficulty strengthening targets, weakening distractors, or both. The study separately assessed target learning from distractor learning, and the results showed that older adults strengthened the targets only slightly and weakened the distractors only slightly. As a result, their search became more efficient but not automatic. Younger adults, on the other hand, showed substantial strengthening of targets and weakening of distractors. The differential between targets and distractors was large enough that attention was not required to detect the presence of the target item. This study provided additional evidence that older adults were deficient in the attention-strengthening mechanism that led to the development of an automatic attention response.

### Summary of the Quest for Understanding

The results of our quest for understanding age-related differences in control and automatic processing led to some general findings that can be summarized as easy as 1, 2, 3:

1. Performance improves with both VM and CM practice for both younger and older adults.
2. VM practice yields primarily quantitative changes for both younger and older adults such that search continues to require control processing, and even with extended practice, age-related differences are most evident for VM tasks that demand working memory.
3. CM practice leads to qualitative changes in performance: (1) Memory search tasks can become automatized through associative learning for both younger and older adults, (2) visual search tasks can become automatized for younger adults through attention strengthening and weakening of targets and distractors, and (3) visual search for older adults may become more efficient, but remains a control process.

### ATTENTION AUGMENTATION

Given what we know about age-related differences in attention, how can we support the everyday activities of older adults? Can we use this fundamental knowledge of aging and attention to develop methods of attention augmentation? Where are there gaps in the knowledge that additional research will be required to fill? These are the questions that we are investigating in our current research efforts.

### Potential of Environmental Support

Within the cognitive aging literature, environmental support has been suggested as a means of minimizing age-related differences in a number of contexts (e.g., Craik, 1986). Although this theoretical proposition has mixed support (Craik & Jennings, 1992; Morrow, 2003), the idea of providing information in the world to support cognition has been espoused in other fields as well. Much support has been provided for the idea that environmental cues support performance (e.g., Hammond & Stewart, 2001). The idea that perception can support cognitive activities has been demonstrated for simple and very complex cognitive activities (e.g., Kirlik, Walker, Fisk, & Nagel, 1996). In addition, Norman (1988) argued that knowledge should be placed "in the world" rather than be required to be "in the head" of the person using a system or performing a task. Similar is the concept

in the human–computer interaction literature that cognitive orthotics or cognitive augmentation can be used to provide external support for cognitive functions (e.g., Bergman, 2002).

The concept of environmental support contends that the cognitive performance of older adults is a direct function of the amount of internal processing required by the task at hand (e.g., Craik, 1986; Craik & Jennings, 1992). That is, as internal information processing demands are decreased (e.g., by the presence of supportive cues in the environment), the performance of older adults will improve and perhaps be equivalent to the performance of younger adults. For example, in an attentional search task, the provision of cues directing attention to a spatial location in a display is a form of environmental support (Hartley, 1992).

Older adults perform less well than younger adults during dual-task conditions, and the magnitude of the age difference increases with the magnitude of single-task difficulty (McDowd, Vercruyssen, & Birren, 1992). Although there are reliable, significant age differences in dual-task studies, such age-related differences probably have multiple sources (e.g., Hartley 1992; Sit & Fisk, 1999). However, task simplification through cognitive supports appears to hold promise to facilitate older adults' ADLs that involve multiple components. For example, the provision of a site map on a Web site can aid older adults in keeping track of where they are and where they have been (Mead, Lamson, & Rogers, 2002) and a step-by step navigational aid can support information search and retrieval for both younger and older adults (Rogers, Stronge, & Pak, 2001). Providing automated reminder messages can support memory for appointments (Morrow & Leirer, 2001), and reminder cues at the appropriate time can improve medication adherence (Park, Morrell, Frieske, & Kincaid, 1992). For other examples see Fisk and Rogers (2002); Fisk, Rogers, Charness, Czaja, and Sharit (2004); Mynatt and Rogers (2002); and Rogers and Fisk (2001).

These few examples of age-related differences in cognition that are relevant to everyday tasks are only illustrative. Based on the literature, one can establish a generalized understanding of the existing cognitive support needs of older adults. Older adults have difficulties with attention, aspects of memory, inferencing, and multitasking. Environmental supports have the potential to improve performance by augmenting the attentional capabilities of older adults. An important question is whether older adults can take advantage of environmental information to improve performance.

## Environmental Consistency as Environmental Support

One potentially promising means of providing environmental support is to add it to the structure of the task incidentally. That is, aspects of the task might be correlated in such a way that attending to and learning the correlated information can support task performance—for example, knowing that the Microsoft Word icon on your desktop is located in the upper left corner of your screen is not necessary to open the program, but it may enable you to open the program more quickly, if that location is consistently correlated with that program. This is an example of environmental consistency serving as environmental support.

We assessed younger and older adults' ability to benefit from environmental consistency in a series of studies. In one study (Caine, Nichols, Fisk, & Rogers, 2005), we found that younger adults could benefit from correlated information (especially if it was 100% consistent), but older adults were unable to do so. In a conceptual replication with different stimuli, a smaller display, and more conspicuous environmental cues, we found the same pattern: Younger adults benefited from the environmental consistency but older adults did not (Caine et al., 2005).

One plausible explanation for the age-related difference was that older adults were not attending to the environmental information, not because they could not, but because their strategy was to focus on the targets in the task, to the exclusion of other potentially helpful information. Age-related differences in task strategies have been shown to account for performance differences in other tasks (e.g., Rogers & Gilbert, 1997; Rogers et al., 2000). We conducted a study with older adults to assess the strategy hypothesis directly (Caine et al., 2005). We investigated the role of strategies by introducing an instructional manipulation to the task. Participants who were told to attend to the incidental information were able to benefit from that correlated information significantly more so than participants who were either given no instructions at all or whose attention was misdirected. These results show that older adults can benefit from environmental consistency as a form of environmental support. However, such benefits may only be evidenced if

older adults recognize and attend to the correlated information.

## ATTENTION GOES HOME

### Attentional Demands of the Home Environment

There is a growing need in society to enable older adults to remain in an independent living environment. Many older adults fear losing their independence and being required to move to an assisted living environment (e.g., AARP, 2000; Shafer, 2000). Moreover, the initial and long-term economic implications of transitioning to one of these settings are substantial to the individual and to society as a whole. Given current demographics, the projection of these costs will increase exponentially.

Older adults who are living in their own home may be faced with situations in which there is a mismatch between the demands in their daily environment and their capabilities. These situations may be the result of both increased demands (e.g., learning to use a new medical device) and deficits in the capabilities of the individual (e.g., age-related changes in cognition, perception, or movement control). To remain fully functional, older adults must find ways to compensate for gaps between task demands required for living and their capabilities. Even healthy, well-educated older individuals still have difficulties with the demands of an independent living situation as a result of diminished cognitive capabilities (Diehl, Willis, & Schaie, 1995).

Although there have been detailed analyses of loss of process such as a slip of action or a lapse of attention (e.g., Norman, 1981; Reason, 1990), these studies have not focused on the methods that people use to recover their process or the cues that inform them that they have made an error. In addition, it is not yet known whether the occurrence of these errors, the recognition that they have occurred, and the recovery of the process differ either quantitatively or qualitatively as a function of age.

A variety of tasks performed in the home environment require carrying out a sequence of actions, such as following a recipe to prepare a meal (Diehl et al., 1995), performing calibration procedures on a medical device (Rogers, Mykityshyn, Campbell, & Fisk, 2001), or loading a medication organizer (Park, Morrell, Frieske, Blackburn, & Birchmore, 1991).

Such sequential tasks are likely to be susceptible to loss of the process—forgetting where one is, skipping a step, or performing the same step more than once—especially if one is interrupted.

Research on the nature of interruptions and the utility of technical supports to aid recovery from interruptions has focused on assisting people in preparing for an interruption (e.g., Trafton, Altmann, Brock, & Mintz, 2003) or using a computer to determine when is the best time to interrupt someone (McCrickard, Catrambone, Chewar, & Stasko, 2003). However, although the fact that interruptions lead to memory and attention issues is well established, the locus of the cause of the problems has yet to be clearly identified.

The nature of interruptions in the home is likely to be unpredictable and uncontrollable (e.g., the telephone or doorbell rings). Understanding the locus of the influence of such interruptions will provide fundamental information about the source of the loss of process. The findings of support for predominantly an encoding issue or predominantly a retrieval issue will also provide guidance for the development of effective cognitive supports. For example, if the problem is primarily the result of an encoding failure, then the type of support will serve as a "memory" because the information was not stored in the first place. If interruption primarily affects retrieval, then helping to recreate the state of memory prior to the interruption would be appropriate as a cognitive aid (e.g., Schneider & Detweiler, 1987).

## Advancing Theory and Practice: Attention Goes Home

There is promise for psychologically based approaches to address many cognitive challenges of daily living. Our focus is on providing support for attentionally demanding tasks in the home environment, based on our research on attention and aging. However, to move toward development of supports to bridge the gap between the demands of the tasks that must be performed and the capabilities of the individuals who must perform them, we need to have more detailed analyses of the sources of the problems, the nature of the problems, and the contexts in which they occur. In particular, more focus needs to be placed on the role of cognition in home functioning.

Our ultimate goal is to develop a framework of task transformations—how tasks should be changed to accommodate the capabilities and limitations of older adults. Development of this framework will require both quantitative and qualitative data concerning the home tasks with which older adults have difficulties. Such a framework can guide the development of prototype supports that capitalize on intact capabilities and provide support for cognitive needs.

There is not an existing framework to guide the transformation of tasks to support older adults' activities required for independent living. Utilizing a theory such as Wickens's (1980) multiple-resource theory is a good first approximation. However, we must first develop a framework to characterize the relationship between cognitive performance and the use of environmental cues. A foundation for our framework comes from attention theory (e.g., Schneider & Detweiler, 1987) as well as from "ecological" theories (e.g., Hammond, 1966; Hammond & Stewart, 2001; Kirlik, 1995; Vicente, 1997). For an adequate theory to emerge from foundations of prior psychological theories, we must understand how the nature of the cues in the environment provide support for cognitive functioning in some cases, yet overload cognitive functioning in other cases. Similarly, it is necessary to determine whether the use of environmental cues interacts with cognitive capabilities (e.g., differs for younger vs. older adults). Moreover, the effects of transformations may be additive or interactive across tasks. A valid representation of the relationships between human capabilities and task demands will lead to predictions about the potential for interventions to support cognitive functioning. These interventions can be tested in the form of technological supports (i.e., cognitive augmentations).

## The Aware Home at Georgia Tech

The idea that intelligence can be designed into the home to support the activities of the people living there is not new. Simple examples of technology supports designed into home products and systems include sensor lights that turn on when one enters a room, programmable thermostats that enable differential temperature settings throughout the day, and alarms that respond to the opening of a window or the presence of smoke. Such efforts are referred to as "smart" homes, or "domotics," and discussions of prototypes are available online (e.g., www.smart-homes.nl, www.sentha.tu-berlin.de/, www.stakes.fi/cost219/smarthousing.htm, www.gdewsbury.ukideas. com/).

Moving beyond simple control of home systems are efforts to provide the home with the intelligence to

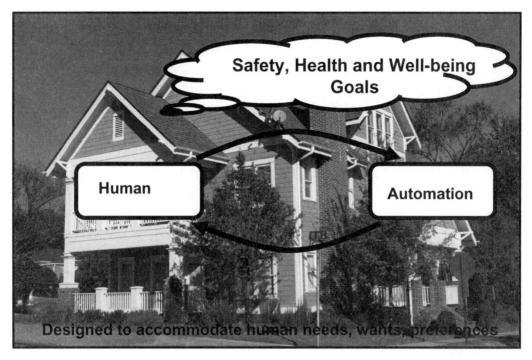

FIGURE 11.4. The Aware Home collaborative environment at the Georgia Institute of Technology (www. awarehome.gatech.edu/).

support complex activities (i.e., developing an "aware" home). An aware home is embedded with computer intelligence that can augment the activities of the people living in the home, supporting their activities, providing interactive information to the home dwellers and selected individuals outside the home, and enabling the development of predictive models of changes in capabilities based on trending information. Such efforts are the focus of research at the Georgia Tech Aware Home (Figure 11.4).

The Aware Home Research Initiative (www. awarehome.gatech.edu) at Georgia Tech brings together specialists in psychology, computer science, engineering, and design. The Aware Home is a laboratory that provides the opportunity to conduct controlled research in a realistic home environment. Participants can be tested during the course of a day or several days, performing typical ADLs. We think of the home as a collaborative environment. Technology in the home can provide augmentation and support to the person living in the home; that person must be willing and able to interact with the technological supports being provide.

The Aware Home Residential Laboratory is a fully furnished, state-of-the-art, 5,040-square foot two-story

residence. The two floors are identical apartments, each consisting of a full kitchen, dining area and living room, two bedrooms, two bathrooms, an office, and laundry room. The apartments facilitate conducting advanced research on one floor while simultaneously being able to support experimentation on another floor. The basement contains a conference room with full multimedia presentation capabilities as well as a machine room, storage rooms, and two large project areas. The facility was constructed to look as much like a normal house as possible, with some concessions to facilitate research. There is a drop ceiling with hidden cable trays to permit rewiring and sensor installation. To facilitate computational perception research, indirect lighting was provided, high-gloss paints and chrome finishes were avoided, and the floor is bleached hardwood.

An aware home can potentially recognize that a crisis has occurred—for example a fire, the stove left on, a person has fallen. It can support everyday cognition such as medical monitoring and memory support, the data gathered can provide insight into daily and long-term trends for individuals, and it may support connectedness and communication with family and friends. Awareness is accomplished through

FIGURE 11.5.  Support systems throughout the Aware Home.

monitoring systems such as cameras and other types of sensors (e.g., motion detectors, weight sensors) as well as audio input and output systems. There are also support systems and displays throughout the house, as illustrated in Figure 11.5.

Just as computer science efforts need to be informed by psychological science, the desire to transform a task to minimize the cognitive demands on older adults needs to be informed by a realistic assessment of current and likely future technology capabilities. Mynatt and others (Mynatt, Essa, & Rogers, 2000; Mynatt & Rogers, 2002; Abowd, Bobick, Essa, Mynatt, & Rogers, 2002) described a set of technologies such as new monitoring techniques and a spectrum of application possibilities such as memory aids that form the underpinnings for investigating realistic technological aids for older adults. Particular capabilities that can be exploited include (1) the ability of computer systems to monitor, capture, summarize, and display records of human activity; (2) direct and "natural" input and output technologies such as touch input and audio output; (3) the ability of computer systems to recognize key human activities such as walking, eating, and manipulating objects; and (4) data visualization techniques for presenting information to older adults, in particular using video-based images that have the potential to convey the rich context surrounding a person's activity.

There is no magic technology bullet to solve the challenges of older adults trying to maintain their independence. Understanding the constraints of technology is just as critical as understanding its potential. For example, computer systems are well suited for capturing, summarizing, and displaying records of human activity. In contrast, these systems are very limited in their ability to predict future actions. Similarly computer systems can easily capture, store, and manipulate natural input such as voice and handwriting, but the recognition of that content in a free-form environment (e.g., not wearing a microphone) at an acceptable accuracy is unlikely in the foreseeable future. A guiding design principle is to investigate the combinations of human and technology capabilities that maximize the strengths of both while trying to compensate for respective weaknesses. As an example, technology can easily serve the role of an external memory aid and, given that resource, older adults should be able to complete previously challenging tasks such as resuming an interrupted activity or retrieving a misplaced object.

## ADVANCING THE RESEARCH AGENDA

These research efforts in the Aware Home environment have grown from our understanding of age-related differences in attentional processes. We have a good understanding of the limitations and capabilities of older adults as they are manifested in well-controlled task environments. Our current research efforts will improve knowledge for the principled development of age-related system design and will enhance basic understanding of cognition for older adults in relatively complex, rich task domains. These data from laboratory and "in-home" tests will allow the formulation of a framework of age-related task interaction for complex tasks to address the important issue of scale of complexity in psychological theory. This will allow categorization and tracking of performance issues across various task domains, improve the generalizability of age-related theories, and improve the accessibility of these theories to designers. The latter benefit leads to more direct benefits, including improvements in the quality of life, independence, and the well-being of older adults.

A serious fear among older adults is becoming dependent on other people and losing their sense of dignity. Current technology has the power to aid in the reduction of such fears by facilitating activities required for successful aging. Such technology can aid performance and can leave intact, and even enhance, a person's dignity. Unfortunately, investigation of the science and engineering of such advanced technology has been lacking from the perspective of the *human* in the human–machine system. For many problems confronting maintenance of quality of life for older adults, we should not be asking what technology *can* do, but rather we should ask what it *should* do. The length of life is increasing and our societies are getting older. As other have pointed out, the effects of increasing the length of life are many and are still unfolding. We would argue that by understanding basic issues of cognitive aging and translating that knowledge into design, longer life does not need to mean more years of decline but rather more years of fulfillment and independence.

Developing technology-based attention augmentation should be informed by data concerning the relative benefits of different cue types, information abstractions, and display formats. The ability to perform assessments of design within a fully instrumented aware home is a unique opportunity. "In-home" assessment can allow researchers to approximate closely actual ADLs.

Such assessments will lead to design guidelines but will also enable testing of fundamental ideas about aging and attention, for example, in a complex environment.

## ACKNOWLEDGMENTS

The authors thank Chris Wickens for his inspiration through the years. Research reported here was supported in part by the following grants: grant no. P01 AG17211 from the National Institutes of Health (National Institute on Aging) under the auspices of the Center for Research and Education on Aging and Technology Enhancement and Award grant no. 0121661 "The Aware Home: Sustaining the Quality of Life for an Aging Population" from the National Science Foundation.

## References

AARP (2000). *Fixing to stay: A national survey on housing and home modification issues—Executive summary.* Washington, D.C.: American Association of Retired Persons.

Abowd, G., Bobick, A., Essa, I., Mynatt, E., & Rogers, W. (2002). *The aware home: Developing technologies for successful aging.* In *Proceedings of AAAI Workshop and Automation as a Care Giver,* Presented at the American Association of Artificial Intelligence (AAAI) Conference 2002. Alberta, Canada.

Bergman, M. (2002). The benefits of a cognitive orthotic in brain injury rehabilitation. *Journal of Head Trauma Rehabilitation, 17,* 431–445.

Caine, K. E., Nichols, T. A., Fisk, A. D., & Rogers, W. A. (2005). Age-related differences in learning incidental environmental information. In *Proceedings of the Human Factors and Ergonomics Society 49th annual meeting* (pp. 1856–1858). Santa Monica, Calif.: Human Factors and Ergonomics Society.

Craik, F. I. M. (1986). A functional account of age differences in memory. In F. Klix & H. Hagendorf (Eds.), *Human memory and cognitive abilities* (pp. 409–422). Amsterdam: Elsevier.

———, & Jennings, J. M. (1992). Human memory. In F. I. M. Craik & T. A. Salthouse (Eds.), *The handbook of aging and cognition* (pp. 51–110). Mahwah, N.J.: Erlbaum.

Diehl, M., Willis, S. L., & Schaie, K. W. (1995). Everyday problem solving on older adults: Observational assessment and cognitive correlates. *Psychology and Aging, 10,* 478–491.

Egeth, H., Jonides, J., & Wall, S. (1972). Parallel processing of multielement displays. *Cognitive Psychology, 3,* 674–698.

Fisher, D. L., & Tanner, N. S. (1992). Optimal symbol selection: A semi-automated procedure. *Human Factors, 34,* 79–96.

Fisk, A. D., & Ackerman, P. L. (1988). Effects of type of responding on consistent and varied memory/visual search: Responding just "yes" or just "no" can lead to inflexible performance. *Perception & Psychophysics, 43,* 373–379.

———, & Kirlik, A. (1996). Practical relevance and age-related research: Can theory advance without practice? In W. A. Rogers, A. D. Fisk, & N. Walker (Eds.), *Aging and skilled performance: Advances in theory and application* (pp. 1–15). Mahwah, N.J.: Erlbaum.

———, McGee, N. D., & Giambra, L. M. (1988). The influence of age on consistent and varied semantic category search performance. *Psychology and Aging, 3,* 323–333.

———, & Rogers, W. A. (1991). Toward an understanding of age-related memory and visual search effects. *Journal of Experimental Psychology: General, 120,* 131–149.

———, & Rogers, W. A. (2002). Psychology and aging: Enhancing the lives of an aging population. *Current Directions in Psychological Science, 11,* 107–110.

———, Rogers, W. A., Charness, N., Czaja, S. J., & Sharit, J. (2004). *Designing for older adults: Principles and creative human factors approaches.* Boca Raton, Fla.: CRC Press.

———, Rogers, W. A., & Giambra, L. M. (1990). Consistent and varied memory/visual search: Is there an interaction between age and response-set effects? *Journals of Gerontology: Psychological Sciences, 45,* P81–P87.

Gilmore, G. C., Tobias, T. R., & Royer, F. L. (1985). Aging and similarity grouping in visual search. *Journal of Gerontology, 40,* 586–592.

Hammond, K. R. (1966). *The psychology of Egon Brunswik.* New York: Holt, Rinehart & Wilson.

———, & Stewart, T. R. (2001). *The essential Brunswik: Beginnings, explications, applications.* New York: Oxford University Press.

Hartley, A. A. (1992). Attention. In T. A. Salthouse & F. I. M. Craik (Eds.), *Handbook of aging and cognition* (pp. 3–49). Hillsdale, N.J.: Erlbaum.

Hasher, L., & Zacks, R. T. (1979). Automatic and effortful processes in memory. *Journal of Experimental Psychology: General, 108,* 356–388.

James, W. (1890/1950). *The principles of psychology* (vol. 1). New York: Holt, Rinehart & Winston.

Kirlik, A. (1995). Requirements for psychological models to support design: Toward ecological task analysis. In J. Flach, P. A. Hancock, J. Caird, & K. J. Vicente (Eds.), *Global perspectives on the ecology of human–machine systems* (vol. 1, pp. 68–120). Hillsdale, N.J.: Erlbaum.

———, Walker, N., Fisk, A. D., & Nagel, K. (1996). Supporting perception in the service of dynamic decision making. *Human Factors, 38*(2), 288–299.

Kristofferson, M. W. (1975). On the interaction between memory scanning and response set. *Memory & Cognition, 3,* 102–106.

Lawton, M. P. (1990). Aging and performance on home tasks. *Human Factors, 32,* 527–536.

Madden, D. J. (1983). Aging and distraction by highly familiar stimuli during visual search. *Developmental Psychology, 19,* 499–507.

———, & Nebes, R. D. (1980). Aging and the development of automaticity in visual search. *Developmental Psychology, 16,* 377–384.

McCrickard, D. S., Catrambone, R., Chewar, C. M., & Stasko, J. T. (2003). Establishing tradeoffs that leverage attention for utility: Empirically evaluating information display in notification systems. *International Journal of Human–Computer Studies, 58*(5), 547–582.

McDowd, J. M., & Shaw, R. J. (2000). Attention and aging: A functional perspective. In F. I. M. Craik & T. A. Salthouse (Eds.), *Handbook of aging and cognition* (2nd ed., pp. 221–292). Mahwah, N.J.: Erlbaum.

McDowd, J., Vercruyssen, M., & Birren, J. E. (1992). Aging, divided attention, and dual-task performance. In D. L. Damos (Ed.), *Multiple-task performance* (pp. 387–414). New York: Taylor and Francis.

Mead, S. E., Lamson, N., & Rogers, W. A. (2002). Human factors guidelines for Web site usability: Health-oriented Web sites for older adults. In R. W. Morrell (Ed.), *Older adults, health information, and the World Wide Web* (pp. 89–107). Mahwah, N.J.: Erlbaum.

Morrow, D. G. (2003). Technology as environmental support for older adults' daily performance. In N. Charness & K. W. Schaie (Eds.), *The impact of technology on successful aging* (pp. 290–305). New York: Springer-Verlag.

———, & Leirer, V. O. (2001). A patient-centered approach to automated telephone health communication for older adults. In W. A. Rogers & A. D. Fisk (Eds.), *Human factors interventions for the health care of older adults* (pp. 179–202). Mahwah, N.J.: Erlbaum.

Mynatt, E. D., Essa, I., & Rogers, W. (2000). Increasing the opportunities for aging in place. In *Proceedings of the 2000 Conference on Universal Usability* (pp. 65–71). Washington, D.C: ACM.

———, & Rogers, W. A. (2002). Developing technology to support the functional independence of older adults. *Ageing International, 27,* 24–41.

Norman, D. A. (1981). Categorization of action slips. *Psychological Review, 88*(1), 1–15.

———. (1988). *The psychology of everyday things.* New York: Harper Collins.

Parasuraman, R. (1998). *The attentive brain.* Cambridge, Mass.: MIT Press.

———, & Davies, D. R. (1984). *Varieties of attention.* San Diego, Calif.: Academic Press.

Park, D. C., Morrell, R. W., Frieske, D., Blackburn, A. B., & Birchmore, D. (1991). Cognitive factors and the use of over-the-counter medication organizers by arthritis patients. *Human Factors*, 33(1), 57–67.

Park, D. C., Morrell, R. W., Frieske, D., & Kincaid, D. (1992). Medication adherence behaviors in older adults: Effects of external cognitive supports. *Human Factors*, 33(1), 57–67.

Plude, D.J., & Hoyer, W. J. (1981). Adult age differences in visual search as a function of stimulus mapping and processing load. *Journal of Gerontology*, 36, 598–604.

———, Kaye, D. B., Hoyer, W. J., Post, T. A., Saynisch, M. J., & Hahn, M. V. (1983). Aging and visual search under consistent and varied mapping. *Developmental Psychology*, 19, 508–512.

Puglisi, J. T. (1986). Age-related slowing in memory search for three-dimensional objects. *Journal of Gerontology*, 41, 72–78.

Reason, J. (1990). *Human error*. New York: Cambridge University Press.

Rogers, W. A. (1992). Age differences in visual search: Target and distractor learning. *Psychology and Aging*, 7, 526–535.

———, & Fisk, A. D. (1991). Are age differences in consistent-mapping visual search due to feature learning or attention training? *Psychology and Aging*, 6, 542–550.

———, & Fisk, A. D. (2001). Understanding the role of attention in cognitive aging research. In J. E. Birren & K. W. Schaie (Eds.), *Handbook of the psychology of aging* (5th ed., pp. 267–287). San Diego, Calif.: Academic Press.

———, & Gilbert, D. K. (1997). Do performance strategies mediate age-related differences in associative learning? *Psychology and Aging*, 12, 620–633.

———, Hertzog, C., & Fisk, A. D. (2000). Age-related differences in associative learning: An individual differences analysis of ability and strategy influences. *Journal of Experimental Psychology: Learning, Memory, and Cognition*, 26, 359–394.

———, Meyer, B., Walker, N., & Fisk, A. D. (1998). Functional limitations to daily living tasks in the aged: A focus group analysis. *Human Factors*, 40, 111–125.

———, Mykityshyn, A. L., Campbell, R. H., & Fisk, A. D. (2001). Analysis of a "simple" medical device. *Ergonomics in Design*, 9, 6–14.

———, & Spieler, D. (In press). Attention and aging. In D. C. Park & N. Schwarz (Eds.), *Cognitive aging: A primer* (2nd ed.). Philadelphia, Penn.: Psychology Press.

———, Stronge, A. J., & Pak, R. (2001). Enabling older adults to successfully use the World Wide Web. *International Journal of Experimental, Clinical, and Behavioural Gerontology*, 47 (supplement 1), 216. Basel: Karger Medical and Scientific Publishers.

Salthouse, T. A., & Somberg, B. L. (1982). Skilled performance: Effects of adult age and experience on elementary processes. *Journal of Experimental Psychology: General*, 111, 176–207.

Schneider, W., & Chein, J. M. (2003). Controlled and automatic processing: Behavior , theory, and biological mechanisms. *Cognitive Science*, 27, 525–559.

———, & Detweiler, M. (1987). A connectionist/control architecture for working memory. In G. H. Bower (Ed.), *The psychology of learning and motivation: Advances in research and theory* (vol. 21, pp. 53–119). San Diego, Calif.: Academic Press.

———, & Shiffrin, R. M. (1977). Controlled and automatic human information processing: I. Detection, search and attention. *Psychological Review*, 84, 1–66.

Shafer, R. (2000). *Housing America's seniors. Executive summary*. Cambridge, Mass.: Joint Center for Housing Studies, Harvard University.

Shiffrin, R. M., & Schneider, W. (1977). Controlled and automatic human information processing: II. Perceptual learning, automatic attending, and a general theory. *Psychological Review*, 84, 127–190.

Sit, R. A., & Fisk, A. D. (1999). Age-related performance in a multiple-task environment. *Human Factors*, 41, 26–34.

Strayer, D. L., Wickens, C. D., & Braune, R. (1987). Adult age differences in the speed and capacity of information processing. 2. An electrophysiological approach. *Psychology and Aging*, 2, 99–110.

Trafton, J. G., Altmann, E. M., Brock, D. P., & Mintz, F. E. (2003). Preparing to resume an interrupted task: Effects of prospective goal encoding and retrospective rehearsal. *International Journal of Human–Computer Studies*, 58(5), 583–603.

Vicente, K. J. (1997). Heeding the legacy of Meister, Brunswik, & Gibson: Toward a broader view of human factors research. *Human Factors*, 39(2), 323–328.

Wickens, C. D. (1980). The structure of attentional resources. In R. Nickerson (Ed.), *Attention and performance VIII* (pp. 79–99). New York: Plenum.

Zacks, R. T., Hasher, L., & Li, K. Z. H. (2000). Human memory. In F. I. M. Craik & T. A. Salthouse (Eds.), *The handbook of aging and cognition* (2nd ed., pp. 293–357). Mahwah, N.J.: Erlbaum.

# Chapter 12

# The Dynamics of Attention and Aging

## *Pamela S. Tsang*

There is perhaps not a more laudable goal in engineering psychology than performance prediction (e.g., Nickerson & Pew, 2003). As many of the pioneers recognized, useful predictions are derived from scientific principles (e.g., Broadbent, 1958; Fitts, 1958; Skinner, 1960). This chapter examines the extent to which the performance predictions of the multiple-resource model are upheld in the midst of many debates about the nature of the attention construct. Because generalizability to individuals of varied characteristics is one of the best indicators of the robustness of any cognitive theory, the current chapter also examines the extent to which the multiple-resource predictions could accommodate the age-related changes in time-sharing and the moderation of the age effects by expertise.

## METAMORPHOSIS OF ATTENTION THEORIES

From Broadbent's (1958) filter theory to Wickens's (2002) structure-specific resource model, the construct of attention has taken on many forms and properties, has been ascribed to many roles and functions, and has been exemplified by many different metaphors. The two major metaphors—a structural bottleneck and a consumable fuel—represent two rather different theoretical viewpoints that have taken their turns on the center stage in the attention literature.

Few would dispute that Broadbent's (1958) filter theory instigated the still ongoing debate on the nature of attention and how it effects dual-task performance. Broadbent's filter (1958) acts as an all-or-none bottleneck that only permits one task to be performed at a time at the bottleneck stage. Whenever more than one task must be performed, the only recourse is to perform the tasks sequentially. This inescapable sequential processing necessitates a selection of which task to process first. Since early on, a central debate among bottleneck theorists has been on the locus of the bottleneck. Half a century later, this debate is far from settled (e.g., Lachter, Forster, & Ruthruff, 2004; McCann & Johnston, 1992; Sanders, 1998). This state of affairs is not the result of a lack of empirical support for either the early perceptual selection (e.g., Broadbent, 1958; Triesman, 1960) or late response selection (e.g., Deutsch & Deutsch, 1963) bottleneck models. To the contrary, there appears to be ample empirical support for both. This is problematic, however, because most bottleneck models have a single bottleneck along the information processing stages. The current dominance of the response selection model in the literature (e.g., Logan & Schulkind, 2000; Pashler & Johnston, 1998) does not squelch the need of many researchers to continue their quest for identifying the definitive bottleneck stage that could best account for dual-task limitations.

Other researchers took on a radically different approach to modeling attention. Moray (1967) and Kahneman (1973) proposed that, rather than being limited by a bottleneck, dual-task performance is constrained to the extent that the demand for attentional resources is met by its supply. Although the overall attentional supply is limited, it can be deployed flexibly in accordance to changing task demand and priority. Successful time-sharing or simultaneously processing two tasks is permitted, although not mandated, by this view. Although this view had enjoyed some prominence in the '70s and '80s, it was seriously challenged in the '80s. In particular, Navon (1984) proposed a host of alternative factors that could account for the supposedly behavioral manifestations of resource limits. Among the factors proposed were motivational factors and peripheral factors such as outcome conflicts. Despite Gopher's (1986) and others' attempts to counter Navon's challenge, Logan (2005) is probably correct in pointing out that resource theories have never fully recovered.

But Logan (2005) may be correct only in a pocket of the basic literature. In the more applied literature, resource theories, and multiple-resource theories in particular, are widely accepted. Gopher (1986) might not have persuaded all the bottleneck theorists, but he carefully laid out a framework that could accommodate both the structural and resource aspects of performance limitations, providing a boost to the notion of multiple resources that first circulated in the literature in the late '70s (e.g., Navon & Gopher, 1979).

Gopher's (1986) main thesis was that the resource construct includes both structural and energetic components. Resource limitation occurs within a structure, such as a specific information processing stage (e.g., Sanders, 1983) or specific brain space (e.g., Kinsbourn & Hicks, 1978). The structural components referred

to here are not to be confused with Kahneman's (1973) peripheral structural interference, which "occurs because the activities occupy the same mechanisms of perception or response" (p. 196). For example, requiring the same hand to reach two separate locations simultaneously would certainly degrade performance, but is not of interest in terms of understanding attentional limits.

Gopher (1986) pointed out that the main difference between a structural bottleneck and resource limitation is that the engagement of a bottleneck is all or none, whereas attentional resources can be modulated to produce performance at various levels. The performance–resource function formalized by Norman and Bobrow (1975) depicts a monotonic relationship between the amount of attentional resources invested in a task and the resultant level of performance. They noted that performance degradation is smooth and not catastrophic, indicating that resources are continuously modulated to meet task demands via a closed feedback loop between demand evaluation and performance monitoring. Subsequent neurophysiological data appeared to have produced converging evidence of such resource modulation. In addition to the activation of the various cortical regions that appear to be somewhat process specific, recent neurophysiological data reveal graded levels of neuronal activation as well as varying volumes of cortical region involvement as a function of task demand (e.g., Corbetta, Miezin, Dobmeyer, Shulman, & Petersen, 1991; D'Esposito, Detre, Alsop, Shin, Atlas, & Grossman, 1995; Just, Carpenter, & Miyake, 2003; Sirevaag, Kramer, Coles, & Donchin, 1989; Wickens, Kramer, Vanasse, & Donchin, 1983).

The attention model that has been applied most widely is the structure-specific resource model proposed by Wickens (1980, 1984, 2002). His initial model had three dichotomous resource dimensions: (1) along the information processing stages, perceptual and cognitive processing resources were proposed to be distinct from those supporting response processing; (2) spatial processing resources were considered distinct from those needed for verbal processing; and (3) separate resources for the different input (visual and auditory processing) and output (manual and speech processing) modalities were postulated.

In a more recent portrayal of attentional resources, Wickens (2002) proposes a four-dimensional model. The dichotomous distinction along the processing stages and processing codes remain unchanged from the previous model. The third dimension in the new conceptualization is perceptual channels with distinct resources proposed for visual and auditory processing. However, Wickens (2002) cautions that it might be difficult to distinguish between peripheral interference and resource competition between the two input modalities. For example, a lower level of dual-task performance from two visual tasks could be a result of competition for visual processing resources, a result of additional visual scanning needed to capture the information for processing both tasks, or both. To help with the distinction, Kramer and McCarley (2003) advocate the examination of eye movement data in addition to the behavioral data. A fourth dimension of resource—visual channels—is subsumed under the perceptual channels. Based on the interference patterns generated from time-sharing two visual tasks, Wickens (2002) distinguishes resources used for focal processing and those used for ambient processing. He further proposes that the common finding that using separate output modalities generally produces superior dual-task performance to using two manual responses could be accounted for by the fact that tasks requiring a manual response tend to be spatial in nature and tasks requiring a speech response tend to be verbal in nature. The mixed output modality advantage over a bimanual condition therefore might reflect a reduced resource competition between a spatial and a verbal task rather than a reduced competition for output resources. In this case, there would not be a need to hypothesize a distinct resource dimension for the output modalities.

The acceptance of Wickens's multiple-resource model rests largely on the utility of its predictions, which are based on the similarity of the resource demand of the time-shared tasks. Wickens (2002) highlights the application of the prediction that pertains to the extent of dual-task interference attainable and the amount of mental workload that is likely to result. This *time-sharing efficiency prediction* states that tasks that rely on dissimilar resources could be time-shared more efficiently and lead to a higher level of dual-task performance. A lessened degree of resource competition should lead to a lower level of mental workload and more spare resources that could be reserved for other duties.

Another major prediction of Wickens's multiple resource model is the *resource allocation prediction* that states that resource allocation could be facilitated by the similarity of the resource demand of the time-shared tasks. As task demand or task priority fluctuates, it should be more feasible to maintain a stable level of performance of a high-priority task by borrowing resources from and returning resources to the low-priority task as needed. Empirically, resource allocation is commonly induced by varying the relative task priority between the time-shared tasks. Being an instructional variable, task priority is not expected to alter the structural aspects of the tasks, and its effect is taken to reflect the strategic workings of a central executive control.

In the following sections, three data sets are examined for behavioral manifestations of the underlying attentional mechanism. To explore fully how time-shared tasks are performed together, both discrete and continuous tasks are examined. The generalizability of the multiple-resource predictions to different age groups and expertise levels in time-sharing is also examined.

## RESOURCE MANIFESTATION IN TIME-SHARING TWO DISCRETE TASKS

Tsang (2006; Tsang, Stork, Schieltz, Krum, Flinn, Reis, et al., 2003) had subjects between the ages of 20 years and 70 years time-share two discrete tasks: a spatial orientation task called the Planikin task and a short-term memory Sternberg task. The stimulus for both tasks was a twin-engine airplane symbol with the two engines appearing in different colors. The airplane symbol could be presented in 1 of 16 possible orientations. For the Planikin task, the target engine had the same color as a reference cross. Subjects mentally oriented the airplane symbol to determine whether the target engine was on the left or right wing of the airplane. For the memory task, subjects determined whether the airplane symbol, without regard to engine colors, belonged to one of five airplane symbols in the memory set. Subjects responded to the Planikin task manually by button presses and responded to the Sternberg task manually or by speech. Both tasks were presented visually, had spatial stimuli, and placed a heavy demand on perceptual/cognitive processing resources.

Two task pairs were generated from the single tasks: the manual Planikin task with the manual Sternberg task (manual task pair) and the manual Planikin task with the speech Sternberg task (speech task pair). The two task pairs differed only with regard to the similarity of the output modality between the time-shared tasks. More important, the two tasks shared a single stimulus, minimizing visual scanning between the processing of the two tasks and potential response order bias. Subjects were asked to process the two tasks simultaneously.

Relative task priority between the time-shared tasks was manipulated to exercise the subject's attentional control. Under the equal-priority condition, subjects were asked to divide their attention equally between the tasks. Under the differential-priority condition, Navon's (1985) *optimum–maximum procedure* with *multiple priority levels* was used. The high-priority task was designated the optimized task and subjects were given an explicit performance standard to attain for that task. Three individually established performance standards generated three graded levels of priority. The low-priority task was designated the maximized task and subjects were instructed to perform it as well as possible without interfering with attaining the optimized task performance standards.

Figure 12.1 displays the dual-task performance decrement (difference between single- and dual-task performance) for the manual and speech task pairs obtained during the equal-priority condition. As predicted by the structure-specific resource model and as commonly observed in the literature (e.g., McLeod, 1977; Nelson, Vidulich, & Bolia, 2004; Tsang & Wickens, 1988; Vidulich, 1988; Wickens, 1976), the structurally more similar (manual) task pair produced a larger dual-task decrement than the less similar (speech) task pair. But this modality effect could not be attributed easily to a difference in the processing codes associated with the manual and speech tasks because both the Planikin (spatial orientation) and the Sternberg (spatial memory) tasks required spatial processing. Although bimanual processing could entail additional requirements, such as the need to manage two motor programs simultaneously (e.g., Meyer & Kieras, 1999; Navon, 1984), the priority and practice effects discussed later show that a resource account remains viable.

Figure 12.2 shows that regardless of whether the Planikin or the Sternberg task was optimized, it was the low-priority maximized task that bore more of the burden of making two manual responses. This was indicated by the maximized task exhibiting a larger slope between the speech and manual task combinations than the optimized task.[1] Furthermore, Figure 12.3 shows that, in accordance to the multiple-resource

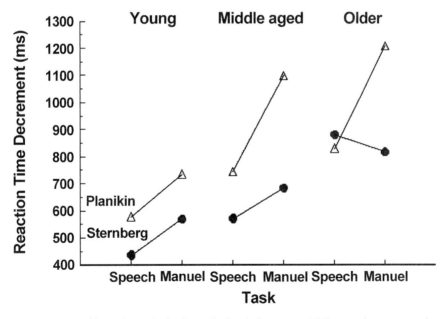

FIGURE 12.1. Older subjects had a large dual-task decrement (difference between single- and dual-task performances) in the Planikin task, especially when it was time-shared with another manual task. Speech, speech Sternberg task time-shared with manual Planikin task; Manual, manual Sternberg with manual Planikin.

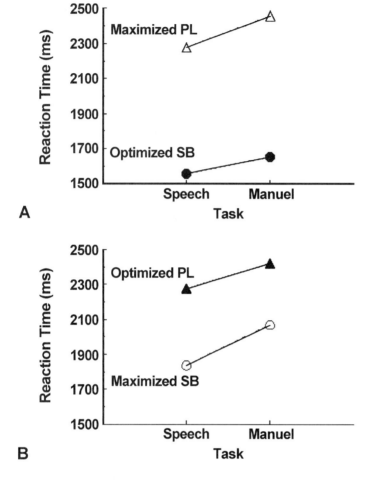

FIGURE 12.2. (A, B) Response modality of the Sternberg task affected the low-priority, maximized task more than the high-priority, optimized task regardless of whether the Sternberg or Planikin task was maximized. Note that the optimized Planikin task had a slower absolute reaction time than the maximized Sternberg task because the Planikin task naturally required more processing time. PL, Planikin task; SB, Sternberg task; Speech, speech Sternberg with manual Planikin; Manual, manual Sternberg with manual Planikin.

prediction, the task pair with a higher degree of resource similarity exhibited a larger degree of performance tradeoff, implicating a greater extent of resource exchange between the two manual tasks than between the manual and speech tasks. With practice, resource allocation improved even for the speech task pair, even though it never achieved the same extent of performance tradeoff as the manual task pair.

These results showed that although the extent of task interference (performance decrement, Fig. 12.1) and performance tradeoff (Fig. 12.3) was constrained by the exchangeability of the resources between the time-shared tasks, they could be modulated, to some extent, by effort, by practice, and by active resource allocation. In addition, that an instructional variable could modulate the response modality similarity effect implicated a resource-like property for the response modality.

### Age Effects

As Figure 12.1 illustrates, the response modality similarity effect increased with increased age. This is consistent with the finding from an earlier study that systematically manipulated the degree of structure similarity between the time-shared tasks along different dimensions of the structure-specific resource model (Tsang & Shaner, 1998). In both sets of results, the structure-specific resource prediction applies to young as well as older people, but increased age exacerbated the magnitude of the dual-task interference with increased structural similarity. Empirically estimated performance-resource functions (PRFs) from both studies showed that increased age was associated with a shallower PRF slope. This implicated an age-related reduction in processing efficiency that naturally would lead to a greater performance decrement

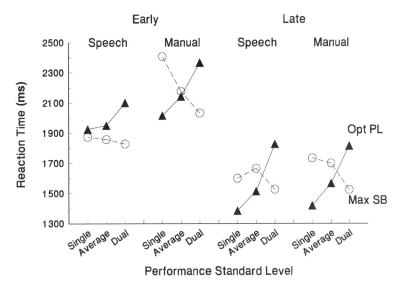

FIGURE 12.3. The manual task pair had a greater extent of performance tradeoff than the speech task pair, and the extent of the tradeoff increased with practice. This was observed among the young subjects. Three performance standards were used: single, average, and dual. PL, Planikin task; SB, Sternberg task; Opt, optimized; Max, maximized; Early, early in practice; Late, late in practice; Single, subjects were asked to perform the optimized task at the single-task level; Average, subjects were asked to perform the optimized task at a level that was an average of the single- and dual-task standards; Dual, subjects were asked to perform at the dual-task level.

with increased resource competition produced by increased structural similarity.

An age-related difficulty in resource allocation was also evident: The graded performance tradeoff displayed in Figure 12.3 was observed only among young subjects, even though subjects of all ages managed the global task priority effectively. That is, high-priority performance was consistently superior to low-priority performance, but the older subjects had greater difficulty with attaining the graded performance standards provided for the high-priority task even though the standards were individually determined. As Figure 12.4 illustrates, departure from the performance standards increased with increased age. The problem lay not in the older subjects failing to reach an excessively difficult standard. In some instances they exceeded the more relaxed performance standard. In contrast, the young group's adherence to the optimized performance standards (left of Fig.12.4) appeared to come at a cost to the low-priority task (right of Fig.12.4). That is, the young subjects did not simply time-share more efficiently; they also had more precise allocation control than the older subjects.

## RESOURCE MANIFESTATION IN TIME-SHARING A CONTINUOUS TASK AND A DISCRETE TASK

In another study (Tsang, Flinn, Stork, Ranieri, & Schieltz, 2003), subjects between the ages of 20 years and 70 years time-shared a continuous task with a discrete task. The continuous task was a one-dimensional compensatory tracking task. The discrete task was the Planikin task described earlier, only now it could be responded to manually by button presses or by speech. There were two task pairs: the manual Planikin task with the manual tracking task (manual task pair) and the speech Planikin task with the manual tracking task (speech task pair). The two task pairs differed only with regard to the similarity of the output modality between the time-shared tasks. The secondary task technique (see Ogden, Levine, & Eisner, 1979; Rolfe, 1971) was used to manipulate task priority to induce attentional control. More specifically, subjects were asked to perform at an individually established performance level for the primary or high-priority task.

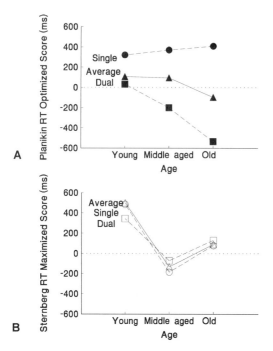

FIGURE 12.4. (A, B) Departure from the optimized standards increased with age. A zero optimized score (difference between the optimized performance and the performance standard) indicates perfect attentional control. A zero maximized score indicates that the maximized performance was the same as the equal-priority dual-task performance. Single, single-task standard; Average, average standard; Dual, dual-task standard; RT, response time.

Subjects were to perform the secondary or low-priority task as well as possible without interfering with attaining the performance level specified for the primary task.

The continuous–discrete task combination offered a unique opportunity to examine the time course of the interference. In a 195-second trial, the Planikin stimulus was presented every 5 seconds. The analysis focused on a segment of tracking performance that was time locked to the discrete Planikin response. The tracking segment spanned from 1 second before the discrete response to 4 seconds after with a 100-msec resolution. The tracking segments from all the correct responses from a trial were "ensembled" over subjects and across practice blocks.

Figure 12.5 displays the tracking error and the control speed for the different age groups and task priorities. Control speed is a measure of the amount of control activity from one moment to the next and is considered to be a closer reflection of motor control

than tracking error. Most noticeable in Figure 12.5 is the transient perturbation in the tracking error and control speed that appeared to be tied temporally to the discrete response. Subjects appeared to have to give up some, if not all, tracking when a discrete response had to be made with the other hand. This phenomenon has been observed by a number of other researchers (e.g., Kramer, Larish, Weber, & Bardell, 1999; McLeod, 1977; Netick & Klapp, 1994; Tsang, Shaner, & Vidulich, 1995). The pattern of interference is suggestive of a bottleneck that operated at the response processing stage. However, it will be shown later that a resource mechanism can provide a better account for several aspects of the data than a bottleneck mechanism.

In Figure 12.5, relative to the secondary task (right of Fig. 12.5), the primary task (left of Fig. 12.5) had a lower *overall level* (which spanned the 5-second segment) of tracking error and exhibited a less pronounced *transient perturbation* (localized around the discrete response) in both the tracking error and control speed. These priority effects are remarkable in several ways.

First, because priority was an instructional variable, it would be difficult to attribute the priority effect to structural causes because structural interference could not be overcome simply by increased effort. It is difficult to conceive a bottleneck mechanism that could account for the reduced overall level of tracking error when the tracking priority was increased. It is just as difficult to conceive a bottleneck mechanism that could account for the heightened level of secondary tracking error level in the 2- to 3-second intervals between the recovery from the transient perturbation and the arrival of the next stimulus. During this interval, the discrete task required no additional response to select, prepare, or execute.

Second, task priority affected the two tracking measures differently. Priority affected the magnitude of the overall level of the tracking error but the magnitude of the transient control speed decrease. That is, the secondary task (right) had a higher level of tracking error throughout the tracking segment, not just around the moments that the discrete response was made. In contrast, the overall level of the control speed was not affected by priority; the magnitude of the transient decrease (height of arrows in Fig. 12.5) that seemed to be synchronized to the discrete response was. This dissociation between the tracking error and the control speed suggested that tracking error was not governed entirely by the amount of motor activity produced,

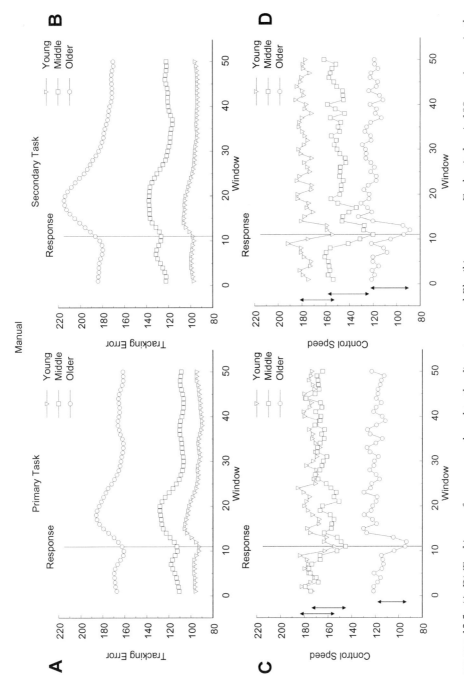

FIGURE 12.5. (A–D) Tracking performance anchored to the discrete manual Planikin response. Each window is 100 ms. Arrows in the control speed graphs (C and D) indicate the amplitude of the transient decrease in control activity.

but a cognitive or strategic component was involved (see also Netick & Klapp, 1994).

Third, priority affected primarily the magnitude rather than the temporal aspect of the tracking performance. This would be more in line with a resource mechanism capable of modulations in resource allocation than a bottleneck mechanism that prioritizes by microscheduling the various stages of processing to minimize the temporal overlap of demand for the bottleneck service.

Whereas Figure 12.5 displays the priority effect when the manual Planikin task was time-shared with the tracking task, Figure 12.6 displays the priority effect when the speech Planikin task was time-shared with the tracking task. Here, the transient perturbation synchronized to the discrete response was conspicuously absent. Note that the response selection demand had not changed. There remained two response choices for the Planikin task (left vs. right) regardless of its response modality. Furthermore, despite the absence of the transient perturbation in the tracking performance as in the manual task pair, it was clear that there was interference between the speech Planikin and tracking tasks that was sensitive to task priority. The secondary tracking task exhibited a higher overall level of tracking error than the primary tracking task. However, regardless of task priority, the discrete speech response would have to be carried out at some point. If there was any response postponement of one task resulting from an ongoing response of a concurrent task as prescribed by the bottleneck mechanism, it was not apparent anywhere in the tracking segment. There is always the issue of resolution and it is possible that interruptions of duration briefer than 100 msec could have occurred but remained undetected. But as Navon and Miller (2002) have pointed out, the distinction between a mechanism capable of simultaneous processing and a mechanism capable of many rapid microswitching between tasks to get through the bottleneck would seem rather futile on theoretical and practical grounds.

## Age Effects

When the tracking task was time-shared with the manual Planikin task, Figure 12.5 shows that increased age was associated with a higher overall level of and a more pronounced transient perturbation (larger amplitude and longer duration) to the tracking error.

Increased age was also associated with a lower overall level of and a larger transient decrease in (amplitude only) control speed. More important, the larger control speed decrease did not last a longer period of time as would be expected for an age-related larger bottleneck (Allen, Smith, Vires-Collins, & Sperry, 1998). When the tracking task was time-shared with the speech Planikin task, Figure 12.6 shows no hint of a bottleneck operation for the young or the older groups. That is, a consistent response modality similarity effect was observed across age groups. That a larger age effect was observed in the manual than in the speech task pairs could be explained by an age-related reduction in processing efficiency as discussed earlier, an age-related difficulty in bimanual processing (e.g., Stelmach, Amrhein, & Goggin, 1988), an age-related difference in motor control in general (e.g., Liao, Jagacinski, & Greenberg, 1997), or a combination of these factors. But there was no indication of an age-related larger bottleneck.

## Age by Expertise Interactions

In another set of task conditions (Tsang, 1997), subjects again time-shared the continuous tracking task with the manual Planikin task. Figure 12.7 displays the characteristic transient perturbation in both the tracking error and control activity by the discrete manual response. The graphs on the left present the data from flight-naive subjects (nonpilots) whereas the graphs on the right present the data from a group of pilots with an average total flight hours of 4801. Pilots were included in this study for their presumed expertise in time-sharing (Carretta, 1987; Damos, 1993; Gopher, 1993; Griffin & McBride, 1986; Jorna, 1989).

Figure 12.7 displays the characteristic age effects described in Figure 12.5, but there were also interesting age-by-expertise interactive effects. Pilots in general had a lower overall level of tracking error (top of Fig. 12.7) and exhibited a smaller age effect than nonpilots. Although pilots in their 30s had only a slightly lower tracking error level than nonpilots of comparable age, pilots in their 60s had a significantly lower tracking error than nonpilots of comparable age. In addition, although the three younger groups of pilots had a higher level of control activity than their nonpilot counterparts, pilots in their 60s had just as low a level of control activity as their nonpilot counterparts. But despite their low level of control activity, the older

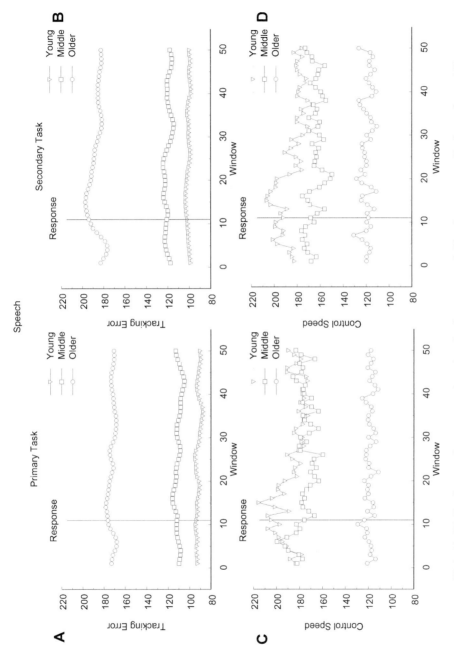

FIGURE 12.6. (A–D) Tracking performance anchored to the discrete speech Planikin response. Each window is 100 ms.

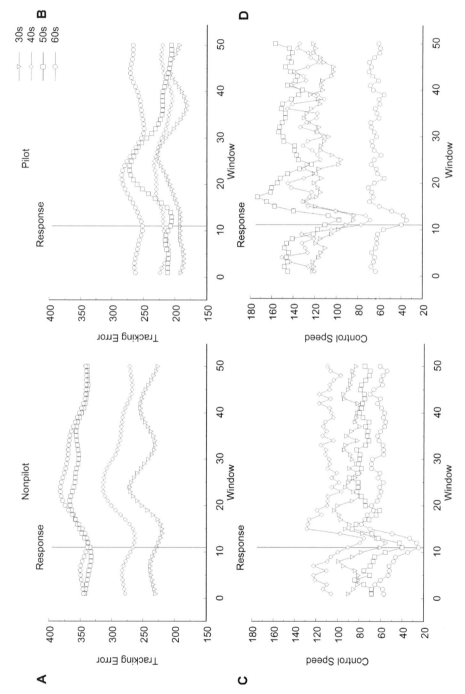

FIGURE 12.7. Tracking performance anchored to the discrete manual Plamikin response. Each window is 100 ms. Older pilots exhibited a low level of control activity comparable with that of the older nonpilots, but the older pilots had significantly lower tracking error than the older nonpilots.

pilots had a considerably lower tracking error than the older nonpilots. If the decrease in tracking control activity that was time locked to the discrete response was a result of a motor interference, pilots were not immune to it. If there was an age-related reduction in motor control activity, pilots were not immune to it. These results implicated a more central cause for the expertise advantage and the age-related difficulty in time-sharing.

## SUMMARY

A key distinction between the resource account and the structural bottleneck account of dual-task interference is that the former allows flexible modulation of the resource supply that governs the level of performance. The data reviewed provided several indications of graded levels of performance in response to changes in task priority and training that are difficult to accommodate by an all-or-none structural bottleneck mechanism. Examination of the effects of structural similarity of the time-shared tasks in the current chapter was restricted to those of response modality similarity. Although there certainly could be nonresource interference generated by bimanual response processing, it could not by itself account for the effects of priority or practice. The notion that manual and speech response processing are supported by distinct attentional resources remains plausible. More important, the multiple-resource predictions applied not only to the "college sophomore" population but extended to people between the ages of 20 years and 70 years, and to people with extensive experience in time-sharing (beyond what could be developed in a laboratory experiment). In fact, the multiple-resource model was found to be able to provide a more satisfactory account of the age-related difficulty with dual-task performance than the bottleneck model.

## DISCUSSION

Since Broadbent's filter theory (1958), there have been waning and waxing of the various theoretical positions over the decades. Although the response selection bottleneck model has dominated the basic literature in recent years, data like those discussed here cannot be reconciled with a single bottleneck mechanism. Indeed, the literature is witnessing a renewed interest

in reconsidering the merits of structural bottleneck and resource accounts of performance (e.g., Navon & Miller, 2002; Ruthruff, Pashler, & Hazeltine, 2003; Tombu & Jolicoeur, 2002; Tsang, 2006).

In particular, Navon and Miller (2002) point out the temptation of embracing a model because of its simplicity. A potential danger is that its applicability may be highly circumscribed. For example, one major difficulty with the single-bottleneck models is that of localizing the bottleneck. Although the response selection bottleneck model has been shown to account ably for the data when the response selection demand is manipulated, the perception selection bottleneck model has been shown to account ably for the data when perceptual demand is manipulated. That is, predictions of either model may hold only under rather specific circumstances. In contrast, the limiting factor for the resource models is not where the limitation or bottleneck occurs, but how much of the task demand is met by the available supply of processing resources. Although the multiple-resource model takes into account the availability of resource within a structure, no single structure has an exclusive gate-keeping or filtering responsibility.

Another major difficulty with the bottleneck model is its strict mandate for an all-or-none sequential processing at the bottleneck. Several researchers (e.g., Meyer & Kieras, 1999; Navon & Miller, 2002) have raised the concern that the preponderance of the extant evidence of sequential processing has been produced by one commonly adopted methodology—the psychological refractory period paradigm. These researchers note that several aspects of the procedures inherent in the paradigm may have unintentionally biased the subjects to respond sequentially. When these procedures are controlled for, many indicators of the all-or-none sequential processing could not be replicated as demonstrated, by the data presented earlier (see also Hazeltine, Teague, & Ivry, 2002; Schumacher, Seymour, Glass, Fenscik, Lauber, Kieras, et al., 2001; Tsang, 2006; Tsang, Velazquez, & Vidulich, 1996). As painstakingly discussed by Navon and Miller (2002), resource theory subsumes the bottleneck theory but not the other way around. There is no question that sequential processing occurs sometimes. If all of one's attention is required to meet the intense demand of one task, other tasks would have to wait for their turns. Modulation of one's effort or resources to meet task demands permits but does not mandate simultaneous processing of the time-shared tasks.

The data reviewed here also show that the resource model could better account for the age-related difficulty in dual-task performance than the bottleneck model. A better understanding of the mechanism underlying the age-related difficulty with dual-task performance has more than just theoretical significance. It is not clear how the effect of a larger age-related bottleneck can be minimized other than by extensive training to produce automaticity (e.g., Ruthruff, Johnston, Van Selst, Witsell, & Remington, 2003). But because only tasks with a consistent stimulus–response mapping could be trained to automaticity (Schneider & Shiffrin, 1977), there are limited circumstances in which extensive training, even if feasible, would be of any help. On the other hand, an age-related reduction in processing efficiency indicates a need for special care when considering task designs that are likely to minimize resource competition. For example, the data reviewed here suggest that adopting a speech response would be especially beneficial for older subjects when a concurrent task has to be responded to manually. An age-related difficulty in allocation control indicates the need for special or additional training for older adults in situations that require dynamic task prioritization. Being conceptualized as a skill, resource allocation control indeed has been demonstrated to be improved by training for the young (e.g., Gopher, 1993) and especially for the old (e.g., Kramer et al., 1999; Tsang & Shaner, 1998). More important, the training effect did not appear to be bound to the specific tasks trained, but appeared to be transferable to new task settings.

## FULL CIRCLE

Although the bottleneck filter model and the structure-specific resource model differ in specifics, both try to account for data from laboratory experiments as well as performance in applied settings. Although the filter model was inspired by practical problems that Broadbent perceived to be associated with piloting and radio communications, the structure-specific resource model was inspired by patterns of dual-task interference that existed mostly in the basic literature. Much of these data, of course, would not have existed had it not been for the volume of research activities instigated by the enormously influential filter model. The current recognition of the practical utility of the structure-specific resource model in the applied literature is probably the best validation there can be of Broadbent's (1971) and Wickens's (Wickens & Hollands, 2000) advocacy for the cooperative relationship between science and applications. Not only is the application of science necessary in solving practical problems, there is much potential in applied work to inform, and to serve as test beds for, scientific theories.

As just one example, along with the need to address the many issues that are confronting an aging society is the need for a better knowledge base of the many facets of aging. A better understanding of cognitive aging in particular is expected to serve not just the academic researchers, but to provide a foundation for solving, or improving upon solutions to, practical problems inherent in an increasingly technology-reliant society (e.g., Czaja, 1990; Stern & Carstensen, 2000). Toward this effort, the ability to account for the effects of aging on time-sharing should provide a new arena for testing the viability of the various attention theories and the utility of their implied practical solutions.

## ACKNOWLEDGMENTS

Research was supported by National Science Foundation grant no. BCS-9910750 and National Institute of Aging grant no. AG08589. The author thanks Michael Vidulich for many interesting discussions and his helpful comments throughout the research and writing process.

### Note

1. A more detailed analysis in Tsang (in press) showed that the priority effect could not be attributed to the proportion of time that a particular task was responded to first.

### References

Allen, P. A., Smith, A. F., Vires-Collins, H., & Sperry, S. (1998). The psychological refractory period: Evidence for age differences in attentional time-sharing. *Psychology and Aging, 13*, 218–229.

Broadbent D. (1958). *Perception and communications.* London: Pergamon Press.

——. (1971). Relation between theory and application in psychology. In P. B. Warr (Ed.), *Psychology at work* (pp. 15–30). Harmondsworth, UK: Penguin.

Carretta, T. R. (1987). *Time-sharing ability as a predictor of flight training performance.* AFHRL-TP-86-69.

Brooks Air Force Base, Tex.: Air Force Systems Command.

Corbetta, M., Miezin, F. M., Dobmeyer, S., Shulman, G. L., & Petersen, S. E. (1990). Attentional modulation of neural processing of shape, color, and velocity in humans. *Science, 248*, 1556–1559.

Czaja, S. J. (Ed.). (1990). *Human factors research needs for an aging population.* Washington, D.C.: National Academy Press.

Damos, D. L. (1993). Using meta-analysis to compare the predictive validity of single- and multiple-task measures to flight performance. *Human Factors, 35*, 615–628.

D'Esposito, M., Detre, J. A., Alsop, D. C., Shin, R. K., Atlas, S., & Grossman, M. (1995). The neural basis of the central executive system of working memory. *Nature, 378*, 279–281.

Deutsch, J. A., & Deutsch, D. (1963). Attention. Some theoretical considerations. *Psychological Review, 70*, 80–90.

Fitts, P. M. (1958). Engineering psychology. *Annual Review of Psychology, 9*, 267–294.

Gopher, D. (1986). In defence of resources: On structures, energies, pools and the allocation of attention. In G. R. J. Hockey, A. W. K. Gaillard, & M. G. H. Coles (Eds.), *Energetics and human information processing* (pp. 353–371). Dordrecht: Martinus Nijhoff.

———. (1993). The skill of attention control: Acquisition and execution of attention strategies. In D. Meyer & S. Kornblum (Eds.), *Attention and performance XIV* (pp. 299–322). Hillsdale, N.J.: Lawrence Erlbaum Associates.

Griffin, G. R., & McBride, D. K. (1986). *Multitask performance: Predicting success in naval aviation primary flight training.* NAMRL 1316. Pensacola, Fla.: Naval Aerospace Medical Research Laboratory.

Hazeltine, E., Teague, D., & Ivry, R. B. (2002). Simultaneous dual-task performance reveals parallel response selection after practice. *Journal of Experimental Psychology: Human Perception and Performance, 28*, 527–545.

Jorna, P. G. A. M. (1989). Prediction of success in flight training by single- and dual-task performance. In *AGARD Conference Proceedings # 458* (pp. 53–62). Neuilly Sur Seine, France: North Atlantic Treaty Organization.

Just, M. A., Carpenter, P. A., & Miyake, A. (2003). Neuroindices of cognitive workload: Neuroimaging, pupillometric and event-related potential studies of brain work. *Theoretical Issues in Ergonomics Science, 4*, 56–88.

Kahneman, D. (1973). *Attention and effort.* Englewood Cliffs, N.J.: Prentice Hall.

Kinsbourne, M., & Hicks, R. (1978). Functional cerebral space. In J. Requin (Ed.), *Attention & performance VII* (pp. 345–362). Hillsdale, N.J.: Lawrence Erlbaum Associates.

Kramer, A. F., Larish, J. F., Weber, T. A., & Bardell, L. (1999). Training for executive control: Task coordination strategies and aging. In D. Gopher & A. Koriat (Eds.), *Attention and performance XVII. Cognitive regulation of performance: Interaction of theory and application* (pp. 617–652). Cambridge, Mass.: MIT.

———, & McCarley, J. S. (2003). Oculomotor behaviour as a reflection of attention and memory processes: Neural mechanisms and applications to human factors. *Theoretical Issues in Ergonomic Sciences, 4*, 21–55.

Lachter, J., Forster, K., & Ruthruff, E. (2004). Forty-five years after Broadbent (1958): Still no identification without attention. *Psychological Review, 111*, 880–913.

Liao, M.- J., Jagacinski, R. J., & Greenberg, N. (1997). Quantifying the performance limitations of older and younger adults in a target acquisition task. *Journal of Experimental Psychology: Human Perception and Performance, 23*, 1644–1664.

Logan, G. D. (2005). Attention, automaticity, and executive control. In A. F. Healy (Ed.), *Experimental cognitive psychology and its application* (pp. 129–139). Washington, D.C.: American Psychological Association.

———, & Schulkind, D. (2000). Parallel memory retrieval in dual-task situations: I. Semantic memory. *Journal of Experimental Psychology: Human Perception and Performance, 26*, 1072–1090.

McCann, R. S., & Johnston, J. C. (1992). Locus of the single-channel bottleneck in dual-task interference. *Journal of Experimental Psychology: Human Perception and Performance, 18*, 471–484.

McLeod, P. (1977). A dual task response modality effect: Support for multiprocessor models of attention. *Quarterly Journal of Experimental Psychology, 29*, 651–667.

Meyer, D. E., & Kieras, D. E.(1999). Precis to a unified theory of cognition and action: Some lessons from EPIC computational models of human multiple-task performance. In D. Gopher & A. Koriat (Eds.), *Attention and performance XVII* (pp. 17–88). Cambridge, Mass.: MIT Press.

Moray, N. (1967). Where is capacity limited? A survey and a model. *Acta Psychologica, 27*, 84–92.

Navon, D. (1984). Resources: A theoretical soup stone? *Psychological Review, 91*, 216–234.

———. (1985). Attention division or attention sharing? In M. I. Posner & O. S. M. Marin (Eds.), *Attention and performance XI* (pp. 133–146). Hillsdale, N.J.: Erlbaum.

———, & Gopher, D. (1979). On the economy of the human-processing system. *Psychological Review, 80*, 214–255.

———, & Miller, J. (2002). Queuing or sharing? A critical evaluation of the single-bottleneck notion. *Cognitive Psychology, 44*, 193–251.

Nelson, W. T., Vidulich, M. A., & Bolia, R. S. (2004). Designing speech interfaces for command and control applications. *Human Factors & Aerospace Safety, 4*, 195–207.

Netick, A., & Klapp, S. T. (1994). Hesitations in manual tracking: A single-channel limit in response programming.

*Journal of Experimental Psychology: Human Perception and Performance, 20*, 766–782.

Nickerson, R. S., & Pew, R. (2003). Psychological experimentation addressing practical concerns. In A. F. Healy & R. W. Proctor (Eds.), *Handbook of psychology* (vol. 4, pp. 649–675). New York: Wiley & Sons.

Norman, D. A., & Bobrow, D. G. (1975). On data-limited and resource-limited processes. *Cognitive Psychology, 7*, 44–64.

Ogden, G. D., Levine, J. M., & Eisner, E. J. (1979). Measurement of workload by secondary tasks. *Human Factors, 21*, 529–548.

Pashler, H., & Johnston, J. C. (1998). Attentional limitations in dual-task performance. In H. Pashler (Ed.), *Attention* (pp. 155–189). East Sussex, UK: Psychology Press.

Rolfe, J. M. (1971). The secondary task as a measure of mental load. In W. T. Singleton, J. G. Fox, & D. Whitfield (Eds.), *Measurement of man at work* (pp. 135–148). London: Taylor & Francis.

Ruthruff, E., Johnston, J. C., Van Selst, M., Whitsell, S., & Remington, R. (2003). Vanishing dual-task interference after practice: Has the bottleneck been eliminated or is it merely latent? *Journal of Experimental Psychology: Human Perception and Performance, 29*, 280–289.

———, Pashler, H. E., & Hazeltine, E. (2003). Dual-task interference with equal task emphasis: Graded capacity sharing or central postponement? *Perception & Psychophysics, 65*, 801–816.

Sanders, A. F. (1983). Towards a model of stress and human performance. *Acta Psychologica, 53*, 61–97.

Sanders, A. G. (1998). *Elements of human performance: Reaction processes and attention in human skill.* Mahwah, N.J.: Lawrence Erlbaum.

Schneider, W., & Shiffrin, R. M. (1977). Controlled and automatic human information processing: I. Detection, search, and attention. *Psychological Review, 84*, 1–66.

Schumacher, E. H., Seymour, T. L., Glass, J. M., Fenscik, D. E., Lauber, E. J., Kieras, D. E., et al. (2001). Virtually perfect time sharing in dual-task performance: Uncorking the central cognitive bottleneck. *Psychological Science, 12*, 101–108.

Sirevaag, E. J., Kramer, A. F., Coles, M. G. H., & Donchin, E. (1989). Resource reciprocity: An event-related brain potentials analysis. *Acta Psychologica, 70*, 77–97.

Skinner, B. F. (1960). Pigeons in a pelican. *American Psychologist, 15*, 28–37

Stelmach, G. E., Amrhein, P. C., & Goggin, N. L. (1988). Age differences in bimanual coordination. *Journal of Gerontology, 43*, 18–23.

Stern, P., & Carstensen, L. L. (Eds.). (2000). *The aging mind: Opportunities in cognitive research.* Washington, D.C.: National Academy Press.

Tombu, M., & Jolicoeur, P. (2002). All-or-none bottleneck versus capacity sharing accounts of the psychological refractory period phenomenon. *Psychological Research, 66*, 274–286.

Treisman, A. M. (1960). Contextual cues in selective listening. *Quarterly Journal of Experimental Psychology, 12*, 242–248.

Tsang, P. S. (1997). A microanalysis of age and pilot time-sharing performance. In D. Harris (Ed.), *Engineering psychology and cognitive ergonomics volume one: Transportation systems* (pp. 245–251). Brookfield, Vt.: Ashgate.

———. (2006). Regarding time-sharing with convergent operations. *Acta Psychologica, 121*, 137–175.

———, Flinn, J. T., Stork, B. V., Ranieri, R., & Schieltz, A. R. (November 2003). *Resource allocation in a dynamic task environment.* Presented at the 44th annual meeting of the Psychonomic Society. Vancouver, Canada.

———, & Shaner, T. L. (1998). Age, attention, expertise, and time-sharing performance. *Psychology and Aging, 13*, 323–347.

———, Shaner, T. L., & Vidulich, M. A. (1995). Resource scarcity and outcome conflict in time-sharing performance. *Perception & Psychophysics, 36*, 365–378.

———, Stork, B. V., Schieltz, A. R., Krum, A. K., Flinn, J. T., Reis, G., et al. (2003). *Regarding time-sharing and aging with convergent operations.* Technical report no. EPL-03-1. Dayton, Ohio: Wright State University, Engineering Psychology Laboratory.

———, Velazquez, V. L., & Vidulich, M. A. (1996). The viability of resource theories in explaining time-sharing performance. *Acta Psychologica, 91*, 175–206.

———, & Wickens, C. D. (1988). The structural constraints and the strategic control of resource allocation. *Human Performance, 1*, 45–72.

Vidulich, M. A. (1988). Speech responses and dual-task performance: Better time-sharing or asymmetric transfer? *Human Factors, 30*, 517–529.

Wickens, C. D. (1976). The effects of divided attention on information processing in tracking. *Journal of Experimental Psychology: Human Perception & Performance, 2*, 1–13.

———. (1980). The structure of attentional resources. In R. S. Nickerson (Ed.), *Attention and performance VIII* (pp. 239–257). Hillsdale, N.J.: Erlbaum.

———. (1984). Processing resources in attention. In R. Parasuraman & D. R. Davies (Eds.), *Varieties of attention* (pp. 63–102). San Diego, Calif.: Academic.

———. (2002). Multiple resources and performance prediction. *Theoretical Issues in Ergonomics Science, 3*, 159–177.

———, & Hollands, J. G. (2000). *Engineering psychology and human performance* (3rd ed.). Upper Saddle River, N.J.: Prentice Hall.

Wickens, C., Kramer, A., Vanasse, L., & Donchin, E. (1983). Performance of concurrent tasks: A psychophysiological analysis of the reciprocity of information-processing resources. *Science, 221*(4615), 1080–1082.

# Part V

# Attention and Interface Design

# Chapter 13

# Multiple-Resource Theory as a Basis for Multimodal Interface Design: Success Stories, Qualifications, and Research Needs

*Nadine Sarter*

Multimodal information processing and design has emerged as a major research topic during the past decade (e.g., Oviatt, 2003; Sarter, 2002, 2005; Spence & Driver, 1997, 2004). This development can be explained, in part, by the recognition that most naturalistic situations involve simultaneous multimodal input (Neisser, 1976). It also reflects the growing need for creating artificial multimodal environments and interfaces that effectively support diverse functions, such as creating a sense of immersion in virtual reality environments or supporting multitasking and attention management in a variety of complex, data-rich domains (e.g., Brickman, Hettinger, & Hass, 2000; Ho, Nikolic, & Sarter, 2001; Latorella, 1999; Means, Fleischman, Carpenter, Szczublewski, Dingus, & Krage, 1993; Nikolic & Sarter, 2001; Sklar & Sarter, 1999; Woods, 1995).

To date, the design of most multimodal displays appears to have been based—implicitly or explicitly—on the original version of multiple-resource theory

(MRT) (e.g., Wickens, 1984), which postulated that people possess separate fixed-capacity resources for information processing that can be characterized along three dimensions: (1) the processing stage (early vs. late processing), (2) the processing code (spatial vs. verbal information), and (3) the information modality (visual vs. auditory encoding; other sensory channels were not considered in the original version of MRT). Based on MRT, the concurrent performance of multiple tasks should benefit to the extent that information related to these tasks is presented in different modalities and thus resource competition is reduced.

Since its original conception, Wickens and colleagues have added qualifications to several aspects of MRT (for an overview, see Wickens [2002]). First, they emphasized that the multiple-resource model was intended primarily to predict the performance of two or more time-shared continuous tasks (Wickens, 1991). Also, based on a review of research methods and findings, Wickens and Liu

(1988) pointed out that benefits that have been observed for cross-modal time-sharing may not necessarily be the result of drawing from independent pools of central perceptual resources. Instead, peripheral sensory factors, such as visual scanning or auditory masking, may play an important role. For example, studies that carefully controlled for visual scanning did not always show performance benefits for cross-modal information presentation. Most recently, the notion of independent perceptual resources has been questioned based on a considerable body of behavioral and neurophysiological evidence that suggests extensive spatial and temporal cross-modal links and constraints on attention, which can both enhance and limit multimodal information processing. (For an overview, see Spence and Driver [1997, 2004].)

Although the mechanisms underlying improved time-sharing with cross-modal task and information presentation continue to be a matter of research and debate, the phenomenon itself has been confirmed and exploited in a number of research and development efforts. This chapter presents examples of the successful implementation of multimodal interfaces in support of concurrent task performance and information processing. It describes additional benefits of distributing information across sensory channels, including redundancy, complementarity, and substitution. Finally, critical research needs in the area of multimodal information processing and interface design are discussed.

## SUCCESS STORIES OF MULTIMODAL INTERFACE DESIGN

Interest in multimodal interfaces has increased dramatically during the past decade. These interfaces have become particularly attractive and important for complex event-driven domains that involve a high risk of data overload resulting from their traditional overreliance on visual information presentation. Examples of these domains include aviation, process control, space flight, medicine, and the automotive industry. Auditory and tactile cues are increasingly introduced to these environments in an effort to support time-sharing and attention management, and to provide directional cues and navigation guidance. In the medical domain, for example, researchers have developed and tested multimodal displays for supporting anesthesiologists in monitoring patient status in parallel with performing other visually demanding tasks (e.g., Crawford, Watson, Burmeister, & Sanderson, 2002; Seagull, Wickens, & Loeb, 2001). Modern car cockpits are equipped with multimodal interfaces that present drivers with auditory navigation information, and vibrotactile cues are explored as a means of warning the driver about critical events, such as the presence of a car in the blind spot or a collision risk with other objects and approaching cars (e.g., Kramer, Cassavaugh, Horrey, Becic, & Mayhugh, 2005).

On modern flight decks, where the auditory channel is already used rather extensively for communication and alerting purposes, tactile information presentation as well as peripheral visual displays have recently received considerable attention. For example, directional and distance information was successfully provided to helicopter pilots using a vibrotactile torso display (Van Erp, Jansen, Dobbins, & van Veen, 2004). Multimodal interfaces have also been developed to support divided attention in pilots who need to monitor the status and behavior of automated flight deck systems in parallel with several other visual tasks, such as scanning flight instruments, monitoring for traffic, or reading checklists (see Sarter & Woods, 2000). Simulator-based evaluations of these interfaces have shown that pilots were better able to track the automation status if the corresponding information was presented in peripheral vision (Nikolic & Sarter, 2001) or in tactile form (Sklar & Sarter, 1999). In both cases, detection rates were higher, and response times shorter, for changes in automation status compared with traditional focal visual indications. These benefits were achieved without leading to significant performance decrements for other flight-related tasks.

Vibrotactile cues were also used successfully for indicating to pilots the location (wing or tail plane section) and severity (high, medium, or low) of in-flight icing conditions (McGuirl & Sarter, 2001). Using natural spatial mappings, a tactor located closer to the wrist provided information about icing on the wing and a second tactor closer to the elbow provided information about icing on the tail plane. Three different vibration frequencies were used to indicate the icing severity for each location. In this study, the icing detection and identification performance of participants receiving tactile cues was not significantly different from participants receiving the same information in the form of a visual additive (using

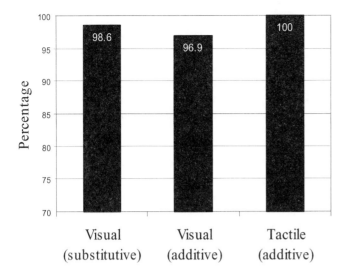

FIGURE 13.1. Detection of icing onset with two types of visual information presentation versus tactile cues.

variations in shading density on the affected flight surfaces) or visual substitutive (using different colors) representation (Fig. 13.1).

However, participants in the tactile condition were significantly more likely to detect an out-of-range oil pressure when it occurred at the same time as the icing cue (Fig. 13.2). Thus, a net gain in monitoring performance was achieved by distributing the information across sensory channels. It is interesting to note that detection performance with tactile cues was, in fact, better for out-of-range values that coincided with an icing onset than for those that appeared in isolation. This finding could be explained by a general arousal effect of the tactile icing cues.

## MULTIMODAL INFORMATION PRESENTATION AND EXCHANGE: BENEFITS BEYOND IMPROVED TIME-SHARING AND INCREASED BANDWIDTH

As the previous examples illustrate, multimodal interfaces are indeed one promising means of increasing bandwidth and supporting time-sharing, as originally suggested by MRT. However, the use and combination of multiple modalities and media can serve many additional purposes and has numerous other advantages. Multimodal input systems (i.e., systems that allow a user to enter data or requests via various channels) can support functions such as increased

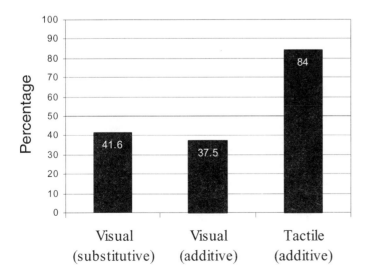

FIGURE 13.2. Detection of out-of-range oil pressure that occurred simultaneously with an icing onset.

system accessibility for diverse users, improved performance of recognition-based systems, and increased expressive power (see Oviatt & Cohen, 2000). Applications of these systems include map-based navigation systems, medical systems for mobile use in noisy environments, person identification systems for security purposes, and web-based transaction systems. (For an overview, see Oviatt [2002].)

Multimodal output systems (i.e., systems that present information to the user via various media) can support functions such as synergy (i.e., the merging of information that is presented via several modalities and refers to various aspects of the same event or process) or redundancy (i.e., the use of several modalities for processing the exact same information). Multimodal output systems are often used for creating a greater sense of immersion in virtual reality environments and, as mentioned earlier, for supporting attention management in data-rich domains (e.g., Brickman et al., 2000; Ho et al., 2001; Latorella, 1999; Means et al., 1993; Nikolic & Sarter, 2001; Sklar & Sarter, 1999).

A review of the multimodal literature shows that, for the most part, research and development efforts are problem driven. In other words, a particular need or difficulty is identified in some application domain (such as the risk of data overload or the need to accommodate a wide range of users with different perceptual or sensory abilities and limitations), and, in response, a multimodal interface is created and tested. Participants in these evaluations usually have no control over the purpose or implementation of the system. They have a rather limited range of modalities at their disposal, and they are usually provided with specific instructions on the purpose and intended use of each channel.

A different, but equally important, question and approach—namely, the exploration of user preferences and strategies for selecting and combining modalities from a wide range of options—has received much less attention. Very little is known also about the evolution of user preferences and strategies over time, as a result of increasing familiarity and experience with multimodal interfaces. Finally, the requirements and effectiveness of multimodal interaction in the context of computer-supported collaborative work is not well understood. These issues were addressed in a recent study by Ho and Sarter (2004), who examined natural tendencies of modality usage in the context of simulated battlefield operations. The ultimate goal

of this study was to inform the design of adaptive multimodal interfaces that adjust to user preferences and task context to support both human–computer interaction and computer-supported collaborative work.

Three groups of three Reserve Officers' Training Corps (ROTC) cadets/officers who were either collocated or distributed each completed a 3-hour training session and four 30-minute simulated military scenarios over another two 3-hour sessions. Throughout the scenarios, participants could communicate with each other via visual (text message, drawing/referring), auditory (two-way radio, face-to-face conversation), and tactile (vibrotactile patterns) means. They could also set system alerts and notifications (to be informed, for example, that an enemy vehicle had been detected or that another unit had crossed a departure line) using various cues and cue combinations in these three modalities. The participants in this research were not given any instructions concerning modality usage, but rather were free to explore all available options and decide as a group, and based on experience during the three sessions, how they wanted to communicate and coordinate their activities.

Overall, the findings from this study show that two-way radio—the primary communication channel in current Army operations—continued to be the primary medium because of participants' familiarity with this channel and because it affords fast exchange of information. However, participants used all other modalities as well, albeit to a lesser extent. For example, text messages were used mostly to substitute for the auditory channel when radio communication was not available. Tactile signals were considered useful for attention capture and for conveying predefined messages. Participants emphasized that tactile cues should be simple and reserved for critical events.

In this study, cadets and officers did not always interact multimodally. Multimodal interaction occurred almost exclusively in the context of spatial tasks and thus often involved drawing or referring on a shared visual map. This confirms earlier findings by Oviatt (1999), who summarized that "users like being able to interact multimodally, but they don't always do so. Their natural communication patterns involve mixing unimodal and multimodal expressions, with the multimodal ones being predictable based on the type of action being performed" (p. 76).

Another important finding is that participants hardly ever used multimodal interaction for the purpose of supporting time-sharing. Instead, complementarity emerged as a major theme and reason for multimodal communication. In fact, 87% of all multimodal exchanges in this study served the purpose of mutual disambiguation of two signals or messages to ensure their proper interpretation. This finding contradicts one of various myths about multimodal interfaces—namely, that multimodal integration involves primarily redundancy of content between modes (Oviatt, 1999).

Finally, the majority of modality combinations occurred in sequence and served what Oviatt (2003) has termed *contrastive functionality*. In most cases, sequential modality combinations were used to capture a participant's attention first and then point out an object or expand on and disambiguate the meaning of a message. Concurrent use of multiple modalities was observed only for participant-selected system alerts to achieve redundancy gains.

Overall, the findings from this study provide important insights into users' choices and preferences for multimodal information presentation and exchange. They show that multimodal interfaces need to be adaptive (in the sense of system-initiated adjustments) and adaptable (in the sense of user-initiated adjustments), because modality usage strongly depends on contextual factors, such as the type of information to be exchanged, the user's tasks, mission context, and group dynamics. The latter factor was one of the main driving forces behind changes in modality choices and preferences over time.

## RESEARCH NEEDS

### Potential Risks and Limitations of Multimodal Information Presentation

Numerous benefits of multimodal information presentation have been derived analytically and demonstrated empirically in a number of application domains. However, recent behavioral and neurophysiological data highlight possible risks and limitations of this approach. In particular, the existence of cross-modal links in attention in the form of (1) modality expectations (i.e., expecting a cue to appear in a certain modality increases the detection rate and reduces the response time to that stimulus), (2) the modality shifting effect (i.e., the strong tendency of people to respond more slowly to a target in one modality if the preceding target was presented in a different modality), and (3) cross-modal spatial and temporal links

(i.e., endogenous shifts in attention to a particular location in one sensory modality lead to concurrent shifts in other modalities, and an unintended close temporal proximity of cues can lead to a reduced ability to process a second unrelated cue) have been established in numerous laboratory studies. (For an overview see Spence and Driver [1997] and Spence and McDonald [2004].) Despite the fact that these types of cross-modal links and constraints have the potential to lead to breakdowns in human–computer interaction and can lead to disastrous outcomes in high-risk domains, they are hardly ever considered in the design of or in guidelines for multimodal interfaces (Sarter, 2002). Instead, multimodal design guidelines tend to emphasize user preferences as the basis for modality choices. They are often not specific to the design of multimodal interfaces, but rather repeat earlier general design guidelines, and they either focus on the choice of individual sensory channels for given tasks and contexts or lay out high-level design objectives, such as the need to support synchronization or symmetry. (For a review of current guidelines, see Sarter [2006].)

Before the available data on cross-modal links in attention are considered in multimodal interface design, their ecological validity and operational significance need to be established. Evidence of cross-modal constraints to date stems almost exclusively from highly controlled laboratory experiments that are not representative of the real-world domains for which multimodal displays are designed. They do not involve highly skilled practitioners, numerous competing attentional demands, or the type of tasks that operators in the real world tend to face. For example, the typical paradigm used in studies of exogenous cross-modal links in attention is an adaptation of the standard spatial-cueing paradigm (Posner, 1980) in which a cue stimulus is used to direct attention to a specific location prior to the appearance of a target stimulus. This cue is typically presented at fixation and may or may not be informative about the likely location of the forthcoming target. To avoid response priming by the distractor location, subjects are then asked to make a speeded elevation discrimination (up vs. down) for the target event, regardless of the side on which it appears. (For a more detailed description of this orthogonal spatial cuing paradigm, see Spence and McDonald [2004] and Calvert and colleagues [2004]). It is difficult to envision real-world tasks that are comparable in terms of attentional settings and response requirements.

In studies of endogenous cross-modal attention, participants are usually instructed to orient their attention toward the expected location of target stimuli within one modality. On few trials, target stimuli in another modality are presented that are equally likely to appear ipsi- or contralaterally to the expected target location. Detection performance tends to be superior for targets on the expected side, independent of their modality. This paradigm more closely resembles real-world situations in which practitioners form expectations—albeit on their own—of relevant cues and cue locations to guide their attention allocation.

One of the few studies that examined cross-modal spatial links in a naturalistic environment (a driving simulation) was conducted by Spence and Read (2003). The findings from this experiment suggest that earlier laboratory-based findings generalize to more complex and dynamic environments. They show that subjects' ability to combine speech shadowing with a simulated driving task was affected by the spatial location from which the speech was presented. Participants found it significantly easier to shadow a relevant speech stream when it was presented from directly in front of them (as opposed to from the side). This effect was more pronounced when participants performed a demanding simulated driving task (requiring a forward visual orientation) at the same time as shadowing than when they performed the shadowing task alone. Thus, collocation of stimuli in different modalities led to more efficient information processing and should therefore be considered in the placement of display elements, which is currently driven primarily by practical considerations, such as the availability of real estate.

### Where Top-down Meets Bottom-up

A second important area for future research on multimodal information processing is the interplay between exogenous (or bottom-up) and endogenous (or top-down) control of cross-modal attention. Top-down control refers to knowledge-driven (voluntary) mechanisms, such as expectations or intentions, which can both enhance and interfere with sensory information processing. Top-down mechanisms can support the discrimination between targets and distractors, and they can bias a person toward locations or forms in which information may appear. In contrast, bottom-up (involuntary) attention control refers to data-driven mechanisms in which properties of the stimulus itself (such as its brightness or sudden onset) determine a person's attentional focus and orientation.

There is considerable evidence that a person's attention allocation results from the interplay of both modes of attention control. For example, Folk and Remington (1998) proposed and provided empirical evidence for the contingent involuntary orienting hypothesis, which states that a stimulus will capture attention only to the extent that its properties (such as color or location) match top-down attentional control settings. Also, Lloyd (1999) demonstrated that exogenous orienting to a tactile stimulus resulted in inhibition of subsequent stimuli at that body site—a supramodal phenomenon known as *inhibition of return* (see Spence, Lloyd, McGlone, Nicholls, & Driver, 2000). In contrast, when subjects endogenously oriented attention to the stimulus site, the processing of subsequent stimuli at that location was facilitated. In both cases, the skin received the exact same stimuli (100-Hz sine waves presented for 50 msec), but very different effects were observed, depending upon the person's attentional setting and strategy.

In real-world environments, this phenomenon can be observed with highly trained practitioners who anticipate the appearance of specific cues based on their knowledge of the system, process, and interface. They are more likely to search for and notice those expected and/or highly critical cues than others that are of lower importance and/or appear unexpectedly (Adams, Tenney, & Pew, 1995). However, when an unexpected cue is presented in a highly salient manner (such as an auditory alarm), it will attract the operator's attention as a result of bottom-up factors overriding top-down control.

The interplay between exogenous and endogenous attention control has been captured in several descriptive and computational models of attention (e.g., Neisser, 1976; McCarley, Wickens, Goh, & Horrey, 2002); yet, there is still little empirical evidence concerning the exact nature of this phenomenon, especially as it relates to cross-modal attention and information processing.

### Concurrent Processing of Cues in More Than Two Modalities

Another important research question for multimodal interface design is how well operators can process signals that are presented concurrently via more than two modalities. In many real-world settings, the simultaneous appearance and processing of multiple cues in visual, auditory, and tactile form is not uncommon.

For example, a pilot may be monitoring flight instruments or receive a visual notification of a problem with one of the aircraft systems while using force feedback from the flight controls to trim the aircraft and, at the same time, an auditory message from air traffic control may be received. Yet, to date, research on multimodal interfaces has studied almost exclusively the processing of concurrent cues in two modalities (most often, a combination of visual and auditory cues).

Data from our research on in-flight icing suggest that adding signals in multiple modalities can result in performance costs that do not necessarily increase linearly and that may vary for different modality pairings (McGuirl & Sarter, 2001). As shown in Table 13.1, when the onset of icing occurred simultaneously with an auditory (air traffic control) message, it was missed in the visual additive and substitutive conditions in 25% and 17% of all cases, respectively, Also, the diagnosis of the icing condition was incorrect in 50% and 25% of those cases. In contrast, during the tactile condition, none of the icing onsets were missed and only 17% of the icing onsets were diagnosed incorrectly; however, participants in this group required a repetition of the auditory message more often than the two visual groups.

### Exploring Underutilized Modalities

A fourth area that deserves more attention is the exploration and development of currently underutilized media and modalities that play an important role in naturalistic environments. Haptic cues have only just begun to be included in multimodal interfaces, and their benefits and limitations have not been fully determined. Olfaction and, even more so, gestation are hardly ever used in multimodal

TABLE 13.1. Performance on Icing Detection, Diagnosis, and Processing of Air Traffic Control Message for Different Modality Combinations

| | Missed Icing Cue, % | Misidentified Icing Cue, % | Requested Repetition of ATC Message, % |
|---|---|---|---|
| Visual additive | 25 | 50 | 6 |
| Visual substitutive | 17 | 25 | 4 |
| Tactile | None | 17 | 11 |

ATC, air traffic control.

interfaces, which, in the former case, may be explained by challenges associated with odor generation and control of the breathing space. Olfactory cues can, in principle, support functions such as conveying high-level assessments of a situation (including alerting to life-threatening situations), increasing vigilance, decreasing stress, and improving retention and recall of learned material (e.g., Knasko & Gilbert, 1990; Krueger, 1995). Kaye (2001), for example, discussed two forms of olfactory outputs: olfactory icons and smicons. The former involve the use of a scent that is semantically related to the information that is to be conveyed (e.g., releasing a gunpowder smell when a shotgun is fired). In contrast, smicons involve the use of scents that have only an abstract relationship with the information they express (e.g., setting an olfactory alarm to be released at certain times each day). To date, only a few applications of cues in these modalities have been explored (see Barfield & Danas, 1996).

### ACKNOWLEDGMENT

The preparation of this document was supported, in part, by a grant from the Army Research Laboratory under the Advanced Decision Architecture Collaborative Technology Alliance (CTA; grant no. DAAD 19-01-2-0009; CTA manager, Dr. Mike Strub; project manager, Sue Archer), and a grant from the National Science Foundation (grant no. 534281; Program Director: Dr. Ephraim Glinert).

### References

Adams, M. J., Tenney, Y. J., & Pew, R. W. (1995). Situation awareness and the cognitive management of complex systems. *Human Factors, 37*(1), 85–104.

Barfield, W., & Danas, E. (1996). Comments on the use of olfactory displays for virtual environments. *Presence: Teleoperators and Virtual Environments, 5*(1), 109–121.

Brickman, B. J., Hettinger, L. J., & Haas, M. W. (2000). Multisensory interface design for complex task domains: Replacing information overload with meaning in tactical crew stations. *International Journal of Aviation Psychology, 10*(3), 273–290.

Calvert, G. A., Spence, C., & Stein, B. E. (Eds.). (2004). *The handbook of multisensory processes.* Cambridge, Mass.: MIT Press.

Crawford, J., Watson, M., Burmeister, O., & Sanderson, P. (2002). Multimodal displays for anaesthesia sonification: Timesharing, workload, and expertise.

In *Proceedings of the 46th annual meeting of the Human Factors and Ergonomics Society.* Santa Monica, Calif.: Human Factors and Ergonomics Society.

Folk, C. L., & Remington, R. (1998). Selectivity in distraction by irrelevant feature singletons: Evidence for two forms of attentional capture. *Journal of Experimental Psychology: Human Perception and Performance, 24*(3), 847–848.

Ho, C. Y., Nikolic, M. I., & Sarter, N. B. (2001). Supporting timesharing and interruption management through multimodal information presentation. In *Proceedings of the 45th annual meeting of the Human Factors and Ergonomics Society* (pp. 341–345). Santa Monica, Calif.: Human Factors and Ergonomics Society.

———, & Sarter, N. B. (2004). Supporting synchronous distributed communication and coordination through multimodal information exchange. In *Proceedings of the 48th annual meeting of the Human Factors and Ergonomics Society* (pp. 426–430). Santa Monica, Calif.: Human Factors and Ergonomics Society.

Kaye, J. N. (2001). *Symbolic olfactory displays.* Master's thesis. Massachusetts Institute of Technology. [Online]. Available: http://web.media.mit.edu/~jofish/thesis/

Knasko, S. C., & Gilbert, A. N. (1990). Emotional state, physical well-being, and performance in the presence of feigned ambient odor. *Journal of Applied Social Psychology, 20*(16), 1345–1357.

Kramer, A. F., Cassavaugh, N. D., Horrey, W. J., Becic, E., & Mayhugh, J. (2005). *Examination of the efficacy of proximity warning devices for young and older drivers.* Presented at the Third International Driving Symposium on Human Factors in Driving Assessment, Training, and Vehicle Design. Rockport, Maine.

Krueger, M. W. (1995). *Olfactory stimuli in virtual reality medical training.* Vernon, Conn.: Artificial Reality Corporation.

Latorella, K. A. (1999). *Investigating interruptions: Implications for flightdeck performance.* NASA/TM-1999-209707. Hampton, Va.: NASA Langley Research Center.

Lloyd, D. M. (1999). Mechanisms of attention in touch. *Somatosensory and Motor Research, 16*(1), 3–10.

McCarley, J. S., Wickens, C. D., Goh, J., & Horrey, W. J. (2002). A computational model of attention/situation awareness. In *Proceedings of the Human Factors and Ergonomics Society 46th annual meeting* (pp. 1669–1673). Santa Monica, Calif.: Human Factors and Ergonomics Society.

McGuirl, J., & Sarter, N. B. (2001). Presenting in-flight icing information: A comparison of visual and tactile cues. In *Proceedings of 20th Digital Avionics Systems Conference (DASC)* (pp. 2.A.2-1–2.A.2-8). Daytona Beach, Fla.: Digital Avionics Systems.

Means, L. G., Fleischman, R. N., Carpenter, J. T., Szczublewski, F. E., Dingus, T. A., & Krage, M. K. (1993). Design of TravTek auditory interface.

In *NRC-TRB: Driver performance: Measurement and modeling* (pp. 1–6). Washington, D.C.: National Academy Press.

Neisser, U. (1976). *Cognition and reality.* San Francisco, Calif: W. H. Freeman.

Nikolic, M. I., & Sarter, N. B. (2001). Peripheral visual feedback: A powerful means of supporting attention allocation and human-automation coordination in highly dynamic data-rich environments. *Human Factors, 43*(1), 30–38.

Oviatt, S. L. (1999). Ten myths of multimodal interaction. *Communications of the ACM, 42*(11), 74–81.

———. (2003). Multimodal interfaces. In J. Jacko & A. Sears (Eds.), *Human–computer interaction handbook: Fundamentals, evolving technologies and emerging applications* (pp. 286–304). Mahwah, N.J.: Lawrence Erlbaum Associates.

———, & Cohen, P. R. (2000). Multimodal systems that process what comes naturally. *Communications of the ACM, 43*(3), 45–53.

Posner, M. I. (1980). Orienting of attention. *Quarterly Journal of Experimental Psychology, 32*, 3–25.

Sarter, N. B. (2002). Multimodal information presentation in support of human-automation communication and coordination. In E. Salas (Ed.), *Advances in human performance and cognitive engineering research* (pp. 13–36). New York: JAI Press.

———. (2006). Multimodal human–machine interfaces: Design guidance and research challenges. *International Journal of Industrial Ergonomics* [Special issue: New Insights in Human Performance and Decision Making], *36*(5), 439–445.

———, & Woods, D. D. (2000). Teamplay with a powerful and independent agent: A full-mission simulation study. *Human Factors, 42*(3), 390–402.

Seagull, F. J., Wickens, C. D., & Loeb, R. G. (2001). Attention and workload in auditory, visual, and redundant patient-monitoring conditions. In *Proceedings of the Human Factors and Ergonomics Society 45th annual meeting* (pp. 1395–1399). Santa Monica, Calif.: Human Factors and Ergonomics Society.

Sklar, A. E., & Sarter, N. B. (1999). "Good vibrations": The use of tactile feedback in support of mode awareness on advanced technology aircraft. *Human Factors, 41*(4), 543–552.

Spence, C., & Driver, J. (1997). Crossmodal links in attention between audition, vision, and touch: Implications for interface design. *International Journal of Cognitive Ergonomics, 1*(4), 351–373.

———, & Driver, J. (Eds.). (2004). *Crossmodal space and crossmodal attention.* New York: Oxford University Press.

———, Lloyd, D., McGlone, F., Nicholls, M. R. E., & Driver, J. (2000). Inhibition of return is supramodal: A demonstration between all possible pairings of vision, touch, and audition. *Experimental Brain Research, 134*, 42–48.

———, & McDonald, J. (2004). The cross-modal consequences of the exogenous spatial orienting of attention.

In G. A. Calvert, C. Spence, & B. E. Stein (Eds.), *The handbook of multisensory processes* (pp. 3–26). Cambridge, Mass.: MIT Press.

——, & Read, L. (2003). Speech shadowing while driving: On the difficulty of splitting attentions between eye and ear. *Psychological Science, 14*, 251–256.

Van Erp, J. B. F., Jansen, C., Dobbins, T., & van Veen, H. A. H. C. (2004). Vibrotactile waypoint navigation at sea and in the air: Two case studies. In *Proceedings of EuroHaptics 2004* (pp. 166–173). Munich, Germany: Technische Universitat Muenchen.

Wickens, C. D. (1984). Processing resources in attention. In R. Parasuraman & D. R. Davies (Eds.), *Varieties of attention* (pp. 63–102). New York: Academic Press.

——. (1991). Processing resources and attention. In D. L. Damos (Ed.), *Multiple task performance* (pp. 3–34). London, UK: Taylor & Francis.

——. (2002). Multiple resources and performance prediction. *Theoretical Issues in Ergonomics Science, 3*(2), 159–177.

——, & Liu, Y. (1988). Codes and modalities in multiple resources: A success and qualification. *Human Factors, 30*(5), 599–616.

Woods, D. D. (1995). The alarm problem and directed attention in dynamic fault management. *Ergonomics, 38*(11), 2371–2393.

# Chapter 14

# Cross-Modal Interactions between Sensory Modalities: Implications for the Design of Multisensory Displays

## Jan Theeuwes, Erik van der Burg, Christian N. L. Olivers, and Adelbert Bronkhorst

In the real "physical" world, people see, hear, talk, and act in a multimodal way. The world consists of pictures, sounds, and touch that coincide in a natural way. This natural integrated environment allows for an intuitive and efficient interaction. Because of technical advancements such as miniaturization (mobile integration), digitalization, and wireless networking (mobile information at the right time and place), it has become possible to design an "electronic" world that has the same natural multimodal properties as the physical world. These future interfaces understand human multimodal communication and can actively anticipate and act in line with human capabilities and limitations. The largest challenge for the near future is the development of natural multimodal interfaces—a topic that requires the active participation of industry, technology, and the human sciences.

Research into multimodal perception and cross-modal interactions has a long history and has addressed a wide range of subjects (e.g., Kohlrausch & van de Par, 1999). For example, in the 1950s it was shown that the presentation of the face of the speaker can improve speech recognition compared with auditory-only presentation. Other well-known multimodal phenomena are the McGurk effect (McGurk & MacDonald, 1976) and the ventriloquist effect (Thurlow & Jack, 1973), which illustrate the dominance of visual over auditory information. Many studies have investigated the behavioral outcome of cross-modal interactions (for a review, see Driver and Spence [1998]). For instance, in a study by Spence and Driver (1996), it was demonstrated that directing attention to a location in space improved not only visual discrimination (as in a classic Posner task; see, for example, Posner [1980]), but also auditory discrimination. Thus, in a task in which participants had to carry out a speeded elevation discrimination task with respect to the location of a target tone, they performed better (i.e., faster and/or more accurately) for an auditory target that appears on the cued rather than on the uncued side. Similarly, when auditory attention was endogenously directed to a location in space, both visual and auditory discrimination at that location were improved. The visual influence on auditory perception is well established (Driver & Spence, 1998); however, there are only a few studies showing a clear advantage of an auditory influence on visual processing. The best example of such influence is a study by Vroomen and De Gelder (2000) in which participants were presented with a rapid sequence of visual displays. A series of tones was also presented from a fixed location concurrently with each visual display. The results showed that the visual target was better detected and localized if it coincided with the unique sound even when the sound was completely noninformative. It appeared that the sound helped to segregate the visual display and improved visual performance quite substantially. (For similar findings with visuotactile stimuli, see Ernst and Banks [2002] and Duncan and colleagues [1997].)

Typically, these studies of *multisensory integration* examined interactions between the modalities occurring within a single task. In general, with these paradigms the different modalities all contribute to the performance on a single task. A completely different line of research has concentrated on *multisensory separation* using dual-task paradigms looking specifically at how well people can perform two tasks at the same time. Typically in these dual-task conditions, performance is better when the tasks used rely on the recruitment of different modalities (e.g., a visual and an auditory task). These results were incorporated in the influential multiple-resource theory proposed by Wickens (1984, 2002), which states that there are fixed-capacity resources available for each modality.

An obvious example of a structural distinction is between the eyes (visual processing) and the ears (auditory processing). In line with the multiple-resource theory, various experiments have demonstrated that performance is less adequate when two visual tasks must be time-shared than when one of these tasks is presented in the auditory domain. For example, Parkes and Coleman (1990) showed that an automobile driver both drives and understands messages better when listening to a set of instructions than when reading the same set of instructions. The multiple-resource theory posits that when tasks share common resources along a given dimension (e.g., both tasks require the visual channel), performance is poorer than tasks that utilize separate resources (e.g., one task uses the visual domain and the other task uses the auditory domain). Wickens (1980) reports several other studies that show similar cross-modal advantages.

Even though there is ample evidence for cross-modal (auditory–visual) over intramodal (visual–visual and auditory–auditory) performance advantages, Wickens (2002) points out that these advantages may not be the result of separable resources as originally assumed. Indeed, the performance costs of an intramodal task (visual–visual or auditory–auditory) may be the result of interference at the peripheral, sensory domain (e.g., masking or visual scanning) rather than interference at the resource level. As Wickens (2002) points out: "The issue of whether the advantage of separating auditory and visual displays is entirely a sensory phenomenon, related to visual scanning and auditory masking in the intra-modality case, or whether there are separate auditory and visual resources within perception, is one that remains unresolved" (p. 165). Even though the multiple-resource theory has been around for more than 25 years, the issue of whether separate resources exist for the visual and auditory domain is still unresolved. The current study seeks to address this issue further by closely monitoring the time course of visual–auditory processing interactions while keeping local sensory-masking effects constant.

We used the attentional blink paradigm to investigate the mechanisms underlying cross-modal interactions. The attentional blink is a laboratory task that originally only involved the detection of visually presented targets. In the classic paradigm, a trial consists of a rapid series of letters presented at the center of the display at a rate of around 10 items per second. Among the letters are two target digits (referred to as $T_1$ and $T_2$), and the observer's task is to report these, "unspeeded," at the end of each trial. The usual result is that detection of $T_2$ suffers considerably if it is presented within a short lag (typically 0.5 second) from $T_1$, a phenomenon referred to as the *attentional blink* (e.g., Chun & Potter, 1995; Olivers, 2004; Raymond, Shapiro, & Arnell, 1992). It appears that upon detection of the first target, the information processing system is shut down for as long as 0.5 second and appears not to be able to process any additional information. In most attentional blink experiments, both $T_1$ and $T_2$ are presented visually. Given the multiple resource theory of Wickens (1984) which postulated that there is only one visual channel one may not be surprised that two visual targets presented in close succession results in interference.

The current study investigated the role of cross-modal dual-task performance by examining the attentional blink across modalities. Arnell and Jolicoeur (1999) used a comparable paradigm in a study in which target modality

$T_1$ and $T_2$ (visual and auditory) were fully crossed. When using spoken letters as auditory targets, they showed large Attentional Blink (AB) effects in all conditions. In our study we focused on pure tones and on auditory–visual interactions only (see also Arnell and Jolicoeur [1999], experiment 3). Participants were asked to attend to a stream of auditory items, and to detect both an auditorily and a visually presented target. If there are separate resources for auditory and visual perception, as proposed within the multiple-resource theory of Wickens (1980, 2002), one expects no cross-modal attentional blink. It should be realized that in an attentional blink paradigm, no speeded responses are necessary, so any interference observed cannot be attributed to interference at the level of response selection and execution. If however, auditory and visual resources are not completely independent, one expects a cross-modal attentional blink effect to occur.

## EXPERIMENT 1

In Experiment 1, participants viewed a stream of letters while simultaneously hearing a stream of tones. The first task was to detect a high or low target tone ($T_1$). At different lags following this tone ($T_1$), participants had to detect a visually presented letter ($T_2$). During the dual-task condition, we examined the performance on $T_2$ as a function of lag. During the control condition, participants only had to detect $T_2$. If the detection of an auditory $T_1$ causes an attentional blink affecting visual processing, we expect a performance decrement in detecting the visually presented $T_2$ for those lags immediately following the presentation of the tone.

## Method

### Participants

Thirteen students (nine male; mean age, 21.1 years; age range, 17–30 years) participated in the experiment as paid volunteers. Each participant received 7 Euros for a single 1-hour session. All participants were naive to the purpose of the experiment. Data from one participant was excluded from further analyses because of an overall $T_1$ accuracy of only 50.6%.

### Design

The design was a $2 \times 2 \times 2 \times 8$ mixed factorial design. $T_1$ (low or high tone), $T_2$ (presence or absence), and lags 1 through 8 were within-subjects variables and were varied randomly within blocks. Control and dual-task conditions were blocked.

### Apparatus and Stimuli

The experiment was run in a dimly lit, air-conditioned cubicle. Participants were seated at a distance of approximately 80 cm from the monitor in one of the six cabins. Participants wore headphones during the experiment. The visual stimuli included all the letters of the alphabet except the letters W, N, F, and S (see Arnell & Jolicoeur, 1999). Letters were presented in black against a gray 9.34-cd/m² background. All letters were capitals and presented in 48-point Geneva font (width, 1.4 deg; height, 1.6 deg) at the center of a gray background. The luminance of the letters was 0.63 cd/m². The auditory stimuli included eight different tones that were used as random filler tones, ranging from 2119 to 2416 Hz, and were spaced equally on a logarithmic scale. The target tone was always one of two tones: One was higher in frequency and one was lower in frequency than the filler tones. Frequency values for both target tones were varied across blocks to keep auditory target accuracy between 78% and 91%. Starting frequencies for auditory targets were 3025 Hz and 1692 Hz for the high and low tones, respectively. The high and low target tones included seven different tones that were equally spaced on a logarithmic scale, ranging from 2860 to 3200 Hz and 1600 to 1790 Hz, respectively. The frequency of the high target tone was decreased by one step and for the low target tone was increased by one step, when the target tone accuracy was more than 91%. The frequency of the high target tone was increased by one step and, for the low target tone, was decreased by one step when the target tone accuracy was less than 78%. This was adapted after each block of 64 trials.

### Task and Procedure

Each trial began with a fixation cross presented at the center of the screen for 500 msec followed by a blank screen for the same period. Then, a rapid serial auditory presentation stream and a rapid serial visual presentation stream were presented synchronously, with an equal number of items. All tones and letters were presented for 16 msec, followed by an 80-msec blank interval, which resulted in 10.4 tones and letters per second. Both streams started with the same number of pretargets (4, 6, 8, 10, or 12), which was randomly determined. Subsequently, the target tone ($T_1$) was presented in the auditory stream. After the target tone, a letter X appeared on 50% of the trials at eight possible lags (lags 1–8). Figure 14.1 presents an outline of the paradigm.

During dual-task blocks, participants were asked to identify the target tone ($T_1$) in the auditory stream and to detect the target letter X in the visual stream. During control blocks, were participants asked to ignore the auditory stream and to detect the target letter X in the visual stream. For the auditory target ($T_1$), a participant was asked to identify the target tone in the auditory stream, and make an unspeeded response after each trial by pressing the 5 and 6 keys for the low and high

tones, respectively. For the visual target, a participant was asked to detect the target letter X in the visual stream, and make an unspeeded response after each trial, by pressing the 0 key when the letter X was absent and the 1 key if the letter X was present. Participants initiated the next trial by pressing the spacebar.

Participants received instructions on the screen, which emphasized accuracy. There were two practice blocks with 16 random trials each. One block was used to practice the difference between the low and high target tone in the auditory stream. The second block was used to practice the dual-task block. After the practice blocks, participants completed five dual-task blocks of 64 trials and five control blocks of 64 trials, with the constraint that a control block was always followed by a dual-task block and vice versa.

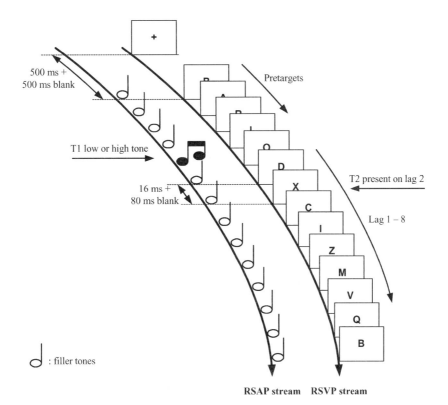

FIGURE 14.1. Outline of the paradigm used. Participants received concurrently a rapid serial auditory presentation (RSAP) stream and a rapid serial visual presentation (RSVP) stream. The task was to identify a target tone ($T_1$) in the RSAP stream, which could be of low or high frequency among filler tones, and to detect the letter X ($T_2$) in the RSVP stream. Note that the letter X was only presented on 50% of the trials at eight different positions (lag 1–8) after $T_1$. Participants were asked to identify both $T_1$ and $T_2$ during the dual-task condition, whereas participants had to identify only $T_2$ during the control condition.

## Results

Data from practice blocks were excluded from further analysis. The data for $T_1$ accuracy was subjected to a two-tailed paired $t$-test, with target tone as a within-subject factor, with alpha set at .05. The data for $T_2$ accuracy was subjected to a repeated-measures univariate analysis of variance, with lag and task as within-subject factors, with alpha set at .05. The reported values for Mean Squared Error (MSE) and $P$ corresponded to the Huynh–Feldt correction.

### $T_1$ Accuracy

The target tone was identified correctly 93.6% of the time in the current experiment.

### $T_2$ Accuracy

Figure 14.2 presents the mean percentage of correct detection of the letter X for those trials during which the target tone was correctly identified as a function of task and lag. As is clear from Figure 14.2, mean accuracy of $T_2$ was not significantly lower when participants did a dual task (85.5%) relative to only a visual task (86.6%, F < 1). Further analyses showed a main effect of lag (F(7, 77) = 3.557, MSE = .004, P < .01). The two-way interaction between lag and task did not reach significance (F < 1), indicating the absence of an AB effect.

## Discussion

The current results are clear. Detecting an auditory target in a stream of auditory nontargets does not cause an attentional blink for detecting targets presented in the visual stream. Participants performed just as accurately during the control condition, in which they only detected the visual target, as during the dual-task condition, in which they had to detect the auditory and visual targets. In line with the multiple-resource theory of Wickens (1980, 2002), it appears to be possible to process an auditory stream and a visual stream in a completely separate fashion without any cross-modal interference. This strongly suggests the existence of separate resources for auditory and visual processing.

### EXPERIMENT 2

The current findings are important in that they show that no auditory and visual interactions occur in a task that requires fast auditory and visual information processing. The results are consistent with claims that the attentional blink is a purely visual phenomenon (Shapiro, Raymond, & Arnell, 1994). In addition, the results are consistent with earlier work by Duncan and colleagues (1997), who showed within-modality interactions (visual–visual and auditory–auditory), but no interactions between the visual and auditory domains

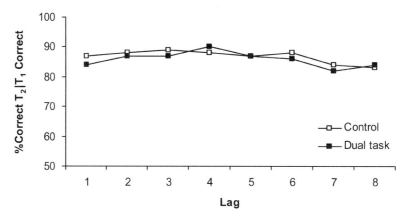

FIGURE 14.2. Experiment 1. Mean percentage of correct $T_2$ given that $T_1$ was identified correctly as a function of lag in the current experiment. During the control condition, participants were asked to detect only the presence or absence of an X ($T_2$). During the dual-task condition, participants were asked to identify the target tone ($T_1$) and to detect the presence or absence of an X ($T_2$).

(visual–auditory and auditory–visual interactions). However, the results are inconsistent with recent findings from Arnell and Jolicoeur (1999), who showed a clear cross-modal attentional blink effect in a task very similar to the one we used. There may be an important difference between Arnell and Jolicoeur (1999) and the current task. In our task, participants had to detect an auditory target that was either higher or lower than the stream of filler tones. In Arnell and Jolicoeur (1999), the auditory target was always higher than the stream of filler tones, and participants had to determine whether the auditory target was high or very high. Possibly because the target detection in our experiment 1 was relatively easy, we did not observe a cross-modal attentional blink. To test this notion, we adapted our task so that it was basically identical to that of Arnell and Jolicoeur's (1999) auditory–visual "pure tones" condition in their experiment 3.

## Method

Experiment 2 was identical to experiment 1 except that the target tones were both higher than the filler tones. Participants had the task to identify the target tone that was either low or high in frequency. The frequency value for the highest of the two target tones was adjusted across blocks to maintain the auditory target accuracy between 78% and 91%. It included six different tones that were equally spaced on a logarithmic

scale, ranging from 1767 to 3200 Hz and starting at a frequency of 2378 Hz. The lowest of the two target tones was kept constant during the experiment (1600 Hz). The frequency of the high target tone was decreased one step when the target tone accuracy was more than 91% and was increased one step when the target tone accuracy was less than 78%. Twelve new students (six male; mean age, 19.6 years; age range, 16–24 years) participated in the experiment as paid volunteers.

## Results

### $T_1$ Accuracy

The target tone was identified correctly 92.6% of the time in this experiment, a result similar to that of Arnell and Jolicoeur (1999).

### $T_2$ Accuracy

Figure 14.3 presents the mean percentage of correct detection of the letter X for those trials during which the target tone was correctly identified as a function of task and lag. There was no significant main effect of task and lag ($F(1, 11) = 1.979$, MSE = .007, $P = .187$ and $F(7, 77) = 1.672$, MSE = .020, $P = .139$, respectively). The two-way interaction between lag and task failed to reach significance ($F < 1$), indicating the absence of an AB effect.

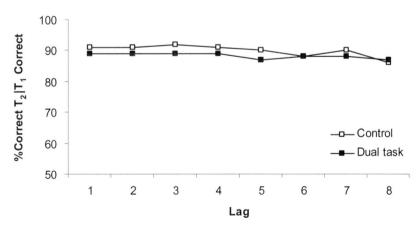

FIGURE 14.3. Experiment 2. Mean percentage of correct $T_2$ given that $T_1$ was identified correctly as a function of lag in the current experiment. During the control condition, participants were asked to detect only the presence or absence of an X ($T_2$). During the dual-task condition, participants were asked to identify the target tone ($T_1$) and to detect the presence or absence of an X ($T_2$).

## Discussion

Even though we used basically the same setup as Arnell and Jolicoeur's (1999) experiment 3 (auditory–visual condition), we were not able to replicate their findings. In fact, there is no hint of a cross-modal attentional blink whatsoever. Arnell and Jolicoeur (1999) indicate that the cross-modal attentional blink in their experiment 3 using pure tones was much smaller than the large AB effects reported in their experiments 1 and 2 that used spoken letters. One way to explain this difference (see, for example, Arnell and Jolicoeur [1999]) is that the phonological codes of spoken letters may automatically induce a visual representation that causes a cross-modal attentional blink. Pure tones as used in our experiments 1 and 2, and Arnell and Jolicoeur's experiment 3 do not have a visual representation, and that is why we reported no AB, and Arnell and Jolicoeur reported an AB that was much reduced.

Even though an interpretation in terms of phonological codes is feasible, an alternative explanation would be that to perform the auditory task adequately, one does not have to process auditory information immediately. If this is the case, the visual task does not suffer because the auditory task is postponed until after the processing of the visual target has finished. To force immediate auditory processing, we changed the task so that participants now had to detect the ear to which a target tone was presented. We assumed that it was impossible to postpone auditory processing when the task required the localization of the target tone.

## EXPERIMENT 3

During this experiment there was a stream of tones presented to both ears. Within this stream, one tone (the target tone) was presented more to one ear (either left or right). Participants had to detect the ear (left or right) to which the target tone was presented.

## Methods and Participants

The filler tones were presented to both ears. The target tone was presented more to the left ear or more to the right ear when the target tone. Filler tones which were presented to both ears had the same amplitude. The target tone was either presented perceptibly left or right. When the target tone was perceptibly right, the amplitude of the right ear was equal to

the amplitude of the filler tones and the amplitude of the left ear was reduced by 13.97 dB. When the target tone was perceptibly left, the amplitude of the left ear was equal to the amplitude of the filler tones and the amplitude of the right ear reduced by 13.97 dB.

Twelve students (six male; mean age, 22 years; age range, 18–29 years) participated in the experiment as paid volunteers. Data from two participants were excluded from further analyses because of an overall $T_1$ accuracy of only 50% was achieved.

## Results

### $T_1$ Accuracy

The target tone was identified correctly 88.8% of the time.

### $T_2$ Accuracy

Figure 14.4 presents the mean percentage of correct detection of the letter X for those trials during which the target tone was correctly identified as a function of task and lag. There was a significant main effect of task ($F(1, 9) = 10.398$, MSE = .018, $P = .01$), indicating that $T_2$ accuracy was higher when participants were asked to detect only the letter X (91.6%) than when participants were asked to identify the target tone and to detect the letter X (84.7%). Furthermore, was there a significant main effect of lag ($F(7, 63) = 2.819$, MSE = .003, $P < .05$). More important was the significant two-way interaction between lag and task ($F(7, 63) = 2.427$, MSE = .003, $P < .05$), indicating the presence of an AB. The interaction was further analyzed in detail by a pair-wise $t$-test for each lag (1–8). The $t$-test showed an AB effect at lag 1 to 4 ($P < .05$, all; except at lag 1, $P < .01$). Note that lag 7 was significant as well ($P < .01$).

## Discussion

Experiment 3 shows clear evidence of a cross-modal attentional blink similar to that demonstrated by Arnell and Jolicoeur (1999) in their experiment 3. At lags 1 to 4, detecting the tone impaired the detection of the visual target. Typically during AB studies, an AB is absent at the later stages (lags 5–8), because enough resources are freed to process the incoming second target. In our data, we basically observed the same

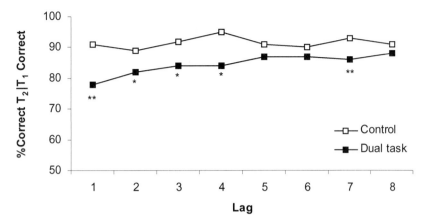

FIGURE 14.4. Experiment 3. Mean percentage of correct $T_2$ given that T1 was identified correctly as a function of lag in the current experiment. During the control condition, participants were asked to detect only the presence or absence of an X ($T_2$). During the dual-task condition, participants were asked to identify the target tone ($T_1$) and to detect the presence or absence of an X ($T_2$). $*P < 0.05$. $**P < 0.01$.

pattern of results for the later stages even though at lag 7 the difference between the control and dual-task condition was reliable. The classic AB effect in studies using visual targets typically shows a U-shaped appearance, in which performance is relatively good at the first lag after $T_1$ (so-called *lag 1 sparing*). Interestingly, in our experiment 3 we do not have lag 1 sparing; in fact, the AB is the largest at the first lag. This result is consistent with Arnell and Jolicouer (1999), who also showed in their experiments the largest effect at the first lag. It may not be surprising that lag 1 sparing does not occur in the cross-modal AB, because the reason for lag 1 sparing in AB studies using visual stimuli is attributed to the proximity in time and space of the two visual targets. Because in the cross-modal AB $T_1$ and $T_2$ are not proximate in the space (one is auditory, one is visual), lag 1 sparing does not occur (see also Potter, Chun, Banks, & Muckenhoupt, 1998).

### GENERAL DISCUSSION

The current study used a cross-modal attentional blink task to investigate whether it is possible to process auditory and visual information simultaneously. If there are completely independent resources for auditory and visual processing, as assumed by the strongest version of the multiple-resource theory (Wickens, 1980),

one would expect that processing the auditory target would have no impact on the processing of the visual target. Our experiments 1 and 2 seem to provide evidence for this claim. Processing the auditory tone had no influence whatsoever on the processing of the visual target. The results of experiments 1 and 2 are in line with those of Duncan and colleagues (1997), who found no cross-modal AB. However, our results of experiments 1 and 2 are not in line with the results obtained by Arnell and Jolicoeur (1999), who found clear cross-modal AB effects in their study. In fact, the task and procedures in our experiment 2 were basically identical to that of Arnell and Jolicoeur's (1999) experiment 3, and we were not able to replicate their results. However, consistent with Arnell and Jolicoeur (1999), our experiment 3 shows a clear cross-modal attentional blink effect.

What should be concluded from these experiments with respect to the multiple-resource theory and the claims of an independence of visual and auditory processing? The current findings seem to suggest that there may be independent resources for auditory and visual processing, but that cross-modal interference will occur when "central" processing is necessary for consolidation. In line with Arnell and Jolicoeur (1999), we assume that encoding information in short-term memory requires a process referred to as *short-term consolidation (STC)*. This process requires central processing. When the detection of the auditory target requires STC, the visual task has to wait until the central processing resources are available. It is assumed that during the period of waiting, the perceptual representation of the visual target decays because the visual target is masked by the subsequent filler items. We assume that cross-modal interference only occurs when both tasks require STC.

Given this notion, it is feasible that in our experiment 3, STC was necessary to encode the correct response in short-term memory. If participants did not encode at which ear the target tone was presented, as a result of masking by the subsequent filler tones, the perceptual representation would immediately decay. It may be impossible to extract this information at a later stage of processing. However, in our experiments 1 and 2, the detection of a tone that popped out from a stream of filler tones may not have required STC. Indeed, it is likely that the information in the auditory task in experiments 1 and 2 may have persisted to bridge the period of central processing required by the visual target. Therefore, under these circumstances, no AB deficit is observed. One possible explanation is that through echoic memory the information regarding the (popping-out) target tone can be extracted later, allowing for the "reconstruction" of the stream of tones that was presented earlier. It is known that there are two different forms of auditory persistence, one more short-lived than the other. The shorter form lasts only hundreds of milliseconds, but the longer one may last between 2 and 10 seconds (Cowan, 1984). Our data suggest that in our experiments 1 and 2, through auditory persistence, one can postpone the central consolidation process until after the processing of the visual stimulus.

The current findings shed some new light on the multiple-resource theory of Wickens (1980, 2002). According to Wickens (2002), resources for perceptual activities and cognitive activities such as the operation of working memory are the same and are separate from those underlying the selection and execution of responses. Even though perception and cognition may indeed be different from response selection and execution, our findings suggest that the resources for perception and cognition (i.e., working memory) are not the same but are different at least at the level of the modalities. Our findings imply that at the level of perception, different resources are available, one for vision and one for audition, but at the level of what Wickens (2002) called "cognition" (and more specifically working memory), there are no separate resources.

Indeed, our findings suggest that central cognitive processing (i.e., short-term memory consolidation) is sharply capacity limited. Independent of the perceptual modality (whether it is visual or auditory) in which the information is processed, only one operation that requires central processing, such as working memory consolidation, can be performed at any given time. Because of these capacity limitations, serialization between central operations is needed, resulting in uni- and cross-modal blink effects.

What are the implications of our findings for the design of multisensory displays? There are several important conclusions to be drawn. First, the usage of different modalities can have large advantages, because peripheral interference (such as masking) observed in unimodal displays is reduced. Indeed, perceptual processing can proceed without cross-modal interference. Second, even though it is possible to process information from two different modalities (auditory and visual) simultaneously, it should be realized that as soon as one of these modalities require central processing (such as STC) serialization is enforced, and processing of one event is postponed until central resources are freed up. If either one of these modalities require immediate action (such as an auditory alert indicating an upcoming collision), then missing the event can have severe implications. It is important to realize that central processes are capacity limited even when different modalities are used. Third, if one is able to use signals that do not need the immediate recruitment of central processing, it is possible to have near-perfect cross-modal dual-task performance. In our experiments 1 and 2, central processing was not immediately necessary because the auditory signal was designed in such a way that the recruitment of central processing could be postponed. Through adequate design of multimodal displays, the serialization of central processing does not need to become a "bottleneck," because information extraction from one of the modalities may be postponed until a moment that central processing resources are available. Note, however, that even though (from performance measures) it may appear that the auditory and visual tasks are perfectly time-shared (as in our experiments 1 and 2), this is not the result of shared resources at the central level, but of adequate scheduling of a single capacity-limited central processing resource. Fourth, given the notion that some signals may not require immediate central resource recruitment and therefore do not cause dual-task interference, it may be valuable to speculate what type of signal these may be. In the auditory domain, signals that easily can be stored in echoic memory would fulfill these requirements. Therefore, a salient warning tone (high or low tone) would be suitable; alphanumerical information such as spoken words that convey some type of warning would be less suitable because they may require immediate consolidation. In the visual domain, simple salient (pop-out) signals that require hardly any attentive processing conveying their information through spatial coding (e.g., a flashing red light located at a particular well-defined location in the car implies braking) may require the least central processing.

In summary, in line with the multiple-resource theory, there appear to be separate resources for auditory and visual perception. However, as soon as cognitive processing is required to consolidate the input, a central, single-resource, limited-capacity process is necessary that forces serialization between the operations requiring central processing.

## References

Arnell, K. M., & Jolicoeur, P. (1999). The attentional blink across stimulus modalities: Evidence for central processing limitations. *Journal of Experimental Psychology: Human Perception and Performance, 25,* 630–648.

Chun, M. M., & Potter, M. C. (1995). A two-stage model for multiple target detection in rapid serial visual presentation. *Journal of Experimental Psychology: Human Perception and Performance, 21,* 109–127.

Cowan, N. (1984). On short and long auditory stores. *Psychological: Bulletin, 96*(2), 341–370.

Driver, J., & Spence, C. (1998). Attention and the cross-modal construction of space. *Trends Cognitive Science, 2,* 254–262.

Duncan, J., Martens, S., & Ward, R. (1997). Restricted attentional capacity within but not between sensory modalities. *Nature, 387,* 808–810.

Ernst, M. O., & Banks, M. S. (2002). Humans integrate visual and haptic information in a statistically optimal fashion. *Nature,* (1980). *415,* 429–433.

Kohlrausch, A., & van der Par, S. (1999). Auditory–visual interaction: From fundamental research in cognitive psychology to (possible) applications. *Proceedings of SPIE, 3644,* 34–44.

McGurk, H., & MacDonald, J. (1976). Hearing lips and seeing voices. *Nature, 264,* 746–748.

Olivers, C. N. L. (2004). Blink and shrink: The effect of the attentional blink on spatial processing. *Journal of Experimental Psychology: Human Perception and Performance, 30,* 613–631.

Parkes, A. M., & Coleman, N. (1990). Route guidance systems: A comparison of methods of presenting directional information to the driver. In E. J. Lovesey (Ed.), *Contemporary ergonomics 1990* (pp. 480–485). London: Taylor & Francis.

Posner, M. I. (1980). Orienting of attention. *Quarterly Journal of Experimental Psychology, 32,* 3–25.

Potter, M. C., Chun, M. M., Banks, B. S., & Muckenhoupt, M. (1998). Two attentional deficits in serial target search: The visual attentional blink and an amodal task-switch deficit. *Journal of Experimental Psychology: Learning, Memory, and Cognition, 24,* 979–992.

Raymond, J. E., Shapiro, K. L., & Arnell, K. M. (1992). Temporary suppression of visual processing in an RSVP task: An attentional blink? *Journal of Experimental Psychology: Human Perception and Performance, 18,* 849–860.

Shapiro, K. L., Raymond, J. E., & Arnell, K. M. (1994). Attention to visual pattern information produces the attentional blink in rapid serial visual presentation. *Journal of Experimental Psychology: Human Perception & Performance, 20,* 357–371.

Spence, C., & Driver J. (1996). Audiovisual links in endogenous covert spatial attention. *Journal of Experimental Psychology: Human Perception & Performance, 22,* 1005–1030.

Thurlow, W. R., & Jack, C. E. (1973). Some determinants of localization adaptation effects for successive auditory stimuli. *Journal of the Acoustical Society of America 53,* 1573–1577.

Vroomen, J., & De Gelder, B. (2000). Sound enhances visual perception: Cross-modal effects of auditory organization on vision. *Journal of Experimental Psychology: Human Perception and Performance, 26,* 1583–1590.

Wickens, C. D. (1984). Processing resources in attention. In R. Parasuraman & D. R. Davies (Eds.), *Varieties of attention* (pp. 63–101). New York: Academic Press.

———. (2002). Multiple resources and performance prediction. *Theoretical Issues in Ergonomics Science, 3,* 159–177.

# Part VI

# Attention and Training

# Chapter 15

# Emphasis Change as a Training Protocol for High-Demand Tasks

## Daniel Gopher

This chapter summarizes the experimental results and discusses the theoretical underpinnings of a large body of training studies conducted at our and several other laboratories with a protocol labeled *the emphasis change protocol*. This protocol was found to be especially robust for training performers to cope with complex, high-demand tasks. Throughout my professional career I have always been interested in studying and modeling the limits of attention, mental workload, and the processing and response limitations of humans coping with high-demand tasks (Erev & Gopher, 1999; Gopher, 1994; Gopher, Armony, & Greenshpan, 2000; Gopher & Donchin, 1986; Navon & Gopher, 1979). The emphasis change protocol, directed to improve the ability of performers to cope with high demands, is a direct outgrowth of this research (Gopher, 1993). It concurs with a firm belief in an old statement attributed to the famous psychologist Kurt Lewin: "There is nothing more practical than a good theory (1951, p. 169)."

THE PROTOCOL

Emphasis change is a training protocol under which subjects are required, during training, to change systematically their emphasis, effort, attention allocation policy (these terms are used interchangeably) on major subcomponents of the performed tasks. Emphasis levels are varied between few-minute practice trials or among prespecified short durations of task performance. There are four major variants of the emphasis change protocol:

1. *Variable priorities*—Manipulation of attention allocation policies in concurrent task performance (Gopher, 1993; Gopher & North, 1977; Kramer, Larish, & Strayer, 1995)
2. *Emphasis change*—Change of emphasis on comonents of a complex task through instructions and augmented feedback indicators (Fabiani, Buckley, Gratton, Coles, Donchin, & Logie, 1989; Gopher, Weil, & Bareket, 1994;

Gopher, Weil, & Siegel, 1989; Shebilske, Goettl, Corrington, & Day, 1999; Shebilske, Jordan, Goettl, & Day, 1999; Shebilske, Reigan, Arthur, Jordan, 1992)

3. *Introduction of a secondary task*—Change of primary task performance strategies by adding a secondary task (Seagull & Gopher, 1997; Yechiam, Erev, Yehene, & Gopher, 2004)

4. *Task switching*—Training under changed computations or task-switching requirements (Carlson & Shin, 1996; Goettl, Yadrick, Connolly-Gomez, Regian, & Shebilske, 1996; Gopher et al., 2000; Kramer, Hahn, & Gopher, 1999)

The following sections illustrate and briefly describes each of these variants.

### Variable Priorities Training

Figure 15.1 presents a schematic diagram of the display and control panels of subjects in the concurrent performance of tracking and typing tasks. It is taken from Gopher (1993) and describes the tasks used by Michael Brickner in his doctoral dissertation (Brickner & Gophen, 1981).

Subjects performed a two-dimensional, pursuit tracking task using a right-hand joystick. They controlled the X symbol and followed the square moved by a random forcing function generated by the computer. In parallel, they performed a letter-typing task, using the Hebrew letter shape chord keyboard (Gopher, 1984). Hebrew letters were presented within the tracking square and had to be responded to by entering the correct letter chord on the left-hand keyboard. A new letter was generated each time the chord for the displayed letter was correctly entered. In addition to the two tasks, subjects were also presented with feedback indicators, displayed at the upper part of the screen. Indicators comprised a vertical desired performance line and two moving bar graphs, indicating for each task the difference between actual and desired performance levels. Moving the desired performance line to the left or right of the center changed priority levels on the two tasks. When moved to the left, less effort had to be allocated to the tracking task and more to the typing task to reach the desired performance line and vice versa when the line was moved to the right of the center. Priority changes were commensurate and summed to 1.0. The center of the screen represented equal priorities.

Subjects were trained under five priority levels: .75, .65, .50, .35, and .25. Priority levels were changed between 3-minute practice trials. Training under variable priorities was compared with training under equal priorities with the augmented feedback display

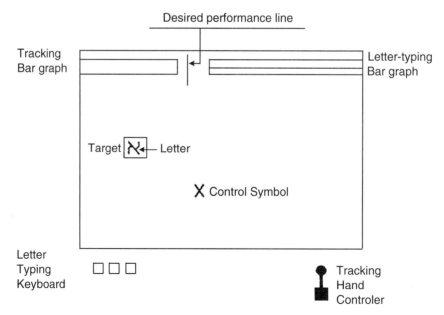

FIGURE 15.1. Variable priorities. Tracking and typing under five priority levels (Gopher, 1993; Gopher & North, 1977).

and training under equal priorities without the feedback display. Subjects in the latter condition were aurally instructed to attend equally to both tasks. They were given feedback on their performance at the end of each 3-minute trial. In addition to training, subjects were also tested in two transfer sessions. During one session they performed the same two tasks with equal priority, without feedback, but with commensurate changes of the difficulty of each tasks. During the second, transfer was tested to the performance of new tasks.

Figure 15.2 is taken from a variable priority training study by Kramer and colleagues (1995). Subjects were trained in the concurrent performance of two tasks: a visual monitoring task of six gauges for critical changes in process status and an alphabet arithmetic task. Here, again, desired and actual performance feedback displays and six priority levels were used. As in the previous example, subjects' performance in training and transfer was compared with a group trained only under fixed, equal-priorities condition.

## Emphasis Change Training

All complex and demanding tasks can be subdivided into many subcomponents. Think, for example, of the daily tasks of driving a car or playing tennis. Each task comprises many elements and segments, and performers have to acquire a variety of skills. Drivers should be able to control their car, monitor and interpret instruments and gauges to maintain its proper functioning, monitor the out-the-window field of view to adjust direction and speed, follow the rules of the road, orient themselves geographically, and so on. Tennis playing can be segmented in the same manner. In both cases all task segments should be attended to concurrently, under severe time and space constraints. Because the tasks as a whole are too difficult for beginners to cope with, conventional training protocols decompose the tasks to segments and train subjects on parts before practicing the complete tasks (e.g., Fredricksen & White, 1989). In contrast, the emphasis change protocol maintains the complete task intact, as a whole, but during different practice sessions changes the emphasis on components and segments through instructions and augmented performance indicators.

Figure 15.3 depicts the task display in a study in which subjects were trained in the performance of a complex computer game named Space Fortress (Gopher et al., 1989). This study was conducted in the framework of an international collaboration directed to compare learning strategies for complex high-demand tasks (Fabiani et al., 1989).

In the Space Fortress game, subjects control the movement of a spaceship in a frictionless atmosphere and are required to hit and destroy the space fortress located at the center of the screen. The fortress itself tracks the ship and attempts to hit it. Mines are intermittent, dynamic hostile elements that actively chase the spaceship to destroy it. Other considerations are efficient use of ammunition, resource scarcity, operational restrictions, complicated reward structure, and point

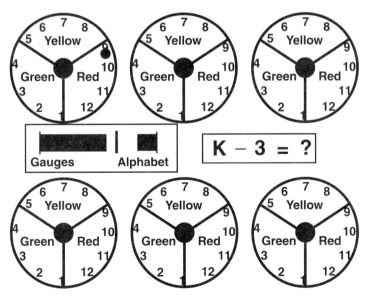

FIGURE 15.2. Variable priorities. Visual monitoring and letter arithmetic under five priority levels: .20, .35, .50, .65, and .80 (Kramer, Larish, & Strayer, 1995).

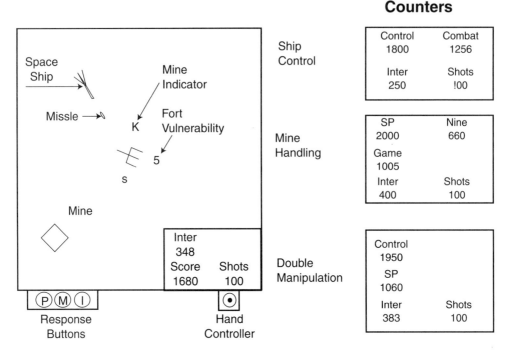

FIGURE 15.3. Emphasis change. Changed emphasis on subcomponents in the Space Fortress computer game (Fabiani, Buckley, Gratton, Coles, Donchin, & Logie, 1989; Gopher, Weil, & Siegel, 1989).

bonus opportunities. The game includes difficult dynamic and discrete manual control, visual scanning, short- and long-term memory demands—all performed under severe time constraints and attention load. The overall objective of subjects is to obtain the highest number of points in each few-minute game.

Within the emphasis change training protocol, subjects are instructed during a specific game trial to pay special attention to one of the several major subcomponents of the game. Examples are ship control or mine handling. They can attend to other game elements only in their spare capacity. Emphasis is changed through instructions and by adding counters dedicated to specific aspects of performance relevant to the emphasized element (Fig. 15.3). Emphasized elements are changed between game trials. It is important to note that under the emphasis change protocol, subjects are exposed and respond to the whole task throughout training. An emphasized element is advanced forward and is made a figure and all the others become ground, but the whole task—its dynamic and requirements—is active at all times.

Figure 15.4 depicts a version of the Space Fortress task that was used in a study that investigated the transfer of training from a computer game to actual flight in the Israeli Air Force (Gopher et al., 1994). It replicated the protocol used by Gopher and associates (1989); however, the display was redesigned to create a closer similarity to an airplane piloting task. The upper part of the display can be likened to an out-the-window, bird's-eye view of the flight practice area. The lower part grouped together all the game indicators to create an analog of a cockpit instrument panel. Flight cadets had no difficulty in observing the similarity between the computer game and actual flight task requirements to share attention and move back and forth between out-the-window and in-the-cockpit events.

### Introduction of a Secondary Task

Dual-task performance has been a major experimental paradigm in studying mental workload and investigating the processing and response limitations of the human processing system (Gopher, 1994; Wickens, 1992).

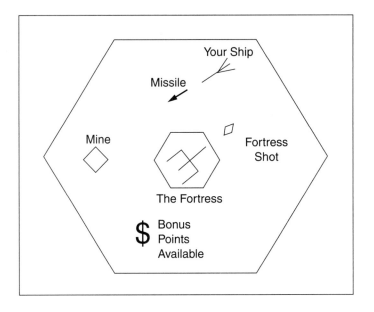

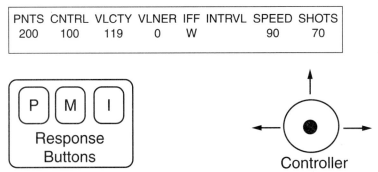

FIGURE 15.4. Emphasis change. Transfer from the Space Fortress computer game with emphasis change to actual flight (Gopher, Weil, & Bareket, 1994; Shebilske, Goettl, Corrington, & Day, 1999; Shebilske, Jordan, Goettl, & Day, 1999; Shebilske, Regian, Arthur, & Jordan, 1992).

The secondary task methodology is a variant of this paradigm, in which the level of performance on one task—the secondary task—is used to evaluate the difficulty and demands of the other, concurrently performed primary task. Subjects are required to protect the performance of the primary task at all times and perform their secondary task only to the extent that they have spare capacity. When the same secondary task is paired with a battery of different primary tasks, it can be used as common ruler. Its performance is argued to reflect the relative demands of these tasks (Gopher, 1994). In the current context of skill training and the emphasis change protocol, the introduction of a secondary task has been used as a tool to force subjects to change their response and coping strategies with primary task demands. Similar to the two variants described earlier, the introduction of a secondary task during training represents an emphasis change in the appeal of some response strategies over others in terms of achieving overall task goals (primary + secondary), compared with task performance without a secondary task. These arguments are illustrated in the following paragraphs.

Figure 15.5 is taken from a study by Yechiam and coworkers (2001), who trained subjects to acquire touch-typing skills. Blind touch typing, the most efficient mode of work with standard computer keyboards, is a difficult skill, which most users do not have. The vast majority of people working daily with computers are slow-pace, visually guided typists. In this mode, performers use vision to guide their fingers, and hence move continuously back and forth between monitoring the text on the screen or their fingers on the keyboard. In their training protocol, the researchers introduced a secondary task—a blue wire square—displayed intermittently at random locations on the screen (Fig. 15.5). Subjects who practiced typing had to eliminate the square by pressing the left

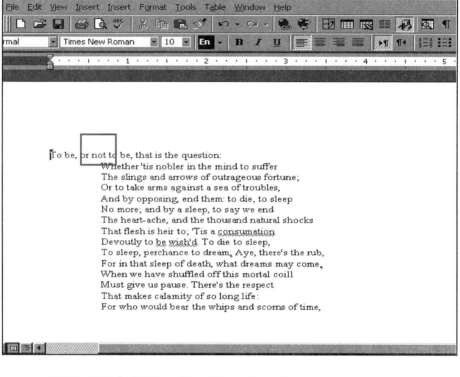

FIGURE 15.5. Adding a secondary task. Touch-typing training (Yechiam, Erev, Yehene, & Gopher, 2004).

square bracket ([) key on the keyboard. If not pressed within 2 seconds, the whole screen went blank and resumed only when the Alt key was pressed. Blanking the screen was a minor but very annoying penalty, which required the subjects to reorient themselves each time the screen went away and came back. To avoid this event, subjects had to monitor the screen closely and respond quickly to the squares. It is easy to see how the introduction of blue squares reduced the appeal of visually guided typing while increasing the value of touch typing, which enabled better concurrent typing and blue square monitoring.

A second example comes from a study by Seagull and Gopher (1997) on training pilots to fly with a helmet-mounted display (HMD). Single-eye HMDs are night

vision systems that enable pilots to fly at night and during limited-vision conditions (fog, smoke, sandstorms, and so on). They were first installed in military helicopters, but were rapidly adopted for civil uses, mainly for emergency rescue operations. The system is based on a thermal sensor, which is sensitive to the heat emission of objects. Thermal radiation is converted to the optical range and is displayed as a visual image of the outside world on a small monitor display attached to the pilot helmet and presented to the right eye (Fig. 15.6) Because of its weight and size, the sensor is located on a servomotor at the nose of the helicopter. The visual angle of the sensor and image are limited to 20 to 40 deg, and hence the servomotor is connected and sensitive to pilot head movements. Consequently, to scan

# Helmet-mounted displays

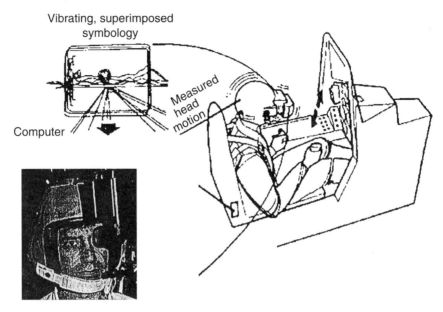

FIGURE 15.6. Adding a secondary task. Flying and capturing targets with a single-eye helmet-mounted night vision system (Seagull & Gopher, 1997).

and get an adequate coverage of their field of view, pilots have to move their head (and the sensor). Note, this mode of response is radically different from scanning behavior under normal viewing conditions in which scanning is performed by an automatic and unconscious coordinated movement of eyes and head. Normally, one does not know when and how eye and head motion is combined when scanning the visual field.

It is clear from the previous description that when flying with this system, the use of head movements in scanning the visual field is a critical adaptive behavior. However, pilot reports and field data have indicated that head movements substantially increase the probability of disorientation. Consequently, with experience, pilots teach themselves to limit their head movement. If it cannot be avoided, they use a very conscious and controlled procedure to move their head. In addition to the requirement for the exclusive use of head movement in visual scanning, there are several other contributors that increase the likelihood of disorientation: Visual information is monocular, coming from a single sensor to a single eye; peripheral information and visual flow are very limited in the dark; because the sensor is located forward, on the nose,

pilots do not see the outside world though the cockpit windshield and cannot use its features and structure for orientation. Visual motion on the display at the pilot's eye level can occur because terrain features have changed, the helicopter changed its heading, wind gusts introduced random motions, or the pilot moved his or her head. These determinants are hard to separate, in particular when co-occurring. Thus, head movement that is a crucial adaptive skill is also a major source of confusion. The training protocol, which was developed to teach trainees to gain confidence and apply head movements, was based on the introduction of a secondary task while practicing flying with an HMD.

Trainees practiced 3-minute missions of low-level canyon flights with an HMD in a helicopter simulator with a computer-generated visual field. Flight performance and head movements in HMD flights were compared before and after training, with flying under normal out-the-window viewing conditions. During training, trainees received a secondary task in addition to their primary flight mission. The secondary task concerned a diamond-shaped target that appeared intermittently for 10 seconds at random locations along the forward flight path. Subjects had to capture and eliminate the target by moving their head and superimposing on the target a cross-hair presented at the middle of their display screen. If not eliminated, the target would disappear and it would be counted as a miss. Similar to the touch-typing study, the introduction of the target-capturing task changed not only the overall framework and demands of the whole task, but required and trained subjects to perform multiple accurate head movements while flying with an HMD. The posttraining flight tests, conducted without the secondary task, showed equal flight performance levels for this group under HMD and normal viewing conditions. In addition, subjects increased considerably their head movements not only during HMD flights but also under normal viewing conditions. In contrast, control groups trained with the HMD but without a secondary task, or only under normal viewing conditions, showed substantially lower flight performance with an HMD and, with accumulated experience in HMD flights, also had a significant reduction in the number of head movements.

### Emphasis Change in Task Switching

The fourth and last variant of the emphasis change protocol to be described is training within the task-switching paradigm. Task switching is an experimental paradigm within which subjects are asked within a block of trials to switch from the performance of one task to another and vice versa. Task switching is a popular experimental paradigm in contemporary research of control processes in human information processing and response. Control processes are the class of processes that initiate, coordinate, synchronize, and regulate the conduct of goal-directed behavior. They can be conceptualized as the working tools of intentions. They represent the ensemble of top-down forces that guide, constrain, and influence task performance, and are closely related to

the study of executive functions (Gopher & Koriat, 1999; Monsell & Driver, 2000). Voluntary switching between tasks is a clear act of control, and the costs of switching are argued to reflect, on the one hand, the reconfiguration and adaptation required for the initiation of the new task, and on the other hand, the effort to stop and inhibit all processes associated with the performance of the previously performed task (e.g., Allport, Styles, & Hsieh, 1994; Mayr & Keele, 2000; Meiran, 1996; Rogers & Monsell, 1995). Switching costs are conventionally evaluated by comparing performance levels on repeating trials, in which the measured trial belongs to the same task performed during the previous trial, with switch trials, which are the first trials of a new task. In the current context we consider the influence of training within the task-switching paradigm as a variant of the emphasis change protocol.

Figure 15.7 illustrates a typical switching task from a study by Gopher and colleagues (2000). Subjects were presented, during each block of trials, with a sequence of screens displaying a single row of equal-value digits. They could be instructed to perform one of several possible tasks, such as press one key if the value of the digits is more than five, press another key if it is less than five, do the same but count the number of digit elements in each row, or judge the value of digits and press a different key for odd and even numbers, and so on. The type of stimuli, required responses, or nature of transformations could change, as could the display time and structure of trial sequences. Figure 15.7 illustrates the case of a continuous alternation condition during which subjects continuously alternate between tasks, as indicated by the different background screen color of trials. Switch and repetition trial probability can be manipulated, and the change of tasks can be random or predictable. These have all been important variables in comparative experimentation.

Before considering the paradigm from a skill-training vantage point, I would like to present another variant

FIGURE 15.7. Task switching. Continuous alternations, digit value/ number of elements or odd/even (Goettl, Yadrick, Connolly-Gomez, Regian, & Shebilske, 1996; Gopher, Armony, & Greenshpan, 2000; Kramer, Hahn, & Gopher, 1999).

AND #        A = \$  (0,1)            A = \$  (0,1)

OR \$         B = ▲ (1,1)            B = ▲ (1,1)
NAND *
              C = # (1,0)             C = # (A,B)
NOR ▲
              D = # (0,0)             D = # (0,0)

              E = * (A,B)             E = * (0,1)

              F = ▲ (C,D)             F = ▲ (D,E)

              **X = \$  (E,F)**       **X = \$  (C,F)**

FIGURE 15.8.  Computations change. Seven-step Boolean algebra problems (Carlson & Shin, 1996).

of the task-switching paradigm, in which switching is performed between computation types rather than tasks.

Carlson and Shin (1996) conducted a study in which they trained their subjects to solve seven-step Boolean algebra problems. They taught their subjects the four basic operations in Boolean algebra—And, Or, Nor, Nand—and gave them seven-step problems of the kind illustrated in Figure 15.8. The two problems in Figure 15.8 are ones in which all four operations appear in random order. Note also that the products of some steps are the input to later steps. The researchers compared training and transfer performance for groups of subjects who were trained in single-operation problem blocks with groups who were trained in four-operation problem blocks. In each training group, subjects practiced the four operations; however, for the single-operation group, problems contained only one of the operations in all seven steps whereas the mixed-operation condition used all four operations in each problem (as in Fig. 15.8).

From the perspective of the emphasis change protocol, the important distinction between conditions is that subjects who are trained in single-operation blocks are exposed to a very different training experience from those who are trained in mixed operation blocks. In task switching and mixed-operation problems, subjects, although focusing each time on a single component, are also introduced from start with the richness of the situation and the need to perform rapid transitions between task components or alternative computations. In this respect, task and computation switching are very similar to emphasis change in the Space Fortress computer game, the change of priorities under variable priorities training,

and the introduction of a secondary task. In all variants, while focusing on one element, one task, or one operation, all others coexist in the background and should not or cannot be easily ignored. This is the most important feature of the emphasis change protocol and the common denominator for its four described variants.

### MAIN FINDINGS

A detailed review of the experimental results of the studies conducted with the emphasis change protocol is beyond the scope of this chapter and is not required for a discussion of its general principles and the sources of its power. The following presents a global four-point summary of the most important outcomes of this work:

1. Emphasis change proved to be a robust training protocol. In all studies, for all tasks variants and subject populations, variable priority and emphasis change protocols led to substantially higher levels of task performance at the end of training compared with equal-priority or no-priority training protocols.
2. Emphasis change training led to better transfer and adaptation to changed conditions, new tasks, and operational environments.
3. In all the studies, emphasis change and variable training were shown to have slower progress at early stages of training compared with no change or uniform training protocols, but subjects excelled at advanced stages of training and in subsequent transfer tasks (e.g., Carlson & Shin, 1996; Yechiam et al., 2001).

4. When compared with part-task training protocols, emphasis change was shown to be poorer
or equal at the end of training on the same task,
but superior in transfer to different conditions
and new tasks (e.g., Fabiani et al., 1989; Gopher
et al., 1994).

## APPLICATIONS

Emphasis change training protocols have been, thus
far, applied and found useful in the performance of
five complex and highly demanding daily tasks:

1. Piloting high-performance airplanes. A 10-hour
   training program on the modified Space Fortress
   game, under the emphasis change protocol, was
   found to increase by 30% the flight performance
   scores of cadets at the Israel Air Force flight
   training school (Gopher et al., 1994).
2. Flying with an HMD. HMD flight performance following training equaled flight levels
   under normal viewing conditions (Seagull &
   Gopher, 1997).
3. Acquisition of touch-typing skills. Using the
   secondary task variant of the emphasis change
   protocol, the study by Yechiam and coworkers
   (2001) demonstrated much faster acquisition,
   higher typing rates, and better retention of
   touch-typing skills.
4. Teaching older adults to cope with high-attention
   management demands. The variable-priority protocol was found to be especially powerful in
   improving the coping ability of older adults with
   high-demand tasks (Kramer et al., 1999; Kramer
   et al., 1995).
5. Training basketball players at the individual
   and team levels. The principles and the knowledge acquired in the study of the emphasis
   change protocol were used by Ace, an Israeli-
   based company, to develop a cognitive trainer
   for basketball players. The trainer was beta
   tested during the 2005 season in 12 teams of
   the US college league. It was found to improve
   substantially the game performance of individuals and the overall achievements of their
   team (www.ace4sports.com).

Note that these five applications demonstrate a performance advantage both within and between tasks.
With the HMD, touch typing, and older adult applications, emphasis change training helped trainees in
the acquisition of competence on the task and
improved their performance in subsequent performance with the same task. In the flight and basketball
applications, earlier training with this protocol as a
specially developed computer game improved the
performance of trainees on a different task.

The obvious questions that need to be addressed
are: What is the power of emphasis change? Why is it
so helpful in training? What is its power in transfer?
These are the questions that will guide our discussion
in the remainder of the chapter. We first examine
emphasis change as a specific and special case of
introducing variability to training. We then consider
the special contribution of emphasis change to the
training and transfer of complex, high-demand tasks.

## THE CONTRIBUTION AND SIGNIFICANCE OF VARIABILITY IN TRAINING

An important basic feature of the emphasis change
protocol is the introduction of systematic variability to
training. We first consider this aspect of the protocol.
Several lines of experimental research provide
evidence for the influence of introducing variability to
training on the nature and performance characteristics of the acquired skill. Four groups of such studies
are briefly described: effects of training in uniform versus mixed-trial blocks, using intermittent versus full
schedules of feedback and knowledge of results,
encouraging subjects to explore alternatives and avoid
local optima, and introduction of random noise to
neural networks in machine learning.

### Training in Uniform versus Mixed-Trial Blocks

When a study includes several conditions or several
tasks, a uniform blocks design is one within which only
one condition or a single task is presented to subjects in
each block of trials. In contrast, in a mixed experimental design, several conditions or tasks are mixed within
each block of trials. It should be recognized that mixing
implies variability, because within each block subjects
are required to cope with and switch between several
conditions or tasks. Researchers have long been well
aware of the performance differences resulting from
these two types of designs (e.g., Poulton, 1982).
Throughout the years there have been a number of
studies that compared blocked and mixed schedules in

the training of motor and of verbal skills (as reviewed by Schmidt and Bjork [1992]). More recent examples include studies by Strayer and Kramer (1994), Carlson and Shin (1996), Gopher and colleagues (2000), and Meiran (2000). All studies show that both the influence of experimental manipulations and general performance levels on tasks are significantly different in the two design variants. For example, Shiffrin and Schneider (1977) have shown convincingly that the quantitative and qualitative differences created between the responses to stimuli that were trained under consistent mapping (CM) versus variable mapping (VM) protocols. This work generated an influx of experimental replications and modeling efforts, all supporting the proposed distinctions, but all conducted under the uniform block design. However, Strayer and Kramer (1994), who compared responses to CM and VM stimuli trained in uniform versus mixed-block designs, found that mixed-block training changed considerably the performance and transfer characteristics of these two types of mappings. It brought performance levels and response strategies of the two much closer to one other in ways that undermine some of strong theoretical claims on their nature, and the resultant predictions. Carlson and Shin (1996) report similar results from their seven-step Boolean algebra problems. Meiran and colleagues (2000) obtain the same pattern of outcomes in the performance of task switching.

### Using Intermittent versus Full Schedules of Feedback and Knowledge of Results

Schedules of reinforcements have been known, from the early days of learning research, to influence the learning and extinction curves of animals and human (Skinner, 1961; Adams, 1987). Random, partial rate or interval, reinforcement schedules were shown to be slower in acquisition but also more persistent and have lower and slower extinction rates. When describing human learning in subsequent cognitive psychology and information processing research, the term *reinforcement* was replaced by *feedback* and *knowledge of results*. The importance of this change was the emphasis on the contribution and importance of the information value of feedback, above and beyond its role as a motivator. Research with both verbal and motor tasks has shown that intermittent feedback schedules may slow down acquisition, but are superior in retention and transfer. Schmidt and Bjork (1992), who review this literature, argue that intermittent

feedback forces trainees to a deeper processing and less dependence on external information, leading to improved retention and transfer.

### Encouraging Subjects to Explore Alternatives and Avoid Local Optima

Another justification for introducing variability to training comes from the decision-making literature. It is related to the widely documented limited willingness of subjects to explore spontaneously the response alternative space of a given situation. Herrnstein and Prelec (1991) labeled this tendency melioration. It implies that in a multiple alternative space, when the value of alternatives is not known, subjects will stop exploring as soon as they hit an acceptable response alternative, and thus converge to a local optima (Herrnstein, Loewenstein, Prelec, & Vaughan, 1993; Herrnstein & Prelec, 1991). Melioration has been documented in a variety of tasks. It was also clearly observed in the learning studies with the Space Fortress computer game, in which subjects in the control group, who practiced the game without instruction, progressed but converged to a suboptimal response strategy relative to the game heuristics and their own ability. Yechiam and coworkers (2004), who studied this issue experimentally, showed that encouraging subjects to explore led them to identify better response strategies and avoid local optima. Encouraging exploration introduces variability to training.

### Introduction of a Random Noise Component to Neural Networks

The last example for the influence of introducing variability to training comes from machine learning in the domain of neural networks. Albeit not human, neural networks are powerful bottom-up learning algorithms that capture the regularities (conditioned probabilities) of input–output relationships in a given set of examples. The power of the acquired knowledge in a neural network is conventionally tested by generalization to a new set of examples. Neural networks have been used as a modeling tool for a wide variety of human behaviors. It is one of the main computational approaches in contemporary cognitive psychology (McClelland, McNaughton, & O'Reilly, 1995; Rumelhart, McClleland, & the PDP Research Group, 1986). In the framework of the current chapter, it is interesting to note that a common "trick" used in the development of neural networks to increase their stability and generalization power is to add a random noise component (Miglino, Pedone, & Parisi, 1993) during the learning phase. Such a component introduces variability and uncertainty to learning situations; it influences the trained network behavior much the same way as variability in human skill acquisition.

Taken together, the results of these lines of study present arguments and provide strong evidence for the contribution and value of introduced variability in training to the acquisition and transfer of skills.

### Local Sources of Variability in the Demands of Ongoing Task Performance

The role of introducing variability to training can be further evaluated in the light of the inevitable local variability in the performance demands of ongoing tasks. Such variability exists in the performance of every task, but is expected to be much more significant in performing complex, high-demand tasks. Figure 15.9 illustrates the possible ingredients of a task. As the figure shows, every task is the collective set of a large number of individual items, which vary in their formative features — stimuli, responses, required transformations, time intervals, and so on. Items in each set may also vary in their difficulty in a variety of ways, some digits may be more difficult than other to perceive and encode,

some responses may be harder to perform, and some transformations are more difficult and demanding than others. Each trial in a task is a joint product of all these ingredients; hence, individual trials are bound to vary in their difficulty and demands. These are external sources of variations. In addition, there are also internal, performer-related sources of variability. Individual performers vary considerably in their past experience, knowledge, skills, and abilities. These differences may make some elements of an ongoing task more difficult and demanding than others for an individual performer. Moreover, during the course of task performance, performers may encounter a temporary decrease of efficiency, lapses of attention, or loss of orientation, all of which may lead to fluctuations in task difficulty and demands. There are, hence, both external and internal causes for variability in task demands. When evaluating performance on a task, we normally average across such fluctuations. Alas, performers have to cope with them trial by trial.

Instances of local variability in difficulty and demands are expected to be much more frequent and pronounced in complex, high-demand tasks. The vast majority of such tasks are composed of many covarying components, performed under time pressure, and impose a high workload. Local variability and fluctuations in demands in these tasks are likely to be more frequent and robust. The introduction of emphasis change training to high-demand tasks can hence be

## THE INGREDIENTS OF A TASK

**Display**  2,6,3,7,1,8,9,4

**Responses**  A Key, B Key

**Presentation mode**  Visual, auditory

**Time and trial sequence structure**

===============   ===============

**Possible assignments**
- A <5, B >5
- A odd, B even
- Sum of pairs, larger/ smaller than 10
- A a digit with a close circle, B no close circle

**Performance instructions Reward structure**

? ? ? ?

FIGURE 15.9. The dimensions of a task.

viewed as a specific and special case of training in a subset of tasks in which coping with local fluctuations in demands is highly needed. It is mandatory for successful performance (Gopher, 1993).

## THE POWER OF EMPHASIS CHANGE TRAINING

What is the power and what are the benefits of the emphasis change training protocols? The previous two sections have laid the ground work for an attempt to address these questions by describing sources of local variability in the performance demands of tasks and by reviewing evidence for the effects and benefits of introducing variability to training. The main emerging conclusions from the two sections are the following:

1. Variability in difficulty, workload, and demands is an inherent property in the performance of every task, and is particularly viable in the performance of complex, high-demand tasks.
2. The sources of variability are twofold: task features and individual differences.
3. Trainees are limited explorers. Unless specifically encouraged, they are likely to converge to suboptimal strategies that become more consistent and persistent with the progress of training.
4. Introduced variability changes the process of training and influences its scope. Trainees may be slower and perform less well during earlier acquisition stages, but demonstrate better final performance, retention, and transfer to new conditions and tasks.

How does the emphasis change protocol apply to the four points?

### The Value of Guided Exploration

One obvious contribution of the protocol is that it encourages subjects to explore the response alternative space. As in many individualized training programs, such an exploration may lead to revealing the best (optimal) fit between an individual performer and the requirements of the task. This match is of particular importance in complex, high-demand tasks. Individuals vary in their skills, abilities, and experiences. Tasks vary in their elements and requirements. Good performance depends on the best correspondence between the two and there are no uniform, general solutions.

Think, for example, about the game of tennis. Competitors at Wimbledon are, no doubt, the highest level expert players, yet champions vary considerably in their game style, strength, and weaknesses. There are many degrees of freedom in the game of tennis. Some weaknesses can be compensated by other strengths and vice versa. A good coach first explores the abilities of his trainee to find and develop the best match between a specific player and game requirements. The emphasis change protocol leads trainees through a very similar procedure. In this context, it is important to emphasize that unlike an introduction of a random or uncontrolled variability factor (e.g., Schmidt & Bjork, 1992), emphasis change leads subjects through a controlled and well-planned exploration scheme that is based on a detailed task analysis. Exploration not only gives trainees the opportunity to examine their abilities, but its content comprises elements and behaviors that are of major significance for task performance and underline critical performance strategies. Again, the more complex and demanding a task, the higher the importance of an exploration, strategy evaluation, and a match between the performer's skills and task requirements.

### Development of an Adaptive "Task Shell"

Exploration may help trainees to develop the best correspondence between their capabilities and task requirements, but it cannot provide answers to problems of coping with variability and changes in task demands, or a better transfer of training to new conditions and tasks. To this end, I briefly introduce here the theoretical construct of a "task shell." I first proposed it in a keynote address presented at the 2004 28th International Congress of Psychology in China (Gopher, 2006) to distinguish it from the conventional use of the term *task* in psychology. In the following paragraph I summarize major claims from this chapter that are relevant for the current discussion of emphasis change training. Although the term *task* is one of the most fundamental and frequently used terms in psychology, and is included as a mandatory section in any report of scientific work, its meaning and use are rather fuzzy. It does not have a formal, agreed upon definition. Researchers do seem to have a general agreement on the elements describing a task, the main dimensions of which are summarized in Figure 15.9.

Stimulus types, response modes, transformation requirements, time constraints, and others are all important composites of a task, but they are only its separate elements. The "task" is the binding framework. It is the inclusive entity that represents the joint product of properties and constraints encapsulated in these elements, in the service of purposive, goal-directed behavior. Stimulus types, processing and transformation modes, response characteristics, memory representations, and performance competency are all defined, bounded, and developed within their respective task shells. The term *task shell* denotes the integrated joint product of all structural and dynamic properties that compose a task. Task shells have an independent status, which is akin to the fundamental Gestalt idea of a whole being more than the sum of its parts (Kellman, 2000; Koffka, 1935). Similarly, it is argued that task shells have a marked influence on the work of their elements. Shells are important for the understanding of interaction, facilitation, and interference effects on performance, within and between tasks. Shells also delineate the boundaries of an acquired skill, the value of practice, and the cost of transfer. Task shells are integrative constructs that do not occur immediately. They gradually develop with experience and training. They evolve around leading dimensions (dominant features, environmental constraints, control strategies). Once established, the global properties of the shell link together and influence the work of its composing elements in ways that cannot be predicted from a separate study of the elements. Psychology has generally overlooked the importance of incorporating the construct of a task shell in its models, and the need to study its formation and influence on behavior. This is despite the fact that the formation of a task shell is the building block of the conduct of purposive behavior.

The relevance of the task shell construct for the current discussion of training is that differences in practice and training protocols are likely to lead to the development of different task shells. Thus, uninstructed practice, part-task, equal-priority, and emphasis change training may lead to the development of radically different task shells, although the same task elements are being practiced. When performing multielement, high-demand tasks, uninstructed practice and equal-priority training are likely to lead most subjects to focus on a single suboptimal performance strategy. Part-task training practices subjects on separate segments of a task and does not expose them, until late stages, to the complete, dynamic environment. In contrast, emphasis change training leads trainees through a well-constructed exploration of the

intact task. The protocol requires trainees to perform the task from different perspectives and vantage points, to evaluate the influence of alternative strategies, and to learn to change their behavior, adopt different attention management strategies, and cope with differential demands. The task shell developed under such a training protocol is bound to be different. It is likely to include the requirement to change and adapt behavior, as an inherent property of the shell, which is complemented by an acquired ability to respond to elements and allocate graded levels of effort from different perspectives. A task shell developed through emphasis change training may lead subjects to be more sensitive to changes in task difficulty and load, and be better adapted to coping with changes through reallocation of efforts.

Along the same line of thinking, we can reason the pronounced advantage of the emphasis change protocols in the transfer to new tasks and conditions. Beyond learning during the very early years, most acquired skills can be considered secondary, in the sense that they are based heavily on preexisting more elementary skills, which are recombined and organized in new ways. The inclusion of existing skill components in newly developed capabilities becomes more and more dominant as we move from childhood to adulthood. Flexible and adaptive task shells developed through emphasis change training make their composites easier to adapt and be incorporated in the framework of new tasks and developed skills. It should be noted that such a generalization is constrained by content relevance. Indeed, this is one of the major challenges in developing training programs for operational environments, and was a key consideration in the development of the computer games environments for the flight and basketball applications presented earlier (Gopher et al., 1994).

Another possible and more general value of emphasis change training to transfer is if subjects have learned the value of exploration. Controlled explorations are a general strategy that is likely to have a positive effect on any new acquisition process. Although the effects on transfer of a larger flexibility and adaptiveness of the acquired task shell should be immediate, the influence of enhanced exploration is more gradual.

In conclusion, the power of the emphasis change protocol is argued to stem from enabling the development of a better match between individual performers and task demands, increasing trainees' sensitivity and ability to cope with dynamic changes in demands, and establishing flexible and adaptive task shells that ease the coping, transfer, and incorporation of the acquired skill components in new tasks and changed conditions.

## References

Adams, J. A. (1987). Historical review and appraisal of research on the learning, retention, and transfer of human motor skills. *Psychological Bulletin, 101,* 41–47.

Allport, A., Styles, E., & Hsieh, S. (1994). Shifting intentional set: Exploring the dynamic control of tasks. In C. Umilta & M. Moskovitch (Eds.), *Attention and performance, XV* (pp. 421–452). Cambridge, Mass.: MIT Press.

Brickner, M., & Gopher, D. (1981). Improving time-sharing performance by enhancing voluntary control on processing resources. *Technion, Research Centre for Work Safety and Human Engineering, HEIS-81-3.*

Carlson, R. A., & Shin, J. C. (1996). Practical schedules and subgoals instantiation in cascaded problem solving. *Journal of Experimental Psychology: Learning, Memory and Cognition, 22*(1), 157–168.

Erev, I., & Gopher, D. (1999). A cognitive game theoretical analysis of attention strategies, ability and incentive. In D. Gopher & A. Koriat (Eds.), *Attention and performance XVII—Cognitive regulation of performance: Theory and application* (pp. 343–372). Cambridge, Mass.: MIT Press.

Fabiani, M., Buckley, J., Gratton, G., Coles, M. G. H., Donchin, E., & Logie, R. (1989). The training protocol of complex task performance. *Acta Psychologica, 71,* 259–299.

Fredricksen, J. R., & White B. Y. (1989). An approach to training based upon principled task decomposition. *Acta Psychologica, 71,* 89–146.

Goettl, G., Yadrick, R. M., Connolly-Gomez, C., Regian, J. W., & Shebilske, W. L. (1996). Alternating task modules in isochronal distributed training of complex tasks. *Human Factors, 38*(2), 330–346.

Gopher, D. (1982). A selective attention test as a predictor of success in flight training. *Human Factors, 24,* 173–183.

———. (1984). On the contribution of vision-based imagery to the acquisition and operation of a transcription skill. In W. Prinz, A. Sanders, & H. Heuer (Eds.), *Cognition and motor processes* (pp. 195–208). New York: Springer-Verlag.

———. (1993). The skill of attention control: Acquisition and execution of attention strategies. In D. Meyer & S. Kornblum (Eds.), *Attention and performance XIV: Synergies in experimental psychology, artificial intelligence, and cognitive neuroscience—A silver jubilee* (pp. 290–322). Cambridge, Mass.: MIT Press.

———. (1994). Analysis and measurement of mental workload. In G. d'Ydewalle, P. Eelen, & P. Bertelson (Eds.), *International perspectives on cognitive sciences* (vol. II, pp. 265–291). London: Lawrence Erlbaum.

———. (2006). Control processes in the formation of task units. In Qicheng Jin (Ed.), *Psychological science around the world, volume 2, social and applied issues.* Oxford: Oxford University Press.

———, & Donchin, E. (1986). Workload: An examination of the concept. In K. Boff & L. Kaufman (Eds.), *Handbook of human perception and performance* (vol. II, pp. 1–49), New York: John Wiley.

———, Armony, L., & Greenshpan, Y. (2000). Switching tasks and attention policies. *Journal of Experimental Psychology: General, 109,* 306–339.

———, & Koriat A. (Eds). (1999). *Attention and performance XVII. Cognitive regulation of performance: Interaction of theory and application.* Cambridge, Mass.: MIT Press

———, & North, B. (1977). Manipulating the conditions of training in time-sharing performance. *Human Factors, 19*(6), 583–593.

———, Weil, M., & Bareket, T. (1994). Transfer of a skill from a computer game trainer to flight. *Human Factors, 36*(3), 387–405.

———, Weil, M., & Siegel, D. (1989). Practice under changing priorities: An approach to training of complex skills. *Acta Psychologica, 71,* 147–179.

Herrnstein, R. J., Loewenstein, G. F., Prelec, D., & Vaughan, W., Jr. (1993). Utility maximization and melioration: Internalities in individual choice. *Journal of Behavioral Decision Making, 6,* 149–185.

———, & Prelec, D. (1991). Melioration: A theory of distributed choice. *Journal of Economic Perspectives, 5,* 137–156.

Kellman, P. J. (2000). An update on Gestalt psychology. In B. Landau, J. Sabini, J. Jonides, & E. Newport (Eds.), *Perception cognition and language: Essays in honor of Henry and Lila Gleitman.* Cambridge, Mass.: MIT Press.

Koffka, K. (1935). *Principles of Gestalt psychology.* New York: Harcourt Brace.

Kramer, A., Hahn, S., & Gopher, D. (1999). Task coordination and aging: Exploration of executive control processes in the task-switching paradigm. *Acta Psychologica, 101,* 339–378.

———, Larish, J. F., & Strayer, D. L. (1995). Training for attentional control in dual task settings: A comparison of young and old adults. *Journal of Experimental Psychology, 1*(1), 50–76.

———, Larish, J. L.,Weber, T. A., & Bardell, L. (1999). Training for executive control: Task coordination strategies and aging. In D. Gopher & A. Koriat (Eds.), *Attention and performance XVII. Cognitive Regulation of performance: Interaction of theory and application* (pp. 617–652). Cambridge, Mass.: MIT Press.

Lewin, K. (1951). *Field theory in social science: Selected theoretical papers.* New York: Harper & Row.

Mayr, U., & Keele, S. W. (2000). Changing internal constraints on action: The role of backward inhibition. *Journal of Experimental Psychology: General, 129,* 4–26.

McClelland, J. L., McNaughton, B. L., & O'Reilly, R. C. (1995). Why there are complementary learning systems in the hippocampus and neocortex: Insights from the successes and failures of connectionist models of learning and memory. *Psychological Review, 102*(3), 419–457.

Meiran, N. (1996). The reconfiguration of processing mode prior to task performance. *Journal of Experimental Psychology: Learning, Memory and Cognition, 22*, 1423–1442.

———. (2000). Modeling cognitive control in task switching. *Psychological Research, 63*, 234–249.

Miglino, O., Pedone, R., & Parisi, D. (1993). A noise gene for Econets. In M. Dorigo (Ed.), *Proceedings of Genetic Algorithms and Neural Networks* (pp. 768–771). Reading, Mass.: Addison Wesley.

Monsell, S., & Driver, J. (2000). *Control of cognitive processes*: Attention and performance XVIII. Boston, Mass.: MIT Press.

Navon, D., & Gopher, D. (1979). On the economy of the human processing system. *Psychological Review, 86*, 214–253.

Poulton, E. C. (1982). Effects of one strategy on another in the within-subjects design. *Psychological Bulletin 91*, 673–690.

Rogers, R. D., & Monsell, S. (1995). Costs of a predictable switch between simple cognitive tasks. *Journal of Experimental Psychology: General, 124*, 207–231.

Rumelhart, D. E., McClleland J. L., & the PDP Research Group. (1986). *Parallel distributed processing: Exploration in the microstructure in cognition* (vols. 1 and 2). Cambridge, Mass.: MIT Press.

Seagull, F. J., & Gopher, D. (1997). Training head movement in visual scanning: An embedded approach to the development of piloting skills with helmet mounted displays. *Journal of Experimental Psychology: Applied, 3*, 463–480.

Schmidt, R. A., & Bjork, R. A. (1992). New conceptualization of practice: Common principles in three paradigms suggest new concepts for training. *Psychological Science, 3*, 207–217.

Schneider, W., & Shiffrin, M. R. (1977). Controlled and automatic human information processing: Detection, search and attention. *Psychological Review, 84*, 1–66.

Shebilske, W. L., Goettl, B., Corrington, W. L., & Day, E. A. (1999). Interlesson spacing and task-related processing during complex skill acquisition. *Journal of Experimental Psychology: Applied, 5*(4), 413–437.

Shebilske, W., Goettl, B., & Regian, J. W. (1999). Executive control and automatic processes as complex skills develop in laboratory and applied settings. In D. Gopher & A. Koriat (Eds.), *Attention and performance XVII: Cognitive regulation of performance: Interaction of theory and application.* Cambridge, Mass.: MIT Press.

———, Regian, J. W., Arthur, W., Jr., & Jordan, J. A. (1992). A dyadic protocol for training complex skills. *Human Factors, 34*(3), 369–374.

Shiffrin, R. M., & Schneider, W. (1977). Controlled and automatic human information processing: II. Perceptual learning, automatic attending, and a general theory. *Psychological Review, 84*, 127–190.

Skinner, B. F. (1961). *Cumulative record.* New York: Appleton.

Strayer, L. S., & Kramer, F. K. (1994). Strategies and automaticity: Basic findings and conceptual framework. *Journal of Experimental Psychology: Learning, Memory and Cognition, 20*(2), 318–341.

Wickens, C. D. (1992). *Engineering psychology and human performance*, 2nd ed. New York: Harper Collins Publishers.

———, & Gopher, D. (1977). Control theory measures of tracking as indices attention allocation strategies. *Human Factors, 19*, 349–365.

Yechiam, E., Erev, I., & Gopher, D. (2001). On the potential value and limitation of emphasis change and other exploration enhancing training methods. *Journal of Experimental Psychology: Applied, 4*, 277–285.

———, Erev, I., Yehene, V., & Gopher, D. (2004). Melioration and the transition from touch typing training to everyday use. *Human Factors, 45*, 671–684.

# Chapter 16

# Prospective Memory, Concurrent Task Management, and Pilot Error

## *Key Dismukes and Jessica Nowinski*

In 1991, a tower controller at Los Angeles International airport (LAX) cleared a commuter aircraft to position and hold on runway 24L while she worked to clear other aircraft to cross the other end of the runway. There were several communications delays because one of the other aircraft was on the wrong radio frequency. Visibility was poor at twilight because of haze and glare. The controller's workload was considered moderate by air traffic controllers, although laypeople might consider it quite busy. The controller forgot to clear the commuter aircraft to take off and cleared another aircraft to land on 24L, which it did, destroying both aircraft and killing 34 people.

Similar errors by pilots have also led to major accidents. In 1994, an airliner ran off the runway at LaGuardia airport after the crew rejected the takeoff at high speed because they observed anomalous indications on their airspeed indicators. The National Transportation Safety Board (NTSB) determined that the anomalous indications occurred because the crew failed to turn on the pitot heat, a normal procedural step that keeps the pitot input to the airspeed indicators from freezing in cold, wet weather. Two previous major airline accidents occurred in the 1980s when the crews forgot to extend wing flaps and slats to takeoff position, a normal procedural step required before takeoff. More recently, in 1996, an airliner landed gear-up in Houston when the landing gear failed to extend because the crew forgot to set the hydraulic pumps to the high position, which was part of the normal procedure for preparing their type of aircraft for landing. Obviously, multiple factors were at play in each of these accidents, but a central aspect of each accident was the failure of the crew to execute a simple procedural step that they had performed many thousands of times during previous flights.

In everyday life we are all susceptible to forgetting to perform intended actions. These everyday lapses are mainly annoying and sometimes embarrassing, but in the operational world memory lapses can be fatal, as these accidents testify. Memory lapses during airline flight operations are particularly striking because the airline industry has erected elaborate safeguards against errors, including written standard operating procedures, checklists, and requirements for the captain and first officer to cross-check each other's actions.

Prospective memory—remembering to perform an action that cannot be executed when the intention is formed—is a fairly new but rapidly growing topic in cognitive psychology (see reviews by Brandimonte and colleagues [1996] and Ellis and Kvavilashvili [2000]). Prospective memory is distinguished by three features: (1) an intention to perform an action at some later time when circumstances permit; (2) a delay between forming and executing the intention, typically filled with activities not directly related to the deferred action; and (3) the absence of an explicit prompt indicating that it is time to retrieve the intention from memory—the individual must "remember to remember." This third feature distinguishes prospective memory from traditionally studied retrospective memory. (Arguably, prospective memory has some similarity to implicit memory, which is a form of retrospective memory.) Typically, if queried after forgetting to perform an action, individuals can recall what they intended to do. If the LAX controller had been asked what she planned to do with the holding aircraft, she almost certainly would have been able to report her intended sequence of actions. Thus, the critical issue in prospective memory is not how we retain the content of our intentions, but how we remember to perform those intentions *at the appropriate moment*, and why we sometimes fail to remember. What would have helped the controller remember to clear the commuter aircraft to take off *before* she cleared the second aircraft to land?

Aided by new laboratory paradigms, researchers are beginning to elucidate the cognitive processes underlying prospective memory, although many questions remain unanswered. The most common paradigms are variations of a procedure developed by Einstein and McDaniel (1990): Experimental participants are given an *ongoing task*, such as evaluating the pleasantness of a series of words displayed on a computer screen, and are told that if they encounter a particular word (or set of words or class of words) they should take a specified action, such as pressing the slash key on a keyboard. This second task is the *prospective memory task*. This particular type of prospective memory task, which we will call *episodic*, has been studied extensively in recent years; however, in this chapter we present evidence that this paradigm represents only one of several types of prospective memory situations encountered in the real world.

Our research group is attempting to link real-world prospective memory phenomena with the emerging picture of underlying cognitive processes. Our approach is congruent with the approach that Chris Wickens (1992) has pioneered for many years. We believe that understanding human performance of complex real-world tasks requires converging evidence from several very different types of research methods. This chapter examines findings from ethnographic studies, analyses of accident and incident reports, and laboratory studies, all of which we attempt to pull together in a theoretical framework grounded in cognitive psychology. Well-controlled laboratory studies are essential to understand cognitive processes underlying human performance, but taken by themselves often miss important phenomena and major sources of variance in the real world. Field studies (ethnographic observations and analyses of accident and incident reports) identify crucial phenomena and the influence of task, individual, organizational, and social factors, and raise theoretical issues that might not be apparent from laboratory studies alone. Working back and forth between field and laboratory studies enriches both approaches.

## FIELD STUDIES

Airline operations lend themselves to the study of skilled human performance and human error because these operations are highly standardized, with formal written operating procedures that cover almost every aspect. Because most aspects of flight operations are explicitly scripted, we can readily observe deviations from what is prescribed. In addition, a fair degree of consensus exists among subject matter experts over what actions are appropriate or inappropriate in most normal situations.

We conducted three studies that helped us to identify the kinds of tasks involving prospective memory in airline flight operations and the most common forms of associated error. An ethnographic study focused on a particular aircraft type to allow in-depth analysis (the Boeing 737—one of the most commonly used airplanes in the transport industry). We reviewed written operating procedures, participated in classroom and flight simulation training at two major airlines, and observed a large number of flights from the cockpit jump seat (Dismukes, Loukopoulos, & Barshi, 2003; Loukopoulos, Dismukes, & Barshi, 2003). A second study analyzed NTSB reports for the 19 major US airline accidents attributed to crew error between 1990 and 2001 (Dismukes, Berman, & Loukopoulos, 2005), and a third study sampled 20% of all air carrier reports submitted to the Aviation Safety Reporting System (ASRS) over a 12-month period to obtain reports involving any type of memory error (Nowinski, Holbrook, & Dismukes, 2003).

From these studies (which also address topics beyond prospective memory), we concluded that prospective memory demands in cockpit operations emerge during five types of task situations:

1. *Episodic tasks.* During these situations, pilots must remember to perform at a later time some task that is not habitually performed at that time. For example, an air traffic controller may instruct a crew to report passing through 10,000 feet while the crew is still at 15,000 feet, creating a delay of perhaps 5 minutes. Another example occurs when circumstances force pilots to perform a habitual task out of its normal sequence. Most laboratory research on prospective memory has focused on these types of episodic tasks.

2. *Habitual tasks.* Crews perform many tasks and many subtask steps during the course of a normal flight. On the order of a hundred action steps are required just to prepare a large aircraft for departure. Most of these steps are specified by written procedures and are normally performed in the same sequence. Thus, execution of tasks becomes highly habitual for experienced crews. For example, flaps are normally set to takeoff position after the engines have been started and before taxiing to the runway. Pilots do not have to form an episodic intention to perform each of these action steps; rather, the intention to perform each step is *implicit in the action schema* for the task, stored in procedural memory. Pilots do not have to form an explicit intention in advance each time they must set the flaps.

   One might argue whether performing highly habitual tasks fits the definition of prospective memory. Although habitual tasks differ substantially from episodic tasks, we include them as a form of prospective memory because the individual must retrieve the action to be taken when circumstances are appropriate without receiving any explicit prompt to retrieve the memory item. Individuals who forget to perform habitual tasks typically report that they intended to perform the task.

3. *Atypical actions substituted for habitual actions.* Circumstances sometimes require crews to deviate from a well-established procedural sequence. For example, through long experience departing from a certain airport, a crew would come to know that the standard instrument departure procedure (a written instrument procedure) requires them to turn left to 300 deg upon reaching 2,000 feet. This would become habitual for the crew. If on rare occasion a controller told them to turn to 330 deg instead of 300 deg, the crew would have to form both an episodic intention to turn to 330 deg and an intention to inhibit their habitual response of leveling the wings at 300 deg. Reason (1984) discussed memory errors in such situations as *habit capture.*

4. *Interrupted tasks.* Interruptions of procedures occur fairly frequently, especially when crews are at the gate preparing the airplane for departure. Flight attendants, gate agents, mechanics, and jump seat riders frequently interrupt the pilots as they work to complete preflight procedures. Pilots may try to finish the immediate task they are working on before addressing the person interrupting them, or they may suspend the ongoing task to handle the interruption. In either case, attention is diverted at least momentarily by the intrusion, and pilots must remember to resume where they left off. A common form of error is to move on to the next task in the normal procedural sequence, failing to return to and complete the interrupted task.

5. *Interleaving tasks.* Pilots must often "multitask," interleave two or more tasks concurrently, somewhat like a circus performer twirling plates on poles. For example, first officers must sometimes reprogram the flight management system while the airplane is taxiing to the runway (perhaps because the original runway or the original departure clearance has changed). But during taxi, the first officer is also responsible for other tasks, including monitoring the course of the taxi (to catch potential errors by the captain), handling radio communications, and—depending on the airline—various other tasks. If the reprogramming can be accomplished with a few keystrokes, the first officer may do this all at one time. But if the reprogramming takes longer, it is necessary to interleave performing some programming steps with performing other

cockpit duties, switching attention back and forth. It is easy for pilots to become preoccupied with one attention-demanding task (for instance, if a programming glitch occurs) and forget to interrupt themselves to check the status of other tasks frequently enough. (Dismukes, Young, & Sumwalt, 1998)

The ASRS study revealed a startling finding: Of the 75 reports with sufficient information to identify a memory failure clearly, 74 involved prospective memory, rather than retrospective memory (Nowinski et al., 2003). We cannot conclude from this that prospective memory failures occur more often than retrospective memory errors. The frequency of reporting of various error types reflects factors beyond the frequency of occurrence. For example, pilots are motivated to submit ASRS reports in part because submission provides immunity from prosecution for the reporter's errors; thus, pilots are more likely to submit reports about the kinds of error that might get them in trouble. However, this finding suggests that prospective memory errors are more consequential, more frequent, or more memorable than retrospective memory errors, or combine some of these three aspects. The high level of expertise of airline pilots greatly reduces their vulnerability to retrospective memory errors, but that expertise appears to provide less protection against prospective memory errors, and indeed may contribute to some forms of prospective memory error, as discussed further in later sections of this chapter. Flight operating procedures are designed to safeguard against crew errors, but in the case of prospective memory tasks, the safeguards are themselves vulnerable to errors of omission.

Although our discussion focuses on aviation operations, we have conducted other studies revealing that comparable prospective memory tasks occur in everyday life situations (Holbrook, Dismukes, & Nowinski, 2005), and other workplace settings are very probably similar in prospective memory demands.

## A THEORETICAL PERSPECTIVE

Phenomenologically, these five prototypical prospective memory situations seem quite diverse, but we argue that they share some cognitive features and can best be understood within a common conceptual framework. To make that argument requires a theoretical perspective on the cognitive processes underlying

prospective memory, and this perspective can in turn help us to understand the nature of vulnerability to prospective memory errors and point to countermeasures to reduce vulnerability.

Several theoretical accounts of prospective memory have been published in recent years (e.g., McDaniel & Einstein, 2000; Smith, 2003). In some accounts a stored intention is retrieved from memory automatically when the individual notices some cue associated in memory with the intention. This has been called the *automatic* view (Guynn, McDaniel, & Einstein, 2001; McDaniel, Robinson-Riegler, & Einstein, 1998). A cue can be a specific physical stimulus or combination of stimuli in the external environment (I remember to take the cookies out of the oven when I hear the timer go off), or an internal event such as a thought or a state (I remember to go grocery shopping when I think about a recent meal or when I feel hungry). Two critical features determine the effectiveness of a cue. The cue must have a strong enough association to the intention (either through rehearsal or previous experience) to bring the intention to mind when the cue is encountered, and the cue must be present within the window of opportunity for performing that intention. A cue to remind pilots to extend the flaps for takeoff is not effective if it appears after takeoff.

A competing theoretical perspective, which has been dubbed the *strategic* view, is that retrieval requires individuals to monitor for an opportunity to perform a delayed task (Smith, 2003; also, see the discussion in McDaniel and Einstein [2000]). This monitoring makes demands on limited cognitive resources. The critical difference between the two theoretical perspectives is that they predict different effects of a delayed task on ongoing task performance, and different effects of ongoing task difficulty on prospective memory performance. The strategic view posits that the monitoring required to identify the window of opportunity for a prospective memory task requires cognitive resources that must be shared with the ongoing task. Therefore performance on an ongoing task should always be affected to some degree by a prospective memory task, and, likewise, performance on the prospective memory task should decline when the ongoing task is particularly difficult and resource demanding. In contrast, the automatic view suggests that performance on the ongoing task is not necessarily affected by the presence of a deferred intention. Also, some authors have assumed that the demands of the ongoing task should not affect automatic retrieval of intentions; however, we argue that these demands could impair retrieval if they prevent individuals from attending cues associated with the intention or reduce the extent to which those cues are processed. We believe the automatic view suggests that prospective memory performance should vary directly with the extent to which the ongoing task directs attention toward relevant cues when they appear. McDaniel and Einstein (2000) combined the two perspectives in their multiprocess framework, arguing that individuals sometimes use automatic processing and sometimes use strategic processing, depending on the nature of the prospective memory task.

Neither the proponents of the strategic view nor the proponents of the automatic view have provided a detailed account of the cognitive processes that might be involved in the retrieval of intentions. Both views have been presented exclusively in terms of episodic intentions. The *associative activation* model of Nowinski and Dismukes (2005) is an elaboration of the automatic view that also provides a framework for examining all five types of prospective memory situation. This model posits that in most situations, after forming an intention, individuals turn their attention to other tasks. The intention resides in long-term memory and is retrieved when the individual processes cues associated with the intention. Thus, retrieval is dependent on the presence of adequate cues and may or may not occur during the window of opportunity for intended execution of the deferred task. Even if the ongoing task does not direct attention to cues that were encoded to define the window of opportunity for execution, other cues associated with the intention may trigger retrieval. Retrieval may also occur at other times that are not appropriate for execution because associated cues are present. For example, one might form an intention to ask a colleague for a copy of his paper when seeing him, but might also be reminded of this intention while reading another paper related to his.

Our model posits that automatic retrieval processes are always at play, however individuals may, in some situations, supplement those processes with some strategic process, such as monitoring for opportunities to execute intentions (although it seems unlikely that in most real-world situations individuals could perform ongoing tasks adequately and monitor for cues related to intentions for long periods, especially because at any moment individuals have various and diverse

intentions stored in memory). At the heart of this model is a simple system consisting of (1) only two separate information stores (focal attention and long-term memory), (2) activation mechanisms that allow memory representations to move within and between those stores, and (3) an associative network of representations through which activation is delivered to and distributed among those representations. Our formulation draws directly from the ACT-R cognitive architecture developed by Anderson and colleagues. See Anderson and Lebiere (1998) and Cowan's (1995) framework for integrating attention and memory processes. Like Cowan, we do not consider working memory a separate store, but rather treat it as a small subset of highly activated items in long-term memory.

Deferred intentions are a form of goal; however, unlike some theorists, such as Goschke and Kuhl (1993) and Anderson and Lebiere (1998), we argue that goals have no special status in cognitive processes, and we treat goals simply as memory representations consisting of actions to be executed under specified conditions. Retrieval of deferred intentions follows the same rules and involves cognitive processes underlying retrieval of other types of memory items. Thus, our account of retrieval of deferred intentions is couched within an existing framework of memory retrieval.

Following the ACT-R framework, we posit that items are stored in long-term memory in associative networks, and that items that have been encountered together form links through which activation can spread. Retrieval of an item from memory occurs when the representation receives sufficient activation to pass some threshold and enters awareness. The activation of an item at any given time is the sum of activation from two sources. The first, *baseline activation*, is determined by history. It increases with rehearsal of an item and with the frequency of retrieval, and it decreases with the length of time since the item was last retrieved. The second type of activation, *source activation*, is determined by the proportion of attentional resources directed to a cue at a given moment. The source activation received by a given item spreads to its associates, is distributed among them, and in turn spreads from them to their associates. The level of activation spread from one item to another is proportional to the strength of association between the two items. Source activation is a limited resource, thus the amount of activation reaching a given item in memory is inversely proportional to the number of competing associates.

The content of focal attention is in a constant state of flux, and once a cue exits attention, source activation to its associates in memory decays rapidly. However, decay is not instantaneous, and we speculate that this allows source activation received by a memory item from a series of associated cues passing through attention to be summated over brief intervals. The item retrieved from memory at a given moment is the item with the highest total activation, baseline activation plus source activation received through associative links.

Prospective memory, by its nature, involves dual-task processing. Once an intention is delayed, retrieval of that intention must occur during progress of whatever task is ongoing. Thus, retrieval of intentions must compete with retrieval of memory items directly associated with the goals of the ongoing task. The ongoing task has an advantage in this competition as it guides attention to environmental information needed to achieve its goal. The overarching goal, when in focal attention, provides activation for retrieval of subgoals, and subgoals, when in focal attention, in turn provide activation to help maintain the overarching goal as well as to retrieve specific information relevant to the task. So how are deferred goals ever successfully retrieved when we are in the midst of performing ongoing tasks? We attempt to answer that question in the following section.

### SOURCES OF VARIANCE IN PROSPECTIVE MEMORY PERFORMANCE IN THE REAL WORLD

Our theoretical account of prospective memory suggests that the probability of retrieval of an intention (at the desired time or otherwise) is determined by several factors, one of which is the effectiveness of cues associated with the stored intention that may be noticed and processed attentively. The effectiveness of a cue hinges on the level of activation delivered to the intention from the cue. Therefore, the strength of a cue's association to the intention, the number of intentions associated with that cue, and the number of intermediate links though which source activation must spread before reaching the stored intention should influence prospective memory performance. Direct and indirect experimental evidence supports these predictions. A number of studies have demonstrated a substantial effect of the strength of association between a cue and

an intention—either by choosing cues with a strong *a priori* association to the intention (Mantyla, 1993; McDaniel & Einstein, 2000; Nowinski & Dismukes, 2005) or by encouraging participants to rehearse the association (Guynn, McDaniel, & Einstein, 1998; Passolunghi, Brandimonte, & Cornoldi, 1995; Taylor, Marsh, Hicks, & Hancock, 2004). Fewer studies have examined the effect of the number of associations to the cue on prospective memory performance, but McDaniel and Einstein (1993) demonstrated that words that were likely to have fewer associations, unfamiliar words such as *bole* and *monad*, were more effective prospective memory cues than more common words. Finally, several studies have demonstrated that cues associated only indirectly to an intention are less effective than are directly associated cues. These studies found that prospective memory performance was better when specific cues rather than general-category cues were used to define the conditions for executing intentions. For example instructions to participants might read: "Press the slash key when you see the word apple," versus "Press the slash key when you see the name of a fruit" (Cherry, Martin, Simmons-D'Gerolamo, Pinkston, Griffing, & Gouvier, 2001; Ellis & Milne, 1996). When a general-category instruction is used, cue activation must spread across two associative links from the specific target presented at retrieval to the category concept to the intention.

The encoding of an intention is another major factor influencing prospective memory performance. We suggest that intentions are encoded in a form similar to if-then statements, with the *then* part specifying what is to be done and the *if* part specifying the conditions under which the intention is to be executed. The diary study by Holbrook and associates (2005) found substantial variation in the way that individuals encoded intentions to perform everyday tasks. Often individuals encoded only a vague notion of the window of opportunity for executing an intention, and did not identify specific cues they were likely to encounter that could trigger retrieval of the intention at the appropriate time. For example, one might form an intention to go to the grocery store without specifying when to execute the intention. In these circumstances, retrieval depends on chance encounters with cues that have preexisting associations with the intention—for example, one might be reminded of the need to get groceries while eating lunch in the office cafeteria. The effects of variation in encoding of intentions have not been explored experimentally until recently. In most laboratory paradigms the instructions to participants specify a particular cue that narrowly defines the condition under which the prospective task is to be executed (e.g., encountering a particular word or category of word while performing the ongoing task of evaluating the pleasantness of a series of words). Later in this chapter we report an experimental study of interruptions in which encoding was manipulated and which supports the associative activation model.

## IMPLICIT INTENTIONS

Our studies of interruptions and habitual tasks in the cockpit have led us to conclude that intentions are sometimes implicit rather than explicit. In episodic situations, individuals explicitly form an intention to perform an action at some later time when conditions become appropriate. But interruptions of real-world tasks sometimes occur so quickly and forcefully that individuals do not think explicitly about the need to resume the interrupted task after the interruption. In these situations, we argue that an intention does exist; however, it is implicit in the individual's original plan to execute the interrupted task. If queried, the individual is likely to say that they do intend to complete the interrupted task, or if they forget to complete it, they are likely to say they intended to do so. When individuals do not form an explicit intention to resume an interrupted task, they may be especially vulnerable to forgetting because they do not encode specific cues likely to be encountered after the interruption that can trigger retrieval of the need to go back to the interrupted task.

Implicit intentions are also involved in highly practiced tasks that are always performed in a particular situation—for example, setting flaps to the takeoff position after starting the engines and before taxiing to the runway. Pilots do not need to think in advance of each flight "I must remember to set the flaps," thus no explicit advance intention is formed for each episode of setting the flaps. However, we argue that the intention to set the flaps exists implicitly as part of the action schema for preparing the aircraft for flight. Normally, highly practiced tasks such as this are performed with great reliability, but they become vulnerable to inadvertent omission if the cues that normally trigger execution of an action are absent.

For the sake of discussion, let us suppose that a captain normally calls for the flaps to be set when the engine after-start checklist is completed. Performing the checklist is strongly linked in procedural memory to the next action, calling for flaps to be set. Contextual cues from the environment at the airport gate may also contribute to remembering to set the flaps. Nowinski and Dismukes (2005) reported an experiment in which contextual cues enhanced the effectiveness of primary cues in a prospective memory task. But what happens if the crew must defer setting the flaps until after taxi because of freezing slush on the taxiway? The cues that normally trigger crews to set the flaps are removed. This action is now out of sequence, temporally separated from completion of the after-start checklist and is removed from the normal environmental context provided by being at the gate. Unless the pilots form an explicit intention to set the flaps at a specific point and identify or create cues to remind them, they become vulnerable to forgetting to perform this essential action.

Cues that normally trigger habitual action can also be removed for reasons other than crew actions. For example, Nowinski and colleagues (2003) found that landing without a clearance at a controlled airport was one of the prospective memory errors most frequently reported by airline pilots. Normally, crews are instructed to switch radio frequencies and contact tower immediately by approach control, and crews apparently come to rely on this prompt. However, approach controllers on occasion tell crews to delay switching to tower frequency until reaching a specified distance from the airport. Nowinski and colleagues (2003) found that 12 of the 13 reports citing an incident of landing without clearance occurred under these circumstances in which the normal prompt to change frequency immediately did not occur.

## INTERLEAVING TASKS

Our model predicts that any prospective memory situation in which the ongoing task does not direct attention to cues strongly associated with the intention is vulnerable to error. Interleaving two or more attention-demanding tasks is an important example of this situation. Pilots are required to monitor the state and path of the aircraft and the actions of the other pilot while performing other tasks, and monitoring is considered an essential defense against threats to safety and crew errors (Sumwalt, Thomas, & Dismukes, 2002, 2003).

Although task switching has been studied extensively in fundamental research on attention mechanisms (Pashler & Johnston, 1998), much less research has been conducted to determine the cognitive mechanisms involved when individuals attempt to interleave tasks in real-world situations. In contrast to typical laboratory paradigms for studying attention mechanisms, many real-world situations do not provide strong environmental cues for both tasks being interleaved, and switching between tasks occurs relatively slowly—typically on the order of minutes. In these situations, individuals cannot maintain the intention to check the status of other tasks continuously in focal attention, and thus must somehow retrieve that intention to interrupt the ongoing task periodically. Pilots report becoming preoccupied with one attention-demanding task, such as reprogramming the flight management computer, and forgetting to check the status of another task, such as monitoring the progress of the taxi by the captain (Dismukes et al., 1998; Loukopoulos et al., 2003).

We suggest that interleaving may be accomplished in one of two ways. First, individuals may attempt to remember to interrupt the ongoing task after some period of time has passed. However, because they cannot consciously monitor the passage of time continuously while performing the ongoing task, and because the ongoing task often directs gaze away from the other task or tasks to be monitored, it is not clear how individuals retrieve the intention to switch attention to the other task. (See Cicogna and coworkers (2005) and Logie and associates (2004) for theoretical discussions.) What is clear is that individuals are more vulnerable to forgetting to perform time-based prospective memory tasks than they are when performing prospective memory tasks in which salient physical cues are available (Holbrook et al., 2005; Einstein & McDaniel, 1996).

Second, we speculate that in practice individuals do not depend entirely on time cues to perform time-based prospective memory tasks such as interleaving. Rather, retrieval of the intention to switch tasks may be prompted by happenstance noticing of cues associated (to some degree) with the intention, and this prompting may be facilitated by the environmental context. Also, individuals may implicitly learn rules of thumb to help them remember to switch tasks; for example, first officers might learn to limit the number of actions taken to program a flight management computer before looking up to check taxi progress.

Either of these two possibilities converts the time-based prospective memory task to an event-based task. However, both processes seem rather haphazard, and performance is not likely to be highly reliable.

## AN EXPERIMENTAL STUDY OF INTERRUPTIONS

We describe here an experimental study that illustrates some of the issues discussed in this chapter and provides support for our theoretical account of some of these sources of errors of omission in prospective memory. Interruptions by external agents are a major source of errors of omission in cockpit operations (Dismukes et al., 1998), maintenance (Hobbs & Williamson, 2003), and everyday tasks (Holbrook et al., 2005), and presumably contribute to errors in other domains, such as medicine (Gawande, Studdert, Orav, Brennan, & Zinner, 2003), although these other domains have not been studied extensively.

The associative activation model suggests that individuals may be vulnerable to forgetting to resume interrupted tasks in large part because of three reasons. First, the salient intrusion of many interruptions quickly diverts attention and discourages encoding explicit intentions and identifying cues to resume the interrupted task. If no explicit intention is encoded, then remembering to resume the interrupted task will depend on noticing happenstance cues that remind the individual of the status of the interrupted task and the implicit intention of completing all tasks. Even if an intention is explicitly encoded, the conditions for resuming the interrupted task are likely to be framed only as "after the end of the interruption." Individuals are often not in a position to identify and encode specific perceptual cues likely to be present at the end of the interruption. Second, cues indicating the window of opportunity for resuming the interrupted task at the end of the interruption may not closely match the form in which the intention (implicit or explicit) to resume the interrupted task is encoded. The end of the interruption is not a perceptual cue but a state of affairs that requires cognitively interpreting diverse perceptual cues to recognize. If the individual does not consciously monitor for the end of the interruption, the diverse perceptual cues may fail to trigger recognition that the interruption has ended. Third, the end of interruptions in real-world situations is often followed immediately by other task demands that may not allow the individual sufficient time to process and interpret environmental conditions fully signifying that the interruption is over or to retrieve the associated intention (Holbrook et al., 2005; Loukopoulos et al., 2003). Furthermore, activation from environmental cues associated with these other task demands may support retrieval of the goals associated with these task demands preferentially over retrieval of the goal to resume the interrupted task.

Dodhia and Dismukes (2005) designed an experimental paradigm to investigate these three themes. Experiment participants were required to answer a series of questions resembling the Scholastic Aptitude Test, arranged in blocks of different question types (e.g., analogies, vocabulary, math). They were instructed that when blocks were interrupted by the sudden onset of a different block of questions they should remember to return to the interrupted block (after completing the interrupting block) before continuing to the next block in the series. During the baseline (control) condition, these occasional interruptions were abrupt—the screen with the question participants were currently working on was suddenly replaced with a screen with a different type of question, and the background color of the screen changed.

After the end of the interrupting block, a screen appeared for 2.5 seconds with the message "Loading next section" (this screen also appeared between all blocks that were not interrupted) and then the next block of questions appeared without any reference to the interrupted block. Without receiving any explicit prompt, participants had to remember to return to the interrupted block by pressing a key. Participants of the baseline condition frequently forgot to resume the interrupted task and instead continued with the next block in the series after an interruption. The proportion of successful resumptions of the interrupted task was 0.48. These failures to return to the interrupted block were the result of memory failures, rather than a misunderstanding of the task requirements, as shown by participants' correct description of task requirements when debriefed after the experiment and by the distribution of errors among the five prospective memory trials for each participant.

To address our first hypothesis—that the intrusion of a sudden interruption discourages adequate encoding of an intention to resume the interrupted task—we implemented an *encoding reminder* condition during which the interruption began with a 4-second text message "Please remember to return to the block that

was just interrupted." This manipulation increased the proportion of resumptions from the baseline condition of 0.48 to 0.65, which was highly significant statistically (as were the results of all other manipulations, discussed later). It was not clear whether the encoding reminder manipulation was effective at improving performance because of the explicit reminder or because of the additional 4-second delay before participants had to start performing the interrupting task. We therefore performed an *encoding pause* manipulation in which participants saw only a blank screen for 4 seconds at the beginning of the interruption. This manipulation also improved performance to 0.65. We interpret these results to indicate that a pause before starting to perform an interrupting task allows individuals time to recognize the implications of being interrupted and to encode information that helps them to remember to resume the interrupted task. The explicit reminder to resume the interrupted task apparently did not provide any additional encoding advantage.

We also addressed our second hypothesis that individuals are likely to forget to resume interrupted tasks because they do not encounter explicit cues signaling the end of the interruption. During the *retrieval reminder* condition, participants received a message "End of interruption" for 2.5 seconds while the next block was loading. This message appeared above the "Loading next section" message that appeared during all conditions. This manipulation increased the proportion of interruptions resumed to 0.90.

Finally, we addressed our third hypothesis, that individuals sometimes forget to return to an interrupted task because the end of interrupting tasks is often quickly followed by other task demands that do not allow the individual time to process and interpret environmental conditions fully and to retrieve the intention to resume the interrupted task. One might imagine that the "Loading next section" message that appeared for 2.5 seconds after the end of interrupting blocks (and between all blocks) would give participants enough time to reflect on whether they should do anything else before starting the block after the interruption. However, we suspected that this short pause, coupled with the message that the next section was about to start, might orient participants toward mentally preparing to start the next section and make them less likely to think about the implications of the start of a new block of questions. Thus we created a *retrieval pause* condition during which the delay between the end of the interrupting task and the beginning of the next block was increased to 8 to 12 seconds, and a countdown clock appeared to display the remaining time to the next block. This manipulation was intended to make clear to participants that they had plenty of time before new task demands would begin. Resumption performance increased to 0.88, supporting the idea that people fail to resume interrupted tasks in part because their attention is quickly diverted to new task demands arising after interruptions end.

## CONCLUSION: IMPLICATIONS AND COUNTERMEASURES

The results of this experimental study of interruptions are consistent with the associative activation model, although of course much more empirical research is required to validate such a broad conceptual framework. Equally important, these results suggest practical ways individuals can reduce their vulnerability to forgetting to resume interrupted tasks. Individuals may be able to improve performance by (1) pausing when interrupted to form an explicit intention to resume the interrupted task and to identify cues that may be available to remind them after the interruption and (2) pausing after completing all tasks to ask which task should be performed next, which may not necessarily be the most salient task. We are currently conducting experiments to determine whether individuals can implement these two techniques, after being given only general instructions, without reminders on each trial from experimenters.

More broadly, we suggest that individuals may improve their prospective memory performance by (1) deliberately encoding information about environmental cues that may be encountered during the window of opportunity for executing deferred intentions, (2) by creating salient cues they will be likely to encounter at the appropriate time, (3) by making and consulting lists of deferred intentions, and (4) by periodically pausing to search memory for deferred intentions.

Although a relatively new topic in cognitive psychology, prospective memory is clearly of great importance for safe, effective human performance in many real-world situations. Continued theoretical and experimental studies are needed to elucidate the cognitive mechanisms underlying prospective memory, particularly to address questions about the form in which intentions are encoded, how intentions are retrieved, and how prospective tasks interact and compete with ongoing tasks. However, we hope that investigators will not forget that we must also study prospective memory in diverse real-world situations to identify the full range of phenomena and sources of variance that theoretical and experimental studies must attempt to explain.

## ACKNOWLEDGMENTS

Different aspects of this research were supported by the National Aeronautics and Space Administration's Aviation Safety Program and Aviation Systems Program and by the Federal Aviation Administration (Eleana Edens, program manager). The authors thank Loukia Loukopoulos, Jon Holbrook, and Barbara Burian for helpful comments on this manuscript, and are most grateful to their laboratory manager, Kim Jobe, who supports all their efforts skillfully, graciously, and diligently.

### References

Anderson, J. R., & Lebiere, C. (1998). *The atomic components of thought*. Mahwah, N.J.: Lawrence Erlbaum.

Brandimonte, M., Einstein, G. O., & McDaniel, M. A. (1996). *Prospective memory: Theory and applications*. Mahwah, N.J.: Lawrence Erlbaum.

Cherry, K. E., Martin R. C., Simmons-D'Gerolamo, S. S., Pinkston, J. B., Griffing, A., & Gouvier, W. D. (2001). Prospective remembering in younger and older adults: Role of the prospective cue. *Memory*, 9(3), 177–193.

Cicogna, P., Nigro, G., Occhionero, M., & Esposito, M. J. (2005). Time-based prospective remembering: Interference and facilitation in a dual task. *European Journal of Cognitive Psychology*, 17(2), 221–240.

Cowan, N. (1995). *Attention and memory: An integrated framework*. London: Oxford University Press.

Dismukes, R. K., Berman, B., & Loukopoulos, L. D. (March 2005). *The limits of expertise: the misunderstood role of pilot error in airline accidents*. Presented at the ASPA/ICAO regional seminar on cross-cultural issues in aviation safety. International Civil Aviation Organization, North American, Central American and Caribbean Office,. Mexico City. [Online]. Available: http://human-factors.arc.nasa.gov/ihs/flightcognition/Publications/KD_ICAO3_05.ppt

Dismukes, R. K., Loukopoulos, L. D., & Barshi, I. (November 2003). *Concurrent task demands and pilot error in airport surface operations*. Presented at the joint meeting of the 56th Annual International Air Safety Seminar IASS, IFA 33rd International Conference, and IATA. Washington, D.C. [Online]. Available: http://human-factors.arc. nasa.gov/ihs/flightcognition/Publications/KDfsfIASS1.ppt

——, Young, G. E., & Sumwalt, R. L. (1998). Cockpit interruptions and distractions: Effective management requires a careful balancing act. *ASRS Directline*, *10*, 4–9.

Dodhia, R. M., & Dismukes, R. K. (January 2005). A task interrupted becomes a prospective memory task. Presented at the biennial meeting of the Society for Applied Research in Memory and Cognition. Wellington, New Zealand. [Online]. Available: http://human-factors.arc.nasa.gov/ihs/flightcognition/Publications/Dodhia_SARMAC'05.pdf

Einstein, G. O., & McDaniel, M. A. (1990). Normal aging and prospective memory. *Journal of Experimental Psychology: Learning, Memory & Cognition*, *16*(4), 717–726.

——, & McDaniel, M. A. (1996). Retrieval processes in prospective memory: Theoretical approaches and some new empirical findings. In M. Brandimonte, G. O. Einstein, & M. A. McDaniel (Eds.), *Prospective memory: Theory and applications* (pp. 115–142). Mahwah, N.J.: Lawrence Erlbaum.

Ellis, J., & Kvavilashvili, L. (2000). Prospective memory in 2000: Past, present and future directions. *Applied Cognitive Psychology*, *14*, 1–9.

——, & Milne, A. (1996). Retrieval cue specificity and the realization of delayed intentions. *The Quarterly Journal of Experimental Psychology*, *49A*(4), 862–887.

Gawande, A. A., Studdert, D. M., Orav, E. J., Brennan, T. A., & Zinner, J. J. (2003). Risk factors for retained instruments and sponges after surgery. *The New England Journal of Medicine*, *348*, 229–235.

Goschke, T., & Kuhl, J. (1993). Representation of intentions: Persisting activation in memory. *Journal of Experimental Psychology: Learning, Memory & Cognition*, *19*, 1211–1226.

Guynn, M. J., McDaniel, M. A., & Einstein, G. O. (1998). Prospective memory: When reminders fail. *Memory & Cognition*, *26*(2), 287–298.

——, McDaniel, M. A., & Einstein, G. O. (2001). Remembering to perform actions: A different type of memory? In H. D. Zimmer, R. L. Cohen, J. Engelcamp, R. Kormi-Nouri, & M. A. Foley (Eds.), *Memory for action: A distinct form of episodic memory?* (pp. 25–48). London: Oxford University Press.

Hobbs, A., & Williamson, A. (2003). Associations between errors and contributing factors in aircraft maintenance. *Human Factors*, *45*, 186–201.

Holbrook, J. B., Dismukes, R. K., & Nowinski, J. L. (January 2005). *Identifying sources of variance in everyday prospective memory performance*. Presented at the biennial meeting of the Society for Applied Research in Memory and Cognition. Wellington, New Zealand. [Online]. Available: http://human-factors.arc.nasa.gov/ihs/flightcognition/Publications/HolbrookSARMAC05.pdf

Logie, R. H., Maylor, E. A., Sala, S. D., & Smith, G. (2004). Working memory in event- and time-based prospective memory tasks: Effects of secondary demand and age. *European Journal of Cognitive Psychology*, *16*(3), 441–456.

Loukopoulos, L. D., Dismukes, R. K., & Barshi, I. (2003). Concurrent task demands in the cockpit: Challenges and vulnerabilities in routine flight operations. In *Proceedings of the 12th International Symposium on Aviation Psychology* (pp. 737–742). Dayton, Ohio: Wright State University. [Online]. Available: http://human-factors.arc.nasa.gov/ihs/flightcognition/Publications/LL_KD_IB_ISAP_03.pdf

Mantyla, T. (1993). Priming effects in prospective memory. *Memory*, *1*(3), 203–218.

McDaniel, M. A., & Einstein, G. O. (1993). The importance of cue familiarity and cue distinctiveness in prospective memory. *Memory*, *1*(1), 23–41.

——, & Einstein, G. O. (2000). Strategic and automatic memory processes in prospective memory retrieval: A multiprocess framework. *Applied Cognitive Psychology*, *14*, S127–S144.

——, Robinson-Riegler, B., & Einstein, G. O. (1998). Prospective remembering: Perceptually driven or conceptually driven processes? *Memory & Cognition*, *26*(1), 121–134.

Nowinski, J. L., & Dismukes, R. K. (2005). Effects of ongoing task context and target typicality on prospective memory performance: The importance of associative cuing. *Memory*, *13*(6), 649–657.

——, Holbrook, J. B., & Dismukes, R. K. (2003). Human memory and cockpit operations: An ASRS study. In *Proceedings of the 12th International Symposium on Aviation Psychology* (pp. 888–893). Dayton, Ohio: Wright State University. [Online]. Available: http://human-factors.arc.nasa.gov/ihs/flightcognition/Publications/Nowinski_etal_ISAP03.pdf

Pashler, H., & Johnston, J. C. (1998). Attentional limitations in dual-task performance. In H. Pashler (Ed.), *Attention* (pp. 155–189). Hove, UK: Psychology Press/Erlbaum.

Passolunghi, M. C., Brandimonte, M. A., & Cornoldi, C. (1995). Encoding modality and prospective memory in children. *International Journal of Behavioral Development*, *18*(4), 631–648.

Reason, J. T. (1984). Lapses of attention. In W. Parasuraman, R. Davies, & J. Beatty (Eds.), *Varieties of attention* (pp. 515–549). New York: Academic Press.

Smith, R. E. (2003). The cost of remembering to remember in event-based prospective memory: Investigating the capacity demands of delayed intention performance. *Journal of Experimental*

*Psychology: Learning, Memory, & Cognition, 29*(3), 347–361.

Sumwalt, R. L., III, Thomas, R. J., & Dismukes, R. K. (2002). Enhancing flight-crew monitoring skills can increase flight safety. In *Proceedings of the 55th International Air Safety Seminar, Flight Safety Foundation* (pp. 175–206). Dublin, Ireland. [Online]. Available: http://human-factors.arc.nasa.gov/ihs/flightcognition/Publication/FSF_Monitoring_FINAL.pdf

——, Thomas, R. J., & Dismukes, R. K. (2003). The new last line of defense against aviation accidents. *Aviation Week & Space Technology, 159*(8), 66.

Taylor, R. S., Marsh, R. L., Hicks, J. L., & Hancock, T. W. (2004). The influence of partial-match cues on event-based prospective memory. *Memory, 12*(2), 203–213.

Wickens, C. D. (1992). *Engineering psychology and human performance*. New York: HarperCollins.

# Part VII

# Future Directions

# Chapter 17

# Attention to Attention and Its Applications: A Concluding View

## *Christopher D. Wickens*

---

Attention, as we know, has represented an integral part of psychology (with some ups and downs) since the writing of William James (1890), who observed that:

> Everyone knows what attention is. It is the taking possession by the mind, in clear and vivid form, of one out of what seems several simultaneous possible objects or trains of thought. Focalization, concentration, of consciousness are of its essence. It implies withdrawal of some things in order to deal effectively with others. (pp. 403–404)

My own fascination with the topic of attention was triggered by three formative influences during my graduate work at Michigan: (1) learning about the pioneering analysis of pilot's eye movements carried out by Fitts, Jones and Milton (1950), (2) studying the "British school" of early attention researchers (Broadbent, Cherry, Welford, Treisman, Moray), and reading the beautiful little book on *Attention and Effort*, written by

Kahneman (1973), which became a foundation of my dissertation research. As my academic work at Michigan, and then at Illinois, gravitated toward human factors, and particularly toward human factors in ground and air transportation, I rapidly became fascinated by the critical role that attention plays as a "glue" or emergent feature that binds together all the various components of cognition and human information processing (memory, perception, action selection) or, on some occasions, fails to do so, creating mishaps, errors, and accidents.

It has been useful for me to conceive of attention in two different, and somewhat orthogonal orientations. First, as *varieties of attention* manifest in behavior (Parasuraman, Davies, & Beatty 1984), I have distinguished between:

- Selective attention—a serial "spotlight" on selected elements of the external world or the mental representations that must switch in series between these

- Focused attention—which characterizes the goal-directed orientation of the spotlight and which breaks down when processing of selected elements is disrupted by unwanted distractions (Eriksen & Eriksen, 1974)
- Divided attention—which characterizes the efforts to process multiple channels of information or carry out multiple tasks in parallel, the latter being characterized as successful multitasking
- Sustained attention—which characterizes the mobilization of concentrated effort for some duration of time

Second, in terms of a simplified model of human information processing, I have dichotomized between two ways or *metaphors* in which attention supports human perception, cognition, and action, as shown in Figure 17.1 as a *selective filter* to the external world of environmental events and to mental activities, and as a *limited resource* that can be distributed to tasks and mental operations. Both the fourfold behavioral distinction and the information processing dichotomy are different ways of looking at the same picture, and are certainly not mutually exclusive. Indeed, the close linkage between selective and divided attention on the one hand, and the filter and resource metaphors on the other, should be evident.

Considered within this general framework, the presentations in this book have yielded an impressive array of research that, on the one hand, beautifully bridges the gap between theory and applications and, on the other hand, spans the range between the different manifestations of attention I have outlined earlier. For example, the chapters by Fisher, Pollatsek and

Moray concern the selective attention aspects relevant to driving and train safety, respectively, whereas Strayer also addresses driving safety issues but in the context of divided attention, the same context in which Dismukes has addressed aviation safety. Theeuwes and Sarter both consider aspects of divided attention in processing environmental events (the filter metaphor), and so on.

These chapter represent the best practices of where applied attention research stands, and point to the challenges to attention researchers to be relevant to human factors and applied psychology in general, and to the human factors of safety in complex systems in particular. Before I describe my own current perspective on applied attention theory, I will take some time to outline what I see are three of these challenges.

## CHALLENGES TO APPLIED ATTENTION RESEARCHERS

### Paradigms and Phenomena

It has been my observation that researchers in psychology often get quite immersed in *paradigm-driven* research (e.g., the "psychological refractory period" or dual-stimulation paradigm, the "task-switching" paradigm, the "Eriksen flanker" paradigm) or in *phenomenon-driven* research (e.g., the current interest in change blindness) (Rensink, 2002; Simons, 2000). Although there is nothing intrinsically wrong about such high levels of engagement, particularly on the part of the basic researcher, applied researchers must realize two things. First, paradigms are typically only one of many

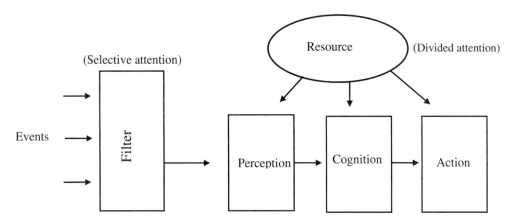

FIGURE 17.1. A simplified information processing model showing two metaphors of attention: as a filter and as a limited resource.

possible ways to study a phenomenon (that may be relevant to real-world behavior), and there is a danger of becoming "paradigm bound" such that the phenomenon in question becomes redefined by the paradigm in question (e.g., "successful focused attention" *is* success on the Eriksen flanker task, "successful divided attention" *is* a "flat slope" in the visual search paradigm, or "failure of divided attention" *is* the response time delay in response to the second stimulus in the psychological refractory period paradigm).

Second, phenomena may make for fascinating demonstrations, but applied researchers need to continue to search for *where* in real-world (extralaboratory) behavior, the phenomenon is manifest and, if it is, *why* understanding that phenomenon has implications for design or training. A nice positive example of this search has been the association of change blindness with breakdowns in driving hazard monitoring (McCarley, Vais, Pringle, Kramer, Irwin, & Strayer, 2004.). This second need highlights the importance of cognitive task analysis of real-world (extralaboratory) people engaging in attention-relevant behavior. Real attentional problems, particularly those inducing safety concerns, can then guide the applied researcher's agenda and lead her to seek the appropriate tasks, paradigms, and phenomena to research and understand the *collective* implications of multiple phenomena to the applied environment in question.

## Statistics

There is no doubt that the past 50 years of attention research has been heavily driven by what I call "statistics of the mean" (e.g., *t*-tests, analyses of variance, null-hypothesis statistics testing [NHST]) (Wickens, 1998, 2001). The challenge is that much of the relevance of research (on attention, or other psychological phenomena) to safety is defined by "statistics of the tails." This is because, fortunately, accidents happen rarely. Therefore, the attentional behavior that may produce the accidents is also relatively rare, manifesting itself only a small proportion of the time, by people who themselves may be out on the lowest tail of the ability distribution (e.g., the slowest responder or the slowest task switcher). In this book, Moray's analysis of a train accident in England elegantly demonstrates the importance of focusing on the tail of the distribution—in this case, the distribution of scanning intervals—to understand attention-related accidents.

To these tails are added the characteristic that many safety-critical attentional phenomena result from

exposure to surprising unexpected or "off-normal" events (failure to notice or delayed noticing) (Foyle & Hooey, 2003). A truly unexpected event, imposed in an experimental setting designed to assess the phenomenon in question, may occur only once per participant. As a consequence, the statistical error in estimate of the response (time or accuracy) to this event will be quite high, and the resulting statistical power to assess effects on the phenomenon will be quite low.

An example in our laboratory relates to the phenomenon of display-driven attentional tunneling (Alexander, Wickens, & Hardy, 2005; Thomas & Wickens, 2004; Wickens, 2005). This phenomenon was experimentally created by presenting pilots with an unusual event in the airspace outside the simulated airplane, while pilots were engaged in processing a very compelling three-dimensional head-down display within the cockpit. A small sample of pilots using this display (e.g., n = 3) showed the phenomenon of failing to notice the outside world event, although none of the pilots using a more conventional display did so. Given the small sample size, the difference in proportion of those who noticed between the two groups was far less than that required to show .05-level "significance," but the attentional tunneling phenomenon, observed in the expected direction, was of sufficient potential importance to be of some concern in considering the adoption of the new technology (or the required training for its use).

These issues of assessing attentional response (failure to notice) to surprising events have two important implications:

1. Researchers should be advised to consider statistics at the tails of the distribution. In the previous example, even if all pilots had noticed the unexpected outside world event, and the time to notice not been found to be "significantly" different ($P < .05$), if the longest 10% of responders within the compelling display group were, for example, 5 seconds slower than those in the 10% tail of the control group, this difference would be potentially quite important.

2. Echoing a point that I have made elsewhere (Wickens, 1998, 2001; see also Loftus, 1996), researchers should consider relaxing the stringent and somewhat arbitrary $P < .05$ criterion for "difference" fostered by NHST, *when the statistical power may be low*, because of necessary restrictions on sample size (limited number of observations per participant, which will increase the error of estimate per participant, or limited

number of participants available for complex, real-world research with domain expert participants). Such a relaxation of the .05 criterion better balances the relative cost of type 1 versus type 2 statistical errors. In this regard, when safety is at stake, it is often just as egregious to commit a type 2 error (e.g., concluding that a new procedure or technology does *not* affect safety when it does) as to commit a type 1 error (Wickens, 1996).

## Modeling

The third challenge I offer to applied attention researchers is that of modeling, and, in particular computational modeling. There are at least two important reasons why this challenge is leveled. First, it has always been the mantra of human factors that it is nice to be able to predict that a system will or not be successful before "metal is bent" (that is, before the system is actually put into development and production). This prediction, if negative, will of course avoid the waste and time of developing and fielding a system that will turn out not to work, or it may reveal necessary modifications in the design prior to expensive and time-consuming human-in-the-loop evaluation. Thus, models of attention, like models of other processes, could conceivably be harnessed to answer such questions (McMillan, Beevis, Salas, Strub, Sutton, & Van Breda, 1989; Pew & Mavor, 1998; Wickens, McCarley, Alexander, Thomas, Ambinder, & Zheng, in press; Foyle, Hooey & Goodman, in press).

The second reason why attentional modeling is offered as a challenge is that human factors design questions are often based on a tradeoff between attention and some other factor (or between two aspects of attention). Models that can accurately compute the predicted strength of both factors can allow prediction of which one will dominate as they trade off in design. A relevant case that has dominated a lot of our research is the tradeoff between focused and divided attention demands imposed when display sources are contrasted that are physically separated or overlaid. Divided attention is challenged by physical separation; focused attention is challenged by overlay, as the distracting effects of clutter and close spatial separation become manifest (Kroft & Wickens, 2003; Wickens 2000; Wickens & Carswell, 1995; Wickens, Goh, Helleberg, Horrey, & Talleur, 2003).

A specific example is in asking the question of whether information should be presented on a head-up display (clutter, but reduced attentional switching to access information between the display and the world beyond) or on a head-down display (reduced clutter, but increased demands of selecting and switching attention) (Wickens, Ververs, & Fadden, 2004). Recently we have evaluated and modeled the relative "strength" of these two forces as collectively revealed in a number of studies (Wickens, 2005), noting that the advantage of overlay for divided attention "wins" by a small margin, but this advantage is modulated by a number of other categorical and quantitative variables that themselves can be modeled.

Thus, in general, computational models can reveal the conditions in which one versus the other design philosophy is superior (Wickens, 2005), and by how much. It is important to realize that such models need not be highly complex, nor account for a great deal of variance to be useful (Wickens, Vincow, Schopper, & Lincoln, 1997).

## TWO ATTENTIONAL MODELS

Having laid down the attention modeling challenge, I now turn to describing in some detail two computational models of attention that have occupied a good portion of my own time and research effort during the last 35 years: the *multiple-resource model* (MRM) of divided attention and the *SEEV* model of selective attention. Both of these are described in detail elsewhere (e.g., Wickens, 2002; Wickens, Goh, Helleberg, Horrey, & Talleur, 2003; Wickens et al., in press), so here I briefly review them and then focus on the challenges imposed by integrating the two models.

## The Multiple-Resource Model

The MRM is familiar to many in its somewhat awkward "cube"-like form as a model of time-sharing or multitask divided attention performance (Fig. 17.2) (Wickens, 1980, 1984, 1991, 2002). It was derived from the implications of a set of dual-task studies carried out by many investigators in the '50s, '60s, and '70s. The fundamental prescription of the model is that, to the extent that two tasks share demands for common levels on the four dichotomous dimensions of multiple resources shown in Figure 17.2 (stages, codes, modalities, and visual channels), divided attention will degrade, dual-task decrements will be larger, and increases in the demand of one task will be more likely to degrade performance

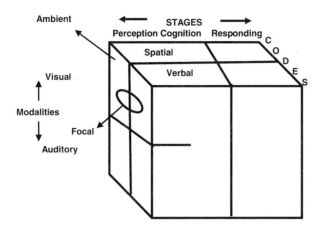

FIGURE 17.2.  The multiple resource model depicting the four dimensions of stages, codes, modalities, and visual channels (ambient versus focal).

of the other. More important, the particular set of four dimensions were chosen for three convergent reasons (two theoretical and one applied): (1) all were found to account for significant variance in time-sharing efficiency in dual-task studies in both the laboratory and the real world, (2) all were associated with *physiologically plausible* dichotomies in the brain, and (3) all had direct implications that designers could harness in configuring tasks for users in dual-task settings (e.g., presenting navigational directions by arrows or words, inputting data by keyboard or voice). Computational versions of the MRM (Wickens, 1989, 2002, 2004) have been used to predict multiple-task performance in both flying (Wickens et al., 2003) and driving (Horrey & Wickens, 2003).

It is critical to think of the "multiple" in the MRM as only one of a trilogy of mechanisms responsible for successes (or failures) in divided attention. These three are shown at the top of Figure 17.3. The other two elements are *resources* and the *allocation policy* by which resources (whether single or multiple) are allocated between tasks (Navon & Gopher, 1979).

When considering first the concept of "resources," I have always been heavily influenced by a dominant theme of Kahneman's (1973) book: the association of attentional resources with a mental effort that can be allocated to tasks. Such a representation of attention, preceded by Moray's classic 1967 paper, and heavily invoked in an important related paper by Norman and

MULTIPLE RESOURCE MODEL

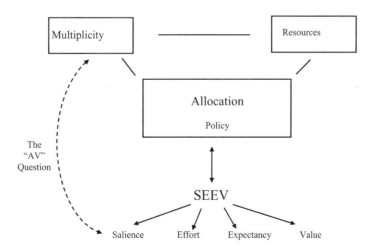

FIGURE 17.3.  Schematic representation of the relation between the multiple resource model (top) and the SEEV model (bottom).

Bobrow (1975), can be considered entirely orthogonal to whether those resources are single or multiple. That is, the *multiplicity* and the *resource* elements are relatively independent of each other.

The concept of resources as effort is closely linked to the vast body of applied research on mental workload (Moray, 1979; Williges & Wierwille, 1979), in which the dominant issue has been to measure the demands imposed upon the brain's resources by tasks of varying difficulty (effort or resource demands) to predict when such demands, whether from single or multiple tasks, would exceed the brain's limited supply and cause performance to falter. Many workload researchers, therefore, modeled this supply in terms of a limited, depletable "pool" of mental effort (Hockey, Gaillard, & Coles, 1986), and the multiplicity aspect of this pool is but one component.

It is also true that the concept of effort has a value in its own right, entirely independent of the divided attention, multitask research in at least two important domains: (1) as a limited commodity that people like to conserve, thereby leading people to chose effort-conserving decision heuristics, over more effort-consuming decision algorithms (Gigerenzer, Todd et al., 1999; Kahneman, Slovic, & Tversky, 1982), and to the selection of different task strategies (Gray & Fu, 2004); and (2) as a depletable commodity that leads to performance decrements when that effort should be sustained over long periods of time, as in vigilance watches (Warm, 1984).

Turning now to the third component of the trilogy, allocation policy, the MRM states that multiplicity and resource demand jointly can predict the debt (or surplus) of resources necessary to time-share two tasks successfully. However, the allocation policy determines the extent to which one or the other of these tasks suffers when there is a debt. In the early dual-task research, this allocation policy was typically described in terms of a "primary" (favored) and "secondary" (more neglected) task. Then, following the conception of allocation policy as a more continuous variable (Kahneman, 1973; Norman & Bobrow, 1975; North & Gopher, 1976; Sperling & Dosher, 1986; Wickens & Gopher, 1977; see also Gopher, this volume), the concerns for allocation policy have more recently migrated to conceptions of task management (Hart & Wickens, 1990), workload management (Raby & Wickens, 1994), queuing theory (Freed, 2000; Kleinman & Pattipati, 1991), task switching (Rogers & Monsell, 1995), interruption management (McFarlane & Latorella, 2002; see also Dismukes, this

volume), and executive control Pashler, 1998). Indeed the allocation element becomes the dominant member of the MRM trilogy in circumstances when parallel processing (resource sharing between tasks) is no longer possible, because either peripheral structures hinder this (e.g., both tasks demand access to foveal vision and are separated by several degrees of visual angle so scanning is required) or because demands within a resource are extremely high (e.g., dual reaction time tasks, typical of the psychological refractory period paradigm) (Kantowitz, 1974; Keele, 1968; Pashler, 1998).

At this point, the "multiple" and "resource" components of the MRM become relatively less important, other than perhaps modulating the level of resource competition at which parallel concurrent processing becomes impossible and task switching (with all its manifestations mentioned above) becomes dominant. Then the important challenge becomes to identify the "rules" of task management. In applied environments, what leads drivers sometimes to "neglect" the higher priority tasks of driving in favor of cell phone conversations? How are interruptions managed and what factors lead to forgetting to return to uncompleted tasks? At this point, my own interests in the MRM and its allocation policy component have joined my interests in selective attention, as represented by the SEEV model, to which we now turn.

## The SEEV Model

Shifting from the metaphor of attention as a resource allocated to multiple-task performance in divided attention to the metaphor of the filter or spotlight in selective attention, my interests during the last decade have been heavily driven by the desire to model the factors that govern this allocation in real-world environments. This is captured by the SEEV model. Just as the MRM was heavily influenced by early psychological research on dual-task performance, so the SEEV model has been heavily influenced by early engineering research on optimal allocation scheduling (Carbonell, Ward, & Senders, 1968; Moray, 1986; Senders, 1964; Sheridan, 1970; see also Moray and Sheridan, this volume). Indeed in this area, Neville Moray will be pleased that, in large part through his consistent advocacy, I have become a convert to his view that "the eyes have it" (see Moray, this volume), even though I am still far away from a being a card-carrying single channelist!

As shown in Figure 17.3, the SEEV model links the allocation of attention to the movement of the eyeball (visual scanning). Accordingly, our eyes move to events that are *salient* (the "S"), but that movement is inhibited when it requires extensive *effort* (the first "E"), as when long scans or head movements are required (Wickens, 1993). The eye tends to look to locations where information is *expected* (the second "E"), particularly when such information is of high *value* (the "V"), because it serves a task that is of particular importance. I have joined the four factors in the order I have, not only because it makes a nice pronounceable acronym, but because it readily segregates the first two factors, salience and effort, as bottom-up drivers of attention, from the second two, expectancy and value, as top down, knowledge-driven factors.

To elaborate, high levels of both salience, which captures attention, and effort, which inhibits its movement, can be thought of as characteristics of the physical properties and location of information sources, respectively. Furthermore, these are unwanted "nuisance" factors in guiding attention, *unless* they are explicitly correlated with expectancy and value. It is the goal of designers of display layout to impose these correlations, first by making valuable information salient and second by keeping highly expected (high-bandwidth) sources of information close together, so that they can be accessed in sequence with little effort. The reader may recognize the second component here as a key element of the *proximity compatibility principle* of attention-guided display design (Wickens & Carswell, 1995).

Turning directly to the top-down factors, expectancy is clearly a property of the knowledge of the attender, as he or she has internalized the statistical properties of events in the world (e.g., formed a mental model). Such properties include both the bandwidth (event frequency) and the contingencies of and between events along channels in the world. Value can relate to the value of the *task* served by the event at its location, but also to the value of a channel in serving a task that is already activated. (For example, once I have decided to perform a given task that depends on two sources of input, both sources increase their value, relative to other competing sources.)

An interesting, unresolved point remains the extent to which these two terms should be combined in an additive fashion (E + V) or a multiplicative (E × V) one, the latter characterizing the "optimal" properties of an expected value model. This leads to a provocative question: Should a source of input along which potentially valuable input (V > 0) *never occurs* (E = 0) be sampled (Moray, 2003)? Optimal sampling theory dictates that it should not be. But in the real world, how confident of "never" can we really be?

We have now completed three different validations of the SEEV model, across six different experiments, and it is successful in predicting the probability that the eyes will land on certain areas of interest in both driving (Horrey, Wickens, & Consalus, 2006) and flying (Wickens et al., 2003; Wickens et al., in press). In all these efforts, we have found a high degree of validity reflected by correlations between model predictions of how often an area of interest should be scanned (in a particular condition) and how often it is scanned, with correlations ranging from 0.60 to 0.96. Such correlations tend to be lower to the extent that ambient vision can effectively carry out the task, without foveal scanning (as in driving [Horrey et al., 2006]). Note the role of ambient vision as a separate resource from scan-driven focal vision (as depicted in Fig. 17.2). More important, when expert pilots are involved as participants in the experiment, their scan performance appears to be little influenced by effort (that is, inclusion of the effort parameter does not improve model fit), Here the simple expected value model nicely discriminates better pilots (whose data are better fit by the model) from poorer performing pilots (Wickens et al., in press).

## CHALLENGES FOR MODEL INTEGRATION

As depicted in Figure 17.2, the SEEV model acts as a computational model of selective attention, the "filter" or spotlight of Figure 17.1, feeding to the allocation component of the MRM, which can act as a computational model of divided attention. In theory, the two components can be joined in a comprehensive model of attention. However, there are several challenges to researchers in the process of achieving this integration, two of which currently engage my own attention, as I describe next.

### The Rules of Allocation

I actually define three subchallenges to this challenge area. The first subchallenge is to map the boundary between parallel and serial behavior, and identify the levels of total resource demand, at which what clearly may be parallel processing (e.g., lane keeping and radio listening in a vehicle) regresses to a more distinct serial mode of processing, where the rules of allocation become critical.

Following this, and once the domain of serial processing has been entered, researchers are challenged to identify those "rules" of task management (e.g., Freed, 2000), that capture actual, and not just optimal, human behavior. A particular challenge is to account for and predict long instances of *cognitive lockup* or *attentional fixation*, which define the failure to switch attention from a "compelling" or "engaging" task, to deal with a neglected task of higher expected value. Such behavior is clearly a violation of the optimal expected value prescriptions of the SEEV model. From the behavior of cell phone users in cars (Strayer, this volume) to pilots in the airplane (Dismukes, this volume), we know that such behavior exists, but the ability to predict when it does and does not take place remains limited. A key element here is the ability of researchers to define "engagement" or "compellingness" operationally, before the impact of these forces on task switching behavior has been observed.

The final subchallenge within the rules–challenge area, and one that is well represented by many of the chapters in this book, is the development of training strategies to address the issues of attention flexibility (see chapters by Gopher, Tsang, Fisher, and Dismukes, this volume), and bring the actual allocation strategies more closely in line with those of optimal task management.

## Coupling of Attention to the Eye

The SEEV model was primarily designed to predict visual scanning. The MRM predicts performance. In many circumstances these two can be tightly linked (e.g., visual monitoring or monitoring coupled with vehicle control). However, simple intuition informs us of the many circumstances when this coupling is much looser. These include performance of mental tasks freed of visual inputs (rehearsal, mental imagery, problem solving); use of peripheral ambient vision that is less reflected by scanning, as in driving lane keeping (Horrey et al., 2006); and, of particular interest in our laboratory, the use of the auditory modality.

There is no intrinsic reason why the ear (or any other sensory modality for that matter) (see Sarter, this volume) cannot be represented by the same selective attention filtering model as the eye (Moray, 1969), and indeed we have recently tried to incorporate auditory delivery into SEEV (Wickens et al., in press, application 1). However, the data predicting the relative costs and benefits of auditory (versus visual) presentation of task information in a visually dominant working environment have proved to be very puzzling and challenging (Wickens, Dixon, & Seppelt, 2005; Wickens & Liu, 1988; see also Theeuwes, this volume).

One of the biggest sources of this challenge, with direct relevance to Figure 17.3, is that it pits features of the two models directly against each other in a sort of head-to-head competition. On the one hand, the MRM clearly predicts a superiority to both tasks in a dual-task pair of a cross-modal auditory–visual (AV) combination, over an intramodal configuration (AA or, particularly, VV). Naturally this benefit can be predicted when the two visual sources are widely separated, but there are also strong basic laboratory data that indicate a cross-modal AV advantage even when both visual tasks are foveal (see Wickens [1980] for a summary), suggesting that modality-specific resources are central as well as peripheral.

On the other hand, emerging research on auditory processing in multimodal environments often signals the clear *preemptive* or attention-capturing properties of this modality relative to visual information (Spence & Driver, 2000; Wickens & Liu, 1988). Such preemption directly maps to the salience component of SEEV. This situation dictates that the performance of a discrete task, in the company of an ongoing visual task, will benefit from auditory (versus visual) delivery, as predicted by both multiple resources and SEEV (assuming the auditory modality is intrinsically more salient than the visual). However, the two models make precisely *opposite* predictions for the ongoing visual task (typical, for example, of vehicle control). The MRM predicts that this, too, will benefit from auditory delivery of the concurrent task. SEEV predicts that it will suffer.

Our research has continued to reveal instability and volatility in the conclusions of which modality is "better" in high-demand multitask environments (Wickens & Colcombe, in press; Dixon, Wickens, & Chang, 2005; Horrey & Wickens, 2004; Iani & Wickens, in press; Latorella, 1998; Wickens et al., 2001). We also believe that this question will grow in its importance and in the complexity of its answer when tactile presentation is thrown into the mix (Sarter, this volume). I am hoping that the joining of the models can assist in answering this critical question of concern to designers of alarms (Dixon et al., in press; Wilkens & Colcombe, in press), of task reminders (Herrmann, Brubaker, Yoder, Sheets, & Tio, 1999), of in-vehicle technology (Horrey & Wickens, 2004; Wickens et al., 2003), and of a variety of multimedia environments (Sarter, this volume).

## CONCLUSION

In concluding my discussion of these and many other important emerging areas of attention research, my plea to applied attention researchers (or even those basic researchers who hope that their work will become relevant to near-term design and training problems) is that attention be paid to the first of the research challenges laid out at the beginning of the chapter: Do not become paradigm bound. Examine the manifestations of the examined phenomena in real-world behavior, with all of its multitask complexity. Be willing to sacrifice some elements of experimental control in the effort to carry that complexity into your scientific investigation. The chapters in this volume provide me with great optimism that researchers are doing this. William James and Paul Fitts would be pleased.

## ACKNOWLEDGMENTS

I would like to acknowledge the contributions of scores of graduate students at the University of Illinois with whom I have had the pleasure to work during the past three decades and who helped stimulate many of the ideas in this chapter, as well as others not covered here. I owe special gratitude to that National Aeronautics and Space Administration Ames Research Center human factors division for the research support and encouragement of scientific thinking that links research to applications. Dick Pew, Stan Roscoe, and Hank Taylor have all been mentors who encouraged my formation of these links. Finally, a particular debt of gratitude goes to Art Kramer, who inspired the Symposium that led to this book Alex Kirlik and Doug Weigmann, who worked with Art to develop the program; and to Mary Welborn, whose invaluable assistance was essential to carrying it through. Mary also had the patience to put up with my own cognitive style and (lack of) computer skills for the 25 years that she has worked with me.

## References

Alexander, A., Wickens, C. D., & Hardy, T. J. (2005). Synthetic vision systems: The effects of guidance symbology, display size, and field of view. *Human Factors*, 47(4), 693–707.

Carbonell, J. R., Ward, J. L., & Senders, J. W. (1968). A queuing model of visual sampling experimental validation. *IEEE Transactions on Man–Machine Systems*, MMS-9, 82–87.

Dixon, S. R., Wickens, C. D., & Chang, D. (2005). Control of multiple UAVs: A quantitative workload analysis. *Human Factors*.

Eriksen, B. A., & Eriksen, C. W. (1974). Effects of noise letters upon the identification of a target letter in a nonsearch task. *Perception & Psychophysics*, 16, 143–149.

Fitts, P. M., Jones, R. E., & Milton, J. L. (1950). Eye movements of aircraft pilots during instrument-landing approaches. *Aeronautical Engineering Review*, 9, 24–29.

Foyle, D. C., & Hooey, B. L. (2003). Improving evaluation and system design through the use of off-nominal testing: A methodology for scenario development. In Foyle, Hooey, & Goodman (Eds.), *Proceedings of the 12th International Symposium on Aviation Psychology* (pp. 397–402). Dayton, Ohio: Wright State University.

Freed, M. (2000). Reactive prioritization. In *Proceedings of the 2nd NASA International Workshop on Planning and Scheduling in Space*. Moffett Field, Calif.: NASA.

Gigerenzer, G., Todd, R., et al. (1999). *Simple heuristics that make us smart*. New York: Oxford University Press.

Gray, W. D., & Fu, W. T. (2004). Soft Constraints in Interactive Behavior: Ignoring perfect knowledge in-the-world for imperfect knowledge in-the-head. Cognitive Science, 28, 359–382.

Hart, S. G., & Wickens, C. D. (1990). Workload assessment and prediction. In H. R. Booher (Ed.), *MANPRINT: An approach to systems integration* (pp. 257–296). New York: Van Nostrand Reinhold.

Herrmann, D., Brubaker, B., Yoder, C., Sheets, V., & Tio, A. (1999). Devices that remind. In F. T. Durso (Ed.), *Handbook of applied cognition* (pp. 377–407). Chichester, England: Wiley.

Hockey, G. R. J., Gaillard, A. W. K., & Coles, M. G. H. (Eds.). (1986). *Energetics and human information processing*. Dordrecht: Martinus Nijhoff.

Horrey, W. J., & Wickens, C. D. (2003). Multiple resource modeling of task interference in vehicle control, hazard awareness and in-vehicle task performance. In *Proceedings of the Second International Driving Symposium on Human Factors in Driver Assessment, Training, and Vehicle Design, Park City, Utah* (pp. 7–12). Satt Lake City: University of Utah.

——, & Wickens, C. D. (2004). Driving and side task performance: The effects of display clutter, separation, and modality. *Human Factors, 46*(4), 611–624.

——, Wickens, C. D., & Consalus, K. P. (2006). *Modeling drivers' visual attention allocation while interacting with in-vehicle technologies. Journal of Experimental Psychology Applied, 12*(2), 67–78.

Iani, C., & Wickens, C. D. (in press). Factors affecting task management in aviation. *Human Factors.*

James, W. (1890). *Principles of psychology.* New York: Holt.

Kahneman, D. (1973). *Attention and effort.* Englewood Cliffs, N.J.: Prentice Hall.

——, Slovic, P., & Tversky, A. (Eds.). (1982). *Judgment under uncertainty: Heuristics and biases.* London: Cambridge University Press.

Kantowitz, B. H. (1974). Double stimulation. In B. H. Kantowitz (Ed.), *Human information processing* (pp. 83–131). Hillsdale, N.J.: Erlbaum Associates.

Keele, S. W. (1968). Movement control in skilled motor performance. *Psychological Bulletin, 70,* 387–403.

Kleinman, D. L., & Pattipati, K. R. (1991). Engineering models in supervisory control. In D. Damos (Ed.), *Multiple task performance* (pp. 35–68). London: Taylor & Francis.

Kroft, P., & Wickens, C. D. (2003). Displaying multi-domain graphical database information: An evaluation of scanning, clutter, display size, and user interactivity. *Information Design Journal, 11*(1), 44–52.

Latorella, K. A. (1998). Effects of modality on interrupted flight deck performance: Implications for data link. In *Proceedings of the 42nd annual meeting of the Human Factors and Ergonomics Society.* Santa Monica, Calif.: Human Factors and Ergonomics Society.

Loftus, G. R. (1996). Psychology will be a much better science when we change the way we analyze data. *Current Directions in Psychological Science, 5*(6), 161–171.

McCarley, J. S., Vais, M. J., Pringle, H. L., Kramer, A. F., Irwin, D. E., & Strayer, D. L. (2004). Conversation disrupts visual scanning and change detection in complex traffic scenes. *Human Factors, 46,* 424–436.

McFarlane, D. C., & Latorella, K. A. (2002). The scope and importance of human interruption in human–computer interaction design. *Human–Computer Interaction, 17,* 1–61.

McMillan, G., Beevis, D., Salas, E., Strub, M. H., Sutton, R., & Van Breda, L. (Eds.). (1989). *Applications of human performance models to system design.* New York: Plenum Press.

Moray, N. (1967). Where is attention limited: A survey and a model. *Acta Psychologica, 27,* 84–92.

——. (1969). *Listening and attention.* Baltimore: Penguin.

——. (Ed.). (1979). *Mental workload: Its theory and measurement.* New York: Plenum Press.

——, (1986). Monitoring behavior and supervisory control. In K. R. Boff, L. Kaufman, & J. P. Thomas (Eds.), *Handbook of perception and human performance* (vol. 2, pp. 40-1–40-51). New York: John Wiley & Sons.

——. (2003). Monitoring, complacency skepticism and eutectic behavior. *International Journal of Industrial Ergonomics, 31*(3), 175–178.

Navon, D., & Gopher, D. (1979). On the economy of the human processing system. *Psychological Review, 86,* 254–255.

Norman, D. A., & Bobrow, D. G. (1975). On data-limited and resource-limited processes. *Cognitive Psychology, 7,* 44–64.

North, R. A., & Gopher, D. (1976). Measures of attention as predictors of flight performance. *Human Factors, 18,* 1–14.

Parasuraman, R., Davies, R., & Beatty, J. E. (Eds.). (1984). *Varieties of attention.* Orlando, Fla.: Academic Press.

Pashler, H. (Ed.). (1998). *Attention.* East Sussex, UK: Psychology Press.

Pew, R., & Mavor, A. (1998). *Modeling human and organizational behavior.* Washington, D.C.: National Academy Press.

Raby, M., & Wickens, C. D. (1994). Strategic workload management and decision biases in aviation. *International Journal of Aviation Psychology, 4*(3), 211–240.

Rensink, R. A. (2002). Change detection. *Annual Review of Psychology, 53,* 245–277.

Rogers, D., & Monsell, S. (1995). Costs of a predictable switch between simple cognitive tasks. *Journal of Experimental Psychology: General, 124,* 207–231.

Senders, J. W. (1964). The human operator as a monitor and controller of multidegree of freedom systems. *IEEE Transactions on Human Factors in Electronics, HFE-5,* 2–6.

Sheridan, T. B. (1970). On how often a supervisor should sample. *IEEE Transactions on Systems, Science & Cybernetics, SSC-6*(2), 140–145.

Simons, D. (2000). Current approaches to change blindness. *Visual Cognition, 7,* 1–15.

Spence, C., & Driver, J. (2000). Audiovisual links in attention: Implications for interface design. In D. Harris (Ed.), *Engineering psychology and cognitive ergonomics* (Vol. 2, pp. 185–192). Hampshire: Ashgate Publishing.

Sperling, G., & Dosher, B. A. (1986). Strategy and optimization in human information processing. In K. Boff, L. Kaufman, & J. Thomas (Eds.), *Handbook of perception and performance* (vol. I, pp. 2-1–2-65). New York: Wiley.

Thomas, L. C., & Wickens, C. D. (2004). Eye-tracking and individual differences in off-normal event detection when flying with a synthetic vision system display. In *Proceedings of the 48th annual meeting of the Human Factors and Ergonomics Society* (pp. 223–227). Santa Monica, Calif.: Human Factors and Ergonomics Society.

Warm, J. S. (1984). *Sustained attention in human performance.* London: Wiley.

Wickens, C. D. (1980). The structure of attentional resources. In R. Nickerson (Ed.), *Attention and performance VIII* (pp. 239–257). Hillsdale, N.J.: Lawrence Erlbaum.

———. (1984). Processing resources in attention. In R. Parasuraman, R. Davies, & J. E. Beatty (Eds.), *Varieties of attention* (pp. 63–101). New York: Academic Press.

———. (1989). Models of multitask situations. In G. McMillan, D. Beevis, E. Salas, M. H. Strub, R. Sutton, & L. Van Breda (Eds.), *Applications of human performance models to system design* (pp. 259–273), New York: Plenum Press.

———. (1991). Processing resources and attention. In D. Damos (Ed.), *Multiple-task performance* (pp. 3–34). London: Taylor & Francis.

———. (1993). Cognitive factors in display design. *Journal of the Washington Academy of Sciences,* 83(4), 179–201.

———. (1998). Common sense statistics. *Ergonomics in Design, October,* 18–22.

———. (2000). Human factors in vector map design: The importance of task-display dependence. *Journal of Navigation,* 53(1), 54–67.

———. (2001). Keynote address: Attention to safety and the psychology of surprise. In R. Jensen & L. Rakovan (Eds.), *Proceedings of the 11th International Symposium on Aviation Psychology* (pp. 1–11). Columbus, Ohio: Department of Aerospace Engineering, Applied Mechanics, and Aviation, Ohio State University.

———. (2002). Multiple resources and performance prediction. *Theoretical Issues in Ergonomics Science,* 3(2), 159–177.

———. (2004). Multiple resource time sharing model. In N. A. Stanton, E. Salas, H. W. Hendrick, A. Hedge, & K. Brookhuis (Eds.), *Handbook of human factors and ergonomics methods* (pp. 40-1–40-7). London: Taylor & Francis.

———. (2005). *Display formatting and situation awareness model (DFSAM): An approach to aviation display design.* University of Illinois Institute of Aviation technical report no. AHFD-05-14/NASA-05-5. Savoy, Ill.: Aviation Human Factors Division.

———, & Carswell, C. M. (1995). The proximity compatibility principle: Its psychological foundation and relevance to display design. *Human Factors,* 37(3), 473–494.

———, & Colcombe, A. (in press). Performance consequences of imperfect alerting automation assciated with a cockpit display of traffic information. *Human Factors.*

———, Dixon, S. R., & Seppelt, B. (2005). Auditory preemption versus multiple resources: Who wins in interruption management? In *Proceedings of the 49th annual meeting of the Human Factors & Ergonomics Society* (pp. 463–467). Santa Monica, Calif.: Human Factors and Ergonomics Society.

———, Goh, J., Helleberg, J., Horrey, W., & Talleur, D. A. (2003). Attentional models of multi-task pilot performance using advanced display technology. *Human Factors,* 45(3), 360–380.

———, & Gopher, D. (1977). Control theory measures of tracking as indices of attention allocation strategies. *Human Factors,* 19, 354–366.

———, & Liu, Y. (1988). *Codes and modalities in multiple resources: A success and a qualification.* Human Factors, 30, 599–616.

———, McCarley, J. S., Alexander, A., Thomas, L., Ambinder, M., & Zheng, S. (2007). Attention–situation awareness (A-SA) model of pilot error. In D. Foyle & B. Hooey (Eds.), *Pilot performance models.* Mahwah, N.J.: Lawrence Erlbaum.

———, Ververs, P., & Fadden, S. (2004). Head-up display design. In D. Harris (Ed.), *Human factors for civil flight deck design* (pp. 103–140). UK: Ashgate.

———, Vincow, M. A., Schopper, A. W., & Lincoln, J. E. (1997). *Computational models of human performance in the design and layout of controls and displays.* CSERIAC SOAR report no. 97-22. Wright–Patterson Air Force Base, Ohio: Crew System Ergonomics Information Analysis Center.

Williges, R. C., & Wierwille, W. W. (1979). Behavioral measures of aircrew mental workload. *Human Factors,* 21, 549–574.

# Author Index

# Subject Index